Ramban

Commentary on the Torah

Commentary on the Torah

ספר במדבר
NUMBERS

Translated and Annotated with Index
by Rabbi Dr. Charles B. Chavel, PH.B., M.A., LL.B., D.H.L., D.D.

Shilo Publishing House, Inc.
New York, N.Y. 10002

Library of Congress Catalog Card No. 71–184043

Standard Book No. 0-88328-009-4

MANUFACTURED IN THE UNITED STATES OF AMERICA

Preface:

The student of Ramban's Commentary on the Torah who has sought enlightenment in his exegesis from the beginning of the Book of Genesis up to this point, is by now realizing that an essential characteristic of this work is that its provinces encompass the whole treasure-house of Jewish learning. Unlike the commentaries of the other masters that are devoted to one, two or three aspects of the Scriptural text, Ramban's work is as varied as is the mystery of Jewish historical experience. In Ramban's Commentary there are no boundaries on the moods of the spirit. Language, *Halachah, Agadah,* Philosophy, Cabala, Jewish and World history—all these extend the terms of the sacred text of the Torah to give the student some concepts of the higher levels of reality which is the word of G-d. One need but recall the spiritual interpretation of World history that Ramban finds reflected in the chapter of Creation (Vol. 1, pp. 61-64), to realize the truth of this observation.

The Commentary on the Book of Numbers meets this standard in a very significant sense. A brief examination of the volume shows that besides the basic exegesis necessary for the understanding of the Scriptural text, it comprises also a number of themes which are of far-reaching spiritual value and enduring reality. Thus we recognize among the highlights of the Commentary enlightening expositions about our eternal duties toward the Land of Israel; the meaning and significance of the miracle of Chanukah, as alluded to in the Torah; the reason why the building of the *Beth Hamikdash* in Jerusalem was delayed till the days of David and Solomon; the nature of Balaam's prophecy, the differences between it, and that of the Hebrew prophets, especially that of Moses; the four world powers which will rule until the Messianic era, etc. Thus the Commentary on the Book of Numbers, as its preceding volumes, unfolds to us a deep interest in everything which is Torah in its widest sense for all time.

It is my fervent prayer that the translation of Ramban's Commentary on the Book of Numbers be a worthy companion to the three preceding volumes, helping and guiding the arduous student through the garden-rows of *the vineyard of the Eternal.*

In closing, I wish to acknowledge my sincere indebtedness to all persons involved in the production of this volume, for their painstaking care and complete co-operation, in making this sacred project a reality.

C. B. Chavel

4 Marcheshvan 5736
October 9, 1975

Contents

COMMENTARY ON THE TORAH

BY OUR MASTER

RABBI MOSHE THE SON OF NACHMAN

THE GERONDITE

The Book of Numbers

'B'MIDBAR SINAI' (IN THE WILDERNESS OF SINAI). After having explained the laws of the offerings in the third book, He now began to set forth in this book the commandments which they [the children of Israel] were told with reference to the Tent of Meeting. Now He had already given a warning for all times about [the prohibition of] impurity relating to the Sanctuary and its holy things.[1] Here He defined the boundaries of the Tabernacle whilst it was in the wilderness, just as He had set bounds for Mount Sinai when the [Divine] Glory was there,[2] and He commanded *that the common man that draweth nigh shall be put to death,*[3] just as He had said there, *no hand shall touch him* [i.e., the mountain], *but he shall surely be stoned.*[4] He also commanded [here], *And they shall not go in to see the holy things as they are being covered, lest they die*[5] just as He warned there [at Sinai], *lest they break through unto the Eternal to gaze, and many of them perish.*[6] He commanded here. *And ye shall keep the charge of the holy things and the charge of the altar,* [*that there be wrath no more upon the children of Israel*],[7] just as He said there, *And*

(1) Leviticus 5:2-3. See Ramban there (Vol. III pp. 52-54). (2) Exodus 19:12. Ramban here, in stressing the parallels between the Tent of Meeting and Mount Sinai, is developing the idea that he mentions in Exodus at the beginning of *Seder Terumah,* that the Tent of Meeting was, as it were, a continuation of Mount Sinai. See Vol. II p. 435. (3) Further, 1:51. (4) Exodus 19:13. (5) Further, 4:20. (6) Exodus 19:21. (7) Further, 18:5.

let the priests also, that come near to the Eternal, sanctify themselves, lest the Eternal break forth upon them; [8] *and let not the priests and the people break through to come up unto the Eternal, lest He break forth upon them.* [9] Thus He commanded [here] how the Tabernacle and its vessels are to be guarded, and how they [the people] are to pitch round about it and how the people are to stand afar off, and how *the priests that come near the Eternal*[8] are to treat it [the Tabernacle] when it is resting and when it is being carried [during the journeyings], and how they are to guard it. Now these are all [signs of] distinction and honor for the Sanctuary, just as the Rabbis of blessed memory have said,[10] "A King's palace[11] that has guards over it cannot be compared to a palace that has no such guards."

Now this whole book deals only with those commandments which were meant only for a particular time, being the period when the Israelites stayed in the desert, and [it deals also] with the miracles which were done for them, in order to tell all the wondrous deeds of the Eternal which He wrought for them. It tells how He began to destroy their enemies before them by the sword, and He also commanded how the Land should be divided up amongst them. There are no commandments in this book which are binding for all times except for some commandments about the offerings which He had begun in the Book of [the Law of] the Priests [i.e., Leviticus], and whose explanation was not completed there, therefore He finished them in this book.

(8) Exodus 19:22. (9) *Ibid.*, Verse 24. (10) Sifre Zuta *Korach* 18:4. (11) "And it is known that the term 'palace' is a reference to the Sanctuary" ("The Commandments," Vol. I, p. 31). — It is possible, on first thought, to explain Ramban's expression "and how they are to pitch round about it" that the pronoun "they" refers to all the Levites, and in that case the continuing expression "and how *the people* are to stand afar off" would thus complete the thought by contrast: the Levites are to encamp round about the Tabernacle, while the people are to stand afar off. But see in Chapter 2, Verse 2, that Scripture speaks clearly of *the children of Israel* encamping round about the Tabernacle. Hence the words of Ramban are to be understood as follows: the people are to pitch round about the Tabernacle, and when they approach it they are to stand afar off. This interpretation is fully borne out in the following chapters of this book of the Torah.

Bamidbar

1

1. AND THE ETERNAL SPOKE UNTO MOSES IN THE WILDERNESS OF SINAI, IN THE TENT OF MEETING. Because He had interrupted with the commandments about the Sabbatical year and the Jubilee, of which He said that they were spoken *in Mount Sinai*[12] [in contrast to all the other commandments in the Book of Leviticus, which, as mentioned at the beginning of that book, G-d told Moses from the Tent of Meeting], He stated here again that this communication was given from the Tent of Meeting, as were all the communications which He had mentioned since the beginning of the Book of Leviticus. And all of them from now onwards [were said to Moses] from the Tent of Meeting, for since the time that the Tabernacle was set up *and G-d called* him [Moses] *from the Tent of Meeting,*[13] He only communicated with him from there.

Scripture mentions here *in the wilderness of Sinai* in order to tell us that they did not travel away from there until they were counted [the first time, as described here], for the second census[14] was taken in the plains of Moab,[15] but the [actual] communication was in the Tent of Meeting.

(12) Leviticus 25:1. (13) *Ibid.,* 1:1. (14) Further, 26:1-51. (15) *Ibid.,* Verse 3.

3. FROM TWENTY YEARS OLD AND UPWARD, 'KOL YOTZEI TZAVA' (ALL THAT ARE ABLE TO GO FORTH TO THE HOST) IN ISRAEL. "This tells us that no one under the age of twenty goes forth to the host. *'Se'u eth rosh'* [literally: 'take the head' and generally translated: *take ye the sum*] *of all the congregation of Israel.*[16] This is as one says to an executioner: 'take that man's head'."[17] This is Rashi's language.

Perhaps the reason for this [law that a male under twenty years old was not liable to military service] is because he is not strong enough for war under the age of twenty, as the Rabbis have said: [18] "Twenty is the age for pursuit." [19] But it may be that the meaning of the phrase *kol yotzei tzava* is "all who go forth to be assembled in the congregation," because the young men do not take part in such an assembly of the people, and every gathering of the people is called *tzava,* as in '[*litzvo*] *tzava'* (*to be counted among the host*) *for the work of the Tent of Meeting;*[20] *he shall return from the 'tz'va' of the work;*[21] *with the mirrors of the 'tzov'oth' that 'tzav'u'* (*women that congregated together*);[22] and similarly *'tz'va'* (*the host of*) *heaven;*[23] *and all 'tz'va'am'* (*their host*) *I commanded.*[24] Therefore Scripture explains when speaking of men of war: *'mi'tz'va'* (*from the host of*) *the war;*[25] *and the number of them reckoned 'bi'tz'va'* (*by the host*) *for the war.*[26] Scripture states here *all that go forth to the host,* similar to what it says, *all that went out of the gate of the city.*[27] It states, *ye shall number them by their 'hosts'* [in the plural], because they consisted of many hosts, since each and every tribe was a great host.

(16) Verse 2. (17) The meaning of this text which stems from Bamidbar Rabbah 1:9 will be explained further on by Ramban. The final quote is not found in our texts of Rashi, although Ramban quotes it from his commentary.The reason for its disappearance from all other texts of Rashi may well be its sharpness of expression which on first sight baffles the student. Ramban, however, recognizing that it is a genuine text which stems from Midrash Rabbah proceeds to explain it appropriately. (18) Aboth 5:21. (19) The Hebrew is *lirdof,* which is variously interpreted as: "for seeking a livelihood;" or "for seeking one's life-pursuit." Ramban here understands it in its literal sense—"to pursue [the enemy in battle]." (20) Further, 8:24. (21) *Ibid.*, Verse 25. (22) Exodus 38:8. (23) Deuteronomy 4:19. (24) Isaiah 45:12. (25) Further, 31:14. (26) I Chronicles 7:40. (27) Genesis 34:24. Ramban's meaning is that the intention of the verses is: "all that are able to go," even if they have not actually gone.

But as for Rashi's expression when he wrote — "This is as one says to an executioner: 'take that man's head' " — it is not clear to me why the Sages should interpret the verse in this derogatory manner. If it is because [the people counted here] died in the desert [therefore He said, *take the head . . .*] whereas in the case of the tribe of Levi He said *Number the children of Levi,*[28] since they were not included in the decree [that they die in the desert] — [this cannot be so], for in the second census [taken] of those who *were* to come into the Land it also uses the same [expression], *take the head of all the congregation of the children of Israel!*[29] But in the Agadah (homiletic exposition) of Vayikra Rabbah[30] the Rabbis explain it as an expression of praise [for the people]: "The term *se'u* always means 'greatness', as it is written, *Pharaoh 'yisa' (shall lift up) thy head, and restore thee unto thy office.*[31] Said the Holy One, blessed be He, to Israel: 'I have given you an exaltation of the head, and I have likened you to Myself. Just as I am exalted above all inhabitants of the world, as it is said, *Thine is the kingdom, O Eternal, and Thou art exalted as head above all,*[32] so to you also I have given an elevation of the head, as it is said, *Lift up the head of all the congregation of the children of Israel,* thus fulfilling that which is said, *And He hath lifted up a horn for His people,*[33] and similarly it is said, *and the Eternal thy G-d will set thee on high above all the nations of the earth.*' "[34]

I have found further in Bamidbar Sinai Rabbah that the Sages have stated:[35] "Said Rabbi Pinchas in the name of Rabbi Idi: What is [the meaning of] that which is written at the beginning of this book, *'se'u eth rosh'* (*take the head*)? It does not say: 'lift up the head,' 'elevate the head,' but it says *se'u eth rosh,* like a man who says to an executioner: 'take this man's head'. Here He gave a hint to Moses, *se'u eth rosh,* meaning that if the people are worthy they will become exalted, just as it is written, *Pharaoh 'yisa' (shall lift up) thy head, and restore thee unto thy office;*[31] but if they are not worthy, they will all die, just as it is written, *Pharaoh 'yisa' (shall lift up) thy head from off thee, and*

(28) Further, 3:15. (29) *Ibid.*, 26:2. (30) I did not find it there. But a similar exposition is found in Bamidbar Rabbah 1:7. See my Hebrew commentary p. 196, Note 26 for the full text. (31) Genesis 40:13. (32) I Chronicles 29:11. (33) Psalms 148:14. (34) Deuteronomy 28:1. (35) Bamidbar Rabbah 1:9.

shall hang thee on a tree."[36] Thus the expression [*se'u eth rosh* which, as Rashi explained, is used in connection with execution] is to be interpreted according to the intention [of the speaker] — in a good way for those who are good.[37] And since it is [also] an expression of elevation, and it is used [here] in the first census, He used the same expression in the second census.[29]

'TIPHKEDU OTHAM.' The term *p'kidah* is an expression meaning remembrance of and attention to a certain matter, as in the phrase, *And the Eternal 'pakad' (remembered) Sarah as He had said,*[38] and this in my opinion is its interpretation in all places, without any exception. The expression *pikadon* [which means a bailment or deposit of goods] is also [from this root], because his guarding and supervision is on it [i.e., because the bailee must guard it]. And therefore when He commanded that Israel be counted He stated *tiphkedu otham,* in order to hint that he [Moses] was not to count them [by persons] but that they were each to give *half a shekel as a ransom for* their *soul,*[39] and he should supervise them [the half-shekels] and thereby know the number of the people. In the case of David Scripture states: *the sum of 'miphkad' (the numbering) of the people*[40] because he knew their numbers through the counting of [the half-shekel] ransom [that each one gave]. For it appears to me unlikely that David should not be careful about that which Scripture states, *that there be no plague among them, when thou numberest them.*[41] And even if David did perhaps make a mistake,[42] why did Joab [the captain of the host in charge of the census] not take [the census through] shekels, *for the*

(36) Genesis 40:19. (37) See Psalms 125:4: *Do good, O Eternal, unto the good.* Thus Pharaoh said unto the chief executioner: "Take the chief butler and lift up his head and restore him to his office." *But as for such as turn aside unto their crooked ways, the Eternal will lead them away with the workers of iniquity* (*ibid.,* Verse 5). Thus in the case of the chief baker, the same expression signified his downfall. In short, the expression of the Midrash which Rashi quoted can be interpreted either for bad or for good. And since it is an expression of elevation etc. (38) Genesis 21:1. See Ramban there (Vol. I, p. 268). (39) Exodus 30:12-13. (40) II Samuel 24:9. (41) Exodus 30:12. (42) In Exodus, at the beginning of *Seder Ki Thisa,* Ramban in fact does explain that David made a mistake and did indeed count them without half-shekels [a theory to which he reverts here briefly at the end of the verse]. For the reason for his mistake, see *ibid.*, (Vol. II, p. 511).

king's word was abominable to Joab,[43] and Joab [in fact] said to the king, *Why doth my lord require this thing? Why will he be a cause of guilt unto Israel?* [44] So why did he [Joab] not count them through the shekels, so that he should not sin?

But in my opinion the [Divine] wrath was [aroused] against him [David] because he counted them unnecessarily, since he was not going forth to war, nor did he do anything with them [the men he counted, so that he would need to know their number] at that time, and [the census] was only to make him rejoice that he ruled over a large people. Therefore Joab said [to David], *Now the Eternal thy G-d add unto the people, how many soever they may be, a hundredfold, and may the eyes of my lord the king see it; but why doth my lord the king delight in this thing?* [45] And I have seen in Bamidbar Sinai Rabbah: [46] "Rabbi Eliezer in the name of Rabbi Yosei ben Zimra said: Whenever Israel was counted for a purpose, their numbers did not diminish; but when they were counted for no purpose, they became diminished. When were they counted for a purpose? In the days of Moses, and[47] for the [setting up of the] standards and at the division of the Land.[48] [When were they counted] for no purpose? In the days of David."

It is also possible to say by way of explanation that David commanded that every "man" in Israel be counted, meaning thereby to include everyone above the age of thirteen years old, who is regarded as "a man" [and not from the age of twenty years upwards], since it is nowhere mentioned in [describing] his counting: "from twenty years old and upwards", but instead David said, *Go, number Israel from Beer-sheba even to Dan . . . that I may know the sum of them.*[49] And

(43) I Chronicles 21:6. (44) *Ibid.*, Verse 3. (45) II Samuel 24:3. (46) Bamidbar Rabbah 2:17. (47) In our Midrash Rabbah the word "and" is not found in the Hebrew text, so that it refers to only one, not two times: "When were they counted for a purpose? In the days of Moses for the [setting up of the] standards" as described here in Chapter 2. See, however, Rashi on Verse 1 above, who is of the opinion that the people were counted at the exodus from Egypt (Exodus 12:37), and again after the worship of the golden calf to ascertain the number of those left. In that case Ramban's version in the text of Bamidbar Rabbah is fully understandable, for there were numberings in the days of Moses preceding the one at the time of setting up the standards. (48) Further, Chapter 26; *ibid.*, Verse 53. (49) I Chronicles 21:2.

this was [the reason for] his punishment, for Scripture only allowed counting to be done *from twenty years old and upwards*[50] by means of the shekels. It was because this is not clearly expressed in Scripture [that even by means of the half-shekels the people are only to be counted from the age of twenty years and over] that David made this mistake, for he thought that when Scripture says *that there be no plague among them*[41] it is because of the shekels, which are a ransom [of the soul] for them [and therefore he thought that as long as he counted them by means of the shekels and not by direct census there would be no plague even if he counted them from above the age of thirteen years old, instead of twenty], but Joab applied his heart [to understand the matter] and was concerned because of it.

And Scripture [itself] stirs me to this thought by saying: *But David took not the number of them from twenty years old and under, because the Eternal had said He would increase Israel like to the stars of heaven. Joab the son of Zeruiah began to number, but finished not; and there came wrath for this upon Israel.*[51] From this it appears that Joab's census included those under twenty years old, and this was [the reason for] the "wrath", because G-d does not want all Israel to be limited by numbers since He will multiply them like the stars of heaven, as He said [to Abraham], *Look now toward heaven, and count the stars, if thou be able to count them.*[52] And when the verse says concerning that census [of Joab], *And all they of Israel were a thousand thousand and a hundred thousand men that drew sword,*[53] it does not mean to say that they were all eligible for military service [since, as explained above, they included also thirteen-year olds who do not go to war], but its correct interpretation is that they were all sufficiently healthy and strong to be able to go to battle, thus stating that he did not count the sick, the weak, and the old, because *the king's word was abominable to* him.[43] This interpretation is very appropriate.

(50) Exodus 30:14. (51) I Chronicles 27:23-24. It is apparent that Ramban interprets these verses as follows: *But David took not the number of them from twenty years old 'and under'* because *Joab began . . . but finished not* for the reason that he [Joab] applied his heart to understand the matter and was concerned about the breach of the law in taking the census from twenty years old and under. (52) Genesis 15:5. (53) I Chronicles 21:5.

But according to the opinion of the Midrash Agadah [a homiletic exposition[54] from which it would appear] that there was an actual census [i.e., that the people were counted without the use of shekels, we must say that] they all erred. This is why David said [to Joab], *Go, 'number' Israel,*[55] and it is further written, *after that he had 'numbered' the people*[56] [expressions which indicate that there was an actual counting of persons without using half-shekels], for in the Torah the term "numbering" of people is not mentioned at all, and the meaning of the expression *according to the number of names*[16] is that each one should tell his name when he is counted through bringing his ransom [of half a shekel].

18. AND THEY ASSEMBLED ALL THE CONGREGATION TOGETHER ON THE FIRST DAY OF THE SECOND MONTH. Scripture mentions [the date although it is already stated in Verse 1 above, to indicate] the zeal of our teacher Moses in [fulfilling] the command of G-d for on the very day of the communication [that he was to take a census of the people] he took the princes of the tribes and assembled all the congregation and began to count them. The count, however, was not completed in one day, and therefore He states again, *so did he number them in the wilderness of Sinai,*[57] in order to inform [us] that the counting was all done in that place, but was not all [finished] on that day.

'VA'YITHYALDU' (AND THEY DECLARED THEIR PEDIGREES) AFTER THEIR FAMILIES. "They brought the documents of their genealogy and witnesses confirming the birth of each of them, so as to prove their descent from their [respective] tribes." This is Rashi's language. But it does not appear [correct to say] that they should have to bring genealogical documents and witnesses with regard to belonging to a [particular] tribe. Rather,

(54) Berachoth 62 b: "And when he [David] counted them he did not take from them the ransom of soul etc." This would seem to indicate that David's mistake was that he counted them *by persons,* [from twenty years old and upwards], and not, as Ramban suggested above, because he included in the count [which *was* done with shekels] people under twenty but over thirteen years old. (55) II Samuel 24:1. (56) *Ibid.*, Verse 10. (57) Verse 19.

va'yithyaldu means that they were counted by *their generations, by their families, by their fathers' houses,*[58] the sense thereof being to state that the whole congregation assembled, as Moses had commanded them by the order of the Holy One, blessed be He, at the door of the Tent of Meeting, except for *the mixed multitude*[59] who *were not of the children of Israel,*[60] for they were recognizable amongst them from the day that they had gone out of Egypt. Thus each man in the congregation brought his [half-] shekel and said to Moses and the princes: "I so-and-so was born to such-and-such a person of such-and-such a family, which is of the tribe of Reuben," or some other tribe, and Moses put the shekels of each particular tribe in a special place [to be counted later], so that he would know the sum of [each] individual [tribe] and of all the tribes together. And the proof for this[61] is that at the second census [taken when they were about to enter the Land of Israel] where the families [of each tribe] are mentioned,[62] it does not say *va'yithyaldu,* nor does it mention *according to the number of names, by their polls,* [as it says here in Verse 19]. This is because ever since the tribes had pitched by their standards, they were separated from each other and it was clearly known to which tribe each family belonged; thus they only had to know how many families there were in each tribe, and each family counted its men *by their polls,* but not *according to the number of names.*[63] Therefore the princes of the tribes did not have to be present [with Moses] at that [second] census [as was stipulated at the first census — in Verse 4 — since the princes

(58) Verses 20, 22, etc. (59) Exodus 12:38. (60) II Samuel 21:2. (61) I.e., a proof that they did not have to bring their genealogical documents, as Rashi explained, but that *va'yithyaldu* means merely that they declared to which family and tribe they belonged, is that etc. (62) I.e., mentioned by name, in contrast to this census [taken at the arrangement of the people into four main groups headed by the four standards] where the names of the families of each tribe are not listed. (63) But if *va'yithyaldu* means, as Rashi explained that they were to produce their genealogical documents, the question arises why was that not required at the second census? According to Ramban, however, who explains that *va'yithyaldu* means that they each declared to which family and which tribe they belonged, we can understand why *va'yithyaldu* is not mentioned at the second census. For once they pitched by their standards, each person's place would indicate to which tribe he belonged, and the families themselves counted their own numbers, whilst Moses counted the numbers of all the families. Hence it was no longer necessary to declare to which family and which tribe one belonged.

of the tribes were only needed in order to identify which families belonged to which tribe, and this was already known at the time of the second census]. And Rabbi Abraham ibn Ezra explains that *va'yithyaldu* means that they were asked when they were born, in order to ascertain whether they were [over] twenty years of age.

32. OF THE CHILDREN OF JOSEPH, NAMELY, OF THE CHILDREN OF EPHRAIM. Scripture mentioned Ephraim before Menasheh, and stated Joseph's relationship to him [which it does not do in the case of Menasheh],[64] and similarly later [Scripture gave Ephraim precedence] at the [division of the tribes according to their] standards, by making him master of the standard, [whilst Menasheh is mentioned merely as one of the two tribes gathered around him], because in accordance with Jacob's blessing[65] he was to be [given the honor accorded to] the firstborn, and his brother [Menasheh] was to be second to him. Moreover, the sons of Ephraim were more numerous than those of Menasheh[66] [and hence Ephraim was mentioned first]. But at the second census *in the plains of Moab*[67] Scripture mentioned Menasheh first, because at that time his sons were more numerous [than those of Ephraim],[68] and [also because] they took their inheritance first.[69] Similarly when mentioning the princes of the Land [who were to take possession of the Land for their respective tribes] Scripture mentioned Menasheh first, and also Joseph's relationship to him.[70] In [the story of] the spies, however, Scripture mentioned Ephraim first, and Joseph's relationship it stated only in referring to the tribe of Menasheh.[71] It appears to me by way of homiletic exposition that it is on account of the evil report that Joseph brought [to his father] concerning his brothers[72] that Scripture, [in the story of the spies], associates with him the spy who [was among those who] spread

(64) Verse 34. (65) Genesis 48:20. (66) Ephraim totalled 40,500 (Verse 33), whilst Menasheh numbered 32,200 (Verse 35). (67) Further, 26:3. (68) The children of Menasheh were then 52,700 (*ibid.*, Verse 34), whilst Ephraim had only 32,500 (*ibid.*, Verse 37). (69) Half of the tribe of Menasheh joined the tribes of Gad and Reuben in settling during the lifetime of Moses on the east side of the Jordan (*ibid.*, 32:33). (70) *Ibid.*, 34:23: *Of the children of Joseph; of the tribe of the children of Menasheh.* In the following verse Scripture mentions the prince of the children of Ephraim. (71) *Ibid.*, 13:8, 11. (72) Genesis 37:2.

the evil report [about the Land, namely the spy from the tribe of Menasheh, whereas the spy from the tribe of Ephraim was Joshua the son of Nun, who was not among those who spread the evil report]. Or it may be that Scripture [in relating the story of the spies] gave honor to both [tribes who were descended from Joseph], and Ephraim had sufficient honor in its prince [Joshua the son of Nun who ministered to Moses, therefore Scripture mentioned the honor of descent from Joseph only in the case of Menasheh].

45. AND ALL THOSE THAT WERE NUMBERED OF THE CHILDREN OF ISRAEL BY THEIR FATHERS' HOUSES . . . ALL THAT WERE ABLE TO GO FORTH TO WAR IN ISRAEL. It was necessary for Scripture to state the collective number of the people although it had already stated the individual numbers [of each of the tribes], because Moses and Aaron were commanded to ascertain the total number of the people counted, as well as the number of [people in] each tribe, for such is the way of kings when they take a census of their people.

However I have not understood the reason for this commandment, namely why the Holy One, blessed be He, commanded [that they should ascertain the number of the people]. For whilst there was indeed a need for them [the people] to establish their relationship to the [individual] tribes because of the [division of the tribes of Israel according to four] standards, I cannot understand why G-d commanded that they find out the number [of men in each tribe]. Perhaps it was in order to proclaim His mercy over them, for it was *with* [only] *threescore and ten persons* that their *fathers went down into Egypt,*[73] and now they were as the sand of the sea, so many men [above] the age of twenty [not to mention the women and children]. After every epidemic and plague He counted them again in order that they should know that it is *He that increaseth the nations;*[74] *He woundeth, and His hands make whole.*[75] It is for this reason that our Rabbis have said: [76] "Because of His abundant love for them He counts them every now and then." Furthermore, he who comes before the father of the

(73) See Deuteronomy 10:22. (74) Job 12:23. (75) *Ibid.*, 5:18. (76) Mentioned by Rashi, above, Verse 1; see also Bamidbar Rabbah 4:2.

prophets, and his brother [*Aaron*] *the holy one of the Eternal*[77] and becomes known to them by name, receives thereby a merit and life, because he has come *in the council of* the *people and in the register of the house of Israel,*[78] and he receives a part in the merits of the community by being included in their numbers. Similarly, each of the people receive a special merit through being counted by number before Moses and Aaron, for they *will set* their *eyes upon them for good,*[79] and intercede on their behalf for mercy, [just as it is said], *The Eternal, the G-d of your fathers, make you a thousand times so many more as ye are,*[80] and He will not reduce your numbers, and the shekels shall be a redemption for your souls. And in Bamidbar Sinai Rabbah I have seen the following text:[81] "*According to the number of names . . . by their polls.*[82] The Holy One, blessed be He, told Moses to count them each with respect and [to treat] each one of them with [the honor due to] greatness. [Thus He said]: You shall not say to the head of the family: 'How many people are there in your family? How many sons do you have?' but they are each to pass before you with awe and in respect, and you shall count them. — It is with reference to this that it is written, *according to the number of names, from twenty years old and upward, by their polls.*"[82]

It is also possible for us to say that [the reason for ascertaining their numbers] was similar to the practice of governments before fighting a war, since they were now ready to enter into the Land and to fight against the kings of the Amorite that were on the other side of the Jordan [eastward] and all the others, as Moses said [unto Hobab], *We are journeying unto the place of which the Eternal said: This I will give unto you.*[83] Therefore Moses and the princes [of the tribes] had to know the number of those armed for war, and also the numbers of

(77) Psalms 106:16. (78) Ezekiel 13:9. The prophet Ezekiel states it in the negative as a punishment for sinners: *they shall not be in the council of My people, neither shall they be written in the register of the house of Israel.* Ramban, as indicated, applies it in the positive, namely, that those possessing merit will be included in the council of G-d's people and be written in the register of the house of Israel. It is possible that Ramban also hints to the concluding part of that verse: *neither shall they enter into the Land of Israel,* thus intimating that those who are deserving of reward will enter into the Land. (79) Jeremiah 24:6. (80) Deuteronomy 1:11. (81) I have not found the source thereof. (82) Verse 18 above. (83) Further, 10:29.

each and every tribe, [in order to decide] what to command each of them in the plains of Moab [when drawing up] the battle-lines, for the Torah does not rely on the miracle of one chasing a thousand.[84] This is the purport of the expression, *all that go forth to the host in Israel,*[85] namely that the census was for the purpose of [determining the number of] men that will go forth to war; and also so that he should distribute the Land to them according to their numbers, and should know how many parts will be allotted to them of the Land that they capture, since if not for the affair of the spies, they would have entered the Land immediately.

47. BUT THE LEVITES AFTER THE TRIBE OF THEIR FATHERS WERE NOT NUMBERED AMONG THEM. Moses had understood at the beginning of his own accord that he should not count the Levites [with the other tribes], because he had been told, *And with you there shall be a man of every tribe* etc.,[86] meaning that each of the tribes that were to be counted should have their prince present, and since G-d had not appointed a prince for the tribe of Levi, hence he [Moses] did not count them. Therefore he was in doubt about the Levites and did not know what to do with them. And when he had finished all those who were counted of the people, and the Levites remained alone [uncounted], the Holy One, blessed be He, explained to him that he was not to count them *among the children of Israel* but that he should take their sum separately, for he was to *appoint* them *over the Tabernacle of the Testimony.*[87]

He stated *'p'kod'* [*'number'*—in the singular] *the children of Levi*[88] meaning that he [Moses] was to count them by himself without [the assistance of] the princes, and it was he [Moses] who called upon Aaron to be with him,[89] since he [Aaron] was the prince of that tribe,

(84) See Deuteronomy 32:30. (85) Above, Verse 3. (86) *Ibid.*, Verse 4. (87) Further, Verse 50. (88) *Ibid.*, 3:15. (89) *Ibid.*, Verse 39: *All that were numbered of the Levites, whom Moses and Aaron numbered* etc. Thus it is clear that Aaron also participated in the counting of the Levites. Since his name was not mentioned when Moses was commanded to take that census, Ramban suggests that he joined at Moses' invitation, see further in text of Ramban that Moses' action was alluded to in the words of G-d. See Note 93.

and just as the princes of Israel were [present] at [the counting of] their tribes, so was the prince of the Levites to be present when they were counted. Perhaps that is the reason for the dots [in the Torah] on the word *'v'Aharon'* [*and Aaron,* in the phrase: *All that were numbered of the Levites, whom Moses 'and Aaron' numbered*] [89] since his [assistance in the counting] was not by the express commandment of G-d.[90] Afterwards, [however], when the Levites were appointed to their individual services and burdens, Moses called upon the princes of the congregation to be with him, as it is said, *All those that were numbered of the Levites, whom Moses and Aaron and the princes of Israel numbered,*[91] since it was fitting that they should all give their assent to and supervise the establishment of the *mishmaroth.*[92] And Scripture repeats in another place, *These are they that were numbered of the families of the Kohathites . . . whom Moses and Aaron numbered 'according to the commandment of the Eternal' by the hand of Moses*[93] Because He had already hinted through the dots [on

(90) Rashi however, [basing himself on Bechoroth 4a] states that the dots indicate that "Aaron himself was not in the census of the Levites." This will be mentioned by Ramban further on in a somewhat different form (see Note 95). (91) Further, 4:46. (92) A *mishmar* [literally: a guard] is a Division of priests and Levites for duty in the Sanctuary. According to tradition, Moses divided the priests into eight Divisions, four from the families of Eleazar and four from Ithamar, and later on when the Sanctuary was built in Jerusalem, David and Samuel sub-divided them into twenty-four Divisions. Each Division served for a period of one week, and during the three Festivals all the Divisions were in attendance simultaneously (see "The Commandments" Vol. I, pp. 46-47). See also Ramban further, Verse 53, and at Note 96, for additional aspects of this term as used by Ramban.— It should be noted that the concept of *mishmaroth* applied also to the Levites and Israelites, for just as the priests were divided into twenty-four Divisions, so also were the other two groups. Each week a new *mishmar* of priests, Levites, and Israelites would arrive in Jerusalem to attend to the Divine Services in the Sanctuary. The Israelites' function was to "stand by" the daily offerings brought for the whole congregation of Israel, for "how can a man's offering be offered while he does not stand by it?" (Taanith 26a). Such a group of Israelites is referred to as a *ma'amad* (literally: "stand by"). In the text of Ramban before us, however, reference is only to the Divisions of the priests and Levites. (93) Further, 4:37. The verse seems to indicate that G-d had explicitly commanded Aaron's presence at the census, which does not corroborate Ramban's interpretation above. Ramban therefore explains that although there was no *explicit* command, there had been a hint, and *Moses* therefore, in asking Aaron to be present, was indeed acting *according to the command of the Eternal.*

the word *'v'Aharon*[89]] that Aaron had to be there, from which Moses understood that he was to do so, [hence it says *according to the commandment of the Eternal*].[93] But the [presence of the] princes of the congregation [at the numbering of the Levites] [91] was not obligatory, and Moses called them in order to show them respect, [therefore Scripture does not state that their presence was "according to the commandment of the Eternal"]. In Tractate Bechoroth[94] the Rabbis have said that the dots on the word *Aharon*[89] are to hint that Aaron himself was not counted at all in the census of the Levites.[95]

53. AND THE LEVITES SHALL PITCH ROUND ABOUT THE TABERNACLE OF THE TESTIMONY, THAT THERE BE NO WRATH UPON THE CONGREGATION OF THE CHILDREN OF ISRAEL, AND THE LEVITES SHALL KEEP THE CHARGE OF THE TABERNACLE OF THE TESTIMONY. Although this [verse] was said [specifically] about the Tabernacle set up between the standards in the desert, it constitutes a commandment for all times, [and thus applies] also to the Sanctuary [in Jerusalem], and it is on the basis of this [verse] that [David and Samuel] instituted the *mishmaroth*.[96] And the meaning of [the verse before us], *and the Levites shall keep the charge at the Tabernacle of the Testimony* is that they should keep guard of and patrol the Tabernacle at night, just as the

(94) Bechoroth 4a. (95) There is a marked difference on this point between the language of Rashi (see above Note 90) and that of Ramban. According to Rashi, the dots on the word *Aharon* indicate that "he was not in the census of the Levites," which can be interpreted as saying that he did not participate in *counting* the people, and only Moses did it. Mizrachi in fact interprets Rashi in this way, since the verse [*whom Moses and Aaron counted*] refers to those who did the actual counting of the Levites, thus the dots on the word "Aaron" indicate that he did not participate in the counting—but he himself may well have *been counted*. Ramban's language, however, clearly means that "Aaron himself *was not counted* at all in the census of the Levites." This explains why Ramban does not quote this explanation of the Gemara in the name of Rashi, as he is wont to do, since his interpretation of the text of Bechoroth 4a is different than Rashi's. (96) The "guards" of the Sanctuary. Guard was kept in the Sanctuary at Jerusalem at twenty-four places; the guards being priests and Levites. The priests kept watch at three places, the Levites at twenty-one (Midoth 1:1). Thus Ramban understands that the order of the *mishmaroth* was a twofold one: consisting of the Divisions, as explained above in Note 92, and of guards, as explained here. See my Hebrew commentary p. 200.

Rabbis have said:[97] "The priests are to keep watch within [the enclosures or the walls], and the Levites outside," all of them constituting a kind of "guard of the king's head." Similarly we have been taught in the Beraitha of Thirty-two Rules:[98] "What is [an example of] a subject not explained in its [proper] place but explained elsewhere? It is written etc. Similarly, it is stated: *The families of the sons of Kohath were to pitch on the side of the Tabernacle southward;*[99] *The families of the Gershonites were to pitch behind the Tabernacle westward;*[100] *And the prince of the father's house of the families of Merari being Zuriel the son of Abichail, they were to pitch on the side of the Tabernacle northward.*[101] We have not yet heard, however, that the Holy One, blessed be He, commanded [Aaron] that he should divide his sons into twenty-four Divisions.[92] Where, then, have we heard it? [In the verse in I Chronicles 24: 19, following the division of the priests by David and Zadok into twenty-four Divisions, where it is stated]: *These were the orderings of them in their service, to come into the House of the Eternal according to the ordinance given unto them by the hand of Aaron their father, as the Eternal, the G-d of Israel, had commanded him.* We thus learn that this commandment [of dividing the priests into *mishmaroth*][92] was already given to Moses and Aaron."

We have also been taught in Tractate Tamid:[102] "The priests kept watch at three places in the Sanctuary." And in the Gemara there the Rabbis said:[103] "Whence do we know this? Said Abaye: Scripture states, *And those that were to pitch before the Tabernacle eastward*

(97) Sifre *Korach* 116. (98) In interpreting the *legal* precepts of the Torah, there are thirteen basic principles of exegesis formulated by Rabbi Ishmael. For explaining the Agadic (homiletic) teachings of the Torah, there are thirty-two such rules, formulated by Rabbi Eliezer the son of Rabbi Yosei the Galilean. Ramban's quotation here is found in Enelow's edition of the work, page 30. See in Genesis (Vol. I, p. 437) where Ramban refers to this Tannaitic work as "the Midrash of Thirty-two Rules by which Agadah is explained."Thus, although a wider latitude of interpretation was applied to the homiletic teachings of the Torah, they were yet guarded by a set of rules which assured all such elucidations as being authentic expressions of the Torah. (99) Further, 3:29. (100) *Ibid.*, Verse 23. (101) *Ibid.*, Verse 35. (102) Tamid 25 b. (103) *Ibid.*, 26 a. The Mishnah there explains which were the three specific places in the Temple at Jerusalem where the priests used to keep watch.

were Moses, and after him *Aaron and his* [two] *sons, keeping the charge of the Sanctuary.*[104] [This teaches us that] Aaron was [to guard] in one place and his [two] sons in two [other] places etc.," as is explained there. Thus we learn that these commandments apply for all times and not only at the Tabernacle, and the verses in the Book of Chronicles[105] explain the subject of the *mishmaroth*[92] and the [details of the] whole institutions.

2

2. EVERY MAN SHALL ENCAMP BY HIS OWN STANDARD, WITH THE SIGNS OF THEIR FATHER'S HOUSE. "Each standard was to have a colored cloth hanging on it, the color of one being unlike the color of another.[106] The color of each standard corresponded to that of the stone fixed in the breastplate [of the High Priest, on which the name of that tribe was engraved], and by this method everyone would recognize his standard." This is Rashi's language. But Rabbi Abraham ibn Ezra commented: "There were signs on each of the [four main] standards. Thus the ancient Sages said that on Reuben's standard there was a figure of a man decorated with mandrakes,[107] and on Judah's standard there was the form of a lion, to which Jacob had compared him,[108] and on Ephraim's standard was the figure of an ox, based upon [the expression that Moses used in speaking of that tribe], *the firstborn of his ox,*[109] and on Dan's standard was the figure of an eagle.[110] Thus [the four signs on the four main standards] were similar to the four figures that the prophet

(104) Further, 3:38. (105) The twenty-four Divisions of the priests are mentioned in I Chronicles 24:7-18; those of the Levites, *ibid.*, Verses 20-31. Verse 19 there [quoted above in the text] states that the command to make such Divisions was already given to Moses and Aaron. See also *ibid.*, 9:22. It remained, however, an oral tradition among the priests that they would be finally divided into such twenty-four Divisions until Ezra (the author of the Book of Chronicles) came and showed that the total number of these Divisions has been alluded to, in the Torah. (106) There were thus twelve standards, one for each tribe (Maskil l'David in his commentary on Rashi). These twelve standards are not to be confused with the four main standards, around each of which three tribes rallied. (107) See Genesis 30:14. (108) *Ibid.*, 49:9. (109) Deuteronomy 33:17. (110) This was because of the expression, *as an eagle stirreth up his nest* (*ibid.*, 32:11), and of Dan it is written that *he was the rearward of all the camps* (further, 10:25), who stirred the attention of all the camps to any lurking dangers (Tziyoni).

Ezekiel saw [in the Divine Charriot]." [111] The Tent of Meeting was in the exact center, with the camps of the Levites surrounding it in the midst of the camps [of the other tribes], as is mentioned in Sefer Yetzirah: [112] "And the Holy Temple is placed exactly in the middle."

Now the directions [in which the standards were to be set up] begin with the east, like the movement of the sun [in its daily course], and afterwards the south, and then the west and finally the north. They put the [main] standard of Judah in the east because he was the first to start journeying as he was the prince, [113] just as G-d commanded, *Judah shall go up*[114] *first,*[115] and Reuben was [set next to him] in the south to honor him as the firstborn. Thus these two neighboring standards consisted of [the children of] Leah [i.e., Judah, Issachar, Zebulun, Reuben Shimon] together with the firstborn of her maidservant who was born upon her [Leah's] knees [i.e., Gad the son of Zilpah.]. And there was one [main] standard for the children of Rachel [Ephraim, Menasheh, and Benjamin] in the west, and the standard of the [other] children of the maidservants [Dan, Asher, and Naphtali] was last, in the north.

I have furthermore seen in the Midrash [the following text]: [116] "And just as the Holy One, blessed be He, created four directions in the universe, so He surrounded His Throne with four 'living creatures,' [111] and high above them all is the Throne of Glory. The Holy One, blessed be He, told Moses to arrange the standards in a manner corresponding to these directions. Thus He said to him: In the east, whence comes light to the world, shall Judah the sovereign pitch his camp, and next to him shall be the tribe of Issachar, who studies the Torah, [117] and next to him the tribe of Zebulun, who is

(111) Ezekiel Chapter 1. *As for the likeness of their faces, they had the face of a man; and they four had the face of a lion on the right side; and they four had the face of an ox on the left side; they four had also the face of an eagle* (*ibid.,* Verse 10). (112) I have not found it in our editions of the Sefer Yetzirah (Book of Creation). On the book itself, see Vol. I, p. 24, Note 41. (113) I Chronicles 28:4. (114) Judges 1:2. (115) *Ibid.,* 20:18. (116) Bamidbar Rabbah 2:9. (117) "For it is said, *And of the children of Issachar, men that had understanding of the times* (I Chronicles 12:32), and Torah is called 'light,' *For the commandment is a lamp, and the Torah is light* (Proverbs 6:23)" (Bamidbar Rabbah 2:9)—Thus, just as the royal House of David is referred to by Scripture in terms of

wealthy, just as it is written, *Zebulun shall dwell at the shore of the sea,*[118] and it is also said [of Zebulun], *for they shall suck the abundance of the sea.*[119] They were to be the first to journey, just as it is said, *And their king is passed on before them, and the Eternal at the head of them.*[120] From the south come the dews and the rains [which bring] blessing for the world, therefore shall Reuben pitch on that side, for he is the master of repentance,[121] which is a good quality, and the mercies of the Holy One, blessed be He, come to the world when people repent [of their evil ways]. Next to Reuben is Gad, who has the quality of heroism.[122] Thus there were [in the south] Reuben with repentance, Gad with heroism, and in between them Shimon in order to atone [for his having caused anguish to his father Jacob].[123] *And they shall set forth second,*[124] because repentance is second to Torah [for by studying Torah one is coming to repent of evil ways]. In the west are the storehouses of snow, and the storehouses of hail, cold, and heat, and corresponding to them were [the tribes of] Ephraim, Menasheh and Benjamin, and the Divine Presence is always

light — as it is said, *that David My servant may have 'a lamp' always before Me in Jerusalem* (I Kings 11:36) — so also is Issachar, student of the Torah which is called light. The position of these two tribes is therefore rightfully in the east whence comes light to the world. And as for Zebulun (see further in text). (118) Genesis 49:13. (119) Deuteronomy 33:19. And riches are also referred to as "light" (Midrash Rabbah *ibid.*). Thus the three tribes that pitched on the east—Judah (sovereignty), Isaachar (knowledge), and Zebulun (wealth)—all represented aspects of "light" which originates in the east. (120) Micah 2:13. (121) See Sotah 7b and Rashi *ibid.*, that Judah's repentance in admitting his guilt in the case of Tamar (Genesis 38:26) was motivated by Reuben's prior repentance in the case of Bilhah (*ibid.*, 35:22). Reuben was also first of the brothers who tried to save Joseph in order to return him to his father (*ibid.*, 37:22). According to a Midrash, G-d then said: " 'You [Reuben] were first in making an effort to bring back a beloved son to his father. By your life! A descendant of yours will be the first [of the prophets] to bring back Israel to their Father in heaven.' And who was that? Hosea the son of Beeri, as it is written, *When the Eternal spoke at first with Hosea*(Hosea 1:2) [and it was that prophet *who proclaimed: Return, O Israel, unto the Eternal thy G-d, for thou hast stumbled in thine iniquity*"(*ibid.*14:2)] (Yalkut Shimoni, at the beginning of the Book of Hosea). That Hosea was of the tribe of Reuben is indicated in I Chronicles 5:6, where his father Beerah is counted among the descendants of Reuben. Beeri and Beerah, according to the Rabbis, refer to the same person. (122) Genesis 49:19. In our Bamidbar Rabbah: "master of the troop," as stated in Genesis *ibid*: (123) *Ibid.*, Verses 5-7, and in Chapter 34:30. (124) Verse 16 here.

in the west within the border of Benjamin, as it is said, *Of Benjamin he* [Moses] *said: The beloved of the Eternal shall dwell in safety by Him.*[125] *And they shall set forth third,*[126] for heroism is fitting to Torah and repentance, in order that a person may grow strong in Torah and overcome his [bad] inclinations. From the north comes darkness to the world, and corresponding to it was the tribe of Dan. For what reason? It is because the tribe of Dan darkened the world through the idols which Jeroboam made, as it is said, *and the one idol he put in Dan.*[127] Next to him was the tribe of Asher, to illuminate the darkness, as it is said [of Asher], *and he shall dip his foot in oil,*[128] and next to him was the tribe of Naphtali who is full of blessings.[129] *They shall set forth hindmost,*[130] for whoever worships idols *goes backward and not forward.*"[131]

There [in Bamidbar Rabbah][116] the Rabbis also interpret [the division of the tribes of Israel according to four standards as] corresponding to the four groups of angels [surrounding the celestial Throne]. The Midrash also explains there that [the division of the tribes was not arbitrary but] it was all in wisdom, [showing] honor and greatness to Israel, and that therefore Scripture mentions everything in detail.

4. AND HIS HOST, AND THOSE THAT WERE NUMBERED OF THEM. The meaning thereof, as well as of *all that were numbered of the camp of Judah,*[132] and so also all [such verses in this chapter], is that these are the words of G-d to Moses, connected with [the opening statement], *And the Eternal spoke unto Moses and unto Aaron,*[133] since they did not count them now a second time. This is also the sense

(125) Deuteronomy 33:12. This is an allusion to the fact that the Sanctuary proper, in which the Divine Presence resided, was in Benjamin's territory. The eastern part of the Temple was in the territory of Judah. These three tribes of Ephraim, Menasheh and Benjamin, to whom G-d grants might (see Psalms 80:3) are thus the most able to resist the destructive aspects of the natural elements (Eitz Yoseph on Bamidbar Rabbah). (126) Verse 24 here. (127) I Kings 12:29. (128) Deuteronomy 33:24. (129) As it is said of that tribe, *O Naphtali, satisfied with favor, and full with the blessing of the Eternal* (*ibid.,* Verse 23). (130) Verse 31 here. (131) Jeremiah 7:24. (132) Further, Verse 9. (133) Verse 1.

of the verse, *These are they that were numbered of the children of Israel,*[134] because He stated [in that same verse] *all that were numbered of the camps according to their hosts* [which indicates that He is referring to a census which had previously taken place, and not to a new census]. He mentioned all this in order to tell us that from the day of the census [which was on the first of Iyar] [135] until the camps were established [according to the four standards] *and they so pitched by the standards, and so they set forward*[136] [which was on the twentieth of Iyar],[137] not one man was missing. This was miraculous, in that not one person of this great multitude died [in the period of twenty days].

The change in the name of the father of the prince of the children of Gad [who is called Deuel above in 1:14, and here in Verse 14 is referred to as Reuel], is because it is customary in the Sacred Language to change names of the same meaning, such as Zerah[138] [one of the sons of Shimon], and Zohar[139] [referring to the same son of Shimon, both names meaning "brightness"], of the expression *as 'tzachar' (white) wool.*[140] Now [the father of the prince of the children of Gad] was called "Deuel" [of the root *dei'ah,* "knowledge"] because he "knew" G-d, [and he was also called] "Reuel" [of the root *ra'ayon,* "thoughts," or *re'uth,* "longing" "striving"] because "he set all the thoughts of his heart on G-d," similar to the expression in these verses: *How weighty also are 'rei'echa' (Thy thoughts) unto me, O G-d;* [141] *Thou understandest 'l'rei'i' (my thought) afar off.*[142] Since people used to call that person by two names [e.g. Deuel and Reuel], therefore the Torah mentioned both of them.

3 1. NOW THESE ARE THE GENERATIONS OF AARON AND MOSES IN THE DAY THAT THE ETERNAL SPOKE WITH MOSES IN MOUNT SINAI. "And yet [in the following verse] Scripture only enumerates the sons of Aaron, [as it is said, *And these*

(134) Further, Verse 32. (135) Above, 1:1. (136) Further, Verse 34. (137) *Ibid.*, 10:11, and see Taanith 29a ["on that day they turned aside" and hence they became subject again to death] (138) I Chronicles 4:24. (139) Genesis 46:10. (140) Ezekiel 27:18. (141) Psalms 139:17. (142) *Ibid.*, Verse 2.

are the names of the sons of Aaron! If so, why does it say here *and Moses?*] They [were indeed the sons of Aaron, but] they are called *the generations of Moses* because he taught them Torah. This establishes the principle that if one teaches the Torah to one's fellow man,[143] Scripture accounts it to him as though he had begotten him. *In the day that the Eternal spoke to Moses* did these children [of Aaron] become his [Moses'], because he taught them then what he learned from the mouth of the Almighty." This is Rashi's language.

However, the expression *in the day that the Eternal spoke to Moses* is intended [not to convey the idea mentioned by Rashi, but] only to say that these were [Aaron's four] sons [namely, Nadab and Abihu, Eleazar and Ithamar, as mentioned in Verse 2] *in the day that the Eternal spoke with Moses in Mount Sinai,* and then Scripture states [in the following verses] that Nadab and Abihu died, and that therefore they[144] have no children now except Eleazar and Ithamar. Now Scripture mentions this in order to state that *in the day that the Eternal spoke with Moses in Mount Sinai* these [sons of Aaron] were chosen to be anointed, and *their anointing shall be to them for an everlasting priesthood,*[145] but as for the rest of the tribe [of Levi], Moses was not commanded that they be chosen [for service in the Tabernacle] until now. And the reason why He mentioned *the generations of Aaron and Moses* at this place is that since He had completed the census of all Israel *by their generations and by their fathers' houses,*[58] and He now wanted to mention the generations of the tribe of Levi, He began with the leaders of that tribe.

According to the plain meaning of Scripture, the sense of [the expression] *the generations of Aaron and Moses* is that the sons of Aaron were anointed priests separated from [the rest of] the tribe [of Levi] so that they be *most holy,*[146] and the generations of Moses were *the family of the Amramites* which He mentions further on, since of

(143) In our Rashi: "the son of his fellow man." (144) I.e., Aaron and Moses. — Ramban is following the verse which speaks of the children as *the generations of Aaron and Moses,* for the reason that Rashi explained, but he is of course referring to Aaron's sons. (145) Exodus 40:15. (146) I Chronicles 23:13.

the Amramites there were only the children of Moses,[147] and they are counted among the Levites. This [verse] is thus similar to that which it is written, *The sons of Amram: Aaron and Moses; and Aaron was separated, that he should be sanctified as most holy.*[146] *But as for Moses the man of G-d, his sons are named among the tribe of Levi.*[148] And the homiletic interpretation [which Rashi mentioned, that the generations of Aaron are also attributed to Moses because he taught them Torah], the Rabbis based upon [the fact that] Scripture does not state "and these are the names of the sons of Moses," as it does with the sons of Aaron [stating in Verse 3: *These are the names of the sons of Aaron* — therefore the Rabbis explained that the verse says: *Now these are the generations of Aaron and Moses*] to allude to [the principle that] the sons of Aaron are also the generations of Moses because he taught them Torah, for it is the way of the Torah to explain and to allude [to spiritual truths].

4. AND ELEAZAR AND ITHAMAR MINISTERED 'AL PNEI' AARON THEIR FATHER — "that is, during the lifetime [of Aaron their father]." This is the language of Rashi. Now [Rashi] does not mean to say that they *ministered* during their father's lifetime, for all priests of the family of Aaron may minister during their fathers' lifetime [so why should Scripture single out Eleazar and Ithamar in this respect?] Rather, [the verse says that they were *anointed* during Aaron's lifetime], because He had stated [that Aaron's sons were] *the priests that were anointed,*[149] meaning that they too were like the High Priests in that they were anointed during Aaron's lifetime, just as he [Aaron] was anointed, a procedure which was not applicable in later generations.[150]

But the correct interpretation is that the expression *al pnei* refers to

(147) Further, Verse 27. Of Amram's two sons, the sons of the first, Aaron, are already mentioned above; thus the verse must be speaking of Moses' children only. (148) I Chronicles 23:14. (149) Verse 3. (150) In later generations ordinary priests did not have to be anointed; they automatically entered into the priesthood by descent. Only High Priests were anointed. Scripture thus alludes here to the unusual fact that Eleazar and Ithamar were anointed at this time, although they were ordinary priests, in the same way that Aaron the High Priest was anointed, a procedure which was not followed in later generations, see Vol. III, p. 117.

the beginning [of the verse, and the order of the phrases is to be understood as if inverted, as follows]: "And Nadab and Abihu died before the Eternal *'al pnei'* (in the presence of) Aaron their father, when they offered strange fire." [151] And so indeed it is stated in the Book of Chronicles: *And Nadab and Abihu died before their father, and had no children, and Eleazar and Ithamar executed the priest's office.*[152] The meaning of [the expression] *before the Eternal* is that they died a miraculous death which came [directly] from Him. Similarly it is stated in the case of the spies that they died *by the plague before the Eternal.*[153]

14. AND THE ETERNAL SPOKE UNTO MOSES IN THE WILDERNESS OF SINAI. The reason for this statement is that since Scripture said above *in the day that the Eternal spoke with Moses in Mount Sinai,*[154] it refers back and says [here] that the command for counting the Levites was not given in Mount Sinai; for only the choosing of the [four] children of Aaron [as priests] took place in Mount Sinai on the day that He commanded Moses about the making of the Tabernacle, but he was not given the command about the choosing of [all] the Levites [as ministers to the priests] at Mount Sinai, but *in the wilderness of Sinai* in the Tent of Meeting, just like the commandment mentioned [above] concerning [the counting of] the children of Israel [about which it is clearly stated that it was *in the wilderness of Sinai, in the Tent of Meeting*].[135]

Now the tribe of Levi was not like all the other tribes, for [even though they were counted] *from a month old and upward*[155] [unlike the other tribes who were counted only from the age of twenty years and over], they were still only *twenty and two thousand,*[156] and from thirty years old and over they were all together [only] *eight thousand* [*and five hundred and fourscore*].[157] Thus, their number from twenty

(151) The order of the phrases according to the Hebrew text is as follows: *And Nadab and Abihu died before the Eternal when they offered strange fire before the Eternal, in the wilderness of Sinai, and they had no children; and Eleazar and Ithamar ministered in the priest's office in the presence of Aaron their father.* (152) I Chronicles 24:2. (153) Further, 14:37. (154) Above, Verse 1. (155) Verse 15 here. (156) Further, Verse 39. (157) *Ibid.*, 4:48.

years old and over does not reach even a half of the [number of the] smallest of [the other] tribes of Israel! [158] And they did not as yet carry the ark, [that we should say] that its holiness took a toll of them! [159] This is indeed astonishing, that His servants and His pious ones should not be *blessed of the Eternal*[160] as were the rest of the people!

Therefore I am of the opinion that this is a confirmation of what our Rabbis have said,[161] that the tribe of Levi was not [subject to] the enslavement of Egyptian bondage and the rigorous work [that was imposed on the rest of the tribes]. Now since the children of Israel's *lives* were *made bitter* by the Egyptians *with hard work*[162] in order to diminish them, the Holy One, blessed be He, increased them [miraculously] to overcome the decree of the Egyptians, just as He said, *And as they afflicted them, so they multiplied and so they grew,*[163] and just as it is said also with reference to the decree that *if it be a son, then ye shall kill him*[164] — *and the people multiplied, and waxed very mighty*[165] — since the Holy One, blessed be He, said: "We shall see *whose words shall stand, Mine or theirs.*" [166] But the tribe of Levi [which was not subject to bondage] reproduced and increased in a normal way, and therefore they did not become as numerous as the other tribes. Perhaps also [their small numbers were] on account of the anger of the patriarch [Jacob] towards them,[167] for the tribe of Shimon which now had a large population[168] decreased, so that at the time of their entry into the Land [they numbered only] twenty-two thousand

(158) The smallest tribe was that of Menasheh, which numbered — from the age of twenty and over — 32,200 (above, 1:35). Thus the Levites, who numbered 8000 men above the age of thirty, certainly do not reach half of the numbers of Menasheh, even after taking into consideration a few more thousand between the ages of twenty and thirty. (159) According to tradition, the carrying of the ark involved great risk. Any of the Kohathites who was unworthy of carrying it immediately suffered a punishment; so also anyone who attended to it with an unwilling heart (Bamidbar Rabbah 5:1). But, as Ramban points out, when this census of the Levites was taken, they were not yet carrying the ark, since they only journeyed from Mount Sinai on the twentieth of Iyar. So the question reappears, why were their numbers so few? (160) Isaiah 65:23. (161) Tanchuma *Va'eira* 6. See also Ramban on Exodus 5:4. (162) Exodus 1:14. (163) *Ibid.*, Verse 12. (164) *Ibid.*, Verse 16. (165) *Ibid.*, Verse 20. (166) Jeremiah 44:28. See Vol. I, p. 457. (167) Genesis 34:25-30, and 49:5-7. (168) See above, 1:23, where the verse numbers them at *fifty-nine thousand and three hundred.*

[and two hundred[169] — whereas most of the other tribes increased in the same period, or decreased relatively slightly]; similarly, Levi, the tribe of His pious ones,[170] was not decreased in the plague [caused because of Peor,[171] and yet at the time of entry into the Land they numbered only one thousand more[172] than their present twenty-two thousand! Thus we see that it was the anger of the patriarch which affected the numbers of both Shimon and Levi.]

23. THE FAMILIES OF THE GERSHONITES WERE TO PITCH BEHIND THE TABERNACLE WESTWARD. Scripture did not begin from the east in [explaining] the charge of the [various families of the] Levites as it did in the case of the standards [of the other tribes],[173] because the Levites had no charge there, except for Aaron and his sons the priests and Moses[174] the priest of the priests.[175] Therefore it began from the west, which was the position opposite the east. But He put the sons of Kohath who were the most honored of the Levites in the south [of the Tabernacle], which is the most distinguished direction [after the east],[176] and He gave them [the charge of carrying] the ark and [all] holy vessels; [177] and in the west [of the Tabernacle] He placed the sons of Gershon, since he was the firstborn [of Levi],[178] and gave them [the charge of carrying] *the Tabernacle and the Tent,*[179] and in the north, which is the last of the [four] directions, He put the sons of Merari, and gave them [the charge of] the implements of the sacred things.[180]

45. TAKE THE LEVITES INSTEAD OF ALL THE FIRSTBORN AMONG THE CHILDREN OF ISRAEL. The firstborns had become sanctified to G-d from the time that He commanded *Sanctify unto Me*

(169) Further, 26:14. (170) See Deuteronomy 33:8. (171) Further, 25:9. (172) *Ibid.*, 26:62. (173) Above, 2:3. (174) Further, Verse 38. (175) See Zebachim 101-102. During the seven days of installation when the Tabernacle was first erected, Moses acted as the priest, and showed the future priests how to do the Service. He was thus "priest of the priests." (176) Tur. (177) Further, Verse 31. (178) Exodus 6:16. (179) Above, Verse 25. "The Tabernacle" refers to the lower ten curtains which formed the ceiling, and were visible inside the Tabernacle. "The Tent" refers to the upper layer of curtains made of goat's hair, which were visible on top of the Tabernacle (Rashi). (180) Verses 36-37.

all the firstborn . . . among the children of Israel etc.[181] There were thus many firstborns in Israel who had not been redeemed until now, since it had not yet been said who would "redeem" them, for it was only now that the priests became sanctified, and [Israel] had not yet been commanded about the gifts of the priesthood.[182] Thus they [the firstborns] continued without restriction in their sanctity, and it is possible that they performed the Service of the offerings, as our Rabbis have said.[183]

The correct opinion appears to me to be that not all these firstborns were born in the desert in one year, for the people did not increase there so rapidly [that there should have been twenty-two thousand firstborns in one year, corresponding to the twenty-two thousand Levites, with an excess over the Levites of two hundred and seventy-three].[184]Rather, all firstborns of Israel [alive at that time, even those born many years previously] were counted, for they were all sanctified, as I have explained there.[185] Now, He exchanged them for the Levites, and this was their "redemption," and He commanded to redeem those that exceeded [the number of the Levites by means of each one giving five shekels]. And He gave the redemption-money to Aaron and his sons, as is the commandment for all generations [that a firstborn son be redeemed by giving five shekels to a priest].

4 6. AND THEY SHALL PUT THEREON [on the ark of the Testimony] A COVERING OF 'TACHASH' [186] SKIN, AND THEY SHALL SPREAD OVER IT A CLOTH ALL OF BLUE. Because of the importance of the ark, the covering of *tachash* skin was not visible [at all] upon it; for they covered [the ark firstly] with the Veil as a screening partition,[187] and then they covered both of them [the ark and the Veil] with the covering of the *tachash* skin [as a protection] against the rains, and above them all they spread *a cloth all of blue* so that this distinguished garment, which was *the like of the very heaven for clearness,*[188] should be seen upon it. But as for all the other vessels

(181) Exodus 13:2. (182) Further, 18:8-20. (183) Zebachim 115 b. (184) Verse 46. (185) Exodus 13:11. See my Hebrew commentary here p. 204. (186) "*Tachash* was a kind of wild animal which only existed at the time [when Israel built the Tabernacle]. Its hide was multicolored" (Rashi, Exodus 25:5). (187) Verse 5. (188) Exodus 24:10.

— the table, the candelabrum, and the altars — the covering of the *tachash* skin[186] was visible over them.[189] And some scholars[190] say that the meaning of the verse [before us] *and they shall spread over it a cloth all of blue* refers to the screening partition Veil [mentioned in the preceding Verse 5, thus meaning: "and they had already spread over it a cloth all of blue"], *and they shall put thereon,* that is, on the ark and the Veil, *the covering of the 'tachash' skin.*[191]

And they shall set the staves thereof. This means, they shall put them on the shoulders of the priests.[192] The correct interpretation is that the word *v'samu* (and they shall set) means that they should adjust them [the staves] so that they should protrude outside [the ark] in such a way that they can carry it by means of them, for the rings [in which the staves were permanently fixed] were wide, so that they were able to lengthen the staves at will, provided only that they were not taken out from them.[193]

7. AND THE CONTINUAL BREAD SHALL REMAIN THEREON. On the table itself was to be the bread,[194] and upon them [i.e., the twelve loaves of bread] a cloth of blue, and upon this cloth which was on the table they put all the vessels, and afterwards they spread upon the vessels and the table a cloth of scarlet.[195] For in honor

(189) Verses 8-14. (190) This opinion is stated here by Ibn Ezra. (191) Thus according to this interpretation, it was the covering of the *tachash*-skin that was visible on top of the ark when it was carried, and beneath it was the cloth all of blue, and not, as explained before, that the cloth of blue was spread on top over the *tachash* skin. (192) In Ibn Ezra, who quotes this interpretation in the name of "some scholars", the reading is: "those who are to carry the ark," namely the Levites of the Kohath family, instead of: "the priests". See my Hebrew commentary p. 205, Note 74. — Ibn Ezra also mentions another interpretation, namely, that the meaning of the expression *and they shall set the staves thereof* is that they should replace the staves which they had previously removed while the ark was being wrapped. Ramban evidently rejects this interpretation because of the verse, *The staves shall be in the rings of the ark; they shall not be taken from it* (Exodus 25:15), which clearly states that the staves are to remain in the rings permanently. See text further. (193) See Note 192. (194) The verse reads: *And upon the table of showbread they shall spread a cloth of blue, and put thereon the dishes, and the pans . . . and the continual bread shall remain thereon.* Ramban interprets the verse to mean: "and upon the table of showbread, on which the continual bread shall remain, they shall spread a cloth of blue etc." (195) Verse 8.

of the bread which was arranged on the table according to the precept [of the Torah], they spread this cloth of blue in order to divide between the table and its bread [beneath the cloth], and the vessels [which lay above the cloth]; and the upper cover was a cloth of scarlet, which was a hue of red, because the table is a sign of the crown of royalty, which is [manifested by] the attribute of justice. But the ark and the golden altar were [covered on top] with a cloth of blue,[196] alluding to the attribute which is comprised of *hakol* (the All),[197] and the altar of the burnt-offering [was covered] with a purple cloth,[198] which is redder than the first [i.e., the cloth of scarlet which was upon the table], for it is there [on the altar of the burnt-offering] that the blood of the offerings, which is a ransom for the souls [of those who offer them], is sprinkled.

16. AND THE CHARGE OF ELEAZAR THE SON OF AARON THE PRIEST SHALL BE THE OIL FOR THE LIGHT, AND THE SWEET INCENSE, AND THE CONTINUAL MEAL-OFFERING, AND THE ANOINTING OIL: HE SHALL HAVE THE CHARGE OF ALL THE TABERNACLE, AND OF ALL THAT THEREIN IS, IN THE SANCTUARY, AND IN THE VESSELS THEREOF. Scripture is stating that Eleazar was in charge of all these things, and the meaning of [the end of the verse] is that "he was in *charge of all the Tabernacle and* in charge of *all that therein is.*" And Rabbi Abraham ibn Ezra explained that it means that "Eleazar's charge extended also to the Tabernacle and to all its vessels, together with his brother Ithamar,[199] and that due to Eleazar's great distinction, he alone was in charge of the oil [for the light], and the incense." But this is not

(196) Verse 6 (the ark); Verse 11 (the golden altar). (197) See Vol. I, p. 292. (198) Verse 13. (199) Ibn Ezra's interpretation is intended to answer the following point: Scripture further on (4:28, 33) explains that it was *Ithamar* the son of Aaron who was in charge of the work of the sons of Gershon [in carrying the curtains, etc.] and of the work of the sons of Merari [in carrying the boards and bars of the Tabernacle, etc.]. Why then does Scripture state here that the charge of *Eleazar* was *all the Tabernacle* etc.? Ibn Ezra answers that Eleazar shared together with his brother Ithamar in the charge of *all the Tabernacle* etc., and that the first part of our verse is pointing out that in addition to sharing the general charge of the Tabernacle, Eleazar was, due to his great distinction, solely in charge of *the oil for the light* etc. Ramban objects to this interpretation and suggests his own explanation.

correct, since Scripture states [that the services of the sons of Gershon and Merari were] *under the hand of Ithamar*[200] [which thus indicates that Eleazar had no share in it]! And [Scripture] explained here [that Eleazar's charge was] *in the Sanctuary and in the vessels thereof,* and similarly it stated above, *And Eleazar the son of Aaron the priest, was prince over the princes of the Levites and had the oversight of them that keep the charge of the Sanctuary*[201] meaning to say that he was the prince [who supervised] the charge of those that guarded the Sanctuary, which was in the hands of the Kohathites[202] [i.e., he supervised the most holy things — the ark, the table, candelabrum, altars, Veils and the vessels used in the Divine Service]. But the meaning of *the charge of all the Tabernacle* is that *"the charge of . . . the oil for the light, and the incense, and the meal-offering, and the anointing oil,* and *the charge of all the Tabernacle — in the Sanctuary, and of all that therein is* of the holy vessels — they were all under the hand of Eleazar," [202] and they are those mentioned here when He stated, *And when Aaron and his sons have made an end of covering the Sanctuary and all the vessels of the Sanctuary.*[203] Eleazar was thus officer over the three princes[204] [of the Levites], and [also] overseer of the charge of the Kohathites, and Ithamar was overseer of [the charges of the families of] Gershon and Merari. Now since Scripture does not say that Eleazar "shall bear" [the oil for the light

(200) Further, 4:28, 33. (201) Above, 3:32. (202) Ramban's meaning is as follows. It is clear from Scripture's explanations that Eleazar was *the prince of the princes of the Levites* inasmuch as he supervised the most holy things. In Verse 4 above it is clearly stated that the sons of Kohath — *alone* — were in charge of the most holy things, thus disproving Ibn Ezra's explanation quoted above. If so, the phrase *the charge of all the Tabernacle* must be in apposition to the end of the verse namely *in the Sanctuary, and in the vessels thereof,* and the meaning is as follows: "the charge of the oil for the light, etc., *the charge of all the Tabernacle,* that is, *in the Sanctuary, and in the vessels thereof* which refers to the most holy things [the ark, etc.] they were given over to the Kohathites — and all these were under the charge of Eleazar," just as Ithamar was in charge of the work of the sons of Gershon and Merari. In addition to supervising the Kohathites, and assigning each one his particular duty, Eleazar was also chief of all three main Levite families, as will be explained. (203) Verse 15. (204) The prince of the Gershonites was Eliasaph the son of Lael (above, 3:24); of the Kohathites, Elitzaphan the son of Uzziel (*ibid.*, Verse 30), and of the families of Merari, Tzuriel the son of Abichail (*ibid.*, Verse 35). The prince over the princes of the Levites was Eleazar the son of Aaron (*ibid.*, Verse 32).

etc.] as is said of the Levites,[205] it would appear that Eleazar did not carry them, but was in charge over them and would give them from hand to hand to those Kohathites whom he chose because of their zeal and piety. It was they who carried them, and they returned them to his control when the Tabernacle was set up. This also [is the meaning of the verse which says that Eleazar was *the prince over the princes of the Levites,*] *having the oversight of them that keep the charge of the Sanctuary,*[206] and the verse stating, *and by name ye shall appoint the vessels of the charge of their burden*[207] [conveying the same thought, that the individual families of the Levites were to be told by the overseer what their particular kind of work would be, and Eleazar, as the prince over the princes, was the overseer of all the service of the Levites].

But according to the opinion of the Yerushalmi[208] mentioned in the commentaries of Rashi[209] that he [Eleazar himself] carried them [all the objects enumerated], it would be a heavy load! For the incense consisted of three hundred and sixty-eight manehs,[210] and [surely] Moses our teacher would not have prepared [only] half of the required quantity,[211] and the oil for the light for a whole year was a large amount, namely one hundred and eighty-three logs,[212] and as for [the ingredients required for] the continual meal-offering, we do not know

(205) Further, Verse 25: *And they shall bear . . .* (206) Above, 3:32. (207) Further, 4:32. (208) Ramban is not referring to Rashi here, but to Rashi's commentary to Shabbath 92 a. On the term "Yerushalmi," see Leviticus, *Seder Metzora,* (p. 192, Note 44). (209) This expression ["mentioned in the commentaries of Rashi"] clearly indicates that Ramban does not mean Rashi's commentary on the Torah, as he never refers to it by that description. Rather, the reference is to Rashi's commentary on the Talmud. See Note 208. (210) Kerithoth 6 a. There was one for each day of the solar year, and 3 extra manehs for the Service on the Day of Atonement. (211) "If he compounded only half the required amount [i.e., 184 manehs] it would be valid" (Yerushalmi Yoma IV, 5). This rule applies to the compounding of the incense, which was to be done once every year. But, continues Ramban, although valid if done in this manner, surely Moses would prepare the complete, and not just half, the required amount. Hence Eleazar carried the full quantity [except, of course, for the amount that had been used up from the time of the erection of the Tabernacle until the camps set forth]. (212) Half a log of oil was used up every night of the year (Menachoth 89 a). This was the measure that was estimated to be sufficient for the longest night of the year; if any of the oil was left over on the shorter nights, it did not matter (*ibid*).

how many days' supply he carried! But [we would have to say that] Eleazar was very strong and powerful, as was our patriarch Jacob,[213] and so also were Moses our teacher[214] and his brother Aaron,[215] and *they that wait for the Eternal shall renew their strength.*[216]

20. AND THEY [i.e., the Kohathites] SHALL NOT GO IN TO SEE THE HOLY THING 'K'VALA' (AS THEY ARE BEING COVERED) — "as they [the priests] put each vessel into its wrapping, as I have explained above in this section: 'and they shall spread upon it such-and-such a garment, and they shall cover it with such-and-such a cover,' the [term] *'k'vala'* referring to its 'covering.' " This is Rashi's language. It is also Onkelos' opinion [who translated the verse as quoted above]. But our Rabbis have said in Tractate Sanhedrin[217] that this verse constitutes a prohibition against stealing a sacred vessel, for which one suffers death [by the hand of Heaven], and zealous people have the right to strike such a thief, for stealing and robbing are referred to as *b'liah* (swallowing, devouring), as in the expressions: *'bala' (he hath swallowed down) riches, and he shall vomit them up again;*[218] *and I will bring forth out of his mouth 'eth bil'o' (that which he hath swallowed up).*[219]

But Rabbi Abraham ibn Ezra explained [the verse] in its plain sense: that [the Kohathites] should not come in to see when the screening Veil is removed and the ark becomes exposed; only afterwards when it is covered are they to come in to carry it. Accordingly, the expression *k'vala eth hakodesh* means [they shall not come in to see] "when the structure [i.e., the screening Veil] is being removed from the ark, which is *hakodesh* (the holiness)," [the word *'k'vala'*] being related to the expressions: *'bila Hashem' (the Eternal hath swallowed up) unsparingly*[220] [which means that He "destroyed

(213) *And Jacob went near, and rolled the stone from the well's mouth* (Genesis 29:10) — "as easily as one draws the stopper from the mouth of a bottle. Scripture thus informs you how strong he was" (Rashi *ibid.*, on the basis of Bereshith Rabbah 70:10). (214) Nedarim 38 a. (215) Vayikra Rabbah 26:10. Proof for his great strength is brought there from the fact that he lifted twenty-two Levites in one day (further, 8:21). (216) Isaiah 40:31. (217) Sanhedrin 61 b. (218) Job 20:15. (219) Jeremiah 51:44. (220) Lamentations 2:2.

the structure" of the habitations of Jacob mentioned further on in the verse]; *Thy hands have framed me . . . together round about; yet 'va'tval'eini' (Thou dost destroy me).*[221]

Thus the Levites are warned not to touch the holy ark lest they die, and only by means of its staves are they to carry it. He furthermore warned them against coming in at all to see the dismantling of the structure, while Aaron is taking down the screening Veil, in a similar way to that which is said [of the people of Beth-shemesh that they were punished] *because they had gazed upon the ark of the Eternal.*[222] He [i.e., Ibn Ezra] has explained it well [i.e., the simple meaning of the verse]. But the [true] intention of the verse is that since the Glory that resides upon the cherubim [on the cover of the ark] is there, the Levites were warned not to break through "to see the Eternal" [223] until the priests take down the Veil, for then the Glory is seen in *the hiding of His power,*[224] and it returns to its former place[225] in "the Holy of Holies." [226] In this way the expression *k'vala eth hakodesh* is to be understood in its literal sense. The student learned in the mysteries of the Cabala will understand.

(221) Job 10:8. (222) I Samuel 6:19. (223) See Exodus 19:24. (224) Habakkuk 3:4. (225) See Hosea 5:15. (226) "In the Holy of Holies on Above" (Abusaula).

Naso

26. "V'EITH KOL ASHER 'YEI'ASEH' LAHEM."[1] "[This is to be understood] as the Targum [of Onkelos rendered it]: 'and with whatever is handed over to them,' that is, to the sons of Gershon [*so shall they serve*]." This is Rashi's language. But if so [if the pronoun *lahem* refers to the Gershonites, and not to *all the vessels of* the Tabernacle and altar mentioned in the first part of the verse], then the word *yei'aseh* [does not have its usual meaning of "doing," but is to be understood as "possessions" or "articles in a person's control," the sense of the verse being: "and all 'the objects handed over' to them—they, the Gershonites shall serve with"], as in the verse: *And there was a man in Maon 'uma'aseihu' were in Carmel,*[2] which means "his possessions with which he 'does' [his occupation]."A more correct interpretation [of our verse] is that it means: "and with whatever [accessories] are made 'for them'—the Tabernacle and the altar—for they had many vessels [*so shall they*—the sons of Gershon—*serve*]."

(1) The verse is part of the section dealing with the work to be done by the families of the Gershonites in carrying the parts of the Tabernacle and its equipment. The verse before us states that they are to carry *the hangings of the court . . . and their cords, and all the vessels of their service 'v'eith kol asher yei'aseh lahem'* [literally: "and all which will be made to them"]. The question Ramban discusses is what the pronoun *lahem* ("to them" or "for them") refers to, and what the meaning of *yei'aseh* is. (2) I Samuel 25:2. The verse obviously cannot be understood in its literal sense, "his deeds," because if he was in Maon, how could "his deeds" be in Carmel! The context of the verse also indicates that it means "his possessions."

27. AT THE COMMANDMENT OF AARON AND HIS SONS SHALL BE ALL THE SERVICE OF THE SONS OF THE GERSHONITES — "and which of Aaron's sons shall be appointed over them? Ithamar" [as is stated in the following verse]. This is Rashi's language. But it is not correct for [if only Ithamar was appointed], why mention Aaron [at all — *at the commandment of Aaron* etc.]? Rather, the meaning of [the expression] *at the commandment of Aaron and his sons shall be all the service* is that the services of the Gershonites shall be at their command. They are to appoint the Gershonites to their work, saying: "This particular Gershonite shall be the overseer for such-and-such a matter" — "This one shall sing [at the services] in such-and-such a way, or attend to the gates[3] in a certain manner, or shall carry a certain number of the curtains." At the time of journeying they were also not permitted to dismantle the Tabernacle or to begin loading it until Aaron and his sons commanded them to do so. Thus all of them [Aaron and his sons] were needed for the appointed charge, Eleazar being the chief over the three princes [of the three main families of the Levites],[4] and Ithamar being the overseer over the sons of Gershon[5] and Merari.[6]

Scripture states *and 'ye' shall appoint unto them in charge* [*all which they have to carry*] [7] because Moses was to be with them at the time of the appointments, when the charges were given to them; but their charge shall be *under the hand of Ithamar,*[5] meaning that each one was to return the vessels to his control when the Tabernacle came to rest, saying to him: "Here you have the vessels that were handed over to me."

32. AND THE PILLARS OF THE COURT ROUND ABOUT, AND THEIR SOCKETS, AND THEIR PINS, AND THEIR CORDS. "[These sockets, pins and cords refer only to] those of the pillars, because the pins and cords of the hangings were part of the burden of the Gershonites [as stated above in Verse 26, and here Scripture is

(3) See further Note 31. and for Scriptural basis see my translation of Sefer Hamitzvoth ("The Commandments," Vol. I, pp. 32-33). (4) See in *Seder Bamidbar* Note 204. (5) Verse 28. (6) Verse 33. (7) Verse 27.

speaking of the work of the sons of Merari]. For there were pins and cords for the curtains and hangings on their lower edges, so that the wind should not raise them, and there were [also] pins and cords round about the pillars, in order to suspend the hangings on them at their upper edges with poles and rails, as we have been taught in [the Beraitha] on the work of the Tabernacle." This is Rashi's language. But I do not understand what pins have to do with the pillars! [8] Moreover, [even if the pillars did have pins], why were the pins of the pillars different from the other pins, in that [the other pins were given] to the sons of Gershon, and those [of the pillars were given] to the sons of Merari? Nor have I found in the Mishnah[9] on the work of the Tabernacle that there were pins to the pillars! Instead, the Rabbis taught there the following: [10] "He [Moses] joined the rails by means of cords to the pillars, and attached them to the pins of the Tent. And just as there were pins to the Tabernacle, so were there pins to the court, as it is said, *All the instruments of the Tabernacle in all the service thereof, and all the pins thereof, and all the pins of the court,* round about, *shall be of brass.*"[11] This is the language of the Beraitha. And it does not teach there that there were pins to the pillars.

But we must rather explain that the pins and cords of *the hangings of the court*[12] were in the hands of the sons of Merari [not, as Rashi understands, that they were in the charge of the Gershonites]; whereas it is the cords and pins of the Tabernacle and Tent[13] that were in the hands of the Gershonites, for [the prepositions] *and 'their' cords, and all the instruments of 'their' service*[12] [mentioned in connection with

(8) The pins were made of brass (Exodus 27:19) and their purpose was to secure the hangings to the ground so that the wind would not blow them from side to side. The poles and rods to which the *upper end* of the hangings was fixed, however, were made of wood, not of brass, and are not included in the Hebrew word for pins. Therefore Ramban asks what do the pins [made of brass] have to do with the pillars? (Kur Zahav). (9) See further in the following text, and also in Ramban on Exodus 26:17, from which it is clear that Ramban when referring to the "Mishnah", is in fact referring to the Beraitha on the construction of the Tabernacle. For the nature of this book, see Vol. II, p. 448, Note 108. (10) M'lecheth Hamishkan, Chapter 5 (p. 33, in Ish Shalom's edition). (11) Exodus 27:19. The expression "round about" is found *ibid.*, 38:20. (12) Above, Verse 26. (13) See Note 179 in *Seder Bamidbar*.

the charge of the Gershonites] are a reference to *the curtains of the Tabernacle and the Tent of Meeting*[14] mentioned in [the beginning of] the previous verse [relating to the work to be done by the Gershonite], and do not refer to [the hangings of] the court [as Rashi wrote]. Similarly, when He said above [with reference to the charge of the Gershonites], *and the cords 'of it'* [15] [the preposition "it"] alludes to the Tabernacle mentioned there [in the *preceding* verse],[16] and not to the hangings of the court [mentioned in the same verse]. A similar case [of a Scriptural reference to a prior subject] is [G-d's command addressed to Aaron]: *only 'they' shall not come nigh unto the vessels of holiness and unto the altar*[17] [where the pronoun "they"] refers back to the more distant [phrase, namely: *thy brethren, the tribe of Levi*] *the tribe of thy father*[18] [mentioned] in the preceding verse, and does not refer to the nearer [phrase] *thy sons.* So also the verse, *And 'their' redemption-money — from a month old shalt thou redeem them*[19] [where the word "their"] refers back to *the firstborn of man*[20] [mentioned in the earlier part of the preceding verse], and not to *the firstling of unclean beasts* [stated at the end of the preceding verse]. There are many cases like this.

However, it appears to me that according to the text of the Beraitha [mentioned further on] the Gershonites only carried cloths, but [did] not [carry] any brass and wood at all. This is the Beraitha wherein we are taught: [21] "The sons of Gershon were assigned [to pitch] on the west[22] [of the Tabernacle], and they were in charge of all woven materials." If so, the meaning of the term *and their pins* [mentioned in the verse before us dealing with the charge of the sons of Merari] is: "[the pins] of the Tabernacle *and* of the pillars of the court," while

(14) *Ibid.*, Verse 25. (15) *Ibid.*, 3:26. (16) *Ibid.*, Verse 25: *And the charge of the sons of Gershon in the Tent of Meeting, the Tabernacle and the Tent* etc. — Ramban is thus, interpreting the preposition "it" [*and the cords of 'it'*] — in 3:26 — as referring back to Verse 25 which mentions the Tabernacle and Tent and does not refer to *the hangings of the court* mentioned in the selfsame Verse 26. To prove this method of exegesis, Ramban proceeds to bring examples from other places in Scripture where this principle perforce applies. (17) Further, 18:3. (18) *Ibid.*, Verse 2. (19) *Ibid.*, Verse 16. (20) *Ibid.*, Verse 15. (21) M'lecheth Hamishkan, Chapter 13 (p. 80, in Ish Shalom's edition). (22) Above, 3:23.

[the term] *and their cords* refers only to those of the pillars of the *court* [since the cords of the Tabernacle itself were in the hands of the Gershonites]. Similarly He said above [with reference to the burden of the sons of Merari]: *the boards of the Tabernacle, and the bars thereof, and the pillars thereof, and the sockets thereof, and all the instruments thereof, and all that pertaineth to the service thereof,*[23] including [in general terms] the pins thereof [i.e., of both the Tabernacle and the pillars of the court]. Therefore He mentioned the cords [in speaking of] both [the burdens of the sons of Gershon[24] and those of Merari,[25] because the cords of the Tabernacle were carried by the sons of Gershon, and those of the pillars of the court by the sons of Merari], but the pins He mentioned only [in the verse before us] with reference to the sons of Merari [because the Gershonites carried no objects of brass or wood at all, but which instead were carried by the sons of Merari].

AND BY NAME YE SHALL APPOINT THE INSTRUMENTS OF THE CHARGE OF THEIR BURDENS. This means that he [Ithamar] should put the vessels which they were to carry in the hands of each man, *according to the number of names, by their polls.*[26] He [Ithamar] is to say: "This person shall carry a certain number of the boards, and that person a certain number of the bars or of the pillars," rather than commanding [generally]: "The sons of Merari as a whole shall carry all the boards, sockets and pillars." He mentioned this first in the case of the sons of Merari although this principle applied also to the work done by the sons of Kohath and Gershon because of the weight of their burdens, for each one [of the sons of Merari] might [be inclined to] make his load lighter by putting it upon his fellowman, [therefore the command had to be given to each person individually].

49. 'UPHKUDAV' (THUS WERE THEY NUMBERED OF HIM) 'ASHER' THE ETERNAL COMMANDED MOSES. "A *Masorah*[27]

(23) *Ibid.*, Verse 36. (24) Verse 26. (25) In this verse. (26) Above, 1:18. (27) The *Masorah* is the tradition handed down from generation to generation of the exact Scriptural text, and also refers to a collection of exegetical notes on the Scriptural text. The comment before us is of this second class.

has it: Five [words in the Scriptures] are written *asher* ('which,' or 'that') but they are to be understood as *ka'asher* ('as'),[28] [this being one of the five cases, and therefore the above expression is to be interpreted as follows: *thus were they numbered of him 'as' the Eternal commanded Moses*]. And those counted were, in accordance with the command, from thirty to fifty years old." This is Rashi's language. If this is so, the word, *uphkudav* refers to Moses [*thus were they numbered 'of him'* — by Moses]. But Rabbi Abraham ibn Ezra commented that [the meaning of the verse is as follows]: *every one,* that is to say, of the three [Levitical] families — namely, Gershon, Kohath, and Merari — Moses appointed *to his service, and to his burden* as Scripture mentioned above [that he should appoint them]. And this is the meaning of [the word] *uphkudav,* namely "[the appointment] of every one" mentioned.

But it is possible that the expression *'asher' tziva* be understood in its plain sense [i.e., "which" He commanded, and not, as Rashi has it, as if it said *'ka'asher' tziva* — "as" He commanded]. Scripture would thus be saying that Moses appointed [each of the sons of] these three brothers [i.e., Gershon, Kohath, and Merari] *to his service and to his burden* as explained above; *'uphkudav'* (*and the numbered individuals*) of each of them *'which' the Eternal commanded Moses* to count *by their polls,* he appointed *to his service, and to his burden.* Thus the verse mentioned that Moses numbered them by their families, and also that he appointed the [numbered] individuals by their polls, *every one to his service, and to his burden.*[29] And such

(28) This whole sentence is not found in our texts of Rashi. See however, Berliner's edition of Rashi, p. 286. — The point though is clear. The Hebrew text reads: *asher tziva Hashem* literally meaning: [and his countings] "which the Eternal commanded," and Rashi on the basis of a *Masorah* interpreted it to mean: *ka'asher tziva Hashem* — [thus were they numbered] " 'as' the Eternal commanded." Ramban later on interprets the text *asher tziva Hashem* in its literal meaning. (29) In brief: a) according to Rashi *asher tziva* is to be understood as *ka'asher tziva* ("as" the Eternal commanded). b) Rashi explains *uphkudav* as meaning "his countings," i.e., those of Moses. Ibn Ezra interprets it as "his appointments," the pronoun "his" referring to each of the three Levitical families. c) Ramban explains *asher tziva* in its literal sense, "which" the Eternal commanded [as explained in the text], the word *uphkudav* he

indeed is the law, that a Levite [of one group] is not permitted to do the work of another group or to assist therein, just as the Rabbis have said:[30] "It once happened that Rabbi Yehoshua the son of Chananyah wanted to help [his fellow-Levite] Rabbi Yochanan the son of Gudgada to close the gates [of the Sanctuary]; whereupon [the latter] said to him: 'Turn back, [for if you do not do so] your life is already forfeit, since I am one of the gatekeepers, and you are one of the singers.' "[31]

5 2. AND THEY SHALL SEND AWAY FROM THE CAMP EVERY LEPER etc. After he [Moses] had erected the Tabernacle, He commanded that the impure should be sent away from the camp in order that the camp should be holy and fit for the Divine Presence to reside therein, this being a commandment which was applicable immediately and in [all subsequent] generations.[32] And because He counted Israel *after their families, by the house of their fathers,*[33] and separated from them the mixed multitude[34] which was among them, He concluded with [the law of] the guilt-offering for robberies[35] [which has to be brought] by one who robs a proselyte.[36]

6. WHEN A MAN OR WOMAN SHALL DO ANY OF THE SINS OF MAN. [The sense of the verse] is as follows: "If a man does any of the sins by which one can transgress, of any sin which man commits against another man, *and he deals falsely with his neighbor*[37] [*—that soul shall be guilty*]." He states [here] *to commit a trespass against*

understands as does Rashi, i.e., as "countings," but the pronoun ["his"] Ramban explains as referring to each of the three brothers [Gershon, Kohath, and Merari — not personally, but in the sense of the descendants of each of them] *'which G-d commanded'* Moses to count *by their polls* — each of them he assigned to his individual work. (30) Arakhin 11b. (31) All the Levites were divided into two groups, those who attended only to the gates in the Sanctuary, and those who attended to the singing at the Services. It was forbidden for a Levite of one group to do the work generally assigned to one of the other group (see "The Commandments," Vol. II, pp. 70-72). (32) See *ibid.*, Vol. I, pp. 39-40 . (33) Above, 1:2, etc. (34) Exodus 12:38. See Ramban above, 1:18. (35) Leviticus 5:21-26. See Vol. III, pp. 56-57. (36) Further, Verse 8. (37) See Leviticus 5:24. A fifth must be paid in addition to repaying the capital.

the Eternal, which means that he swears by His Name falsely and is thus guilty before Him [as well]. Now because this sin has already been mentioned,[35] and here it only comes to introduce the new point concerning robbing a proselyte,[36] He deals with it briefly. He stated here *a man or woman* because since it is not usual for a woman to rob, [we might think that] perhaps Scripture does not make her liable to pay the additional fifth[37] or to bring a guilt-offering [when she confesses the sin] [38] like a man, [therefore He stated here *a man or woman,* teaching that her liability is in all respects the same as that of a man]. He mentioned [here], *And every heave-offering of all the holy things of the children of Israel, which they present unto the priest, shall be his,*[39] meaning to say that once they have given the heave-offering to the priest it becomes his [personal property], and he who robs it from him is to be dealt with in accordance with the law of the guilt-offering for robberies.[35] That is the reason why He mentioned it here. Or it may be that [this verse] comes to complete the laws of the priests regarding the heave-offering, since till now He only mentioned them by way of allusion, [stating] *Thou shalt not delay to offer of the fulness of thy harvest, and of the outflow of thy presses,*[40] and so also, *they may eat of his bread,*[41] but He did not explain the law of the heave-offering at all, that it is to be given to the priest; and as for the tithe, He [only] mentioned at the end of Torath Kohanim [i.e., the Book of Leviticus] that *it is holy unto the Eternal.*[42] Now, therefore, He came to command that the heave-offering and the holy gifts should belong to the priests by the grant of the owners, who may give them to them as they please, meaning to say that the benefit of satisfaction [of choosing to whom to give it] belongs to the owner [and the priest may not come and take it by force, since the owner may have the pleasure of giving it to any priest he chooses].

The meal-offering of the *sotah*[43] is not mentioned together with the other meal-offerings in Torath Kohanim [i.e., Leviticus Chapter 2]

(38) *Ibid.*, Verse 25. (39) Verse 9. (40) Exodus 22:28. See Ramban *ibid.*, (Vol. II, pp. 398-400). (41) Leviticus 22:11. (42) *Ibid.*, 27:30. (43) A *sotah* is a woman suspected of adultery, and is subject to the laws explained further on in Verses 11-31. The law concerning her meal-offering is found in Verse 15, where it is called *a meal-offering of jealousy.*

because it is *a meal-offering of jealousy*[43] and does not come for atonement, therefore He completed the law thereof here [in the Book of Numbers]. Besides, since He traced the genealogy of the people by their fathers' houses, He now gave them a law and judgment to ascertain who are the *mamzerim*[44] who are not the children of their mothers' husbands, when there arises a suspicion in a man's heart concerning his wife.

Similarly He completed here [the laws of] the offerings with the law of the Nazirite, for [only] after the Tabernacle was put up and the impure people separated from the camp, He took *of* their *young men for Nazirites,*[45] *who crowded at the entrance of the Tent of Meeting,*[46] *to stand before the Eternal to minister unto Him, and to bless in His name.*[47] Furthermore, a woman who makes the Nazirite vow is the opposite of the *sotah,*[43] [and for this reason the law of the Nazirite follows that of the *sotah*]. Therefore He stated in the section [of the Nazirite], *when either man 'or woman' utter a vow, the vow of a Nazirite.*[48] Our Rabbis have furthermore said: [49] "Why is the section dealing with the Nazirite placed next to the section dealing with the *sotah?* [43] [It is to tell us] that whoever sees a *sotah* in her disgrace should abstain [by means of a vow] from wine," the reason being that *harlotry, wine, and new wine, take away the heart.*[50] And [the commandment that] the Nazirite should let his hair grow loose is because this is the opposite of [the habit of] young men who curl their hair in order to beautify themselves, for allowing the hair to grow loose *causes anxiety in man's heart,*[51] and therefore the Nazirite is holy[52] and must guard himself from impurity,[53] for he is like the priest who ministers before his G-d [who likewise must be pure for service at the Sanctuary].

(44) The word *mamzer,* according to the final decision of the law, refers to a child born of a union which is prohibited, with the penalty of excision. It thus covers a child of any incestuous or adulterous relationship. (45) Amos 2:11. (46) Exodus 38:8. (47) Deuteronomy 10:8. (48) Further, 6:2. Since the law of vows applies equally to men and women, why did Scripture mention here *or woman*? It is to hint that this woman who takes upon herself the Nazirite vow, is the opposite of the *sotah* whose law has just been stated in the preceding section. (49) Sotah 2 a. (50) Hosea 4:11. (51) Proverbs 12:25. (52) Further, 6:8. (53) *Ibid.,* Verse 7.

9. AND EVERY HEAVE-OFFERING OF ALL THE HOLY THINGS OF THE CHILDREN OF ISRAEL, WHICH THEY BRING UNTO THE PRIEST, SHALL BE HIS. Scripture is saying that the heave-offering which the children of Israel hallow, that is to say, which they set aside [of the produce] and declare holy, shall be the priest's, for since there is no specific measure [required by law of the Torah[54] when setting aside] the heave-offering, therefore Scripture said that however much they set aside of the produce [as the heave-offering] shall belong to the priest when the owners bring it and give it to him, but the priest may not take it by force. This is the plain meaning of the verse. And so the Rabbis have said in the Sifre: [55] "Rabbi Akiba says: 'Scripture comes [here] to teach you that if the owner wishes to declare his whole granary heave-offering, he may do so, provided that he leaves over a small amount' [as ordinary food]." [56]

We have furthermore been taught there in the Sifre: [55] "*Which 'yakrivu' (they bring) unto the priest.* Said Rabbi Yishmael: But do they bring the heave-offering to the priest? What then is the meaning of the expression, *which 'yakrivu' (they bring) unto the priest, shall be his?* [It is as follows:] Since He stated, *The choicest first-fruits of thy land thou shalt bring unto the House of the Eternal thy G-d,*[57] but we have not been informed yet what shall be done with them, therefore Scripture states [here], *which 'yakrivu' (they bring) unto the priest, shall be his* — Scripture comes and teaches you that the first-fruits are to be given to the priest." Now Rashi [in citing here this text of the Sifre] explained [the question] "But do they bring the heave-offering to the priest?" in the following way: "Does not the priest have to go around the granaries asking for it?" But this is not clear.[58] But the

(54) But the Sages laid down a measure: a generous person should give one fortieth of his produce; an average man, one fiftieth, and an ungenerous person must give nonetheless a sixtieth part (Terumoth 4:3). (55) Sifre *Naso* 5. The "Sifre" is the Tannaitic Midrash on the Books of Numbers and Deuteronomy. It is equivalent to the Mechilta on Exodus, and the Sifra or Torath Kohanim on Leviticus. (56) From this text in the Sifre it is also obvious that there is no prescribed measure for the heave-offering. (57) Exodus 23:19. (58) From Rashi's comment it is obvious that even if the priest does not take it by force, but goes around the granaries to obtain the heave-

[correct] explanation is that in the opinion of Rabbi Yishmael [in the above text of the Sifre] the root *hakravah* in the Torah ["bringing" — as in *yakrivu* mentioned here] refers only to things which are offered up on the altar. Therefore he interpreted the expression *'asher yakrivu'* (*which they bring*) as referring to the first-fruits, which require waving and bringing to the altar, Scripture thus stating [here] that all first-fruits which the owners bring to G-d shall belong to the officiating priest. And when Rabbi Yishmael said [in the Sifre above], "Since it is stated, *The choicest first-fruits of thy land thou shalt bring unto the House of the Eternal thy G-d,*[57] but I do not know what is to be done with them," he means to say that we have not yet been taught at all that the first-fruits are amongst the gifts of the priests, and it is here that He taught us for the first time that they are to be given to the priest. But afterwards He taught it again in the section dealing with [the gifts of] the priests: *The first ripe fruits of all that is in their Land, which they bring unto the Eternal, shall be thine,*[59] for there He also restated the [laws of the] heave-offering,[60] and hallowed objects,[61] in order to include together all gifts given to the priests, and to make *a covenant of salt*[62] for all of them [indicating that just as salt never decays, so will His covenant with Aaron endure]. It also [repeats the laws] for the sake of some new things added in that section, such as, *every one that is clean in thy house may eat thereof.*[63] We furthermore learn from the verse here [i.e., from the expression *asher yakrivu* which, as explained above, refers to some act of service in the Sanctuary] that the first-fruits are to be given to the men of the *mishmar*[64]

offering, it is also prohibited on the basis of the expression stating *which 'yakrivu' (they 'bring') unto the priest, shall be his.* The heave-offering, according to Rashi, is to be "brought" to the priest. In the opinion of Ramban, only the priest's taking it by force is forbidden, while his going around for it, is not prohibited in this verse, since the *yakrivu* as explained by Rabbi Yishmael in the Sifre is to be understood as denoting offering on the altar, and his question is as follows: "Were they [really] (*yakrivu*) 'bringing' the heave-offering on the altar? Certainly not. Therefore it must refer to the first-fruits." In brief, Rashi's interpretation of *yakrivu* as "bringing" the heave-offering to the priest is therefore "not clear" (as Ramban expresses it). (59) Further, 18:13. (60) *Ibid.*, Verse 12. (61) *Ibid.*, Verses 9, 17-19. (62) *Ibid.*, Verse 19. (63) *Ibid.*, Verse 13. The verse is speaking about first-fruits. (64) See Note 92 in *Seder Bamidbar.*

to offer it up [i.e., to the priests who are then on duty in the Sanctuary], and that [the owner] may not give them to any priest he wants to, as is the law of the heave-offering.

10. AND EVERY MAN'S HALLOWED THINGS SHALL BE HIS; WHATSOEVER ANY MAN GIVETH THE PRIEST, IT SHALL BE HIS. The correct interpretation of this verse is that Scripture is saying that *all* hallowed things of a man shall be his, meaning to say that all hallowed things about which He has not commanded that they be given to the priest, [such as the Second Tithe, fourth-year produce of trees and the tithe of the cattle] shall be the owners' [entirely], and they may have benefit from [and eat] them, even though they are called "holy." But *whatsoever any man giveth the priest* as I have commanded him, *it shall be his* [partially], for even in the hallowed things about which Scripture commanded that they be given to the priest, the owners have a certain right, for although they belong to the priest to whom the owner gives them, as his personal property [but the owners have the right in these hallowed things to choose to whom to give them]. Thus the Second Tithe and the fourth-year produce of trees about which Scripture stated that they be *holy to the Eternal*[65] belong to the owner as his personal property, and likewise the tithe of cattle.[66] But as for all other hallowed things concerning which He commanded in the section of *Vayikach Korach*[67] that they should give them to the priest, they are to be given to him directly by the owners, and the priests cannot take them from them by force. From this we may deduce ourselves that the right of choosing to whom to give them [with the consequent satisfaction of so doing] is that of the owners. This is the correct interpretation in accordance with the plain meaning of the verse. It is also the opinion of Onkelos [who rendered the verse: "and every man's hallowed 'tithe' shall be his," thus in-

(65) Leviticus 27:30 (speaking of the Second Tithe): 19:24 (in reference to fourth-year produce of trees). Both of these "holy" things do not have to be given to the priest, but are to be eaten by the owner in Jerusalem. (66) *Ibid.*, 27:32. The tithe of cattle likewise did not have to be given to the priest, but belonged wholly to the owner, after the blood and fat of the animal were offered upon the altar (see "The Commandments," Vol. I, pp. 90-91). (67) Further, 16:1. The reference here is to the section on the gifts given to the priests (*ibid.,* 18:8-32).

dicating that he understood the verse as referring to a tithe which is the owner's, for instance the Second Tithe].[68] It is interpreted in a similar manner in the Sifre, where the Rabbis have said:[69] "All hallowed things are included in the general verse stating, *And every man's hallowed things shall be his.* Scripture took away all hallowed things and gave them to the priests, leaving only the thanks-offering, the peace-offering, and the Passover-offering, because they too belong to the owners" [and they are permitted to eat them]. However, this verse is not necessary at all for these matters [i.e., to teach us that the thanks-offering, peace-offering, and Passover-offering belong to their owners, since in each of these cases Scripture clearly states that the meat is eaten by the owners, hence the verse before us must refer, as indicated above, to the Second Tithe, and fourth-year produce of trees].[70]

15. HE SHALL POUR NO OIL UPON IT — "so that her offering shall not be enriched, for oil is called light, whereas she acted in darkness. NOR SHALL HE PUT FRANKINCENSE THEREON, for the matriarchs are compared to frankincense, as it is said, *to the hill of frankincense*[71] [an allegorical expression explained by the Midrash as an allusion to the matriarchs], but this woman turned aside from their [virtuous] ways. FOR IT IS A MEAL-OFFERING OF JEALOUSIES. This flour arouses against her two jealousies — the jealousy of G-d, and the jealousy of her husband." Thus far is Rashi's language on the basis of the words of our Rabbis.[72]

But in the opinion of all the commentators[73] [the meaning of the expression] *for it is a meal-offering of jealousies* is to say that because

(68) Onkelos' expression "hallowed tithe" may also refer to the First Tithe [given to the Levites] or the Poorman's Tithe (see my Hebrew commentary, p. 212), in which case Ramban understands that Onkelos supports the explanation he mentioned: namely, that these tithes, although given away by the owner, are still partially "his" inasmuch as the choice to whom to give them and satisfaction of so chosing, is his. (69) Sifre *Naso* 6. (70) The Sifre, however, mentioned "the thanks-offering etc." incidentally because it discusses all the hallowed things which belong to the owners. (71) Song of Songs 4:6. (72) Tanchuma *Naso* 3; Sifre *Naso* 8. (73) Found in Ibn Ezra.

this meal-offering [of the *sotah*] [43] is an offering which may bring her punishment [if the charge against her is true], therefore it is of a lesser quality [than all other meal-offerings and is to be brought of] barley without oil and frankincense, for a meal-offering of which the memorial-part is brought to be acceptable before the Eternal, comes of fine wheat-flour with oil and frankincense. But in my opinion the expression *for it is a meal-offering of jealousies* refers to the beginning of the verse, stating that the husband shall bring the offering for his wife, that is to say, instead of her, *for it is a meal-offering of jealousies* bringing her iniquity to remembrance. Thus it is not fitting that she should bring it of her own property, but it is he who is to bring the meal-offering to G-d so that He should take note of his suspicions of her, and punish her on his [the husband's] behalf. And the reason [why this meal-offering comes from] *se'orim* (barley) [74] is so that *'sa'arath' (a storm of) the Eternal is gone forth in fury, yea, a whirling storm; it shall whirl upon the head of wickedness,*[75] like *the cake of barley bread*[76] mentioned in the story of Gideon, which [one of the Midianites who saw it in a dream] interpreted as referring to a storm (*sa'ar*) and great confusion [which would break forth upon the camp of the Midianites]. Similarly, *the earthen vessel*[77] [in which the holy water is put] is a hint that she shall be broken like a potter's vessel,[78] and likewise the dust [which must be taken from the floor of the Tabernacle and put into the water[77] indicates] that she is dust, and into dust shall she return[79] [if she is guilty of adultery]. The meaning of the word *hu* [*ki minchath kna'oth 'hu'*—using the masculine form of "it" in the phrase "it is a meal-offering of jealousies," when it should have used *hi,* the feminine form, since the word *minchah* (meal-offering) is feminine] is because it refers back to the word *kemach* (flour) [which is mentioned above in the same verse, and the word *kemach* is masculine]. But this [unusual usage of the masculine here] has a mystical explanation, for further on when the meal-offering is in

(74) The word *se'orim* (barley) is suggestive of the word *sa'ar* (storm), as is indicated in the next verse quoted by Ramban. (75) Jeremiah 23:19. (76) Judges 7:13. Gideon indeed inflicted later a great defeat upon the Midianite host (*ibid.*, 22-28). (77) Verse 17. (78) See Jeremiah 19:11. (79) See Genesis 3:19.

the hands of the woman[80] Scripture uses the word *hi* [*minchath kna'oth hi* — literally: " 'she' is a meal-offering of jealousies"]. And now [in this verse] Scripture mentions the memorial first, stating that "she" *brings iniquity to remembrance.*[81]

18. AND THE PRIEST SHALL HAVE IN HIS HAND 'MEI HAMARIM' (THE WATER OF BITTERNESS) THAT CAUSETH THE CURSE. The commentators[82] have written that Scripture describes it [i.e., *the water of bitterness*] in terms of its final effect, for there will be a bitterness in it, and *G-d* will *deal very bitterly with her,*[83] and it will effect a curse upon her. So also have our Rabbis said in the Sifre:[84] "the water is called *water of bitterness* because of its final effect, for it effects a curse[85] on the body and brings to light the sin." But in the Gemara [of Tractate Sotah] the Sages have said[86] that the priest put a bitter substance in the water, in order to arouse her. If so, the verse stating, *and the water that causeth the curse shall enter into her and become bitter*[87] should rather have said: "and the bitter water shall enter into her to cause the curse," [since the bitter substance was already present in the water before she drank it]. And in the Sifre it is further stated:[88] "*And he shall blot them out into the water of bitterness.*[89] The verse teaches you that it is the writing [on the scroll of the *sotah* which was blotted out into the water] which makes the water bitter."

(80) Verse 18. (81) The verse here reads: *ki minchath kna'oth hu minchath zikaron mazkereth avon* [literally: "for a meal-offering of jealousies 'he' is, a meal-offering of memorial, bringing iniquity to remembrance"], and the meaning thereof is that in this meal-offering there is both judgment and mercy: judgment, if she is guilty, and mercy if innocent. The word *hu* in this verse thus refers both to *kemach* and *zikaron,* which allude to these two attributes. Hence also the word *hu* is mentioned before *zikaron* ("memorial"), for "the memorial which brings iniquity to remembrance" surely alludes to the attribute of judgment, and the word *hu* which is mentioned *before* "the memorial" therefore alludes to mercy. Further on in Verse 18, however, the text reads: *eith minchath hazikaron minchath kna'oth hi.* There the word *hi* ("she") appears at the *end* of the whole expression, after *hazikaron* ("the memorial"), when the meal-offering is in her hands [as the verse states] it is only "judgment" which brings the iniquity to remembrance. See further my Hebrew commentary p. 213. (82) Rashi and Ibn Ezra. (83) See Ruth 1:20. (84) Sifre *Naso* 11. (85) In our Sifre: "makes the body 'bitter' (sick)." (86) Sotah 20 a. (87) Further, Verse 24. (88) Sifre *Naso* 16. (89) Verse 23.

The correct interpretation appears to me to be in accordance with its plain meaning, for when the woman drinks the water, it will taste to her just like any other water, and only afterwards when it enters into her, will it arouse her if she had become defiled [i.e., committed adultery], and then she will immediately feel the bitterness in her mouth and inside her. Therefore Scripture states, *And when he hath made her drink the water, then it shall come to pass, if she be defiled, and have acted unfaithfully against her husband, that the water that causeth the curse shall enter into her and become bitter,*[90] for it is after drinking, when the water enters her belly, that it immediately becomes bitter in her mouth and inside her, as happens with all substances which make one nauseous and cause vomiting, that they seem very bitter to those that drink them. After that *her belly shall swell, and her thigh shall fall away.*[90] The water is called [in the verse before us] *m'orerim* [from the root *arur*—"cursed"] because of the curses [written on the scroll] which have been erased into the water, and which cause her to suffer their effects.

Now the commentators[91] have said that the word *mei* ['*mei*' *hamarim*] is like *mayim hamarim* ["the bitter water"], the word *mei* [literally: "the water of"] being stated here in a construct form in place of the absolute form, just as we find [an opposite verse]: *mayim birkayim*[92] [literally: "the water the ankles," where the word *mayim* occurs in the absolute form, but is really to be understood in the construct: *mei birkayim* — "the water 'of' the ankles," i.e., water which reached as high as the ankles]. But Rabbi Abraham ibn Ezra wrote that "the word *mei* is [indeed] construct [meaning: *the water*

(90) Verse 27. This shows that the water is called *mei hamarim* in our verse because of its final effect, for if she is guilty, the curses that have been erased into the water will cause a bitter taste and the fatal effects described further on. (91) The commentators quoted above. The point involved is as follows: Since the commentators explain that *mei hamarim* is a reference to the final effect of the water, the word *mei* cannot be in construct ["the water of" bitterness — for it is not yet bitter]; thus the word *mei* here merely means "water" — "the bitter water," and is so called because of its final effect. However, as Ramban continues, according to the Rabbis who said that the bitter substance was mixed with the water, the word *mei* may indeed be understood as being in construct — "the water 'of' bitterness," since the water was already bitter. (92) Ezekiel 47:3.

'of'], but the word *hamarim* is an adjectival noun [meaning: 'the bitter substances'—thus *mei hamarim* means 'the water of bitter substances'], and if so, the secret thereof is known." [93] But [Ibn Ezra's interpretation] does not appear to me to be correct, because the verse states, *and the water that causeth the curse shall enter into her and become bitter.*[89]

19. IF NO 'ISH' (MAN) HAVE LAIN WITH THEE, AND IF THOU HAST NOT GONE ASIDE TO UNCLEANNESS. These two conditions constitute [in reality] one. Thus the verse is stating: "*If no man have lain with thee,* and thus *thou has not gone aside to uncleanness, be thou free from the water of bitterness;*" [for you cannot say that these are two separate conditions], since her husband lay with her and he is "a man" [thus the priest could not say to her, *if no man have lain with thee;* therefore both conditions must be one, as explained]. It is possible that the word *ish* (man) lacks the definite article [making it *ha'ish* — "the man"], and Scripture is stating: "*If 'the man' has not lain with thee, and if thou hast not gone aside to uncleanness* at all," and he makes her swear specifically concerning the particular man about whom he [her husband] had warned her, and in general terms about others. And so have the Rabbis said: [94] "*And the woman shall say: 'Amen, Amen.'* [95] [The double utterance of the word '*Amen*' signifies:] '*Amen* [that I have not committed adultery] with this man, and *Amen* [that I have not committed adultery] with any other man.' "

20. BUT IF THOU HAST GONE ASIDE. This is connected with [the expression in the following verse], *the Eternal make thee,*[95] the verses stating: "*But if thou hast gone aside* to uncleanness, *being under thy husband, and if thou be defiled, and some man have lain with thee besides thy husband — the Eternal make thee a curse, and an oath among thy people.*" [95] But due to the length of the conditions [mentioned in Verses 19-20] Scripture restates [in the following Verse

(93) A reference by Ibn Ezra to the statement of the Sages that a bitter substance had to be mixed with the water, and hence the term *mei hamarim* — "the water of bitter substances." (94) Sotah 18a. (95) Verse 21.

21] *and the priest shall cause the woman to swear* [although that has already been said at the beginning of Verse 19; and accordingly the phrase before us in Verse 20, *but if thou hast gone aside* etc. is connected with the expression *the Eternal make thee* in Verse 21], in order to explain that [*the Eternal make thee a curse* etc.] constitutes *the oath of cursing.*[95] And Rabbi Abraham ibn Ezra commented that the first expression of swearing [*and the priest shall cause her to swear,* in Verse 19] means [that she must swear] by G-d's Name, and the second one [in Verse 21] implies by means of the curse, as is clearly explained there [in Verse 21: *and the priest shall cause the woman to swear with the oath of cursing*]. But it is not correct, for the priest would not have caused her to swear by the Name of G-d using an expression of "if" [as in Verse 19: *and the priest shall cause her to swear, and shall say unto the woman: 'If' no man have lain with thee* etc.].[96]

Now there is nothing amongst all the ordinances of the Torah which depends upon a miracle, except for this matter, which is a permanent wonder and miracle that will happen in Israel, when the majority of the people live in accordance with the Will of G-d; for He *was pleased for His righteousness' sake*[97] to teach *the women that they do not do after the lewdness*[97] *of* the other nations, and to purify Israel from adulterous offspring, so that they are worthy that the Divine Presence dwell among them. Therefore this matter [i.e., the effect of the water on the *sotah*] stopped from the time that the people became debauched with [sexual] sins, as the Rabbis have said: [98] "When adulterers became frequent, the water of *sotah*[43] ceased, for it is said, *I will not punish your daughters when they commit harlotry, nor your daughters-in-law when they commit adultery; for they themselves consort with lewd women, and they sacrifice with harlots, and the people that is without understanding is distraught.*[99] Now this verse does not mean to say that adulterous women will be free from [punishment for their] sin, because their husbands [likewise] commit adultery; it [is only saying] that this great miracle will not be done for

(96) For if she is innocent of the charge, then she will have invoked the name of G-d in vain. (97) Isaiah 42:21; Ezekiel 23:48. (98) Sotah 47 a-b. (99) Hosea 4:14.

them, for it occurs as a sign of honor for them *because of* their *being a holy people,*[100] but they do not understand this goodness, nor do they desire it. Therefore the verse states, *and the people that is without understanding is 'yilaveit' (distraught),*[99] that is to say, trapped by its foolishness. Similarly, *but a prating fool 'yilaveit,'*[101] which the Jerusalem Targum[102] translated: "but the fool is caught by his lips." This is the reason for what the Sages have said:[98] "*And the man shall be clear from iniquity.*[103] When the man is clear of iniquity, the water [of the *sotah*] tests his wife; but if the man is himself not free from iniquity, the water does not put his wife to the proof." Now the "freedom from iniquity" of the husband means [in this context] that he had no sexual relations with her after he had warned her and she [nevertheless] had secret contact [with the suspected adulterer]. And there are scholars[104] who explain that if the husband had ever in his lifetime had a forbidden sexual intercourse, the water [of the *sotah*] no longer tests his wife. And according to the final decision of the law, even if his sons or daughters committed adultery and he did not rebuke them the water did not put his wife to the test [even though he himself is clear from iniquity]. In short, this procedure was miraculous, as [a sign of] honor for Israel.

6 11. AND THE PRIEST SHALL PREPARE ONE FOR A SIN-OFFERING. The reason why a Nazirite must bring a sin-offering *when the days of his Naziritehood are fulfilled*[105] has not been explained.[106] In accordance with the plain meaning of Scripture, [it is because] this man sins against his soul on the day of completion of his Naziritehood; for until now he was separated in sanctity and the service of G-d, and he should therefore have remained separated forever, continuing all his life consecrated and sanctified to his G-d, as it is said, *And I raised up of your sons for prophets, and of your young*

(100) See Deuteronomy 26:19. (101) Proverbs 10:8. (102) Reference here is to the Targum Yonathan ben Uziel. (103) Further, Verse 31. (104) Mentioned in Rashi, Sotah 47b, and in Rambam, *Hilchoth Sotah* 2:8. (105) Verse 13. (106) Generally a sin-offering is brought for atonement of a sin committed in error. But here the Nazirite has kept his days of consecration in complete fulfillment of his vow. So the question arises: Why did Scripture oblige him to bring a sin-offering?

men for Nazirites,[107] where Scripture compares the Nazirite to a prophet, and as it is written, *All the days of his Naziritehood he is holy unto the Eternal.*[108] Thus [when he completes his Naziritehood and returns to his normal life] he requires atonement, since he goes back to be defiled by [material] desires of the world.

21. THIS IS THE LAW OF THE NAZIRITE WHO VOWETH HIS OFFERING UNTO THE ETERNAL FOR HIS NAZIRITEHOOD, BESIDES THAT WHICH HIS MEANS SUFFICE. The correct meaning of the verse is as if it had said: "*This is the law of the Nazirite who voweth* a vow of the Nazirite;[109] *his offering unto the Eternal for his Naziritehood* shall be *besides that which his means suffice.*" Or it may mean: "*This is the law of the Nazirite,* and this is the law of *his offering unto the Eternal for his Naziritehood.*" It is possible that He is saying: "*This is the law of the Nazirite,* that *he vow his offering unto the Eternal for his Naziritehood,*" meaning to say that he should not specify a particular animal as an offering, but should vow: "I shall bring an offering for my Naziritehood," or he should simply say: "I am a Nazirite," for as soon as he vowed to be a Nazirite, it is [already] binding upon him as a vow [to bring] the offering mentioned [in the Torah]. He reverts and states, *besides that which his means suffice,* [meaning to say] that if he is rich he may [voluntarily] increase his offerings [i.e., the burnt-offerings and peace-offerings, as will be explained, but not the sin-offering]; and *according to his vow which he voweth* concerning these offerings, whether [he is] rich or poor, *so he must do after the law of his Naziriteship*—so that he may bring more, but not less [than what Scripture prescribes for him to bring]. He mentioned this in order to teach us that if the Nazirite was rich and wants to bring several offerings, or if he vowed at the beginning: "I am a Nazirite and I shall

(107) Amos 2:11. (108) Verse 8. (109) The verse cannot be understood literally, for "the law of the Nazirite" does not consist of a vow to bring a sin-offering; rather, "the law of the Nazirite" is that he must not eat grapes or drink wine, nor defile himself by contact with the dead, and the offering is brought on fulfillment of the Nazirite vow. Hence Ramban explains that the meaning of the verse is: "this is the law of the Nazirite who vows a vow of Naziritehood, etc."

bring a thousand burnt-offerings and peace-offerings," then he must bring them all on the day of completion [of his time as a Nazirite], and he may not drink wine until he has offered them all up, for they all constitute *the law of his Naziriteship*. It is possible that [the latter half of the verse means]: "*besides that for which his means suffice* so must he do *according to his vow which he voweth*." This He mentioned because it is usually the rich who vow in this way.[110]

23. SPEAK UNTO AARON AND UNTO HIS SONS, SAYING: THUS YE SHALL BLESS. I have already mentioned in *Seder Vayehi Bayom Ha'shemini*[111] that He commanded Aaron to lift up his hands towards the people and bless them on that day [i.e., the eighth day of the initiation of the priests, which was the day of the final erection of the Tabernacle], and here He commanded Aaron and his sons to do so throughout the generations, and He explained what the blessing was with which they are to bless them. He mentioned this blessing in connection with the setting up of the Tabernacle [discussed in the next chapter], *for there the Eternal commanded the blessing, even life forever,*[112] just as our Rabbis have said:[113] "In the Sanctuary [the priests pronounced the blessing] using the Divine Name [i.e., the Tetragrammaton],[114] but in the provinces by a substitute Name. In the Sanctuary they pronounced it as a single blessing, but in the provinces [it was pronounced] as three blessings" [the people responding "Amen" to each of the three verses which comprise the priestly blessing], for the blessing in the Sanctuary was singled out by being pronounced with the Proper Name of G-d [i.e., the Tetragrammaton].

(110) At first Ramban explained the expression *besides that which his means suffice* as referring to the rich, and *according to his vow which he voweth* as applying to the poor, as explained above. Now Ramban interprets both expressions as applying to the rich, for it is usually they who vow to bring several burnt-offerings or peace-offerings. The reason why Ramban gives this interpretation may be because it is unnecessary for Scripture to state specifically that a poor Nazirite must bring the minimum number of offerings, as was explained in the first interpretation, since this is self-understood. (111) Leviticus 9:1. The verse referred to is *ibid.*, 22. (112) Psalms 133:3. (113) Sotah 38 a-b. (114) See in Vol. II, p. 18, Note 84.

24. THE ETERNAL BLESS THEE, AND KEEP THEE. By way of the Truth, [the mystic teachings of the Cabala], the meaning thereof is because "the blessing" comes from on High [downward], and the meaning of *shmirah* ["keeping" – *and He 'keep' thee*] is that you should "keep" it, like *Remember [the Sabbath-day]*,[115] and *'Shamor' (Keep) the Sabbath-day.*[116] Furthermore, *the* Great *Name will make His countenance* that watches over you *shine [upon you]*.[117] And so did the Rabbis say in the Sifre:[118] "Rabbi Nathan says: [*The Eternal make His countenance shine upon thee.*] This is a reference to the light of the Divine Presence." *And He be gracious unto thee,* that you may find favor in His sight, similar to that which the Rabbis have said [that when G-d completed the creation of the world He said]: "My world! My world! Would that you will find favor in My sight all the time [as at this moment]!"[119] Furthermore, *the Eternal lift up His countenance* to the heavens above *and give thee peace*[120] – all in your house. And so the Rabbis said in the Sifre:[121] "[*And He give thee peace.*] Rabbi Nathan said: This is a reference to the peace of the kingdom of David." *So shall they put My* Great *Name upon the children of Israel, and I will bless them,*[122] *for it is I that speaketh, behold, here I am,*[123] and peace.[124]

7 1. AND IT CAME TO PASS ON THE DAY THAT MOSES HAD FINISHED SETTING UP THE TABERNACLE. "Scripture does not say 'on the day that Moses set up' [but it states 'on the day that Moses had finished setting up']. This teaches us that on each of the seven days of initiation [of the priests] Moses erected and dismantled the Tabernacle, and on that day [the eighth day] he erected it but did not dismantle it. Therefore it says, *on the day that Moses had finished setting up the Tabernacle,* since it was on that day that he finished all

(115) Exodus 20:5. See Ramban there. (116) Deuteronomy 5:12. (117) Verse 25. (118) Sifre *Naso* 41. (119) Bereshith Rabbah 9:4. "That is to say: 'I wish that man would not spoil the celestial spheres through which his blessings descend after I endowed him with freedom of action' " (Beiur Ha'lvush to Ricanti, quoting the language of Ramban). (120) Verse 26. (121) Sifre *Naso* 42. (122) Verse 27. (123) Isaiah 52:6. (124) Ricanti in quoting the language of Ramban does not mention "and peace." In the commentary of Ma'or V'shamesh, however, it is explained as meaning: "with the consent of peace."

his erections. This happened on the first of Nisan; on the second day the Red Heifer was burnt, on the third day they sprinkled [upon the Levites] [125] the first sprinkling [of the water of purification in which the ashes of the Red Heifer were mingled],[126] and on the seventh day [of Nisan, after having been sprinkled again] [126] the Levites were shaven[125] [and were ready to be initiated into their service]." This is Rashi's language on the basis of the words of our Rabbis[127] of blessed memory. But it is not a complete proof [that Moses set up the Tabernacle and dismantled it again on each of the seven days of initiation], for the expression *on the day that he had finished* is not connected only with the word *l'hakim* (setting up), but [its meaning is rather as follows]: "*on the day that Moses had finished setting up the Tabernacle* and anointing and sanctifying it, and [doing likewise to] the altar and all the vessels thereof — the princes offered their offerings, when all this was done." Nonetheless [however we explain the verse], it was [indeed] on the eighth day [of the initiation of the priests].

This section was written here because on the first day of the initiation *He called unto Moses out of the Tent of Meeting and G-d spoke to him*[128] all the sections [of the Torah] from the beginning of the Book of Leviticus until the section of *Vayehi Bayom Ha'shemini,*[111] which all deal with the laws of the offerings. From that eighth day on Moses was told all the sections beginning with *These are the beasts which ye may eat,*[129] which contain the laws of forbidden and permitted foods, since they are all related to the subject of the offerings, and these topics continued in their correct order up to this place [before us], as I have explained.[130] Thus when He had completed the commandments which Moses was ordered to say to Israel, all of them being laws of the Divine Service and the offerings, the charge of the Tent of Meeting and its Service, He reverted here afterwards to tell of the freewill offerings of the princes, which took place from the eighth day until the nineteenth day of Nisan,[131] or until

(125) Further, 8:7. (126) *Ibid.*, 19:12. (127) Sifre *Naso* 44. (128) Leviticus 1:1. (129) *Ibid.*, 11:2. (130) In Exodus 40:2, and Leviticus 25:1. (131) This is the opinion of Rabbi Akiba, who says that the first day of the initiation of the priests was the first of Nisan, and accordingly "the eighth day" [which marked the final

the twelfth day of the month in accordance with the words of our Rabbis.[132]

'VAYIMSHACHEIM' (AND HE HAD ANOINTED THEM), 'VAYEKADEISH' (AND SANCTIFIED) THEM. Rabbi Abraham ibn Ezra explains that "Moses anointed them with the oil of anointment, and sanctified them by [sprinkling upon them] the blood of the sin-offering, as it is said there, *and he purified the altar, and poured out the remaining blood at the base of the altar, and sanctified it, to make atonement upon it.*"[133] But it is not so, for it is likewise said about the Tabernacle [in the verse before us], *and he had anointed it, and sanctified it and all its vessels,* and yet the Tabernacle was not sanctified by means of [sprinkling upon it] the blood and any offering. Rather, the meaning [of the phrase *vayimshacheim vayekadeish otham*] is that "he anointed them in order [thereby] to sanctify them."

AND THE ALTAR AND ALL THE VESSELS THEREOF. This is connected with the beginning of the verse, [so that the sense thereof is as follows]: "and it came to pass on the day that Moses had finished setting up the Tabernacle [and the altar][134] and all its vessels, and had anointed them and sanctified them — [that the princes of Israel offered etc.]."

3. AND THEY BROUGHT THEIR OFFERING BEFORE THE ETERNAL. Since the wagons [which the princes brought] were for the purpose of the offerings [i.e., for transporting the Tabernacle, where offerings are made before G-d] they are also called "offering." Similarly, *And we have brought the Eternal's offering, what every man*

erection of the Tabernacle] was on the eighth of Nisan. On that day the twelve princes began their offerings, and each one brought an offering on a separate day, so that they finished on the nineteenth of Nisan. (132) This is the opinion of Rabbi Yishmael, and is also the finally agreed opinion of the Rabbis in general. Hence the language of Ramban ["in accordance with the words of our Rabbis"]. According to this opinion, the Tabernacle was first put up on the twenty-third of Adar, and "the eighth day" was therefore the first of Nisan, so that the princes completed their offerings on the twelfth of Nisan. See further on this matter in my Hebrew commentary p. 217, and in Ramban, Vol. II, pp. 616-622. (133) Leviticus 8:15. (134) Tur. In our editions of Ramban this phrase is missing, but the Tur's reading is clearly correct.

hath gotten, of jewels of gold,[135] meaning "an offering" for the repairs of the Tabernacle. Now the princes thought that it would be impossible for the Levites to carry on their shoulders the boards of the Tabernacle and the sockets, which were very heavy, and therefore they brought the wagons of their own accord, for such is the way that all those who carry houses of kings and their palatial tents adopt, transporting them on wagons.

We may also explain that the expression *And they brought their offering before the Eternal, six wagons 'tzov,'* means six large wagons bearing their offerings, *and twelve oxen* drawing the wagons. Thus they brought the wagons laden [with the offerings], and the oxen [drawing the wagons] *before the Tabernacle.* And G-d commanded Moses, *Take* all of *it of them, and* the wagons and the oxen which were not brought for offerings *shall do the service of the Tent of Meeting.*[136] Afterwards the princes took their offerings down from the wagons and brought them before the Tabernacle,[137] intending to offer them all up on that day since they had been given permission to offer them before Him, but G-d commanded, *each prince on his day*[138] *shall they bring their offerings.* And because of this [i.e., since the wagons that the princes brought contained the animals that they intended to offer up] it was not necessary now that He should say to Moses "take it of them," [as the original statement[136] already implies G-d's consent to the offerings as well].[139] And it is a linguistic expression [in the Sacred Language] to say "wagons" when referring to their contents, just like: *those who eat 'shulchan Izebel'* [140] [literally: "Jezebel's table," which means "the food on Jezebel's table"]. So also: *for all 'sha'ar ami' do know*[141] [literally: for all "the gates of my people" do know, which means: "for all the people in the gates of my people do know"]. And [likewise we find] in the language of the Sages: [142] "a hundred wagons

(135) Further, 31:50. (136) Verse 5. (137) Verse 10. (138) Verse 11. (139) But according to the first interpretation, that the wagons were empty and were brought so that the Levites could transport the Tabernacle in them, and G-d consented by saying to Moses, *Take it of them,* the question arises: when the princes came back and brought the actual dedication-offerings, why did G-d likewise not tell Moses to take the offerings from them? Hence the second interpretation is to be preferred. (140) I Kings 18:19. (141) Ruth 3:11. (142) Baba Bathra 146 a.

of pitchers of wine and pitchers of oil, and of silver and golden vessels" [the meaning being "the amount of wine and oil and vessels that can be contained in a hundred wagons," and not just wagons of pitchers of wine and oil]. It is possible that the word *tzov* [*six wagons 'tzov'*] means "full," and so also: *'uvatzabim' and upon mules,*[143] which means "in wagons full of people." In that case *six wagons 'tzov'* [in the verse before us] means "six wagons laden full," their load being the dedication-offerings which Scripture specifies further on.

Now Scripture mentions the offerings of each of the princes individually and afterwards it includes them all in a general statement, saying, *This was the dedication-offering of the altar, in the day when it was anointed, at the hands of the princes of Israel: twelve silver dishes,*[144] and Rashi wrote: [145] "This teaches you that the vessels of the Sanctuary were exactly equal in weight [as specified in the verses: *one silver dish, the weight whereof was a hundred and thirty shekels* etc.]. If one weighed each one separately and then weighed them all together, it was neither more nor less [than the total should have been]. This is based on [the explanations of] Rabbi Moshe the Preacher."[146] But I cannot understand what they mean in saying this. If we are to consider this a miracle, what benefit is there in the occurrence of this miracle? And if this is the natural result with all weights, why should Scripture specifically mention it? In the Sifre the Rabbis have clearly said: [147] "This is to teach you that the vessels of the Sanctuary[148] were not like ordinary vessels. In the case of ordinary vessels, if one weighs each separately and then weighs them all together, the total is sometimes more or less [than it should have been] etc." [149] And there [in the Sifre] the Rabbis further said: "Rabbi

(143) Isaiah 66:20. (144) Further, Verse 84. (145) *Ibid.*, Verse 85. (146) This final statement ["This is based on . . . "] is not found in our editions of Rashi. Rabbi Moshe the Preacher is however quoted here in Verse 23. He was an older contemporary of Rashi's who lived in the city of Narbonne. His work was in the nature of a Midrashic commentary compiled from earlier sources. See in Vol. I, p. 424 Note 196. (147) Sifre *Naso* 54. (148) Literally: "the Permanent House" (see Vol. II, p. 335, Note 598). Here, however, the term *beith olamim* refers both to the Tabernacle and to the Sanctuary. (149) Now this Sifre "clearly" states [as Ramban wrote above] that there was some special phenomenon in the weighing of the vessels. It does not yet explain what purpose it served; hence Ramban continues to quote from the Sifre the

Nathan says: If one were to weigh all the vessels of the Sanctuary together[148] and then turn them into bullion, and again make vessels of it, they would be neither more nor less [than the original weight]." He means to say by this that [these vessels were made of] a very pure gold [or silver, as the case may be], so that even if one melted them down and turned them into bullion, they still remained at their original weight. This was not because a miracle happened to them, but because they were made of a very pure gold.

The correct interpretation of the verse is that the Holy One, blessed be He, bestows honor upon those who fear Him, just as He said, *for them that honor Me I will honor.*[150] Now all the princes brought this offering on the same day, because they all agreed to it simultaneously. But since it was impossible that one of them should not precede the others, He honored those who came first in [the position of] the standards to bring their offerings on the earlier days. He wanted, however, to mention them all by name and the details of their offerings, and to cite the day of each one, rather than honoring the first one by saying, *This was the offering of Nachshon the son of Amminadab*[51] and then saying "and so did each of the princes offer on his day," for that would have been a diminution of the honor of the others. Afterwards [i.e., after having listed them all separately] He included them all again in a general verse,[144] in order to tell us that they were all equal before Him, blessed be He. And so did the Rabbis say in the Sifre: [152] "Scripture tells us that just as they were all equal in the thought [of bringing these offerings] so were they all alike in merit. *Twelve silver dishes*[144] — these were the same ones that they donated, and nothing which would have invalidated them[153] occurred to them."

There is another explanation of this [chapter] in the interpretations of the Rabbis,[154] namely that each of the princes intended to bring a dedication-offering to the altar which would be of the amount [specified in the verses, each one of them intending to bring the same offerings], but Nachshon [prince of the tribe of Judah] had a

words of Rabbi Nathan. (150) I Samuel 2:30. (151) Verse 17. (152) Sifre *Naso* 53. (153) Such as becoming chipped or perforated, in which case a sacred vessel may no longer be used. (Kether Kehunah, commentary to Sifre *ibid.*). (154) Bamidbar Rabbah 13:13.

particular reason for [bringing] this number [of offerings], and each of the other princes thought of an independent reason. Thus the Rabbis said[155] that Nachshon thought he would bring a *ka'arath keseph* (*a silver dish*),[156] since the numerical value of its [Hebrew] letters is nine hundred thirty,[157] corresponding to the years of the first man; [158] and *the weight thereof was a hundred and thirty shekels*[156] indicating the years when he [Adam] begot children [to maintain the existence of the world, i.e., when he begot Seth,[159] from whom the world was founded] — and likewise the whole Midrash, as Rashi wrote it.[155] Or [the offerings of each prince were,] according to another Midrash,[154] [an allusion to] the tradition each tribe had from our father Jacob about all that would happen to it until the days of the Messiah. And so Nachshon [prince of the tribe of Judah] began by bringing his offerings with reference to royalty. The dish and the basin[156] corresponded to the two kings who would be descended from him, who would rule over the sea and land, these being Solomon and the Messianic King. This was why Nachshon brought a *ka'arah* (silver round dish), to symbolize the ocean which covers the whole world and is like a [round] dish.[160] [The weight of the dish was] a hundred and thirty shekels,[156] since it was on the third day [of Creation] that the Holy One, blessed be He, gathered all seas together to one place and called them *yamim,* the numerical value of these letters being one hundred; [161] and Solomon added one *sea* to the work of the Sanctuary, *and a line of thirty cubits did compass it round about.*[162] Thus you have one hundred and thirty. *One silver basin of seventy shekels*[156] corresponds to the world which is shaped like a sphere. The *seventy shekels* symbolize that they [Solomon and the Messiah] will rule over the seventy nations.[163] *Both of them full,*[156] for gifts will be brought to them from all peoples.[164] '*Soleth*' (*fine flour*)[156] corresponds to these

(155) Mentioned by Rashi (in Verse 19) in the name of Rabbi Moshe the Preacher, who doubtless quoted an older source. (156) Verse 13. (157) *Kuph* is 100; *ayin* 70; *reish,* 200; *tav* 400. *Kaph* is 20; *samech* 60; *pei* 80. The total is 930. (158) Genesis 5:5. (159) *Ibid.*, Verse 3. (160) The basin indicated the earth, as will be explained further on. Incidentally we see clearly that the Midrashic Sages were aware of the spherical shape of the earth. (161) *Yod* is 10; *mem* 40; *yod* 10; *mem* 40 — totalling 100. (162) I Kings 7:23. (163) See Megillah 11b, where Solomon is mentioned as having ruled over the whole world. (164) Isaiah 66:20.

[two kings — as in the expression: *the precious sons of Zion*] *'hamesulaim'* (*who were comparable to*) *'fine' gold.*[165] *Mingled with oil*[156] — *A good name is better than precious oil.*[166] *Silver* — as it is said, *The tongue of the righteous is as choice silver.*[167] *One golden pan of ten shekels,*[168] this corresponds to the ten generations from Peretz to David[169] who were all righteous men full of good deeds, [as pleasant] as the odor of the incense.[168] *One young bullock*[170] — in allusion to Abraham;[171] *one ram*[170] — in allusion to Isaac;[172] *one he-lamb*[170] — in allusion to Jacob.[173] *One male of the goats for a sin-offering,*[174] to atone for the deed of Judah who brought Joseph's coat to his father [dipped in the blood of a he-goat].[175] *And for the sacrifice of peace-offerings, two oxen* — alluding to David and Solomon, who began the royal line [of the House of David], and who were righteous men [during whose reigns] the kingdom was whole.[176] *Five rams, five he-goats, five he-lambs of the first year*[151] — in allusion to the fifteen monarchs from Rehoboam to Zedekiah,[177] who were kings and sons of kings [and may be classified in three groups, just as the fifteen peace-offerings came in three groups], some completely righteous, some average, and some very wicked. This was what Nachshon thought [in bringing these offerings, which symbolized the history of his tribe].

And Nethanel the son of Zuar [prince of the tribe of Issachar] also thought in his heart that he would bring a dedication-offering of this amount, but he had a different reason for it, bringing his offerings in

(165) Lamentations 4:2. (166) Ecclesiastes 7:1. (167) Proverbs 10:20. (168) Verse 14. The continuation of the verse ("full of incense") affords the basis for the allusion to the ten generations full of righteous deeds. (169) See Ruth 4:18-22: *And these are the generations of Peretz . . . and Jesse begot David.* Ten generations are listed there. (170) Verse 15. (171) Of Abraham it is stated, *And Abraham ran unto the herd* (Genesis 18:7). (172) *Ibid.*, 22:13: *and he* [Abraham] *took the ram* — as a substitute for Isaac. (173) *Ibid.*, 30:40: *And Jacob separated the lambs.* (174) Verse 16. (175) Genesis 37:31-32. (176) During the lifetimes of David and Solomon the kingdom was complete, ruling as they did over all the twelve tribes. After Solomon's death the kingdom was divided into two parts — Judah and Israel. Hence the allusion here, *and for the sacrifice of peace-offerings, two oxen.* These are the two kings — David and Solomon — whose reigns were characterized by *shelamim* ["peace-offerings," a term which also suggests "peace" and "completeness"]. (177) See I Chronicles 3:10-16 — where all these fifteen kings of Judah are listed.

allusion to the Torah, because the special merit of the tribe of Issachar was [in their knowledge] of the wisdom of the Torah.[178] *A silver dish*[179] — referring to the Torah which is called "bread," as it is said, *Come, eat of my bread,*[180] and it is said of the showbread, *And thou shalt make the dishes thereof.*[181] And [the prince of the tribe of] Zebulun brought his offerings in relation to commerce, which he engaged in and exerted himself in, and [from the profits of which he maintained [through his generosity the Torah-studying tribe of] Issachar, with whom he [equally] shared the reward [for the studying of the Torah]. The [round] dish[182] was symbolic of the ocean, since he [Zebulun] dwelled *at the shores of the sea.*[183] Similarly the Rabbis found in that Midrash[184] a special reason for the offering of each and every tribe and for the amount of the offerings [in accordance with the subsequent history of the tribe]. It is for this reason that Scripture treated them all equally, giving the details of each one separately as if the others had not been mentioned, after which it mentioned them all together, to hint that at the same moment it occurred to each of them to bring the dedication-offering, and none of them preceded the other either in thought or in the actual bringing of the offerings to the Tabernacle. It is because of this Scripture mentioned them all in identical words.

13. FINE FLOUR (MINGLED) WITH OIL FOR A MEAL-OFFERING. The princes dedicated the altar with all the kinds of offerings that can be brought upon it. Therefore they brought a meal-offering, incense, a burnt-offering, a sin-offering, and a peace-offering. Now the incense and the sin-offering were [permitted to be brought by] a special temporary decree, since they cannot usually be brought as freewill offerings. But [this exception was made] in order to complete the dedication with all kinds of offerings, for no other offerings can be brought in Israel except for these offerings [mentioned here], the sin-offering and the guilt-offering being the

(178) I Chronicles 12:33. See above, in *Seder Bamidbar,* Note 117. (179) Verse 19. (180) Proverbs 9:5. (181) Exodus 25:29. (182) Verse 25. (183) Genesis 49:13. — Generosity in support of the study of Torah is thus evident throughout the generations, and its reward is extraordinary as the generous person becomes an equal partner in the sacred venture. (184) Bamidbar Rabbah, Chapters 13-14.

same thing and having the same name, and *there is one law for them.*[185]

Now *the Glorious G-d*[186] agreed to the intention of the princes and commanded, *they shall present their offering, each prince on his day.*[187] Therefore it is possible that this is a commandment for all generations, that the Sanctuary and the altar should always be dedicated [with special offerings upon their completion]. It is for this reason that Solomon made a dedication of the House [of G-d], as it is written, *So the king and all the people dedicated the House of G-d.*[188] Similarly the men of the Great Assembly dedicated [the Second Temple], as it is written, *And the children of Israel, the priests and the Levites, and the rest of the children of captivity, kept the dedication of this House of G-d with joy.*[189] And so [will it be also] in the days of the Messiah, as it is said in the Book of Ezekiel, *Seven days shall they make atonement for the altar and cleanse it; so shall they consecrate it. And when they have accomplished the days, it shall be that upon the eighth day, and forward, the priests shall make your burnt-offerings upon the altar, and your peace-offerings,*[190] this being the dedication of the altar with offerings to consecrate it. Thus the subject of this commandment is similar to that of the section about the impure people on Passover,[191] and the section concerning the sons of Joseph,[192] whose opinion coincided with the opinion on High, and which we were commanded to observe in all subsequent generations.

(185) Leviticus 7:7: *As is the sin-offering, so is the guilt-offering; there is one law for them.* Hence although no guilt-offering was brought as part of the dedication-offerings, it may yet be said that *all* kinds of offerings were brought on these days of dedication, since the sin-offering was brought. (186) Deuteronomy 28:58. (187) Verse 11. (188) II Chronicles 7:5. (189) Ezra 6:16. (190) Ezekiel 43:26-27. (191) Further, 9:1-13. (192) *Ibid.*, Chapter 36. See also in *Seder Korach,* Note 67.

Beha'alothcha

8 2. WHEN THOU LIGHTEST THE LAMPS. "Why does the section dealing with the candelabrum follow [the section which tells of] the dedication-offerings of the princes? The reason is that when Aaron saw the dedication-offerings of the princes, he became disheartened because neither he nor his tribe participated with them in the dedication; whereupon the Holy One, blessed be He, said to him: 'By thy life! Thy contribution is [of] greater [significance] than theirs, for thou wilt kindle and trim the lamps every morning and evening.' "[1] This is Rashi's language, from a Midrash Agadah.[2]

But it is not clear to me why G-d consoled Aaron [by reminding him of his function] in lighting the lamps, rather than consoling him with

(1) "Every morning and evening." This is not found in our texts of Rashi. (2) Tanchuma *Beha'alothcha* 5. — "Midrash Agadah." Rabbinic texts on the Five Books of Moses are divided into two classes: "Midrash Halachah" (texts dealing mainly with the legal parts of the Torah), which consist of the Mechilta on the Book of Exodus, Sifra [or Torath Kohanim] on the Book of Leviticus, and Sifre on the Books of Numbers and Deuteronomy. Another set of texts deal mainly with the narrative, ethical and homiletical aspects of the Scriptures. These comprise two major works — the Midrash Rabbah and Tanchuma. There is in addition a large group of smaller Midrashim that belong to this category. The generic term "Midrash Agadah" includes all this second group of texts.

the burning of the incense every morning and evening, which is [the specific function of his] with which Scripture praised him, as it is said, *they shall put incense before Thee.*[3] Or [G-d could have reminded him of] all the offerings [performed only by his descendants], and the meal-offering of baked cakes [which is brought daily by the High Priest personally],[4] and the Service on the Day of Atonement which is only valid if done by him [i.e., Aaron and subsequent High Priests], and [by the fact that it is] he who enters into the innermost part of the Sanctuary, and he is *the holy one of the Eternal,*[5] standing in His Temple *to minister unto Him, and to bless in His Name,*[6] and his entire tribe minister to our G-d! Moreover, what reason was there for Aaron's uneasiness of mind [upon seeing the offerings of the princes]? Was not his [dedication-] offering greater than that of the [other] princes, for he offered up during those days—all the [seven] days of the initiation [of the priests]—many offerings? And if you reply that [he was disheartened because] his offerings were obligatory and he had been commanded to bring them, and therefore he was dispirited because he did not bring a *voluntary* offering for the dedication of the altar as they did—[this cannot be so] because the lighting of the lamps with which He consoled Aaron was also a duty which he had been commanded! [Therefore what consolation did Aaron derive for not sharing in the *voluntary* offerings by being given a commandment which was obligatory?]

But the intention of this homiletic text is to derive an allusion from this section [of the Torah] to the Chanukah ("Dedication") of lights which occurred in the period of the Second Temple through Aaron and his sons, namely [Matithyahu] the Hasmonean, who was High Priest, and his sons.[7] And I have found this explanation in the

(3) Deuteronomy 33:10. This was recited by Moses in praise of the whole tribe of Levi consisting of priests and Levites, and he singled out this function of the priests for special praise, thus indicating that the burning of incense was a highly significant act. So why did G-d not console Aaron with this special prerogative of his? (4) Leviticus 6:13-15. (5) Psalms 106:16. (6) Deuteronomy 10:8. (7) See Vol. I, pp. 589-590.

following text of Megillath Setharim[8] of Rabbeinu Nissim,[9] who mentions this tradition, saying: "I have seen in the Midrash: When [the princes of] the twelve tribes brought the dedication-offerings and the tribe of Levi did not etc., the Holy One, blessed be He, said to Moses, *Speak unto Aaron, and say unto him: When thou lightest the lamps.* There is another Dedication in which there will be lighting of the lamps, when I will perform through your sons miracles and salvation for Israel, and a Dedication which will be called by their name, namely, 'the Chanukah of the sons of the Hasmonean.'[10] Therefore He put this section [dealing with the lighting of the lamps] next to the section concerning the dedication of the altar." Thus far is his [Rabbeinu Nissim's] language.

And I have further seen in Yelamdeinu[11] and also in the Midrash Rabbah[12] [the following text]: "The Holy One, blessed be He, said to Moses: Go and tell Aaron—'Fear not! You are designated for something of greater importance than this. The offerings are brought only as long as the Sancutary is in existence, but the lamps will *give light in front of the candelabrum* forever; and all the blessings that I have given you with which to bless My children will never come to an

(8) Literally: "Scroll of Hidden Things." This was a kind of anthology of various subjects — law, tradition, Biblical exegesis, philosophy, as well as explanations of customs. It is possible that they were primarily notes which the author wrote down for his own benefit, not intending them for public use, hence its name — "Scroll of Hidden Things." The book was popular in the era of the *Rishonim* ["the Early Scholars" of the eleventh and twelfth centuries]. It has been lost in the course of time. (9) Rabbeinu Nissim lived in the first half of the eleventh century of the Common Era. He was the son of Rabbi Yaakov of Kairwan in North Africa, to whom Rabbeinu Sherira Gaon (see Vol. I, p. 97) addressed his famous letter, in which he gives a historical account of how the Mishnah was written and how the traditions were passed on through the later generations. After the death of his father, Rabbeinu Nissim together with Rabbeinu Chananel (see Vol. II p. 106, Note 45, and Vol. III, p. 324, Note 286) were the recognized authorities of the Kairwan community. Rabbeinu Nissim wrote a commentary on many tractates of the Talmud which is existing and is outstanding for its clarity of exposition. (10) The sense of the verse here is thus: "It is you [Aaron and sons, through your descendants the Hasmoneans] who will kindle and trim the lamps in the days of the Second Temple." (11) Tanchuma *Beha'alothcha,* 5. On the meaning of the term Yelamdeinu, see Vol. II, p. 131, Note 196. (12) Bamidbar Rabbah 15:5.

end.' " Now it is an obvious fact that when the Sanctuary is not in existence and the offerings are not brought because of its destruction, the lighting of the lamps [of the candelabrum in the Sanctuary] also ceases [so what does the Midrash mean in saying that G-d promised Aaron that the lighting of the lamps would never stop]! Therefore [we must say] that the Sages of the Midrash were alluding to the lights of the Dedication of the Hasmoneans, which applies [on the festival of Chanukah] even after the destruction of the Sanctuary, in our exile. Similarly the priestly blessing[13] which is also juxtaposed to the dedication-offerings of the princes applies forever. Thus the Rabbis interpreted the proximity to the chapter of the dedication-offerings of the princes of both [the section] before and after it, in honor of Aaron who was not included with the princes [in those dedication-offerings].

Rabbi Abraham ibn Ezra explains that this section was placed next to [the verse above, stating, *And when Moses went into the Tent of Meeting that He might speak with him . . .*],[14] in order "to inform us that the Divine communication [to Moses] would come at night as well, for there [in the Tent of Meeting] the lamp would be burning and would not become extinguished." But this is not so according to the opinion of our Rabbis, who say: [15] "Did He not speak to him [Moses] only in the daytime?" And if Rabbi Abraham ibn Ezra would have understood the difference between the prophecy [experienced by] Moses and that of the other prophets,[16] he would not have thought so [i.e., that the Divine communication also came to Moses at night]; as Scripture states, *If there be a prophet among you, I the Eternal do*

(13) Above, 6:24-26. (14) *Ibid.*, 7:89. (15) Mechilta *Pis'cha* 2. (16) Ramban clearly refers to the explanation of Rambam in his introduction to the tenth chapter of Tractate Sanhedrin, where he elucidates the ways in which the prophecy of Moses our teacher differed from that of all other prophets: " . . . Secondly, in the case of all other prophets, prophecy only comes to them either in the course of natural sleep . . . or when overtaken during the day by such a deep sleep as to be deprived of all consciousness, their minds being completely suspended . . . In the case of Moses, however, the word of G-d came to him during the day, and whilst he was standing between the two cherubim [of the ark of the covenant]" (see my translation of this introduction, in "The Commandments," Vol. I, pp. 275-276).

make Myself known unto him in a vision, I do speak with him in a dream. My servant Moses is not so,[17] for his prophecy was not through a dream, since dreams take place when it is actually night. But the order of arrangement of these sections [of the Torah] is as I have explained,[18] for Scripture's purpose in this book is to complete the laws of the offerings and all that must be done in the Tent of Meeting. Now He had said originally, *And thou shalt command the children of Israel, that they bring unto thee pure olive oil beaten for the light, to cause a lamp to burn continually,*[19] but He did not mention the candelabrum there, and therefore [one might have thought] that it indicates that they [only] have to kindle [the lamps] in the candelabrum when it is available, just as He said in [the section concerning] the making thereof, *and he shall light the lamps thereof, to give light over against it.*[20] But if it were perchance lost or broken [we might have thought that] they should light the lamps without the candelabrum, and that the candelabrum is not essential for the lighting, since the commandment is *to cause a lamp to burn continually*[19] for all time. Therefore[21] He commanded again afterwards, [so that it would be applicable] at once and for all generations, *Command the children of Israel, that they bring unto thee pure olive oil,*[22] stating, *He* [Aaron] *shall set in order the lamps upon the pure candelabrum,*[23] meaning that he may only set the lamps in order *upon the pure candelabrum.* And since He completed here the account of the erection of the Tabernacle, He also finished all the laws of the lamps, and commanded that the seven lamps should always be burning for all generations *in front of the candelabrum,*[24] just as He had mentioned at the making of the candelabrum, *and he shall light the lamps thereof, to give light over against it*[20] — but not without the candelabrum, and not unless all the lamps *give light over against it.* He did not mention the Tent of Meeting in this section, in order to instruct [us] that this [law] applies also in the Sanctuary [at

(17) Further, 12:6-7. (18) In thc introduction to this book, and above in *Seder Naso* 7:1. (19) Exodus 27:20. (20) *Ibid.*, 25:37. (21) The word "Therefore" is added in the Tur. (22) Leviticus 24:2. (23) *Ibid.*, Verse 4. (24) In Verse 2 before us.

Jerusalem], for one might have thought that because there were no windows in the Tent of Meeting it was necessary to have this light, whereas in the Sanctuary [at Jerusalem] where there were *windows broad within, and narrow without*[25] [such a light] would not be necessary, therefore He did not mention here the Tent of Meeting.

3. AND AARON DID SO. The meaning thereof is to state that it was Aaron who lighted the lamps all his life. For although the commandment may be validly performed by his sons, as it is said, *Aaron and his sons shall set it in order,*[26] it was he who was zealous in the fulfillment of this great commandment which alludes to an exalted matter and sublime secret.[27] Perhaps he deduced an allusion to this [i.e., that during his lifetime it was he who was to light the lamps] from the verse, *Without the Veil of the Testimony, in the Tent of Meeting, shall Aaron set it in order from evening to morning,*[28] [implying] that it was him whom G-d chose [to light the lamps] as long as he lived. And it is for this reason that now too, He said, *Speak unto Aaron . . . When thou lightest,*[29] and He did not say "Speak unto Aaron and his sons . . . When ye light [the lamps]."

4. AND THIS WAS THE WORK OF THE CANDELABRUM, BEATEN WORK OF GOLD. The meaning thereof is to allude [to the law] that throughout all [future] generations the candelabrum must be beaten [and fashioned out of one solid piece of metal], and that this is essential [for the validity of the candelabrum and lighting the lamps therein]. This is why He expressly mentioned at the beginning [that it is to be] beaten work, but did not mention [here] that in the making thereof there should be branches [going out of the candelabrum], knops, and cups shaped like almond-blossoms.[30] But He did mention [here that it be of] gold, for it is likewise a commandment for all

(25) I Kings 6:4. The windows were made in that way in order to indicate that it is not light from the outside world that comes into the Sanctuary but on the contrary — it is from the Sanctuary that the light goes forth to the world (Menachoth 86b, Rashi). (26) Exodus 27:21. (27) See my Hebrew commentary p. 222. (28) Leviticus 24:3. (29) Verse 2. (30) Exodus 25:33.

generations that it be made of gold, in order *to glorify the House of our G-d.*[31] Then He repeated [in the verse before us] *it was beaten work,* in order to say that it is only [failure to make it] of beaten work that invalidates the candelabrum, but [the requirement] of gold is not [indispensable, since it is valid if made of any metal], and certainly its other embellishments [such as the cups and knops do not invalidate it if they are missing]. And thus have our Rabbis said in the Sifre[32] and in Tractate Menachoth.[33]

ACCORDING TO THE PATTERN WHICH THE ETERNAL HAD SHOWN MOSES, SO 'HE' MADE THE CANDELABRUM — that is, Moses mentioned above, for it was he who made efforts to learn about it and directed the making thereof by command. And so the Rabbis have said in the Sifre:[32] "[This is stated] in order to praise Moses, [by emphasizing] that he made it exactly as the Holy One, blessed be He, told him to make [the candelabrum]." And Rashi wrote: "*So he made* — [the word 'he' refers to] the one who made it [i.e., to whomever it was that made it, and does not refer to Moses]. But a Midrash Agadah[2] has it: [The subject 'he' refers to the Eternal, for] it was made of its own accord [without human intervention], by the Holy One, blessed be He."

Now after the firstborn and the Levites had been counted,[34] and the Levites were commanded about their [individual] work and charges, and He gave them the wagons,[35] He completed the commandments referring to the priests with the [laws of the] candelabrum; then He came to give the commandments concerning the Levites so that they could begin their service, and therefore it was necessary to purify them and to effect atonement for them. This is the reason why this chapter [of the purification of the Levites] is put in juxtaposition to this [section on the candelabrum]. He finished [the laws of the Levites] with a commandment applicable for all generations: *From twenty and five years old and upward 'yavo litzvo tzava' (they shall come to be counted among the host) for the work of the Tent of Meeting.*[36]

(31) Ezra 9:9. (32) Sifre *Beha'alothcha* 61. (33) Menachoth 28a. (34) Above, 3:39-43. (35) *Ibid.*, 7:5-8. (36) Further, Verse 24.

Now Rashi commented: "Here it says, *from twenty and five years old;* but in another place it is said, *from thirty years old*![37] How are these [contradictory verses to be reconciled]? From twenty-five years of age the Levite comes to learn the laws of the service, and he studies for five years, and at the age of thirty he performs the service. From here [we derive the principle] that if a pupil studying under his master does not see progress in his study after five years, he will never see such progress." If this is so, the expression *yavo litzvo tzava*[36] means that "he shall come and assemble among those who are gathered" *for the work of the Tent of Meeting,* meaning that he is to stay with them and continually observe the service [of the older Levites] by day and night, in order to learn the laws of the service in theory and practice. This is why He did not state here "to do service," as He said above [*From thirty years old and upward . . . 'to do' service*],[38] but He stated, *'yavo litzvo tzava' (they shall come to be counted among the host) 'ba'avodath' (for the work of) the Tent of Meeting,*[36] meaning that he is to come among those who are gathered for the purpose of the service. But I do not know whether this [explanation that there was a five-year period of training for the Levites] is the unanimous opinion of our Rabbis, for I find it taught in the name of a single Rabbi in the Sifre:[39] "Rabbi Nathan says: One verse states, *From twenty and five years old* etc." And it furthermore appears that these words [of the Sifre as quoted by Rashi] are merely Scriptural support for the practice of the pupils [i.e., the new Levites] who used to study the laws of the service for five years.

According to the plain meaning of Scripture, the [Levites] counted by the hand of Moses and Aaron were aged thirty years old and over, and it is they whom he appointed *every one to his service, and to his burden.*[40] But here He commanded that every Levite who [although not counted by Moses] knows himself to have reached the age of

(37) Above, 4:3. (38) *Ibid.*, Verse 23. For since Scripture speaks there of the Levites above the age of thirty years, it uses the expression *'la'avod avodah' (to do service)*. Here, however, it refers to the five-year period of their training; hence the expression *'ba'avodath' (in the service)*, as they were not yet permitted to do the actual service. (39) Sifre *Beha'alothcha* 62. (40) Above, 4:49.

twenty-five years, is permitted to do the service, and may *come with all the desire of his soul*[41] to work with them and help them in the service, but he may not be *a chief officer*[42] over any particular task. And the reason for this is that every person pays attention to [the passing of] his decades, since there are physical changes at these stages, therefore he knows when he reaches the age of twenty or thirty; for even his neighbors, relatives, his father and mother and his children notice it and inform him of it. But when a person reaches twenty-five years of age, they do not notice it so much; therefore He only commanded Moses to go to the trouble of counting those Levites above the age of thirty, when a man is recognizable by his years. And so did David say, *And the Levites were numbered from thirty years old and upward.*[43]

And Rabbi Abraham ibn Ezra said that the plain meaning of Scripture is that from thirty years old they were to do the work of bearing burdens, and from twenty-five years old they did work in the Tent of Meeting.[44] But this is not correct. For there also [when speaking of the Levites who were more than thirty years old] it is said, *all that came to perform the service, to do the work in the Tent of Meeting,*[45] and it is also said [of this group], *to serve and to bear burdens.*[46] Moreover, it is written of the Sanctuary: *These were the sons of Levi after their fathers' houses, even the heads of the fathers' houses, according to their numberings, in the number of names by their polls, who did the work for the service of the House of the Eternal, from twenty years old and upward. For David said: 'The Eternal, the G-d of Israel, hath given rest unto His people, and He dwelleth in Jerusalem forever; and also the Levites shall no more have need to carry the Tabernacle and all the vessels of it for the service thereof.' For by the last ordinances of David the sons of Levi were numbered from twenty years old and upward. For their station was at the side of the sons of Aaron for the service of the House of the Eternal, in the courts, and in the chambers.*[47] Thus it is stated that *by the last ordinances of David*

(41) Deuteronomy 18:6. (42) Jeremiah 20:1. (43) I Chronicles 23:3. Thirty is the age when a person attains full strength (Aboth 5:24). (44) On the nature of the work in the Tent of Meeting, see Ramban on the verse that follows. (45) Above, 4:23. (46) *Ibid.*, Verse 24. (47) I Chronicles 23:24-28.

when the House [of G-d] is built and the Levites no longer have to carry [the parts of the Tabernacle] on their shoulders, and their service will be only *in the courts, and in the chambers,* he counted them *from twenty years old and upward,* while at first [before the building of the Sanctuary] he counted them from the age of thirty upwards.[43] And according to Rabbi Abraham ibn Ezra's words, he should have counted them from twenty-five years old [since this is, according to him, the age for general work in the Sanctuary as opposed to the work of carrying its parts]!

25. AND FROM THE AGE OF FIFTY YEARS HE SHALL RETURN FROM THE SERVICE OF THE WORK, AND HE SHALL SERVE NO MORE—"the service of carrying loads upon the shoulders, but he returns [i.e., he may still serve] to close the gates, or to sing, or to load the wagons." This is Rashi's language. But in the Sifre[48] the Rabbis mentioned only that "he returns to close the gates or to the work of the sons of Gershon"[49] [but they did not say that he may return to the service of singing]! And this indeed appears correct [that a Levite above the age of fifty was not allowed to take part in the singing] — for if it were as the Rabbi [Rashi] has written, why were the twenty-year old Levites not appointed to sing, to close the gates and to load the wagons until they reached the required age,[50] and why were they counted from thirty to fifty years old and only for the work of bearing burdens [since both before and after these two age-limits they

(48) Sifre *Beha'alothcha* 63. (49) The reference is also to the work of the sons of Merari, since the work of both of them [the sons of Gershon and Merari] consisted only of loading the wagons during transport, and serving as gate-keepers when the Tabernacle was in its place. The Sifre, however, speaks only of "the sons of Gershon" since they are mentioned (above, in Chapter 4, where the work was assigned to each of the three main families of the Levites) next to the sons of Kohath, whose work consisted of carrying the loads on their shoulders. (50) In other words, since the maximum age of fifty applied to the bearing of burdens, which was the specific work of the Kohathites — see above, Chapter 4 — but not to the service of singing, the minimum age of twenty-five likewise does not refer to the service of singing, and the same reasoning applies to serving as gate-keepers and loading the wagons. If so, why were the Levites [including the Kohathites] not counted from the age of twenty, and with no upper age limit?

could still serve by singing etc., therefore they should have been counted from twenty years, with no upper limit]? Moreover, why were the sons of Gershon and Merari counted in this way [from thirty to fifty] since all their work [i.e., singing, closing the gates and loading the wagons] could be done when they were older?

We must rather say that since they were appointed to carry the ark at the age from thirty to fifty, they [therefore] were not appointed to sing, which was the main function of the Levites, unless they were also qualified to carry the ark, for all those who were appointed to sing were qualified to perform all the services [including the carrying of the ark]. And since the Kohathites [who were the only ones permitted to carry the ark] were counted from thirty to fifty years old, even for singing, they were all counted in this manner, in order that the sons of Gershon and Merari should not be qualified to sing during these years [i.e., *below* the age of thirty and *above* the age of fifty] and the sons of Kohath be disqualified. [Hence the age limits of thirty and fifty applied to the Kohathites' singing, which was their main function, as well as to their carrying of the parts of the Tabernacle, and therefore these age limits applied to the function of singing of the sons of Gershon and Merari as well, and they could not, as Rashi wrote, return to the singing.] But for closing the gates or loading the wagons all of them were qualified [even after the age of fifty, as quoted in the Sifre above]. Furthermore it is written, *from thirty years old and upward even unto fifty years old, every one that entered in to do the work of the service, and the work of bearing burdens in the Tent of Meeting,*[51] and the Rabbis interpreted in the Tractate of Shechitath Chullin:[52] "I might think that in Shiloh and in the Eternal House [at Jerusalem,[53] when the services of the Levites were limited to gate-keeping and singing] it was also so [that the Levites were disqualified

(51) Above, 4:47. "This is the song [of the Levites] accompanied with cymbals and harp, this being 'the service' attached to another 'service' " [i.e., the Service of the Offerings] (Rashi). (52) Literally: "The Slaughtering of Ordinary Animals," now generally called Chullin (Ordinary Animals). The text quoted is found there on 24a. — The name *Shechitath Chullin* is in contrast to the Tractate *Schechitath Kodashim* (The Slaughtering of Hallowed Animals), now generally called Zebachim (Offerings). (53) See Vol. II, p. 335, Note 598, and Vol. III, p. 123, Note 122.

after the age of fifty]; Scripture therefore says, *to do the work of service, and the work of bearing burdens.*[51] I have only said so with respect to a time when there is *bearing burdens* upon the shoulders." Now [the expression] *'avodath avodah'*[51] [*the work of service,* but literally "a service of a service"] is a reference to singing, as Rashi has written above in *Seder Naso;*[51] if so [it is clear that] when there was [the duty of] bearing the burdens upon the shoulders, the Levites were disqualified from singing as well [after the age of fifty]. And so it is said in the words of David, *And the Levites were numbered from thirty years old and upward,*[54] and it is further written there, *Of these twenty and four thousand were to oversee the work of the House of the Eternal* etc.,[55] *and four thousand praised the Eternal with the instruments which I made to praise therewith.*[56] For until the House [of G-d in Jerusalem] was built, when they still had to carry [the ark and the Tabernacle] on their shoulders, they only appointed Levites to sing who were also fit to carry [i.e., from the age of thirty to fifty]; but David counted them again from twenty years old[57] to meet the requirements of the House [of G-d] when it was built, as has been explained [above at the end of Verse 4].

9 1. IN THE SECOND YEAR AFTER THEIR COMING OUT OF THE LAND OF EGYPT, IN THE FIRST MONTH. From here the Rabbis have deduced the principle:[58] "There is no [strict] chronological order in the narrative of the Torah" [for the census mentioned at the beginning of this Book of Numbers was *on the first day of 'the second' month in the second year,* and the present chapter about the Passover was *in the 'first month'* of the same year]! Now the reason for this delay [in mentioning the section concerning the Passover] was that since this fourth book [of the Torah] comes to mention the commandments which Israel was given in the wilderness of Sinai for that particular time, He wanted [first] to complete everything related to the Tent of Meeting and its functioning during all the time [that Israel was] in the wilderness. Therefore He

(54) I Chronicles 23:3. (55) *Ibid.*, Verse 4. (56) *Ibid.*, Verse 5. (57) *Ibid.*, Verse 27. (58) Sifre *Beha'alothcha* 64. Pesachim 6b.

mentioned first the [commandments about the four] standards, and the place of the Tent [of Meeting], and the position of its ministers, and the ordinance concerning the divisions [of the Levites] when carrying [the Tabernacle whilst travelling, and] all services of the Tent. Then He mentioned the dedication-offerings of the princes, who brought the wagons in which they would carry it [the Tent] as long as they were to be in the wilderness, and He finished [the account of] their offerings at the dedication of the altar, which began on the first of Nisan or afterwards.[59] After all this He returned and mentioned the admonition that He had given them not to forget the commandment of the Passover.

Now in the opinion of our Rabbis[60] [the obligation to bring the Passover-offering] only applied in the wilderness in this [second] year, after the exodus because they did not perform circumcision in the wilderness,[61] and the [non-performance of] circumcision of the male children and the servants prevented them [from slaughtering the Passover-offering].[62] It is possible that this [specific] command [to bring the Passover] was necessary because at first they were only commanded about making the Passover-offering in future generations after [entering] the Land of Israel, as it is written, *And it shall come to pass, when ye be come to the Land which the Eternal will give you, according as He hath promised, that ye shall keep this Service.*[63] And it is further stated there, *And it shall be when the Eternal shall bring thee into the land of the Canaanite,* etc., *that thou shalt keep this Service in this month.*[64] And now the Holy One, blessed be He, desired and commanded that they should make it [the Passover-offering] in order that the memory of their redemption and of the miracles which were done for them and their fathers should be transmitted from the fathers who saw them to their children, *and their*

(59) See above. *Seder Naso,* Notes 131-132, which mention two opinions, to which Ramban alludes here. (60) Sifre *Beha'alothcha* 67. (61) The reason for this is that during the years of G-d's displeasure with Israel after the incident of the golden calf (Rashi), or that of the spies (Ramban), the north wind did not blow, and there was nothing to mitigate the effect of the extreme heat, so that it was dangerous to do the circumcision (Yebamoth 72 a, and see Rashi and Ramban there). See also further on in the text here. (62) Exodus 12:44. (63) *Ibid.*, Verse 25. (64) *Ibid.*, 13:5.

children to another generation.[65] Thus He had said at first, *And it shall come to pass, when ye be come to the Land,*[63] meaning to say that this commandment [to bring the Passover-offering] does not apply outside the Land in future generations; therefore now He commanded that they should fulfill it in the desert. And in the opinion of our Rabbis[60] they only brought the Passover-offering in this [second] year [after the exodus], because they begot sons and servants whom they could not circumcise, for the reason that the Rabbis mentioned, that it was dangerous [to observe circumcision], as is explained in Tractate Yebamoth.[61]

However, in the Sifre the Rabbis have said: [66] "*And they brought the Passover-offering in the first month.*[67] Scripture speaks in a critical manner about Israel, inasmuch as [throughout their forty years in the desert] they brought only this Passover-offering, and likewise He said, *Did ye bring unto Me offerings and meal-offerings in the wilderness forty years?*"[68] The Rabbis arrived at this interpretation [that the verse is rebuking them because they only brought the Passover-offering in the second year after the exodus], on the basis of this verse which states, *And they brought the Passover-offering in the first month, on the fourteenth day of the month, at dusk, in the wilderness of Sinai,*[67] since it is a superfluous verse, for it would have been sufficient to say, *and they brought the Passover-offering* "according to all that the Eternal commanded Moses." But Scripture mentioned the [exact] day and [the fact that it was in] the wilderness in order to hint that they only observed it in the wilderness on that day, and this was their "shortcoming" [which is referred to in the text of the Sifre].

It is possible that [the reason why it is considered] their shortcoming is because of their sin in the affair of the spies, on account of which they fell into disesteem[69] and the [cooling] northern wind did not blow upon them, [with the result that on account of the great heat in the desert] they could not circumcise themselves, and therefore they were prohibited to eat any sacred offerings, and they were "rebuked" by [G-d].

65 Joel 1:3. (66) Sifre *Beha'alothcha* 67. (67) Verse 5. (68) Amos 5:25. (69) The Hebrew word is *nithnadu,* which means literally "banished, isolated, or excommunicated."

Or it may be that this Beraitha [of the Sifre which speaks of the "shortcoming" of Israel, as hinted at in this section] is in agreement with the words of the Sage[70] who holds that [non-performance of] circumcision of one's male children or servants does *not* prevent one from eating the Passover-offering, and therefore the people were permitted to bring the Passover-offering, but they did not trouble themselves to do it, and this is indeed a great "shortcoming." The first interpretation, however, appears more likely to be correct, for [had they been obliged to bring it] Moses would have forced them to observe it and would not have allowed them [by not bringing it] to incur the penalty of excision. But as for the Festival of Unleavened Bread for seven days, and the removal [over that period] of leavened bread, Scripture did not have to say that they observed it [in the wilderness], since these are commandments that are obligatory on everyone's person and apply in all places, and it has already been stated [that they are to be observed] *throughout your generations by an ordinance forever.*[71]

3. ACCORDING TO ALL THE STATUTES OF IT, AND ACCORDING TO ALL THE ORDINANCES THEREOF, SHALL YE BRING IT [i.e., the Passover-offering]. Now it is written in the commentary of Rashi: "*According to all the statutes of it* — this refers to the laws concerning the animal itself, [that it should be] *a lamb without blemish, a male of the first year.*[72] *And according to all the ordinances thereof* — this relates to the laws 'upon' the lamb,[73] such as eating unleavened bread for seven days, and the removal of leavened bread." But this is a copyist's error.[74] For the laws which concern the animal itself are as stated above], *a lamb without blemish, a male of the first year;*[72] the laws "upon" the animal are that it should be *roast*

(70) Rabbi Eliezer (Mechilta *Pis'cha* 15). (71) Exodus 12:17. (72) *Ibid.,* Verse 5. (73) Our texts of Rashi add here: "from another place." Ramban interprets this phrase as an independent thought, as explained further on. (74) Ramban's meaning is as follows: Even if we concede that the duty to eat unleavened bread can be called a law "upon the lamb," because the Passover-offering must be eaten together with unleavened bread, in what way can the duty of destroying leavened bread be one that is "upon the lamb"? Therefore it must be a copyist's mistake in Rashi, which thus requires re-interpretation.

with fire; its head with its legs and with the inwards thereof; [75] whereas the laws which are "outside" the animal itself are [the duty to eat] unleavened bread [on the first evening of the festival] and the duty of removing leavened bread, concerning which Scripture does not speak here at all. Similarly, it is said of the second Passover that [it should be observed] *according to the statute of the Passover, and according to the ordinance thereof,* [76] and a person may [then] have both unleavened bread and leavened bread with him in his house, [77] and it applies for only one day. [78]

Now Scripture spoke briefly, saying, *at dusk, ye shall bring it in its appointed season; according to all the statutes of it, and according to all the ordinances thereof, shall ye bring it,* [79] thereby including the laws relating to eating it, that it should not be on the *day* mentioned by the verse [on which the offering is slaughtered], but it is to be eaten on the following night, since He already explained previously, *And they shall eat the flesh in that night* etc. [80] Similarly, *In the second month on the fourteenth day at dusk they shall bring it; they shall eat it with unleavened bread and bitter herbs,* [81] means *they shall eat it* at the time of eating mentioned in the command concerning the first Passover.

10. 'B'DERECH R'CHOKAH' Rashi commented [that the meaning of this expression — literally "on a distant way" — is] "that he was outside the threshold of the Sanctuary Court during the whole time prescribed for slaughtering [the Passover-offering]." According to this opinion, this interpretation is hinted at by the dot [on the letter *hei* in the word *r'chokah* (distant) in the Torah, thus indicating that the journey does not really have to be a distant one, for even if he is only

(75) Exodus 12:9. (76) Further, Verse 14. (77) Pesachim 95 a. (78) Hence the duty to eat unleavened bread and to destroy all leavened bread, cannot be included [as implied in our texts of Rashi] in *the statutes and ordinances* of the second Passover, since we have been taught that on the second Passover one *may* have both unleavened and leavened bread with one in the house! Furthermore, the second Passover applies only for one day; so how can there be a duty to eat unleavened bread for *seven* days included in "the ordinances that are upon the animal" [as our texts of Rashi have it]! (79) In Verse 3 before us. (80) Exodus 12:5. (81) Further, Verse 11.

outside the threshold of the Sanctuary Court during the time of slaughtering of the Passover-offering, it is considered "a distant way", as explained further on].

But I am surprised at him [Rashi]! Why did he adopt the opinion of Rabbi Eliezer,[82] when it would have been correct to accept the opinion of Rabbi Akiba [that *a distant way* means] beyond Modiin [a city fifteen miles from Jerusalem; and the verse would thus be referring to someone who cannot reach the Sanctuary Court in time to bring the Passover-offering].[83] And such is the opinion of the *Amoraim* in the Gemara[84] [of Tractate Pesachim],[82] where Ula said, [*a distant way* is if he is at such a distance from Jerusalem that] he cannot come in, in time *for the slaughtering* [of the Passover-offering].[85] This is indeed the plain meaning of Scripture, that a person who is situated at the

(82) Pesachim 93 b. In other words, the interpretation of Rashi follows that of Rabbi Eliezer, whilst the accepted opinion of the Rabbis in the Gemara is that of Rabbi Akiba, as explained further on. (83) But if he were closer to Jerusalem on the afternoon of the fourteenth of Nisan than a distance of fifteen miles, it is not considered *a distant way*. The difference is important. The punishment of excision for neglecting to bring the Passover-offering is stated primarily with reference to the *first* Passover-offering. A person who was on *a distant way* on the fourteenth of Nisan [or in a state of impurity] must bring the *second* Passover-offering, on the fourteenth of Iyar; but if he did not bring the second Passover-offering, even wilfully, he is not liable to punishment, since at the time of the first Passover-offering, when the main duty arose, he was unable to bring the offering. However, a person who was *not* on a distant way on the fourteenth of Nisan and did not bring the Passover-offering, may nonetheless bring the second Passover-offering on the fourteenth of Iyar; but if he wilfully did not bring it then on the fourteenth of Iyar he is subject to the punishment of excision. See further in my translation of "The Commandments," Vol. I, pp. 67-69. (84) *Amoraim* means literally: the Interpreters. This name is given to the Rabbis of the Gemara, as distinguished from the *Tannaim,* the Rabbis mentioned in the Mishnah or Beraitha. The Gemara is the text containing the collected discussions of the *Amoraim* on the Mishnah. The Mishnah and Gemara together are known as the the Talmud. See also Vol. II, p. 132, Note 204, and Vol. III, p. 192. Note 44. (85) Ramban's thought is as follows: The duty of bringing the Passover-offering commences at the *beginning* of the afternoon of the fourteenth day of Nisan (Exodus 12:6, see also Ramban there). Now since prior to that time there is no obligation to bring the offering yet, and Ula is of the opinion that a person on *a distant way* is "one who cannot come into the Sanctuary Court in time *for the slaughtering* of the

beginning of the afternoon in a place from which he cannot reach the Sanctuary Court [on foot] by the time of the slaughtering, is considered as being on *a distant way,* and therefore he is free [from the obligation of bringing the Passover-offering]. It is possible that [according to Rabbi Akiba] the reason for the dot [on the letter *hei* in the word *r'chokah* (distant) in the Torah] is to indicate that it is too distant for him to bring the Passover-offering, even though it is not actually distant [since fifteen-miles — walking-distance — is the required distance]; therefore when He repeated it He stated, *But the man that is clean, and is not on 'a journey,' [and forbeareth to bring the Passover-lamb],*[86] and did not mention "distant."[87]

Now Scripture commanded that a person who was impure or on a distant way should bring the second [Passover-offering], but the same law, for the same reason, applies to anyone who did not bring the first Passover-offering, even wilfully, namely that he is obliged to bring the second Passover-offering, in accordance with the words of our Rabbis.[88] Scripture, however, mentioned only [those who were impure or on a distant way in order] to say that they are allowed to bring the second Passover-offering, and to forbid an *impure* person to bring the *first* Passover-offering. However, one who was on a [distant] way is free from bringing the first Passover-offering, and *may* bring the second one, but if he wants to fulfill his duty on the first Passover and he told someone [in Jerusalem to include him in a group, and] to slaughter the

Passover-offering," it follows perforce that the term *a distant way* cannot mean in reality far away, since prior to the beginning of that afternoon there was no obligation to bring it yet. Hence even if the distance was actually not far but that person for some reason was not in the Sanctuary Court he is also considered as having been on *a distant way*. The case, however, would be different if he were to hold like Rav Yehudah, who says that a person on *a distant way* is "one who cannot come in, in time *for the eating* of the Passover-offering," which is on the following night. In that case a person on *a distant way* would be one, who from the beginning of the afternoon cannot reach Jerusalem at night, in time for the eating of the Passover-offering, since he is actually on a far distant way. (86) Further, Verse 13. (87) For had Verse 13 said: "and he was not on a *distant* journey," it would have implied that even if he was beyond a distance of fifteen miles and fails to bring the Passover-offering, he is liable to the punishment of excision. But this is not the law, for if he were beyond fifteen miles the punishment does not apply. See Note 83 above. (88) Pesachim 93b. See "The Commandments," Vol. I, pp. 67-69.

offering for him [as well], it is acceptable [for him]. For we accept [as the correct interpretation of the law][89] that the [meaning of the verse is not that he *must* bring it only on the second Passover, but that the] Merciful One dealt kindly with him [and *allowed* him if he prefers to bring the second Passover-offering], but if he did bring [the first one] — he is deserving of a blessing [and he has acted rightly]. It is also possible that the reason why Scripture mentioned "distant" [is because it is referring to a journey which is *actually* far away, and only then *must* he bring the second Passover-offering], but if he is on a "near" journey [i.e., *within* fifteen miles — this distance being considered the beginning of what is technically already "a far way"], he *may* bring the second Passover-offering, *or* the first one, by [telling them] to slaughter it and sprinkle it for him as well [in the afternoon of the fourteenth day of Nisan], and then coming [into the city of Jerusalem] and eating the Passover-offering at night.

14. AND IF A STRANGER SHALL SOJOURN AMONG YOU. The purpose of this is to command the stranger to bring this Passover-offering in the wilderness just as He commanded the Israelites. It is possible that when He said in *Seder 'Bo El Par'oh'* (*Go in unto Pharaoh*),[90] *And when a stranger shall sojourn with thee and will keep the Passover,*[91] it refers [only] to the [original] Passover kept in Egypt, for that section was said with reference to the Passover of Egypt, as I have explained there. In that case we might have thought that those strangers who joined us in going out from Egypt, *the mixed multitude,*[92] should keep the Passover, because they were also included in that miracle [of the exodus], but those who become proselytes afterwards, in the desert or in the Land of Israel, [we might have thought] do not have to bring the Passover-offering, since neither they nor their ancestors were included among [those of whom it is said], *and He brought us out from thence;*[93] therefore He had to make them liable here to bring the Passover-offering in [subsequent] generations, in the wilderness and in the Land.

(89) Pesachim 92b. This is the opinion of Rav Nachman. (90) Exodus 10:1. (91) *Ibid.*, 12:48. (92) *Ibid.*, Verse 38. (93) Deuteronomy 6:23.

15. AND ON THE DAY THE TABERNACLE WAS RAISED UP. Now He resumes the telling of the journey [through the wilderness] and the commandments which they were commanded about it, such as the trumpets, which Moses was now commanded were to be *for the calling of the congregation, and for causing the camps to set forward.*[94] The sense of the expression [*And on the day the Tabernacle was raised up*] *the cloud covered the Tabernacle, even the Tent of the Testimony* is to state that the cloud covered only the Tent of the Testimony, but not the court of the Tabernacle.

19. AND WHEN THE CLOUD TARRIED. This means that if *the cloud tarried upon the Tabernacle many days,* and the place [where they happened to be camped] was not good in their eyes, so that they very much desired and wanted to journey away from there, they were nonetheless not to transgress the will of G-d; this being the meaning of the verse, *and the children of Israel kept the charge of the Eternal, and journeyed not,*[95] namely that [it was only] because of their fear of G-d and because they kept the charge of His command that they did not journey. Similarly, *if* the cloud *was* there only *a few days,*[96] for instance two or three days, and the people were very tired because their *strength had weakened in the way,*[97] they would nonetheless fulfill the will of G-d and walk after the cloud. And Scripture further relates that sometimes they tarried for only one night and journeyed in the [next] morning, although it was a great strain for them. And at times the cloud tarried *a day and a night,*[98] when they had journeyed throughout the night and arrived at that place in the morning, and the cloud stayed there all that day and all the night, *and was taken up* on the second morning *and they journeyed.*[98] This was an even greater trouble for them than the previously-mentioned one, because the people would think that they were to stay there [for a long time], and would unload the wagons and lay down their burdens, as is the custom of those who come from a journey, *and when the cloud was taken up*[98] they began reloading, and could not make any preparations for the journey. *Whether it were two days,*[98] and they journeyed at night.

(94) Further, 10:2. (95) Verse 19. (96) Verse 20. (97) See Psalms 102:24. (98) Verse 21.

It is possible that it happened during their journeys that they had to do as is narrated here, and not in another way, namely that the cloud first tarried *from evening until morning,*[98] then *a day and night,*[98] then *two days,*[99] then *a month* and finally *a year.*[99] This is why Scripture mentioned these periods in detail. It [the cloud] would also tarry for many years, as Scripture mentioned at the beginning [of this section],[100] such as in Kadesh of which Scripture states, *And ye abode in Kadesh many days, according to the days that ye abode there.*[101]

10 6. AND THE CAMPS THAT LIE ON THE SOUTH SIDE SHALL SET FORWARD. Scripture explained the purpose of the two *t'ruoth,*[102] the first one being [the sign] for those encamped eastward to go forward, and the second one for those encamped southward to set out on the journey. And it states [in the verse before us], *a 't'ruah'*[102] *they shall blow for their journeys,* meaning that they should blow [this quavering alarm] *for* all *their journeys,* that is to say, they should blow a third *t'ruah* for the camps on the west side to set forth, and a fourth one for the camps on the north side to set out on the journey, for each standard journeyed by itself, as He explains: *And the standard of the camp of the children of Ephraim set forward;*[103] *And the standard of the camp of the children of Dan set forward.*[104] And thus it is taught in the Beraitha of the Work of the Tabernacle.[105] But in the Sifre the Rabbis have taught:[106] "I might think that just as he blows for the camps in the east and the south to set forward [as Scripture clearly explains], so he is to blow for [those that were encamped in] the west and the north; Scripture therefore states [in the verse before us], *a 't'ruah' they shall blow for their journeys,* that is, one blowing for the two [remaining standards]. And some Rabbis

(99) Verse 22. (100) Verse 19: *And when the cloud tarried upon the Tabernacle many 'days',* which means "many years." (101) Deuteronomy 1:46. They stayed in Kadesh for 19 years (Rashi *ibid.*). (102) A *t'ruah* is a succession of nine tremulous or quavering sounds. A *t'kiah* is a continuous plain sound. The *sh'varim* are broken disconnected sounds, but they are not as broken as those of the *t'ruah.* The three broken sounds of the *sh'varim* are equal [in length of time] to the nine quavering sounds of the *t'ruah.* (103) Further, Verse 22. (104) *Ibid.,* Verse 25. (105) Beraitha of *M'lecheth Hamishkan,* Chapter 13. (106) Sifre *Beha'alothcha* 73.

say that there were three [sounds, i.e., *t'kiah, t'ruah, t'kiah*][102] for [the camps in] each and every direction." Thus far [the language of the Sifre], and such indeed is the plain meaning of Scripture, that they should blow [for the camps] in each direction, as I have explained.

A 'T'RUAH' THEY SHALL BLOW FOR THEIR JOURNEYS. I have already explained in *Seder 'Emor El Hakohanim'* (*Speak unto the priests*)[107] that the *t'ruah* alludes to the [Divine] attribute of justice, for so it is written concerning the journeyings that they were *'al pi Hashem'* (*at the commandment of the Eternal*) *by the hand of Moses*,[108] and it is that [attribute] which brings victory in war, as it is written, *And when ye go to war in your land . . . 'vahareiothem'* (*ye shall sound a 't'ruah'*).[109] Therefore Moses said, *and let them that hate Thee flee 'mipanecha'* (*before Thee*),[110] and I have already explained the secret of the *panim* (face) in the Ten Commandments.[111] And similarly you see that the wall of Jericho fell to the sound of a *t'ruah*, for it is written, *Ye shall not shout . . . until the day I bid you 'hari'u'* (*sound a 't'ruah'*); *'vahari'othem'* (*then shall you sound it*),[112] and it is written, *and the people sounded a great 't'ruah,' and the wall fell down.*[113] It was for this reason that it [the city of Jericho] was declared *cheirem* (devoted) [to the Eternal, and prohibited for private use.].[114] *But when the assembly is to be gathered together 'tithke'u'*[115] — they are deserving that the *t'kiah*[102] be sounded, for the *'p'shutah'* [plain long and continuous sound] alludes to the [Divine] attribute of mercy, for "His right hand is *p'shutah* (stretched out) to receive the penitent" [as it is stated at the Closing Service on the Day of Atonement — a time of mercy]. Therefore, when the ark rested, Moses said, *'Return, O Eternal, unto the myriads of thousands of Israel.'*[116] And it is written, *And in the day of your gladness and in your appointed seasons . . . 'uthkatem'* (*ye shall blow a 't'kiah'*),[117] since war is

(107) Leviticus 21:1. The verse referred to is *ibid.*, 23:24. (108) Above, 9:23. The expression *pi Hashem* alludes to the attribute of justice (Abusaula). (109) Further, Verse 9. (110) *Ibid.*, Verse 35. Literally: "from before Thy face." (111) Exodus 20:3. (112) Joshua 6:10. (113) *Ibid.*, Verse 20. (114) *Ibid.*, Verse 17. (115) Further, Verse 7. (116) Further, Verse 36. (117) *Ibid.*, Verse 10.

[suitable] for *t'ruah* [which alludes to the attribute of justice, as explained above], and the appointed seasons and joyous occasions are for mercy [i.e., for the sound of *t'kiah,* which alludes to mercy].[118] And our Rabbis have received by tradition that there should be a long continuous sound before [the *t'ruah*] and a long continuous sound after it and the *t'ruah* in the middle, on the New Year, the Day of Atonement [of the Jubilee year],[119] and at the bringing of the offerings,[120] in order not "to mutilate the shoots" [of faith]. But as far as their purpose is concerned, the one is for *t'kiah* [which alludes to mercy] and the other for *t'ruah* [which alludes to judgment].[118] The student learned [in the mystic lore of the Cabala] will understand.

14. AND OVER HIS HOST WAS NACHSHON THE SON OF AMMINADAB. I do not know why He mentioned here the names of the princes of the standards, since He has already mentioned them.[121] And if you answer that this was to hint that [on the twentieth of Iyar when they set out on the first journey from the wilderness] these princes were alive— this has already been alluded to in the section of the standards,[121] since from the day of the census [on the first of Iyar] till the time of the journey [on the twentieth of that month] not one of all those who were counted died. Perhaps the verse comes to tell us that even when they travel on the way the prince is to go at the head of his host, who are to follow his command, *and* he is *to dwell as a king in the army,*[122] and they are not to travel *as sheep which have no shepherd,*[123] nor are they to appoint someone else for this purpose, as they do in the case of the priest who was anointed for war purposes.[124]

17. AND THE TABERNACLE WAS TAKEN DOWN; AND THE SONS OF GERSHON AND THE SONS OF MERARI WHO BORE THE TABERNACLE SET FORWARD. The indication of the verses on this subject is as follows: After the standard of Judah had set forward, they would begin dismantling the Tabernacle, and the

(118) Tziyoni. (119) Leviticus 25:9. See Ramban there. (120) See "The Commandments," Vol. I, pp. 70-71. (121) Above, 2:3, 10, 18, 25. (122) Job 29:25. (123) Further, 27:17. (124) See Deuteronomy 20:2-4.

beginning of this dismantling was when Aaron and his sons came [into the Tabernacle] and took down the partition Veil, as it says, *And when 'the camp' setteth forward, Aaron shall go in, and his sons, and they shall take down the Veil* etc.,[125] that is to say, when the first camp [i.e., that of Judah] set forth. When they [the priests] finished covering the ark and all the holy vessels which were to be borne by the Kohathites, the Levites would take down the whole Tabernacle and load it upon the wagons; and the sons of Gershon and Merari then journeyed [with these wagons] after the standard of Judah, the ark and the holy vessels remaining covered and placed upon the staves until the standard of Reuben set forth. And the meaning of the verse *Then the Tent of Meeting, with the camp of the Levites, shall set forward in the midst of the camps*[126] is that the Tent of Meeting together with all the camps of the Levites shall set forward in the midst of those camps perviously mentioned, for the Gershonites and Merarites journeyed between the standard of Judah and that of Reuben, while the Kohathites journeyed between the standard of Reuben and that of Ephraim, as He is to explain. He mentioned the reason [for the Gershonites and Merarites journeying before the Kohathites, namely] so that they might set up the Tabernacle before they [the Kohathites who carried the ark and the holy vessels] arrive[127] [and thus they could immediately deposit the holy vessels therein].

However, in the Beraitha of the Work of the Tabernacle[105] I have seen the following text: "They blew *t'kiah, t'ruah, 't'kiah,*[102] and the standard of Judah would set forth first, as it is said, *And in the first place the standard of the camp of the children of Judah set forward.*[128] The sons of Aaron would then enter [the Tent of Meeting] and take down the Veil, and cover the ark with it, as it is said, *And when the camp setteth forward, Aaron shall go in, and his sons* etc.[125] They then blew *t'kiah, t'ruah, t'kiah,*[102] and the standard of the camp of Reuben would set forth. The sons of Gershon and the sons of Merari would immediately enter and dismantle the Tabernacle, and load it upon wagons and re-erect it [in the new resting-place] by the time the sons of Kohath arrived, as it is said, *And the Kohathites the bearers of the*

(125) Above, 4:5. (126) *Ibid.*, 2:17. (127) Verse 21. (128) Verse 14.

Sanctuary set forward, that the Tabernacle might be set up against their coming.[127] They blew *t'kiah, t'ruah, t'kiah,*[102] and the standard of Ephraim would set forth. The sons of Kohath would immediately enter and dismantle the Sanctuary,[129] and put it upon their shoulders, as it is said, *And when Aaron and his sons have finished covering the Sanctuary* etc."[130] But perhaps the following is the correct interpretation of the Beraitha: "They blew *t'kiah, t'ruah, t'kiah*[102] to alert the standard of Reuben to set forth, [but they did not actually set forth at once, for] immediately the sons of Gershon and the sons of Merari would precede them and dismantle the Tabernacle, but they would journey before the sons of Reuben. Similarly, they blew *t'kiah, t'ruah, t'kiah*[102] that the standard of Ephraim be ready to set forth, and the sons of Kohath would immediately set forth and load the holy vessels upon their shoulders, and they would journey before the sons of Ephraim." Thus the Rabbis taught that the journeying of the Levites should be preceded by blowing [of the trumpets], and immediately after them came the standard which followed them.

29. AND MOSES SAID UNTO CHOBAB. I have already explained[131] that Chobab [of the root *chavav* – love] was the new name which they gave to Jethro when he converted to the Torah of Israel, for such is the way of all proselytes, *for he calls His servants by another name.*[132] Now Moses had begged him to go with them and had told him without explanation, *and we will do thee good.*[133] But

(129) The word *hamikdash* (the Sanctuary) is evidently to be understood as in Verse 21 here: *And the Kohathites the bearers of 'the Sanctuary' set forward,* which Rashi explains as meaning: "the bearers of 'the holy vessels' " [and not of the Sanctuary itself, for it was carried by the sons of Gershon and Merari]. This explanation is also clearly evident from the language of Ramban further on ["and the sons of Kohath would . . . load *the holy vessels* upon their shoulders"]. (130) Above, 4:15. – The Beraitha of the Work of the Tabernacle thus contradicts the previous explanation, that the Gershonites and the Merarites set forward immediately after the standard of *Judah,* since the Beraitha states that they journeyed after the standard of *Reuben.* Ramban now interprets the Beraitha so that it accords with the above interpretation which is in line with the simple meaning of Scripture. (131) At the beginning of *Seder Yithro* (Exodus 18:1). (132) Isaiah 65:15. See my Hebrew commentary, p. 230, for source of this practice of renaming proselytes. (133) In Verse 29 before us.

Chobab thought that they would give him of the spoil, silver and gold, garments, sheep and herd, but that he would not have an inheritance among them [in the Land]. Therefore he did not want [to go with them] and he answered, "*But I will depart to mine own land, and to my kindred,*[134] since there I have an inheritance, wealth and honor." So Moses told him,"'*Leave us not, I pray thee,*'[135] for because of your familiarity with the wilderness *thou shalt be to us instead of eyes*[135] [i.e., a guide] in the conquest of the lands, and you will show us *the way by which we must go up,*[136] and of all *that goodness the Eternal shall do unto us, the same we will do unto thee.*"[137] Moses thus hinted that he would be given an inheritance in the good Land as a reward for his trouble and help that he would extend to them in the conquest of the Land. In my opinion Chobab consented to this offer and he did so [as Moses requested of him], as I have mentioned there.[131] And so the Rabbis said in the Yerushalmi:[138] "The children of the Kenite, Moses' father-in-law, bring first-fruits and read [the section of first-fruits, wherein it is stated, *I have brought the first of the fruit of the soil which Thou, O Eternal, hast given me*],[139] because it is written, *Come thou with us, and we will do thee good.*"[133]

33. AND THEY SET FORWARD FROM THE MOUNT OF THE ETERNAL THREE DAYS' JOURNEY. According to the plain meaning of Scripture, the cloud [of the Eternal] journeyed and went before them for three days and the ark followed the cloud in front of the people, and it did not come to rest in that place until the night of the third day, when the cloud rested in the wilderness of Paran,[140] which was a good place for them to camp in. This is the sense of [the expression] *to seek out a resting-place for them.*[141] And when the cloud rested they erected the Tabernacle and brought the ark into it. Scripture, however, did not explain whether they also journeyed at night.

(134) Verse 30. (135) Verse 31. (136) Deuteronomy 1:22. (137) Verse 32. (138) Yerushalmi, Bikurim I, 4. On the term "Yerushalmi," see Vol. III, p. 192, Note 44. (139) Deuteronomy 26:10. (140) See Ramban further, 12:16 for explanation of this area. (141) Verse 33.

35. AND IT CAME TO PASS WHEN THE ARK SET FORWARD. "He [the Eternal] made for this section [i.e., this verse and the following one] a special mark in front of it and behind it [by placing two inverted letters *nun* at the beginning and end of it] in order to indicate that this section is not in its proper place.[142] Why then was it written here? In order to separate between [the narrative of] one punishment and that of another punishment, as is stated in the Chapter of 'Any of the Holy Scriptures.' "[143] This is Rashi's language. But the Rabbi did not explain to us what is this [first] "punishment" from which it was necessary to separate [the later verses], for there is no "punishment" mentioned here in Scripture before the verse, *And it came to pass when the ark set forward.* The language of the Gemara there is: [144] "The second punishment is [the section], *And the people were as murmurers.*[145] The first 'punishment' is that which says, *And they set forward from the mount of the Eternal,*[141] on which Rabbi Chanina said: This teaches us that they turned aside from the Eternal." On this [statement of Rabbi Chanina] the Rabbi [Rashi] wrote there in his commentaries: "Within three days of their journeying *the mixed multitude . . . fell a lusting*[146] complaining about the [lack of] meat, in order to rebel against G-d." But these are astonishing words, for the "punishment" stated in the verse *And the people were as murmurers* [. . . *and the fire of the Eternal burnt among them* etc.][145] is written first,[145] and that of the lusting is second,[146] and they are both next to each other [so why did Rashi mention the sin of the lusting following upon their journeying as the first "punishment," since that of the murmurers is closer to it]? Perhaps the Rabbi [Rashi] thought that these episodes were not written in their [chronological] order, and that He [already] alluded to the first [punishment] in saying, [*and they set forward*] *from the mount of the Eternal,*[141] for perhaps they already intended to do so [to

(142) "And where does it belong? Said Rav Ashi: In the section on the standards" (Shabbath 116 a). That is, above in Chapter 2, after Verse 17, which states: *Then the Tent of Meeting . . . shall set forward* etc. This section, beginning with *And it came to pass when the ark set forward . . . ,* should have followed on there. (143) Shabbath 115 a. The text quoted is on 115 b-116 a. (144) *Ibid.*, 116 a. (145) Further, 11:1. (146) *Ibid.,* Verse 4.

demand meat] from the time that they set forth on that journey; but He made a break [by writing the section of the ark], and then wrote the second [punishment, i.e., that of the murmurers], and afterwards He went back to [relate the actual realization of their original intention to ask for meat, namely] the first punishment. But there is neither rhyme nor reason in this [explanation].

But the meaning of this interpretation [of the Rabbis that *they set forward from the mount of the Eternal* indicates a punishment, is based on that which] they[147] found in the Agadah, that "they set forward from Mount Sinai with joy, just like a child who runs away from school, saying: 'Perhaps He will give us more commandments [if we stay]!" This then is the sense of the expression, *And they set forward from the mount of the Eternal,*[141] meaning that their intention was to remove themselves from there *because* it was the mount of the Eternal. This is the first "punishment" [i.e., the first sin, as explained further on], and then He interrupted [with the section on the ark] in order that there should not be three punishments one after the other, so that it would have established a basis for further punishment.[148] He called the [first] sin "punishment" even though no actual punishment occurred to them because of it, [but since they deserved to have been punished, it is called a "punishment"]. Perhaps were it not for this sin of theirs He would have brought them into the Land immediately [and so there was indeed a "punishment"].

11 1. AND THE PEOPLE WERE 'K'MITHON'NIM.' Rabbi Abraham ibn Ezra commented that [the word *k'mithon'nim* is] "of the root *aven* (wickedness); similarly, *the thoughts of 'oneich' (thy evil thoughts),*[149] for they spoke words of wickedness." But this is not correct, for why would Scripture have concealed their sin, and not stated [clearly what it was], as it does in all other places! The correct

(147) The reference is to the Rabbis in the Talmud, Sabbath 116 a, and Ramban is saying that their interpretation is not based on the explanation given there by Rashi, but on an Agadah, as brought down in the name of Midrash Yelamdeinu by Tosafoth *ibid.,* (see Preface to Vol. I, pp. vii-viii). (148) A repetition of three similar events establishes a legal presumption of recurrence. See also Amos 2:6 , that G-d's long-suffering is at an end with three sins. (149) Jeremiah 4:14.

interpretation appears to me to be that as they got further away from Mount Sinai, which was near an inhabitable settlement, and entered *the great and dreadful wilderness*[150] in their first journey, they became upset and said: "What shall we do? How shall we live in this wilderness? What shall we eat and what shall we drink? How shall we endure the trouble and the suffering, and when shall we come out of here?" The word *k'mithon'nim* is thus related to the expression, *Wherefore doth a living man 'yithonein' (complain), a strong man because of his sins?*[151] which is an expression indicating pain, and feeling sorry for oneself. Similarly, *ben oni*[152] means "the son of my sorrow;" *'v'anu hadayagim' (and the fishers shall lament) and all they that cast angle into the Nile shall mourn.*[153] Thus when Scripture states that they felt anxious and upset, it has thereby already mentioned and told [the nature of] their sin. It states that they were *k'mithon'nim* ('as' murmurers), meaning that they spoke in the bitterness of their soul as do people who suffer pain, and this was evil in the sight of the Eternal, since they should have followed Him *with joyfulness, and with gladness of heart by reason of the abundance of all* good *things*[154] which He gave them, but they behaved like people acting under duress and compulsion, murmuring and complaining about their condition. It is for this reason that He states with regard to the second [sin, or punishment], *and the children of Israel also wept 'again,'*[155] meaning that their first sin consisted of complaining about their lack of comforts in the wilderness, and now they again did a similar thing, and *they did not receive correction*[156] from the fire of G-d which devoured them.[157]

3. AND HE [Moses] CALLED THE NAME OF THAT PLACE TABERAH (Burning). [The meaning thereof is that] he called the place on which *the fire* came down *in the uttermost part of the camp*[145] by that name, and they did not journey from that place, for whilst still encamped there they *fell a lusting*[146] [for flesh], and called

(150) Deuteronomy 1:19. (151) Lamentations 3:39. (152) Genesis 35:18. (153) Isaiah 19:8. (154) Deuteronomy 28:47. (155) Verse 4. (156) Jeremiah 7:28. (157) As stated in the verse before us.

the name of the city or place Kibroth-hattaavah (the graves of lust).[158]

4. AND THE MIXED MULTITUDE THAT WAS AMONG THEM 'HITHAVU TA'AVAH' (FELL A LUSTING). The meaning of this [double expression, which translates literally as "lusted a lust," is] that they had nothing lacking in the wilderness, for they had plenty of manna and they could make of it all different kinds of delicacies with distinguished flavors, as Scripture relates further on, but they goaded themselves to a great desire, as if they wanted to eat [even] charcoal or earth and other bad foods.

AND THEY SAID: WHO SHALL GIVE US FLESH TO EAT. [They used this expression *who shall give us*] because there was not enough meat for the whole people to have every day, although they did eat it many times, for some of them had herds, but [only] the important people ate it [every day], as happens in camps and places where prices are high. But about fish they said, *We remember the fish,*[159] like one who remembers forgotten things, since they had not eaten any fish from the day that they left Egypt until now.

5. WE REMEMBER THE FISH WHICH WE WERE WONT TO EAT IN EGYPT FOR NOUGHT. According to the plain meaning of Scripture [the explanation of the verse is that] the Egyptian fishermen used to put them to work to bring in the fish that they caught in their trawls and nets, and they would give them some fish [to eat], as is the custom of those *that spread nets* [*upon the waters*].[160] And *cucumbers, melons, leeks, onions and garlic*[159] are very abundant in Egypt, for it is *as a garden of herbs,*[161] and when they dug for the Egyptians in gardens *and in all manner of service in the field*[162] they would eat the

(158) Further, Verse 34. — This explains why it is nowhere stated that they set forth from Taberah. According to Ramban, there were two reasons for this. Firstly, the name Taberah was only given to that part of the camp where the fire struck. Secondly, whilst still encamped there, the events occurred for which the place came to be called Kibroth-hattaavah, and hence that was the name the Torah subsequently used. (159) Verse 5. (160) Isaiah 19:8. (161) Deuteronomy 11:10. (162) Exodus 1:14.

vegetables. Or perhaps the Israelites who were the king's slaves doing his work would be supported by him with *sparing bread and scant water,*[163] and they would be dispersed throughout the city and would enter the gardens and fields, and eat of the vegetables without leaving anything over, as the king's servants do. And [in addition it is possible that] they would give them at the edge of the river [Nile] small fish from the king's portion which have no market-price in Egypt, as I have explained in *Seder V'eileh Shemoth.*[164] This was the complaint of *the children of Israel,*[155] not the complaint of *the mixed multitude*[155] [who were originally not of the stock of Israel and were not enslaved in Egypt, therefore they could not say, *We remember the fish, which we were wont to eat in Egypt for nought;* but after *the mixed multitude fell a lusting*[155] they all] complained to Moses and demanded of him, *Give us flesh, that we may eat,*[165] as Scripture mentions further on.

6. BUT NOW OUR SOUL IS DRIED AWAY. This means that because of their many desires their temperaments had become heated and then dried up, as Onkelos translates it ["but now our soul is lusting"]. Or it may be that [they meant that] *our soul is dried away* because there is nothing with which to moisten it, since food produces [essential] liquids in the body which satisfy the soul. And they said, *we have nought save this manna 'to look to,'* meaning that even the food [i.e., the manna] on which we live is not in our possession so that our soul can be nourished and satisfied with it; but we desire it and look to it [i.e., we are dependent upon it] at all times, in anticipation that it will come to us; thus *we have nothing at all* save our hope for the manna. They thus gave expression to the known proverb:[166] "One cannot compare a person who has bread in his basket with one who does not have bread in his basket."[167] Therefore Scripture tells how many qualities the manna had, stating that *its taste was as the taste of a cake baked with oil,*[168] thus declaring that the souls of those who ate

(163) Isaiah 30:20. (164) Exodus 1:1. The verse referred to is *ibid.,* 11. (165) Further, Verse 13. (166) Yoma 74 b. (167) For since the manna only came down in the quantity required for that day, and none was to be left for the following day (Exodus 16:19), and if it was left it rotted (*ibid.,* Verse 20), they were therefore in constant worry for their next day's food. (168) Verse 8.

it did not dry up, for it [the manna] supplied the body with the [essential] liquids and kept it satisfied, and the souls of those who ate it were *like a watered garden and like a spring of water.*[169]

12. DID I 'HARITHI' ALL THIS PEOPLE? In the opinion of Onkelos [who rendered it: "Am I 'the father' of all this people?" the word *harithi*] is like [the expression] *beyond the blessing of 'horai' (my progenitors),*[170] for a father is called *horeh* [of the root *haroh,* "to conceive" or "become pregnant"] because it is he who causes conception and brings about the pregnancy [of the mother]. Thus Moses is saying: "Am I their father [who has caused their conception], or am I their mother who has given birth to them?"[171] But the masters of the plain meaning of Scripture[172] interpreted the verse in the opposite manner: "Am I their mother who was pregnant with them and gave birth to them?" Similarly, *'Vatahar' eth Miriam v'eth Shammai*[173] means "she was pregnant with them and gave birth to them." "Or am I their father who begot them?"[the word *y'lidetihu* being] like: *'vayoled Noach' (and Noah begot);*[174] *thy father that 'y'ladecha' (begot thee),*[175] and other similar expressions. And Moses said, *as 'ha'omein' carrieth the sucking child,* [the word *ha'omein*] being a reference to the [nursing-] father or mother. In my opinion the whole verse is a figurative reference to the mother, and the meaning thereof is as follows: "Have I conceived all this people *and* have I given birth to them?"[176] Moses mentioned it in this way [speaking as the mother] because it is the woman who suffers the pain of raising children, remembering what she suffered for them from birth, pregnancy, and conception.[177] But Moses said *omein* [in the masculine] since he is speaking of himself as a nursing-father, since he is not an *omeneth* (a nursing-mother).

(169) Isaiah 58:11. (170) Genesis 49:26. (171) The double question in the verse — *Did I 'harithi' all this people? . . . Have I born them?* — is thus explained as referring to the separate functions of father and mother. (172) Ibn Ezra here. See also in Sefer Hashorashim of the R'dak, under the root *haroh.* (173) I Chronicles 4:17. (174) Genesis 6:10. (175) Proverbs 23:22. (176) Ramban thus interprets the two questions (see above Note 171) as one, both referring to the mother. (177) See Hosea 9:11.

14. I AM NOT ABLE TO BEAR ALL THIS PEOPLE MYSELF ALONE. The meaning thereof is not that the elders should help him to give the people flesh, for where should they get it from? Moreover, even if they would have many leaders they would still only complain against Moses our teacher who took them out of Egypt, as they used to say to him, *And wherefore have ye made us to come up out of Egypt?*[178] [asking him] that he should give them through his prayers all that they asked for, and grant them their desires[179] [and so they would still continue to complain to him rather than to the elders]! But Moses thought that if they would have many leaders they would appease their wrath by speaking to their hearts when they would start complaining. Or it is possible that when the elders prophesied, and the spirit [which was upon Moses] was put upon them,[180] the people would know that these elders are established as prophets,[181] and would not all gather against Moses but would ask for their desires from them as well [by means of their prayers].

15. AND IF 'AT' (THOU) DO THUS WITH ME. "[The Hebrew word for *Thou* appears here in the feminine form *at,* instead of *atah* in the masculine, because] Moses' strength grew weak, like that of a woman, because the Holy One, blessed be He, showed him the punishment He was to bring upon them for this [sin of theirs]. Moses then said to Him, 'If so, *kill me, I pray Thee.*'" This is Rashi's language. But I do not understand this. For the pronoun *at* refers here to Him on high, [for since it is Moses who is speaking in the verse, his use of the *second*-person pronoun must be referring to G-d; so how can Rashi explain that the feminine form is used to indicate that *Moses'* strength weakened like that of a woman]! But according to the plain meaning of Scripture, the custom of the [Hebrew] language is [to use the form *at*] even when referring to a man, such as, *'at' (thou) the far-covering cherub.*[182] And by way of the Truth, [the mystic teachings of the Cabala], *And if 'at' do thus with me* refers to the attribute of

(178) Further, 20:5. (179) See Psalms 78:29. (180) Further, Verse 17. (181) See I Samuel 3:20. (182) Ezekiel 28:14. Here the word *at* refers to *k'ruv* (cherub), which is a masculine noun.

justice ["attribute" in Hebrew being feminine, and the meaning of the verse is: "if it be decreed that the attribute of justice encounter me, then *kill me, I pray Thee*], just as it is said, *and the anger of the Eternal was kindled greatly.*[183] Similarly, *'v'at' shalt speak unto us*[184] is a reference to *the great fire,*[185] from which you shall speak the words of G-d *unto us, and we will hear it*[184] from your mouth, *and do it.*[184] Similarly, *'at' the far-covering cherub*[182] alludes to the second cherub.[186] The student versed [in the mystic lore of the Cabala] will understand.

'HORGEINI NA HAROG' (KILL ME, I PRAY THEE). This means that Thou should send upon me those that kill by the sword, *for it is better for me to die*[187] even by the sword of man *than to live*[187] with this grief. It is possible that the sense [of the term *horgeini*] is "take my life" [and not, as explained before, that it means death by human agency]. A similar [usage of the term is found in these verses]: *and let their men be 'harugei maveth' (slain of death), and their young men smitten of the sword in battle;*[188] *and breathe 'baharugim ha'eileh' (upon these slain).*[189]

16. AND THE ETERNAL SAID UNTO MOSES: GATHER UNTO ME SEVENTY MEN OF THE ELDERS OF ISRAEL. Our Rabbis have already mentioned that there are seventy nations[190] with seventy languages,[191] each one having a constellation in the heavens with a prince above it, as it is said in the Book of Daniel, *and the prince of the kingdom of Persia,*[192] and it is [further] written with

(183) Above, Verse 10. (184) Deuteronomy 5:24. (185) *Ibid.*, Verse 22. "Fire" can be feminine or masculine in Hebrew. (186) Reference is to the Glory of G-d (Abusaula). (187) Jonah 4:4. (188) Jeremiah 18:21. (189) Ezekiel 37:9. The reference there [according to the plain meaning of Scripture] is to those who died a natural death in the exile (see in R'dak's commentary there). According to the tradition of the Sages, that the dry bones were those of the tribe of Ephraim who left Egypt thirty years before the exodus and were killed on the way by the men of Gath (see Ramban Vol. II, p. 157), the term *baharugim* is to be understood literally: "upon those that were killed [by the sword]" (R'dak). (190) Bereshith Rabbah 66:8. (191) Sanhedrin 17 a. (192) Daniel 10:13. See Ramban in Leviticus 18:25, and also Vol. I, pp. 349-350.

reference to the kings of Greece, *lo, the prince of Greece shall come;* [193] and it is about this that Scripture states, *And the Eternal will punish the host of the high heaven on high.* [194] The Rabbis have also said[195] that the [seventy] bullocks [brought as offerings on the seven days] of the Festival of Tabernacles allude to them. [A similar reference to the seventy princes we find, in connection with the Tower of Babel] in the Pirkei d'Rabbi Eliezer: [196] "Said the Holy One, blessed be He, to the seventy kings that surround the throne of His Glory: 'Let us come and confound their language.' "[197] It was for this reason that the number of those who went down to Egypt was seventy, [198] and that He commanded that there should be this number of judges in Israel [as is stated in the verse before us], for this number includes all opinions [that are possible in a given case] since it comprises all powers, and *there* will not *be anything too hard* for them.[199] Similarly at the Giving of the Torah [special prominence was given to] *seventy elders of Israel,* [200] and it is fitting that the Glory of the Divine Presence should rest upon [a group of] this perfect number, since it is [comparable to] the camp on high, for Israel are *the hosts of the Eternal*[201] on earth, just as the ark and its cover and the Tabernacle were all made in the likeness of those that minister [before Him] on high. So also were the [four] standards made in the image of the Divine Chariot which Ezekiel saw, [202] in order that the Divine Presence should rest upon them on earth as it is present in the heavens.

Now Moses was above the seventy elders [in authority], thus alluding to Israel, *a nation one in the earth.* [203] And our Rabbis have received by tradition that every Sanhedrin (Great Court) that sits in G-d's House in the place which He shall choose on which to rest His Presence, should consist of this number, seventy, with the head [of the Court] above them [in authority] like Moses our teacher, and thus they comprise [a Court] a seventy-one [judges, and with the Divine

(193) Daniel 10:20. (194) Isaiah 24:21. (195) Succah 58 b. (196) Chapters of Rabbi Eliezer. Chapter 24. (197) Genesis 11:7. (198) *Ibid.*, 46:27. (199) Deuteronomy 17:8-9: *If there arise a matter 'too hard for thee' in judgment . . . then shalt thou arise* etc. — and go to the judges of the Great Sanhedrin and they will answer you. The point is thus clear: there will not be anything "too hard" for them. (200) Exodus 24:1. (201) *Ibid.*, 12:41. See also Vol. I, p. 393. (202) Ezekiel, Chapter I. (203) II Samuel 7:23.

Presence in their midst they are seventy-two]. Similarly the letters in the Great Ineffable Divine Name are seventy-two, corresponding to the seventy princes [of the seventy nations, together with Israel, making seventy-one nations],[204] and the One G-d who is the sole Master over all. It is to this that Scripture hints in saying, *G-d standeth in the congregation of G-d; in the midst of the judges He judgeth,*[205] for the Divine Presence is with them to assent to their judgment. And Scripture further states, *How long will ye judge unjustly?,*[206] thus admonishing [and saying] that since *the Glorious Name*[207] *is with* them *in giving judgment,*[208] how can you not be fearful of Him when you pervert justice, as in the expression, *the people that provoke Me to My face continually.*[209] And it states furthermore [in that psalm], "*I said: Ye are godlike beings, and all of you sons of the Most High,*[210] for your number is the same as the number of the princes above and the One Master, and so *I said* that you *will sit in the seat of G-d*[211] on earth. *But 'k'adam' ye shall die*[212] — like the first man [Adam] who was driven from his glorious place [in the Garden of Eden] and died, so will you [who judge unjustly] be driven out of the House of G-d and die. *And like one of the princes*[212] on high you were, but you fell from that high position." I have already mentioned something of this matter in *Seder V'eileh Hamishpatim.*[213]

17. AND I WILL COME DOWN AND SPEAK WITH THEE THERE, 'V'ATZALTI' (AND I WILL TAKE OF THE SPIRIT) WHICH IS UPON THEE, AND WILL PUT IT UPON THEM. The intention of the verse is to say that the transmission [of the spirit resting on Moses to the seventy elders] will take place at the time when G-d will speak to Moses; and it will be from that [Divine communication that the prophetic power will be transmitted to them],[214] as is stated at the actual occurrance [of the events], *And the Eternal came down in the cloud, and spoke unto him, [and took of the*

(204) Abusaula, and so also in Beiur Ha'lvush to Ricanti. (205) Psalms 82:1. (206) *Ibid.*, Verse 2. (207) Deuteronomy 28:58. (208) II Chronicles 19:6. (209) Isaiah 65:3. (210) Psalms 82:6. (211) Ezekiel 28:2. (212) Psalms 82:7. (213) *And these are the ordinances* — Exodus 21:1. The verse referred to is *ibid.*, 6. (214) So clearly explained in the Tur. See my Hebrew commentary p. 234.

spirit that was upon him, and put it upon the seventy elders].[215] Now Scripture did not explain here what this communication was about, as is [usually] written in the whole Torah, where after [stating that G-d spoke to Moses] it explains what the Eternal said and what He spoke. [The reason for this is] that what happened here was that the elders, of whom Scripture states that they prophesied,[215] did not hear any communication from the mouth of G-d, nor did He appear to them *in a vision* or *in a dream*,[216] but G-d spoke to Moses, and from the *atziluth* [as is explained further on] of the spirit upon Moses, they understood that Divine communication. This is the sense of the expression, *and they prophesied, but they did so no more*,[215] meaning that they did not continue receiving Divine communication on their own, for it was only the communication that G-d said to Moses in which they shared. This is also the meaning of *v'atzalti* [of the root *eitzel* – "near"], that "I will hold back with Me of the spirit which I put upon you, *and I will put it upon them.*" This is not the same idea as in the verse, *and thou* [Moses] *shalt put of thy honor upon him* [Joshua],[217] for the term *atziluth* always means "holding something back," as in the expressions: *And whatsoever mine eyes desired 'lo atzalti' (I did not keep) from them;*[218] *'Halo atzalta' (Hast thou not reserved) a blessing for me?*[219] Similarly, [*Now the upper chambers were shorter, for the galleries took away from these, more than from the lower and the middlemost, in the building. For they were in three stories, and they had not pillars as the pillars of the courts;*] *therefore 'ne'etzal' (room was taken away) from the lowest and the middlemost, in comparison with the ground*,[220] meaning that more [room] was left by them [i.e., the upper chambers] relative to the ground, than by the chambers on the bottom and middle [stories], since their galleries did not take away from these upper chambers.[221] Likewise, *and to the*

(215) Further, Verse 25. (216) See further, 12:6. (217) *Ibid.*, 27:20. (218) Ecclesiastes 2:10. (219) Genesis 27:36. (220) Ezekiel 42:5-6. (221) The meaning is as follows: It is clear from the verses that there were three stories, and that they were not supported on pillars. Thus each floor had to be set in somewhat in relation to the floor below it, leaving "galleries" around it. The top floor was the shortest, since the lower ones protruded and covered more of the ground-area than the highest story; thus more room was left relative to the ground by the top floor than by the other two. This shows that the root *'atzal'* used in the verse signifies "holding back."

'atzilei' of the children of Israel[222] means "those who were left and were separated from them, who were withdrawn to themselves from the rest of the ordinary people." Or it may be that great men are so called [*atzilim* — from the root *eitzel* (near)] because everybody comes to them [for counsel and instruction]. And translators of languages[223] use the term *atziluth* with reference to an emanation of any powers [coming forth] from the Creator and spreading to a created object. Thus they speak of the soul as *atzulah* (emanating) from *Ruach Hakodesh* (*the Holy Spirit*), since they understand *atziluth* as an expression of "drawing forth." But it does not appear to me to be correct that *atziluth* should mean "drawing forth" or[224] "placing upon" [the receiver], something which the bestower has set aside [for him]. Onkelos, however, explained that the term *atziluth* has two meanings. Thus he translated here [*v'atzalti*] — "and I shall make great" [thus indicating that the term *atziluth* is to be understood as a "drawing forth" by the giver for the benefit of the receiver, that he will be made great], and similarly *and to the 'atzilei'*[222] [he translated], "and to the great men;" but he rendered *'Halo atzalta' a blessing for me*[219] — "Have you not 'left' for me a blessing?" Thus it appears that his opinion about the meaning of *atziluth* is that it [sometimes] refers to a drawing forth or bestowing by a giver on a receiver; thus [according to this interpretation] the verse here is saying: "I will draw forth from that which is upon you [Moses] of the spirit of prophecy, *and I will put it upon them*." But we may [also use the term *atziluth* in speaking of] a "drawing forth" which a giver does to himself from that which is given, so that it remains with him, this being the meaning of

(222) Exodus 24:11. (223) Ramban is obviously referring to translators from Arabic into Hebrew. See e.g., in Yehudah Halevi's philosophic work Al Khazari, written in Arabic, which Ibn Tibbon rendered into Hebrew, where he writes of *atziluth ne'etzeleth mimenah sibah shenith* (an Emanation from which emanated a second) etc. (Hirschfeld's translation, I, 1, p. 36). (224) "Or placing upon etc." — In Kur Zahav it is suggested that the reading in Ramban should be [instead of: *o hanachah* — "or placing upon"] : *ela hanachah* — "but placing upon." That is to say, Ramban differs with the translators who understood *atziluth* as an act of both, coming forth from one subject and spreading to another, while Ramban holds it is primarily a concept of "placing upon" a subject, part of something which the bestower has set aside for it. — See further my Hebrew commentary p. 235.

the verse, *'Halo atzalta' a blessing for me*[219] — "Have you not kept to yourself for me one of the blessings with which to bless me?"

The general principle about the elders is that their Divine communication came only from [G-d's] spirit which spoke to Moses, and from him it came to them. Therefore the Rabbis have said in Bamidbar Sinai Rabbah: [225] "This can be compared to a master who gave an orchard to a guardian, and paid him a wage for his service. After a while the guardian said to him: 'I cannot guard the whole orchard alone; bring in some more people to guard it with me.' Thereupon the master said to him: 'I gave you my orchard to guard, and all the fruits for guarding it I gave you [i.e., I gave you a reward for it], and now you tell me to bring in others to guard it with you! I will bring in others to help you guard it, but you should know that I will not give them wages for watching it out of my resources; rather it is from the wages that I have given you that they will take their payment.' So did the Holy One, blessed be He, say to Moses: 'I have given you spirit and knowledge to lead My children, and I did not want anyone else [to help you], in order that you alone should be singled out for this guardianship, and now you want someone else! Know then that from Me they will not take anything, but *I will take of the spirit which is upon thee, and will put it upon them.*' Yet nonetheless Moses did not lose anything [of his spirit]." Thus far is in the Midrash.

It appears likely to me that this [bestowing of the Divine spirit that was upon Moses] happened to the elders throughout their lives, so that they knew whatever G-d commanded Israel by the hand of Moses in connection with the temporary needs of the people and the events which happened to them in the wilderness. This is the meaning of the expression [in the verse before us] *and they shall bear the burden of the people with thee,* that whatever Moses told the people they knew, and each one would pass the Divine communication about it to the people of his tribe, and thus Moses no longer had to bear their complaints alone.

(225) Bamidbar Rabbah, at the end of *Seder Beha'alothcha.*

19. YE SHALL NOT EAT ONE DAY. The meaning thereof is: "*you shall not eat* for only *one day, nor* only *two days* [*but even a whole month*].[226] Similarly, the phrase *not once nor twice*[227] means "*not* only *once nor twice.*" And in my opinion it cannot be said of a person who eats or does something for many consecutive days that he ate or did [that action] for one day.[228] Similarly it cannot be said of one who eats [something] for thirty consecutive days that he ate it for twenty days.[228] Or it may be that the word "one" [*Ye shall not eat 'one' day*] is connected [with the following phrases]: "*Ye shall not eat one day, nor two days,* nor ten or twenty single [non-consecutive] days, but a full month." Thus He gave them the meat which they craved for, but not the fish or the vegetables, for their main demand for which they wept was *give us flesh.*[229] And the meaning of the expression, *But even a whole month, until it come out of your nostrils, and it be loathsome unto you*[226] is that He will give them a lot of meat, and they will eat it for a whole month to such a great extent that they will become sick of it, and they will consider it detestable and like a strange inedible food.

According to the plain meaning of Scripture the following is what happened: On the first day [of their eating the meat] they were smitten *with a very great plague*[230] and the people that were the first to lust died,[231] these being *the mixed multitude that was among them,*[232] also *the children of Israel* mentioned at the beginning who said, *Who shall give us flesh to eat?*[232] But the rest of the people who wept afterwards *family by family, every man at the door of his tent*[233] ate of it for a whole month until it became loathsome to them[226] and they threw away any heaps they had left of it. And so does the psalm state: *He caused flesh also to rain upon them as the dust;*[234] *So they did eat, and were well-filled, and He gave them that which they craved. They were not estranged from their craving, their food was still in their*

(226) Verse 20. (227) II Kings 6:10. (228) Hence the statement *ye shall not eat one day* is to be understood literally, for since they will eat for a consecutive period of thirty days, it cannot be said of them that they ate for one day. Likewise the phrase *nor twenty days* is to be understood in its plain sense: "you will not eat of it twenty days, but thirty days." (229) Verse 13. (230) Further, Verse 33. (231) *Ibid.*, Verse 34. (232) Above, Verse 4. (233) *Ibid.*, Verse 10. (234) Psalms 78:27.

mouths, when the anger of G-d went up against them etc.[235] For some of them ate and were well-filled, but those who lusted did not satisfy their lust at all, for while *their food was still in their mouths . . . the anger of G-d went up against them.*[235]

Now the [Midrashic] interpretations of Rabbi Shimon[236] and of Rabbi Yehudah Hanasi[237] do not fit in properly with the language of Scripture, because He said, *Now shalt thou see whether My word shall come to pass unto thee or not.*[238] And the interpretation of Rabbi Akiba who says that the words [of Moses] are to be taken literally, namely "Will it be enough for them?" is the true sense of Scripture,

(235) *Ibid.*, Verses 29-31. (236) The Verses 22-23 state: 22. *And Moses said: "The people, among whom I am, are six hundred thousand men on foot; and yet Thou hast said: I will give them flesh, that they may eat a whole month!* 23. *If flocks and herds be slain for them, will they suffice them? or if all the flesh be gathered together for them 'umatza lahem' (will they suffice them)?*" Since it is inconceivable that Moses actually doubted G-d's powers, Rashi [in Verse 22] quotes the interpretation of Rabbi Shimon in the Sifre, that Moses' intent was as follows: "The people are so many, and Thou hast said 'I will give them flesh, for a whole month' — and then you will kill them! Shall the flock and herds be slaughtered for them so that they [the people] will be killed immediately, and this eating should be their last, satisfying them forever!" Then G-d said to Moses: *Now shalt thou see* etc. (see note that follows). (237) In our Rashi: "Rabban Gamaliel the son of Rabbi Yehudah Hanasi." This Sage explains that Moses said: "Since they are merely seeking a pretext, Thou wilt never be able to satisfy them, for they will always beg for something else." — Then G-d said to Moses: *"Now shalt thou see whether My word shall come to pass unto thee or not* (Verse 23) — for they will not listen unto thee." Moses then went to appease them and told them what G-d said to him: *Is the hand of the Eternal waxed short?* (*ibid.*) But the people answered that He indeed has no power to grant their request. This is what the following verse [24] means: *And Moses went out, and told the people the words of the Eternal.* Since, however, they refused to listen to him, the verse continues, *and he gathered seventy men* etc. (238) Ramban's intent is as follows: Had Verse 23 stated: "*And the Eternal said unto Moses: 'Is the hand of the Eternal waxed short?'* And Moses said: 'I will go to appease them.' And G-d said to him: 'They will not listen unto thee. *Now shalt thou see whether My word shall come to pass unto thee* [that they will not listen unto thee] *or not . . .* ' " the interpretations of Rabbi Shimon and of Rabbi Yehudah Hanasi would have fitted in with the text of Scripture. But all which is written after the phrase, *Is the hand of the Eternal waxed short?* is: *Now shalt thou see* etc. which implies that Moses, as it were, doubted that G-d would satisfy them. Hence we must offer another interpretation, as set forth in the text that follows.

and this is the opinion of Onkelos [who translated *umatza lahem*[239] – "will it suffice them?"]. But the event itself is amazing, as Rabbi Shimon said [commenting on Rabbi Akiba's interpretation]: "The person of whom Scripture writes, *he is trusted in all My house,*[240] would he say that G-d cannot supply enough for them!" Moreover, all of them had already seen far greater wonders than this! And Rabbi Abraham ibn Ezra answered this [by saying] that Moses thought that G-d would not create a new wonder except to vindicate His prophet [as happened in the affair of Korach, further, Chapter 16; and since the truth of his prophecy was not now in question, Moses thought that no miracle would happen merely to satisfy the people's requests]. But this too, does not appear correct to me, for He had already done for them [a miracle] of this sort with the first quail,[241] and also with the water[242] and the manna,[243] for all of these things were given to them to satisfy their complaints.

The correct interpretation appears to me to be that when G-d does signs and wonders for Israel, they are deeds of kindness from Him, and they are all for their good, for *The Eternal is good to all; and His tender mercies are over all His works,*[244] except when *there is wrath gone out*[245] against those who transgress His Will, when He acts towards them with anger and the attribute of judgment to their complete punishment. Thus miracles can only be [manifestations of] complete and perfect goodness in mercy, or retribution by the attribute of judgment. But now when G-d told Moses that He would fulfill their request and they would eat meat *until it cometh out at your nostrils, and it be loathsome unto you,*[246] Moses our teacher knew that there would not be a wonder from G-d to supply them with flesh as He gave them *the corn of heaven,*[247] similar to which the Sages say:[248] "No evil thing comes down from heaven." Moreover, all miracles He told Moses about beforehand: *Behold, I will cause to rain bread from heaven for you;*[249] *Behold, I will stand before thee there*

(239) See Note 236, quoting Verse 23. (240) Further, 12:7. (241) Exodus 16:13. (242) *Ibid.*, 17:6. (243) *Ibid.*, Chapter 16. (244) Psalms 145:9. (245) Further, 17:11. (246) Verse 19. (247) Psalms 78:24. (248) Bereshith Rabbah 51:5. (249) Exodus 16:4.

on the rock in Horeb; [*and thou shalt smite the rock, and there shall come water out of it*].[250] But here since He told him, *And say unto the people: Sanctify yourselves against tomorrow,*[251] and He did not inform him [that he would then give them meat, as He informed about the other miracles], Moses understood that there would be no miracle from Him, blessed be He. Therefore he asked in astonishment: "What can He do [to satisfy] them by natural means? If all the flocks and herds around them be slaughtered for them they will still not be satisfied, and if all the fish of the sea in the place nearest to them be gathered in for them it would still not be sufficient for them." Therefore G-d answered that His hand is not too short to fulfill their request even by ordinary events, this being the meaning of the expression *'ha'yikrecha'* [of the root *mikreh* — "chance"] *My word or not,* [i.e., *Now shalt thou see whether My word 'shall suffice for thee even by chance'*]. And He said, *Is the Eternal's 'yad' (hand) waxed short,* similar to the expression, *and royal wine in abundance, according to the 'yad' (bounty) of the king,*[252] but He did not say, *Is there anything too hard for me?*[253] since this was not done by a wonder. And so indeed it came to pass, that *there went forth a wind from the Eternal*[254] in accordance with natural events, neither a very strong west wind nor *a strong east wind,* as Scripture mentions in speaking of the miracles, but a normal wind as is usual, *and it brought across quails from the sea,*[254] not that they were now created for their sake, and so there was nothing different in this from the natural events of the world. Besides, this had already happened to them before,[241] and the only new element in it now was that the quails were in great abundance.

28. MY LORD MOSES, 'K'LA'EIM' (SHUT THEM IN). The meaning of this is that Moses had told the people the words of G-d, that He would take of the spirit which was upon him and put it upon those that will stand with him in the Tent of Meeting. Now those that

(250) *Ibid.,* 17:6. (251) Verse 18. (252) Esther 1:7. (253) Jeremiah 32:27. (254) Verse 31. This wind was not an exceptionally powerful wind of a miraculous nature, as e.g., in Exodus 14:21 [at the splitting of the Red Sea].

did not go to the Tent [i.e., Eldad and Medad who had also been designated for that honor], and yet held themselves to be among those upon whom Moses' spirit had been put [by *prophesying in the camp,*[255] as Eldad and Medad did], were as rebels against Moses' words. Therefore Joshua said to Moses, "*Shut them in,* for perhaps *it is a lying spirit*[256] in their mouths, or it is *an evil spirit* that *terrifies* them,[257] and thus they must be put in a prison like *a man that is mad, and maketh himself like a prophet.*"[258] But Moses in his humility answered: "*Would that all the people of the Eternal were prophets, that the Eternal would give His spirit upon them!*[259] — for G-d put His spirit directly upon them without taking of the spirit which was upon me, and would that this would happen to all the people."

However, from the words of our Rabbis it appears that the custom in Israel was that no one would prophesy about future events in the presence of a prophet who is greater than him, but they would follow him as his disciples, and these were *the sons of the prophets.*[260] Thus the Rabbis have said in Tractate Sanhedrin [with reference to the prophecy of Eldad and Medad]:[261] "We can well understand according to that Sage who said that [Eldad and Medad prophesied that] 'Moses will die [before entering the Land],' that Joshua therefore said, *My lord Moses, shut them in* [since he wished to save Moses from grief]. But according to the Sage who said that [they prophesied] about the quails [that they would come from the sea], why should they be shut in [and not prophesy]? It is because the case resembled that of a pupil who renders a decision in the presence of his master." Similarly [this was the reason why they were forbidden to prophesy] according to the Sage who says that they prophesied about Gog and Magog.[262] And the Rabbis have mentioned a similar case in Tractate Megillah in the matter of Deborah.[263] But Moses said that he, being the master,

(255) Verse 27. (256) I Kings 22:22. (257) See I Samuel 16:14. (258) Jeremiah 29:26. (259) Verse 29. (260) I Kings 20:35. Rambam defines *the sons of the prophets* as "those who sought the prophetic gift. And although they directed their minds towards it, the Divine Spirit might or might not rest upon them" (*Hilchoth Yesodei Hatorah* 7:5). (261) Sanhedrin 17 a. (262) Ezekiel 38:17. (263) In Megillah 14 b the Talmud lists the seven prophetesses that prophesied in Israel, mentioning among them Deborah, Huldah, etc. It is related in

foregoes the honor due to him [and the law is that a Rabbi is able to renounce the honor due to him],[264] and he desires and is happy [that they prophesy]. And I have seen that the Targum Yerushalmi[265] rendered: "*k'la'eim* — withhold from them the Holy Spirit." The Targum thus understood the word *k'la'eim* to be like the expressions: *Behold, 'lo echla' (I did not refrain) my lips;*[266] *'lo thichla' (Thou wilt not withhold) Thy compassions from me.*[267]

Now the reason for this matter is that Joshua thought that [Eldad and Medad] were prophesying because *they were of them that were recorded*[268] [among the prescribed number of seventy men that were to join Moses], because the spirit of Moses was transmitted to all *that were recorded,* for he intended that all [seventy of them should become prophets]. Therefore Joshua said to Moses: "It is not fitting that they [Eldad and Medad] should prophesy *in the camp,* since they did not fulfill the word of G-d who commanded: *and thou* [Moses] *shalt bring them unto the Tent of Meeting, that they may stand there with thee,*[269] and thus it might appear that not all of them prophesied through His putting of the spirit which was upon you [on them]. It is therefore fitting for my lord to direct your mind towards the spirit of G-d [which is upon you] and to bring it [completely] back to you, so that it should not be taken from you except for those who stand before you in accordance with the word of G-d. For it was because you intended at first that all *who were recorded* [should be prophets] that some of your glory came upon them, and if you will now intend to withdraw it from them, it will come to rest only upon those who stand before you in accordance with the word of G-d." But Moses answered

the Book of Kings that King Josiah of Judah sent to Huldah a delegation to inquire about a certain matter (II Kings 22:14). On this the Gemara asked: "But how could Huldah prophesy whilst Jeremiah — the leading prophet in Jerusalem — was present?" To this question the answer is given that "Huldah was a relative of Jeremiah and therefore he did not mind her prophesying." Thus it is clear from this text that there was a rule in Israel that no one should prophesy in the presence of a greater prophet. — Ramban's mentioning "Deborah" is merely a reference to the text in the Gemara which begins this discussion, but the actual reference is to Huldah, as explained above. (264) Kiddushin 32 a. (265) This is found in our Targum Yonathan ben Uziel. (266) Psalms 40:10. (267) *Ibid.,* Verse 12. (268) Verse 26. (269) Verse 16.

[Joshua by saying] that he should not be zealous for his sake, for he wishes that they prophesy whether in his presence or outside it, since G-d had put His spirit upon them — either by transmission from Moses or [directly from G-d] without such a transmission.

12 3. NOW THE MAN MOSES WAS VERY MEEK. This [is stated] to tell us that G-d Himself was zealous for Moses' sake on account of his [great] humility, since he would never pay attention to injustice [meted out to him] even if he were to consider it such [and therefore G-d vindicated his innocence]. And Rabbi Abraham ibn Ezra explained [the meaning of this phrase] by saying that Moses never sought superiority over any person, nor did he ever pride himself at all about his high position, and certainly not in relation to his brother, thus they [Miriam and Aaron] sinned by speaking against him for no reason.[270] But in the Sifre [it is said]: [271] "Rabbi Nathan says: They spoke against Moses even in his presence, as it is said, *And the Eternal heard it. Now the man Moses was very meek,*[272] and he restrained himself about the matter." [According to the Sifre, therefore, Scripture] mentions Moses' meekness in that he endured [their insult] and did not answer them back, and that G-d was [therefore] zealous for his sake.

4. AND THE ETERNAL SPOKE 'PITH'OM' (SUDDENLY) UNTO MOSES, AND UNTO AARON, AND UNTO MIRIAM. Now Moses was not with them, but [they are mentioned together because] the Divine communication came to the three of them simultaneously. The sense of the word "suddenly" is that they did not direct their minds towards or intend to receive a Divine communication at that time, it being in honor of Moses that it came to them without any preparation for it; for the word *pith'om* (suddenly) in the opinion of the commentators [as explained in Ibn Ezra] applies to something

(270) The slander was in connection with Moses' separating himself from his wife, which Miriam and Aaron attributed to his pride, as if to show that he was a holy man. "We also receive Divine revelations," they said, "and yet continue our conjugal life." (271) Sifre *Beha'alothcha* 100. (272) Verses 2-3.

which one did not think of, from the root *pethi* (simple-minded). Therefore Scripture uses the term *pith'om* [only] on account of Aaron and Miriam, for Moses our teacher was fit for a Divine communication at any time, and his mind was prepared to cleave to *the Glorious Name* at every moment, as our Rabbis have explained in connection with the reason why he [Moses] separated himself from his wife.[273] Onkelos, however, rendered [the word *pith'om*] as *bithkeiph* (in a hurry), the sense being that whilst Miriam and Aaron were still speaking about Moses, and the words were still in their mouths, they were told: *Come out ye three unto the Tent of Meeting,* and He did not delay [the rebuke] to them at all. The word *pith'om* is thus a term indicating hurry. Similarly, *And I beheld his habitation cursed 'pith'om' (suddenly)*;[274] *whose breaking cometh 'pith'om ' l'pheta' (suddenly at an instant)*;[275] *'b'pheta' pith'om' (very suddenly)*,[276] the double expressions being for emphasis, just like: *'kim'at kot' (a very little while)*;[277] *'harbei m'od' (exceedingly great)*.[278] So also: *'bi'm'od m'od' (very much)*,[279] and similar cases. And *pethaim* (simple-minded ones) are those who are very impetuous, who do not have any deep grasp of a matter and do not reflect on it at all, the usage being similar to the expression *and the counsel of the wily is hurried.*[280] So also: *'petha' (on a sudden) shall he be broken;*[281] *and if 'b'phetha' (suddenly) without enmity,*[282] [which Onkelos renders] *bithkeiph,* which is like *pethi* (simple), of the expression *pith'om* (hurriedly).

The reason [why He said at first] *Come out ye three* and [then in the following verse it says] *and He called Aaron and Miriam* [excluding Moses] is that G-d wanted him to be present [in the Tent of Meeting] and to see how He is zealous for Moses' honor; and so that he would be available [to forgive them], for G-d would not forgive them unless he did, after they would beg him and he agrees to [forgive] them. *And He called Aaron and Miriam,* in order to tell Moses' praise when he was not present.

(273) Shabbath 87 a: Since the Divine Glory reveals itself to me at all times [and there is no definite time fixed for the Divine communication] . . . " (274) Job 5:3. (275) Isaiah 30:13. (276) Above, 6:9. (277) Ezekiel 16:47. (278) Genesis 15:1. (279) *Ibid.*, 17:2. (280) Job 5:13. For any plan which is decided upon in a hurry is folly (Rashi). (281) Proverbs 6:15. (282) Further, 35:22.

6. IF THERE BE 'NEVI'ACHEM' [literally "your prophet"] — if there be a prophet "among you," as Onkelos rendered it ["if there be prophets among you"]. And Rabbi Abraham ibn Ezra commented that the meaning thereof is: "if there be among you a prophet, a prophet of the Eternal, [283] as in [the expression] *and the prophecy of Oded the prophet*."[284] He has explained it well. Thus the meaning of the verse is that "even if there is a prophet among you who is a [true] prophet of the Eternal, he can only prophesy by My Great Name through a vision or in riddles." He mentions this ["if he be a true prophet of the Eternal"] because many prophets did not attain even this [stage], but were prophets by virtue of the Holy Spirit, as it is said, *The spirit of the Eternal spoke by me,*[285] this being the "hand" mentioned in connection with Ezekiel,[286] as is explained in the words of Zechariah.[287]

IN A VISION I DO MAKE MYSELF KNOWN TO HIM. Scripture does not say: "I will appear to him in a vision," but it says '*I will make Myself known.*' This verse is then similar to the one which states, *And I appeared unto Abraham, unto Isaac, and unto Jacob, as G-d Almighty,*[288] [the verse here] stating that the Great Name appears in a vision and through it He becomes known to the prophet, but [the prophet does not know Him] [289] by His Great Name, just as He said, *but by My Name the Eternal I made Me not known to them.*[288] And

(283) The Hebrew text reads: *Im yih'yeh nevi'achem Hashem*. Ibn Ezra explains it by adding the word *navi* (prophet), which is in construct with *Hashem* — "the prophet of the Eternal." The reason why Ibn Ezra is forced to do so is because when a noun is in construct it cannot have a pronoun as a suffix, and here it says *nevi'achem Hashem,* the word *nevi'achem* having such a pronoun as a suffix. Hence Ibn Ezra adds the word *navi* (the prophet of), to be in construct with the noun *Hashem*. The sense of the verse is thus: *Im yih'yeh nevi'achem 'nevi' Hashem*. (284) II Chronicles 15:8. The meaning thereof is: "and the prophecy, a prophecy of Oded the prophet." The point here is that a noun which is in the construct cannot have the prefix *hei,* which indicates the definite article. Here it is stated: *v'hanevua Oded*. Hence Ibn Ezra explains it by adding the word *nevuath* (a prophecy of), making the sense of the phrase: "and the prophecy, a prophecy of Oded the prophet." (285) II Samuel 23:2. (286) Ezekiel 1:3. [*and the hand of the Eternal was there upon him*] etc. (287) "Most of his messages were in riddles and parables and through an angel; but he was nonetheless a prophet as he attained to Divine vision" (Abusaula). (288) Exodus 6:3. (289) Abusaula.

Scripture stated [further] that the communication is *in a vision,* but *My servant Moses is not so,* for *in all My house* in which the prophets see dreams, *he is trusted,*[290] knowing of his own accord all the [Divine] attributes, and from *mouth to mouth*[291] the communication comes to him from Me, and *he beholds the similitude,*[291] not in a dream. In the words of the Sifre:[292] "*And the similitude of the Eternal doth he behold.*[291] This refers to the vision of 'the back.' "[293]

Thus Scripture here teaches us the difference between the Divine communication received by Moses and that of the other prophets of his generation, in the same way that it mentioned this [difference between him and] those who preceded him [as it says in the verse], *And I appeared unto Abraham,* etc.,[288] as I have explained; and likewise it mentions at the end of the Torah in relation to those who came after him, *And there hath not arisen a prophet since in Israel like unto Moses, whom the Eternal knew face to face,*[294] the intention being the same in all these places. Do not be disquieted by the statement of the Rabbis[295] concerning Samuel, that he was equal to Moses, as it is written, *Though Moses and Samuel stood before Me, yet My mind could not be toward this people,*[296] since it is because G-d mentioned Samuel together with Moses that our Rabbis considered it an indication of his [Samuel's] greatness, but not that they were comparing the prophecies [of Moses and Samuel] to each other — far it be for them [to say so]! And the intention of this verse [which mentions Moses and Samuel together is as follows]: He mentioned Moses because *he stood before Him in the breach, to turn back His wrath, lest He should destroy them,*[297] both at the [incident of the] golden calf and that of the spies, when the people were in danger of destruction; and so Scripture also mentioned Samuel, because this verse is in connection with the drought[298] when they needed rain, and He said, *Are there any among the vanities of the nations that can cause rain?* etc.[299] Thus G-d said that even if Samuel — the prophet who brought rain when it was not due, in the days of the wheat-

(290) Verse 7. (291) Verse 8. (292) Sifre *Beha'alothcha* 103. (293) See Exodus 33:23. (294) Deuteronomy 34:10. (295) Rosh Hashanah 25b. See my Hebrew commentary p. 240, Note 72, concerning the source of the statement. (296) Jeremiah 15:1. (297) Psalms 106:23. (298) Jeremiah 14:1. (299) *Ibid.*, Verse 22.

harvest[300] — were to stand [in prayer] before Him, He would not listen to him to bring it for these people in their time of trouble. Thus Scripture mentioned the great men of the tribe whom G-d chose *to minister unto Him, and to bless in His Name,*[301] who prayed for Israel. This is also the sense of the verse which says, *Moses and Aaron among His priests, and Samuel among them that call upon His Name.*[302]

16. AND AFTERWARD THE PEOPLE JOURNEYED FROM HATZEROTH, AND PITCHED IN THE WILDERNESS OF PARAN. The reason [why Scripture mentions the wilderness] is to say that when they travelled from Hatzeroth they did not go from one wilderness to another, as they did on their first journey when they set forth *from the wilderness of Sinai and pitched in the wilderness of Paran,*[303] for [now] they set forth from Hatzeroth which is in the wilderness of Paran, and pitched in another place in that very same wilderness. This [place was called] Kadesh-barnea, for [although its name is not given here], it is from there that the spies [mentioned in the next section of the Torah] were sent, as is said in another place, *unto the wilderness of Paran, to Kadesh,*[304] and so also it is written, *and we came to Kadesh-barnea;*[305] *And ye came unto me every one of you, and said: Let us send men before us.*[306] Now Scripture does not say here: "and they journeyed from Hatzeroth, and pitched in Kadesh-barnea," for perhaps there were many [stages in their] journey between them [i.e., these two places], and this is not now the place to mention them. However, it mentioned [that they pitched] *in the wilderness of Paran,*[303] in order to inform us that this Kadesh [from where the spies were sent] is the Kadesh-barnea which is in the wilderness of Paran, not the Kadesh which is in the wilderness of Sin[307] where the affair of *the waters of Meribah*[308] took place in the fortieth year [of the Israelites' stay in the wilderness].

(300) I Samuel 12:17. (301) Deuteronomy 10:8. — Both Moses and Samuel were of the tribe of Levi. (302) Psalms 99:6. (303) Above, 10:12. (304) Further, 13:26. (305) Deuteronomy 1:20. (306) *Ibid.,* Verse 22. (307) Further, 20:1. (308) *Ibid.,* Verse 13.

Shelach

13 2. SEND 'LECHA' (THEE) [1] MEN. "As you see fit. I do not command you [to send them], but if you wish [to do so], send them. [G-d said this] because the Israelites came [to Moses] and said, *Let us send men before us,*[2] as it is said, *And ye came near unto me every one of you,*[2] and Moses inquired [what to do] of the Divine Presence, whereupon G-d said: 'I told them [at the time of the exodus] that it is a good [Land], as it is said, *I will bring you up out of the affliction of Egypt . . . [unto a Land flowing with milk and honey]*.[3] By their lives! I will give them an opportunity to fall into error through the incident of the spies, so that they should not come to possess the Land." This is Rashi's language, from the words of Agadah.[4]

Here one may ask, if this is so, then Moses himself sinned in this matter, as it is said, *And the thing pleased me well!* [5] And furthermore

(1) Literally: "for thyself," as explained by Rashi. (2) Deuteronomy 1:22. The verse continues that the people said to Moses: '*Let us send men before us, that they may search the Land for us, and bring us back word* etc.' (3) Exodus 3:17. The text of Rashi reads: " . . . *unto a good Land,*" which is taken from Verse 8, *ibid.* (4) Sotah 34 b, briefly, and in Bamidbar Rabbah 16:6, more fully. It is possible, as there is more than one reference for the source of Rashi's text, but none specific, that Ramban refers to it merely as stemming "from the words of Agadah." (5) Deuteronomy 1:23. In other words, since Moses was aware of G-d's displeasure with the whole mission, why did he say that *the thing pleased me well?*

why did he tell [the spies] to find out about the Land, *whether it is good or bad,*[6] since he had already been told at the beginning that it is *a good Land, and a large one?* [7] Moreover, what did the spies do [wrong], since Moses told them, *And see the Land what it is; and the people that dwelleth therein, whether they are strong or weak, whether they are few or many,*[8] and he said to see about the cities [that they dwell in] *whether in camps, or in strongholds,*[6] and at the least they had to give him an answer to [the questions] that he commanded them [to find out about]! And *what was* their *trespass,* and *what was* their *sin*[9] when they told Moses, *Nevertheless the people that dwell in the Land are fierce, and the cities are fortified, and very great?* [10] Did he then send them on the understanding that they would give him a false report! And do not think that their trespass consisted only in their report that *it is a Land that eateth up the inhabitants thereof,*[11] for prior telling this to the people, Caleb already quarrelled with them! [12] And likewise it is written, [that the people said], *Our brethren* [i.e., the spies] *have made our heart to melt, saying: The people is greater and taller than we* etc.,[13] and here it is written, *to fall by the sword; our wives and our little ones will be a prey.*[14] And yet Moses our teacher [himself] said similar things to the children [of the generation of the spies], and he emphasized to them the power of the people and the strength of their cities, and the might of the giants to a much greater extent than what the spies had told their fathers, as it is written, *Hear O Israel: thou art to pass over the Jordan this day, to go in to dispossess nations greater and mightier than thyself, cities great and fortified up to heaven, a people great and tall, the sons of the*

(6) Further, Verse 19. (7) Exodus 3:8. "Why then did he now ask G-d whether to send out the spies, and did not rely on the fact that the Land was, as he was told, *a good Land*?" (Gur Aryeh). (8) Further, Verse 18. (9) See Genesis 31:36. (10) Further, Verse 28. (11) *Ibid.*, Verse 32. (12) *Ibid.*, Verse 30. It is thus clear that *before* the spies made this derogatory statement about the Land, the people already did not want to go there. The trespass of the spies could therefore not have consisted only of their report that *it is a Land that eateth up the inhabitants thereof!* (13) Deuteronomy 1:28. (14) Further, 14:3. Scripture thus implies that both the spies and the people sinned in speaking of the difficulty of capturing the Land. And yet Moses etc.

Anakim, whom thou knowest, and of whom thou hast heard say: 'Who can stand before the sons of Anak!' [15] Now if *the trespass* of the spies and *their sin* consisted of this [discouraging report that they gave about the strength of the people in Canaan], why did he [Moses] dismay the heart of their children[16] in the same way that the spies dismayed the heart of their fathers? Moreover, what reason was there for Moses our teacher to send this mission? If [they would report that] the Land is good, and its inhabitants are weak—well and good; but if [they would say that] it is bad, or that the people are strong — would it enter his mind to take them back to Egypt!

But the explanation of this subject is as follows: The Israelites wanted [to act] in the way that all those who come to wage war in a foreign country do, namely to send out men to become acquainted with the roads and entrances to the cities; so that when they return [from their mission], the scouts will go at the head of the army, to show them the way, in a similar manner to that which it says, *Show us, we pray thee, the entrance into the city.*[17] Thus [the Israelites wanted the reconaissance party] to advise them which city they should attack first, and from which direction it would be easy to capture the Land. This is what they said explicitly, *and they* [the spies] *shall bring us back word of the way by which we must go up, and the cities unto which we shall come,*[2] that is to say, the cities into which we shall come first, and from which we will enter the whole country. Now this is the correct guidance [to give] to anyone who [plans to] conquer a country. And so did Moses himself do, as it is said, *And Moses sent to spy out Jazer,*[18] and Joshua the son of Nun also [sent] *two spies.*[19] It was for this reason that [the people's request to send out scouts] pleased Moses,[5] for Scripture does not [allow man] to rely on a miracle in any of its affairs. Instead, it commands those who go out to battle to arm themselves, to take [all necessary] precautions, and to set ambushes [if needed], as Scripture relates in connection with the battle for [the city of] Ai,

(15) Deuteronomy 9:1-2. (16) See further, 32:7-8. (17) Judges 1:24. (18) Further, 21:32. (19) Joshua 2:1.

which was by command of G-d,[20] and similarly in many places. Then Moses consulted the Divine Presence and G-d gave him permission, saying, "*Send thee men, that they may spy out the land of Canaan* and become acquainted with it, and bring back a report to you, and according to their information you should take counsel regarding the conquest." Now Moses told the spies, *Get you up here into the south,*[21] meaning: "Go up by this road into the south so that you will get to know the people who live in the land of the south — [this being] the direction from which Israel was [approaching] — [and see] *whether they are strong*[8] and [the Israelites] when dealing with them will need to be very much on their guard and well-armed; similarly, [see] *the cities,* and whether they are fortified so that [the inhabitants] are well-entrenched, and it will therefore be necessary to build forts and ramps, or [even] to come against them from another direction." Moses further told them that they should get to know *the Land* itself, *whether it is good or bad,*[6] and if it is bad, they should first conquer other parts [of it]; for they spied out the hill-country of the Amorites from the side of Hebron,[22] and even Joshua did not conquer all [areas of the Land], — this being the meaning of the expression *and what the Land is that they dwell in,*[6] meaning the people who live in the land of the south.

[Furthermore] it is possible that it was because Moses knew that it is a fertile and good land, — as he was told, *unto a good Land and a large one, unto a Land flowing with milk and honey,*[23] — that he told them to set their minds ascertaining this [fact], so that [upon their return] they would tell the people about it, and they would rejoice and gain renewed strength to go up there in joy. Therefore he told them, *And be ye of good courage, and bring of the fruit of the Land,*[24] so

(20) *Ibid.,* 8:2. Thus the method of ambush was also by command of G-d, thereby teaching that in war we are not to rely on miracles. (21) Further, Verse 17. The literal translation is: "Go up this, into the south;" therefore Ramban explains that it means "go up by this road into the south." It is also so explained by Ibn Ezra. In Targum Yonathan it is rendered: "Go up by this side, by the south." (22) *Ibid.,* Verse 22. (23) Exodus 3:8. (24) Further, Verse 20.

that they [the people] would see with their own eyes the goodness of the Land. Now it is well-known that Egypt is not very far from Hebron — approximately a seven-days' journey distant — and the border of the land of Canaan comes close to Egypt, and it is therefore impossible that people who live in Egypt should not know about the land of Canaan *whether it is good or bad.*[6] And indeed Moses' intention was to find out the way by which he should go up, and the cities which he was to capture first, as I have explained. However, since the Israelites in Egypt were slaves doing most rigorous work, *they did not know, neither did they understand*[25] [the nature of the Land], therefore Moses wanted the spies to tell them all the particulars of the Land in order to cause them to rejoice in its qualities, since he [himself] knew of them [as explained above.].

Now it appears to me from the language of Scripture that Moses did *not* [in fact] consult the Divine Presence [as to whether he should send spies at all], but the meaning of *Send thee men* is that they [the people] had decided [already] to send spies, and it was customary to send *two spies secretly, saying:* [*'Go view the Land'*],[19] and that they be taken [only] from some [tribes of the people]; but G-d Who knows the future commanded Moses [here] to send *one man from each of the tribes* of Israel, *every one a prince among them.* [This is because] G-d wanted all the great men to be [represented] equally in this matter, so that perhaps *they* would *remember and turn unto the Eternal,*[26] and if not, so that the decree [of punishment] would apply equally to the whole people, this being the meaning of the expression [that Moses sent them] *according to the commandment of the Eternal,*[27] for it was by command of G-d that they were to be *princes* and *heads of the children of Israel.*[27]

(25) Psalms 82:5. (26) *Ibid.*, 22:28. (27) Verse 3. Thus the burden of punishment, instead of falling heavily upon a particular tribe or tribes, would be more lightly distributed throughout the camp. Moreover, by commanding that the heads of the tribes should lead the mission, the people would avoid total responsibility and thus be spared annihilation. This latter point is made clear by Ramban in the text that follows.

It [further] appears to me according to the plain meaning of Scripture that G-d [in speaking] to Moses did not refer [at all] to the request which the people had made, to send out spies, nor to Moses' consent to that request, for if that were the case, Scripture here would have related: "And the children of Israel approached Moses and said: *Let us send men before us* etc.[2] *And the thing pleased* Moses *well,*"[5] and afterwards it would have written : "*And the Eternal spoke unto Moses, saying: 'Send thee men* as they have spoken to you, *one man* etc.' " But the matter was as follows. The Israelites asked to send [spies], *and the thing pleased* Moses *well,*[5] and afterwards a Divine communication came to Moses, as did all other such communications, merely saying, *Send thee men,* this being the reason [for the necessity of the subsequent explanatory words], *that they may spy out the land of Canaan, which I give unto the children of Israel,* as He is speaking of a new matter about which nothing has [hitherto] been related. All this was because *the Eternal was pleased, for His righteousness' sake*[28] that the mission be at His command, and that it be with [the participation of] all their tribes and their great men, so that [the people] should be saved.

Similarly it appears that they asked of Moses, *Let us send men before us, 'v'yachperu'* (*that they may search*) *the Land for us,*[2] which means spying out the roads and [working out] the strategy of conquest, similar to the expression *from there 'chaphar'* (*he spieth out*) *the prey.*[29] This is the meaning of [the words] *before us* [*Let us send men 'before us'*],[2] for they [the Israelites] would follow them [later on] in their route, similar to the expression, *and the ark of the covenant went 'before them'.*[30] G-d, however, commanded *'v'yathuru' the land of Canaan,* which refers to a choice, as is made by those who come to buy something, similar in expression to the verse, *beside that which 'mei'anshei hatarim'* (*the traffickers*) *and merchants.*[31] Similarly: *into a land that 'tarti'* (*I had sought out*) *for them;*[32] also, *'lathur'* (*to seek out*) *a resting-place for them.*[30] Therefore Moses commanded them to

(28) Isaiah 42:21. (29) Job 39:29. (30) Above 10:33. (31) II Chronicles 9:14. (32) Ezekiel 20:6.

state specifically *whether it is good or bad . . . whether it is fat or lean* etc.,[33] all this being in order to cause them to rejoice, for *it is the beauty of all lands,*[32] and they would go up to it with great eagerness. Thus this subject is related here without explanation [of the exact sequence of events leading up to the sending of the spies], as it occurred, but in the Book of Deuteronomy Moses mentioned to them all the happenings from their beginning, in order *to declare* to them *their transgression,*[34] that they sinned by their [very] request which they themselves initiated.

In the opinion of our Rabbis[35] their sin was in saying *Let us send men before us,*[2] because they had seen *the salvation of the Eternal*[36] which He continually did for them, and they should have followed the cloud *whither the spirit was to go,*[37] and Moses accepted their request to fulfill their desire. The meaning, then, of [the verse] *And the thing pleased me well*[5] is: "I endured your evil plan and directed that it be done". And G-d commanded him that he send *one man of every tribe of their fathers* etc., just like it is said in the case of Samuel, *Hearken unto the voice of the people in all that they say unto thee; for they have not rejected thee, but they have rejected Me, that I should not be King over them.*[38] Now these men [who were sent out as spies] were not *pointed out by name*[39] by the word of G-d, as was the case at the census[39] and at the division of the Land,[40] for no mishap occurs to those who carry out the command of G-d, and *whoso keepeth the commandment shall know no evil thing.*[41] Therefore He, blessed be He, only commanded Moses *one man of every tribe of their fathers shall ye send* etc., and that they be princes, and Moses at his own discretion chose these men and sent them, and *they wrought evil unto themselves.*[42]

(33) Verses 19-20. (34) See Isaiah 58:1. (35) Mentioned by Rashi at the beginning of this verse: "I told them [at the time of the exodus] that it is a good Land etc." (36) Exodus 14:13. (37) Ezekiel 1:12. (38) I Samuel 8:7. In that case too, the Divine consent was given only on account of the people's intransigence for having a king appointed over them. The matter, however, was displeasing to G-d because their devoted leader Samuel was still alive. (39) Above, 1:17. (40) Further, 34:19-28. (41) Ecclesiastes 8:5. (42) Isaiah 3:9.

4. OF THE TRIBE OF REUBEN etc. The verse [here] lists the tribes neither according to [the pattern of encampment of] their standards, nor according to the order of birth [of the ancestors of each tribe]. It appears that Scripture saw fit to mention them here according to the importance of the delegates [on the mission], for they *were heads* and princes of the people, as is related,[27] but they were not all of equal standing, some of them being greater than the others in wisdom and honor; therefore Scripture mentioned first those who were most honored, who were first in status, since it named them according to their personal standing, not that of their tribe. Similarly in [citing the names of] the princes who were to divide the Land up amongst the people,[40] He mentioned them according to their personal standing, not according to the order of birth [of the tribal ancestors].

19. WHETHER IT IS GOOD OR BAD. Rabbi Abraham ibn Ezra commented [that the meaning thereof is that they are to see] "if the Land is good, namely that its air is good, and its waters are good." Then Moses continued, *whether it is fat,*[24] meaning "capable of producing wheat" and many fruits.

The correct interpretation is that *whether it is 'good'* includes all good things, and in the word *ra'ah* [*or 'bad'*] are included all evils. [If so, the question arises why Moses continued with the apparently superfluous command to find out *whether* the Land *is fat or lean,* since it is already included in the phrases *good* and *bad*?] It is possible, however, that a good land is fruitful and its fruits are fat, and it produces fat products such as balsam and oil,[43] dates and figs and similar things. But [it is also possible] that it is good and yet lean, and always needs rain, and must be hoed and fertilized very much, and its fruits have a tendency to be dry although they are better and last longer than the fat ones. In such a land are to be found very many "lean" fruits, such as nuts, almonds, apples, carobs and fruits of the forests. Thus [by saying that the spies are to ascertain *whether* the Land *is fat or lean* Moses] meant "whether it is a fat land, as valleys are, or a lean land like the mountains." Onkelos, however, translated

(43) Ezekiel 27:17.

[*whether it is fat or lean* as] "whether it is rich or poor," for there are countries whose inhabitants are rich because of the low prices prevalent among them, and their neighbors trade with them in all the good things found among them, and there are some countries whose inhabitants are dependent upon their neighbors *and their inhabitants are of small power,*[44] although they are good [lands] and not at all bad.

'And be ye of good courage', and bring [*of the fruit of the Land*]. This means that they are not to be afraid when taking of the fruit of the Land that they might be recognized by the people as spies.

22. AND HEBRON 'NIVNETHAH' (WAS BUILT) SEVEN YEARS BEFORE ZOAN IN EGYPT. "Is it possible that Ham [Noah's son, the father of both Canaan and Mitzraim], built Hebron for Canaan, his younger son, before he built Zoan for Mitzraim, his elder son? Rather, you must say that [the meaning of the word *nivnethah*] is *m'vunah* ("built up" – i.e., furnished, supplied) with all excellent qualities, seven times more than Zoan [in Egypt]. The verse thus comes to tell you of the wonderful quality of the Land of Israel." This is Rashi's language.

It appears to me according to the plain meaning [of Scripture] that Hebron is Kiryath-arba, the greatest man of the Anakim having the name Arba, and it was he who built it [Hebron], therefore it was called by his name; just as it is said, *Now the name of Hebron beforetime was Kiryath-arba, which Arba was the greatest man among the Anakim.*[45] This man begot a son whom he named Anak, and it was after him that they [the inhabitants of Hebron] were called Anakim. Therefore Scripture states [here in our verse] that *there* in Hebron *were Ahiman, Sheshai, and Talmai, the children of Anak, and Hebron was built seven years before Zoan in Egypt,* meaning to say that Arba built it for his son Anak seven years before the building of Zoan in Egypt, which was an ancient city. [Scripture thereby] tells of the longevity of these people, for just as they were exceptional in

(44) II Kings 19:26. (45) Joshua 14:15.

their height so also they lived longer than other peoples; since Hebron was built [by Arba] for their father [i.e., Anak, the father of these giants *Ahiman, Sheshai, and Talmai*] before Zoan in Egypt, and many generations had elapsed since then [the founding of Zoan] until now.

It is possible that [in saying that *Hebron was built seven years before Zoan* Scripture] is alluding to that which it said, *whether it is fat or lean,*[24] [implying] that Hebron was very ancient and nonetheless still produced fat and large fruits, as Scripture tells about the bunch of grapes,[46] and how much more so the newer [parts of the] Land, which was more fertile.

It may be that Arba [and not, as explained above, a son of his, called Anak], was the father of Ahiman, Sheshai, and Talmai, and he was called Arba [literally "four"] because there were [altogether] four *Anakim* ["giants" — the three sons, *Ahiman, Sheshai, and Talmai*, and their father. According to this we would not have to postulate, as explained above, the existence of a son of Arba whom he named Anak, and who was the ancestor of the people called Anakim]. And the verse which states *even Kiryath-arba, which Arba was the father of 'Anak' — the same is Hebron*[47] [from which you might deduce that Arba indeed had a son, called Anak, uses the singular as a generic term and] means "the father of Anakim." Therefore Scripture speaks of [*Ahiman, Sheshai and Talmai* as *the sons of*] *Anak* and as *the children 'ha'anak' (of Anak),*[48] that is, the children of the greatest [giant] of them all [Arba], just as it says, *which Arba was the greatest man among the Anakim;* [45] and therefore [since it refers to the greatest giant, called Arba, and not to an individual called Anak] Scripture mentions the name with the definite article.[49] They [giants] are called

(46) Verse 24. (47) Joshua 15:13. (48) In Verse 33 here, Scripture speaks of [*the sons of*] *Anak,* and in Verse 22 here [also in Joshua 15:14] of *the children of 'ha'anak.'* (49) The definite article [indicated in Hebrew by prefixing the word with the letter *hei*] cannot be prefixed to a proper name of a person. Thus, e.g., you cannot say *'ha'Reuben'* (the Reuben). But if it is not a proper name the *hei* can be used. Thus we find *"ha'Reubeini"* (the Reubenites) — further 26:7, etc. Here too, if "Anak" were the proper name of a person, Scripture could not have said *the children of 'ha'anak,'* but since it means here "the [greatest] giant," it may properly be so used.

Anakim [literally "necklaces"] because of their beautiful stature, for they are like necklaces on the necks of the people [i.e., they were the pride of the people], just as [certain people] were called *bnei ha'elohim*[50] in the section of *Bereshith*, as I have explained there.[50] This is the meaning of the verse, *And Hebron 'nivnethah' (was built)* by this *'anak'* [mentioned in the beginning of the verse], *seven years before Zoan in Egypt,* for since the builder of Hebron [Arba] was well-known and famous, because the name of the city was *Kiryath-arba* ("the city of Arba"), Scripture says "it was built," [and does not say that Arba built it]. Or its meaning might be [to emphasize] that it was built for these [very people whom the spies now found in it], their father Arba having built it for them, and thus very many years had passed *since the day it was founded even until now.*[51]

27. AND SURELY IT FLOWETH WITH MILK AND HONEY. Since Moses had commanded them to see *what the Land is, whether it is fat or lean*[24] the spies reported to him that it is fat, *and surely it floweth with milk and honey.* And in answer to his question *whether there are trees therein or not*[24] they reported to him, *and this is its fruit*[52] for so he had commanded them, to show it to him.[24] Now in all this they said the truth, and gave a report about those matters which they had been commanded [to find out],[53] therefore they should [indeed] have said [as in fact they did] that *the people that dwell in the Land are fierce and the cities are fortified;*[53] for it was their duty *to bring back words of truth to them that sent* them,[54] and Moses had commanded them [to see] *whether they are strong or weak,*[55] *[and what cities they are that they dwell in], whether in camps, or in strongholds.*[56] But the wickedness of the spies consisted in saying the word *ephes* ["nevertheless" — *'Nevertheless' the people that dwell in the Land are fierce*],[53] which signifies something negative and beyond human capability, something impossible of achievement, under any

(50) Genesis 6:2. See Vol. I, pp. 102-3. (51) Exodus 9:18. (52) In Verse 27 before us. (53) Verses 27-28. (54) Proverbs 22:21. (55) Verse 18. (56) Verse 19.

circumstances, similar to the expressions: *'Ha'aphes' lanetzach chasdo* (*Is His mercy 'clean gone' for ever?*); [57] *and there is none else; 'ephes'* (*there is no other*) *G-d.*[58] Thus the spies told Moses that the Land is fertile *and surely it floweth with milk and honey*[53] and the fruits are good, but it is impossible to fight against *the people* because they *are fierce, and the cities are fortified, and very great; and moreover we saw the children of Anak there.*[53] They also said, *Amalek dwelleth in the land of the south*[59] by which they intended to allege that there was no direction from which they could enter the Land, as all [its inhabitants] are strong men, for Amalek dwells in the south, and the Canaanite in the west and in the east, *and the Amorite in the mountains.*[59] Thus they reported that which they had been sent [to find out], in such a way as to discourage the people's confidence by means of allusion [and not openly], because they were afraid of Moses and Aaron. Thus they gave an answer to all that Moses commanded them [to ascertain], except for his statement [that they were to see] *whether they are few or many,*[55] to which they gave no reply at all, nor did they report back [*whether it is*] *good.*[56] This is because they intended to tell the people afterwards by way of an evil report, *it is a Land that eateth up the inhabitants thereof,*[60] [thus implying] that its people are few but very strong. Now the people understood their intention and so all the congregation which was present began to murmur, this being the sense of the expression, *And Caleb stilled the people,*[61] for he silenced them and said, *We should go up at once, for we are well able to overcome it,*[61] meaning: "It is true that the people are strong, but we shall be stronger than them and their fortified cities." Therefore Caleb said *lah* ["it" — *we are well able to overcome 'it,'* the word *'it'* referring to the Land, and including the people and their fortifications]. Then the spies spoke up again, explaining their words clearly, and said, *We are not able to go up against the people,*

(57) Psalms 77:9. The thought implied is clear: It is impossible to think that His mercy has been withdrawn forever. (58) Isaiah 45:14. Here too, the thought suggested is abundantly clear: It is inconceivable that there is another deity beside the true One G-d. (59) Verse 29. (60) Verse 32. (61) Verse 30.

for they are stronger than we,[62] meaning: "Even if *the people came out unto us into the field*[63] we are not able to contest them in battle, and we surely cannot capture any of their great and fortified cities." For the meaning of the expression *to go up 'against the people'* is similar to [what Goliath said]: *choose you a man for you, and let him come down to me,*[64] which is an expression for those fighting in battle formation.

32. AND THEY BROUGHT FORTH 'DIBATH' (AN EVIL REPORT OF) THE LAND WHICH THEY HAD SPIED OUT UNTO THE CHILDREN OF ISRAEL. The meaning of this is that the spies left Moses and Aaron and [went around] saying in the [people's] tents that *it is a Land that eateth up the inhabitants thereof.*[60] For at first when they spoke to the people in front of Moses and Aaron [saying] that *the Land . . . floweth with milk and honey* but that *the people are fierce,*[53] and Caleb said, *for we are well able to overcome it,*[61] the people hesitated [between these two opinions], and there were some of them who [still] trusted in their power and strength, and some of them [who trusted] in *the help of the Eternal against the mighty.*[65] Then the spies spread the evil report in front of the people themselves, as it is written, *the Land through which we have passed to spy it out, is a Land that eateth up the inhabitants thereof,* etc.,[60] until they caused *the whole congregation*[66] to complain, this being the sense of the verse stating, *and they returned, and made all the congregation to murmur against him, by bringing up an evil report against the Land.*[67] This happened because when the spies saw the [Amorite] people *whose height was like the height of the cedars, and he was strong as the oaks,*[68] *the fear of* them *was fallen upon them*[69] and they made the hearts of their brothers melt.[13] And when they saw that the Israelites were still considering going up [to the

(62) Verse 31. (63) II Samuel 11:23. (64) I Samuel 17:8. (65) Judges 5:23. (16) Further, 14:2. (67) *Ibid.*, Verse 36. (68) Amos 2:9. (69) Esther 8:17.

Land], and that Joshua and Caleb were encouraging them to do so, they invented a false report in order to frustrate their [intention of] going up by all possible means.

Know that *he who "bringeth forth 'dibah' " is a fool*[70] who speaks falsely, but he who tells a truthful [bad report] is called "one who 'brings' *dibah,*" as it is said, *and Joseph brought 'dibatham ra'ah' (evil report of them) unto their father.*[71] It was for this [false report] that they were punished by death through a plague, as it is said, *And those men that 'brought forth' an evil report of the Land, died by the plague before the Eternal.*[72]

IT IS A LAND THAT EATETH UP THE INHABITANTS THEREOF; AND ALL THE PEOPLE THAT WE SAW IN IT ARE MEN OF GREAT STATURE. If a land is bad and has scanty and poor water so that *the Land miscarrieth,*[73] it does not sustain men of great [physical] stature, and its inhabitants are weak and flabby, small in size and lacking in strength! [So the question appears in what way is the spies' statement that the Land produces *men of great stature* an *evil report?*] But the *evil report* of the spies consisted in saying that the Land has an overpowering atmosphere and a heavy nature, and its water and fruits are thick and heavy, so that [the fruits] grow to a very large size, such that people of an average temperament cannot take them, unless they are giants and men of powerful build who are naturally strong and exceptional in their height and stature. Therefore the Land supports very tall men but brings [premature] death to the rest of the people, as is the nature of coarse foods. The spies then continued and emphasized the strength of the giants, for at

(70) Proverbs 10:8. (71) Genesis 37:2. This shows that when Scripture uses the expression "he 'brings' *dibah*" it means that he tells the truth as he sees, and when it uses the expression "bringeth forth" [which is in Hebrew a different verb], it means a *false* report. See also Ramban *ibid.*, Vol. I, p. 449. (72) Further, 14:37. Thus, in speaking of the spies having *brought forth an evil report,* Scripture by using the word *ra'ah* (evil) wishes to emphasize that not only was their report false but that it was also of an exceedingly evil nature. (73) II Kings 2:19.

first they said, *and moreover, we saw the children of Anak there,*[53] and now they exaggerated and called them *nephilim* [a word which implies that they were so enormous that the hearts of those who saw them "fell" through fear]; saying to the people, *and there we saw the Nephilim,* the three[74] *sons of Anak* who are of the ancient *Nephilim*[75] about whom you have heard, for *the same were the mighty men that were of old, the men of renown.*[76] And since the nature of the Nephilim who lived in the times of Noah was known throughout the world, the spies mentioned that these sons of Anak were their descendants, in order *to frighten them, and to terrify them.*[77] Therefore the spies said now, *and we were in our own sight as grasshoppers, and so we were in their sight.*[75]

14 1. AND THE PEOPLE WEPT THAT NIGHT. The meaning thereof is that the spies went into the [people's] tents towards evening, after they left Moses, and in the morning they [the people] rose early and they all *murmured against Moses and against Aaron* [as related in Verse 2]. And likewise Moses said,[78] *and ye murmured in your tents,* for it was in their tents that they spoke *words of a murmurer.*[79]

Now our Rabbis have said: [80] ["That day was the ninth of Ab. Said the Holy One, blessed be He:] 'They wept for no good reason; therefore I will establish [that day as one for] weeping throughout their generations'." [81] But I do not know from what allusion in this section [of the Torah] the Rabbis deduced this interpretation. It is, however, a clearly-expressed verse [in the Book of Psalms]: *Moreover, they scorned the desirable Land, they believed not His word. And they murmured in their tents, they hearkened not unto the voice of the Eternal. Therefore He swore concerning them, that He would overthrow them in the wilderness, and that He would cast out their*

(74) Ahiman, Sheshai, and Talmai (Verse 22). (75) Verse 33. (76) Genesis 6:4. (77) II Chronicles 32:18. (78) Deuteronomy 1:27. (79) Proverbs 18:8. (80) Taanith 29a. (81) The First and Second Temples were destroyed on the ninth of Ab, the anniversary of the night when the people wept without cause. Many subsequent misfortunes also befell the Jewish people on that day.

seed among the nations, and scatter them in the lands.[82] Perhaps this [interpretation of the Rabbis concerning the destruction of the two Temples on that night of weeping] is derived from the verse which states, *But your little ones, that ye said would be a prey,*[83] which means: "But as for your little ones — it will be as you said, *they will be a prey* when *the time of their visitation*[84] comes, for I shall *visit the iniquity of the fathers upon the children.*[85] — *them will I bring in* now so that they *will* just *know the Land,*[83] but they will not possess it [uninterruptedly] for all time." Scripture only refers to such matters by means of allusion, for it does not want to decree evil categorically, unless it is a rebuke predicated on a condition.

3. AND WHY DOTH THE ETERNAL BRING US UNTO THIS LAND, TO FALL BY THE SWORD? OUR WIVES AND OUR LITTLE ONES WILL BE A PREY. They did not mention the false report [of the spies] about the Land, saying that *the Land miscarrieth*[73] and is bad, because the people hid this statement [of the spies] from Moses, since the delegates themselves had not said so when they brought back word to him and to all the congregation,[86] for Moses and Aaron would have testified against them that they spoke falsely. The spies themselves hid this from Moses, fully realizing that he knew the nature of the Land from Egypt and Midian which are near to it, as I have explained.[87] Therefore the spies [only] told the people this evil report in their tents, in a secretive manner.

Now Moses said in the Book of Deuteronomy: *And they brought us back word, and said: 'Good is the Land which the Eternal our G-d giveth unto us.' Yet ye would not go up, but rebelled against the commandment of the Eternal your G-d.*[88] The meaning thereof is that the spies did [indeed] tell Moses and Aaron and all the congregation that *the Land is good,*[88] *and surely it floweth with milk and honey,*[89] and the people rebelled against the commandment of the Eternal in

(82) Psalms 106:24-27. (83) Further, Verse 31. (84) Jeremiah 8:12. (85) Verse 18 here. (86) Above, 13:26. (87) At the beginning of this *Seder.* (88) Deuteronomy 1:25-26. (89) Above, 13:27.

not wanting to go up because of the statement [of the spies] that *the people that dwell in the Land are fierce*[90] — for *G-d hath power to help, and to cast down,*[91] as is stated clearly there, *The Eternal your G-d Who goeth before you, He shall fight for you.*[92] Therefore, since there was nothing to deter them [in the Land itself] except for the strength of the people, they should have trusted in the Name of G-d, for *the battle is the Eternal's.*[93] And we do not have to say [as does Rashi] that Moses said this [*And 'they' brought us back word, and said, 'Good is the Land* etc.'] only about Joshua and Caleb, for why should the people listen to two [spies] and not believe [the report of] the ten![94] Moreover it says there [in Deuteronomy 1:23]: *and I took twelve men of you,* and it is with reference to [all twelve of] them that he [Moses] said, *and they brought us back word.*[95]

5. THEN MOSES AND AARON FELL ON THEIR FACES. The reason for this was that they saw that the people were about to decide to appoint a leader and return [to Egypt] immediately; so the righteous ones [Moses and Aaron] arose and prostrated themselves with their faces on the ground saying to them, *'I pray you, my brethren, do not so wickedly,'*[96] *and let this be no stumbling-block unto you.*[97] Therefore it says [that they fell on their faces] *before all the congregation of the children of Israel,* for it was for their sake that they prostrated themselves on their faces [imploring them to abandon their plan to return to Egypt].[98] Similarly, *and he* [David] *fell on his*

(90) *Ibid.*, Verse 28. (91) II Chronicles 25:8. (92) Deuteronomy 1:30. (93) I Samuel 17:47. (94) But according to Ramban, even the ten spies only spread an evil report about the Land in the people's tents, secretly, but in the presence of Moses they all spoke well about it. Hence the word *they* in the verse, *and 'they' brought us back word, and said: 'Good is the Land* etc.' (Deuteronomy 1:25) refers to *all* the spies. (95) *Ibid.* (96) Genesis 19:7. (97) See I Samuel 25:31. (98) Ramban here is excluding the possibility of interpreting their falling on their faces as a preparation for prayer (see further, 16:22). Therefore he points out that here it says that they [*fell on their faces*] *before all the assembly of the congregation of the children of Israel,* thus indicating that they did so in order to implore them to abandon their plan of returning to Egypt. See also Note 155 further.

face to the ground and bowed down three times[99] [before Jonathan, is an expression of conciliation and supplication]. And the meaning of the word *liphnei* ["before" — *'before' all the assembly* is like *lahem* ["for them" — to implore them, for their good, to renounce their plan of returning to Egypt]. Similarly, *And his brethren also went and fell down 'l'phanav ('before' him)*[100] [also means "to" him — Joseph — to beg him for forgiveness]. There are many examples of this usage.

7. IT IS 'M'OD M'OD' (AN EXCEEDING) GOOD LAND. The reason [for this emphasis] is in order to contradict the false report [of the spies] and to state that it is not [*a Land*] *that eateth up the inhabitants thereof,* for the air is good, and it is *a Land flowing with milk and honey.*[3]

9. ONLY REBEL NOT AGAINST THE ETERNAL. This means that [Moses and Aaron told the people]: "Your being afraid [to go up] because of the strength of the people that dwell in the Land is [in itself] a rebellion against *the Glorious Name,*[101] for it was not because of your [own] strength that you came out of Egypt, but it was the hand of the Eternal *that hath dealt wondrously with you.*[102] And He has assured you that He will drive them out from before you; if so, believe [in Him] and you will succeed." They [Moses and Aaron] continued: *neither fear ye the people, for they are bread for us,* meaning that "even in the natural course of events and through normal methods of [warfare as practiced in] the world, they will fall before us, for the fear of us has overcome them and they will let us consume them like bread."

'TZILAM' (literally: "their shadow") IS REMOVED FROM THEM. "That is, their shield and their strength [are departed from them]. The worthy ones among them have died. Another

(99) I Samuel 20:41. (100) Genesis 50:18. Here too, it could not mean that the brothers did so in order "to pray" to Joseph, but only to plead with him on their behalf. (101) Deuteronomy 28:58. (10) Joel 2:26.

interpretation: the shade (protection) of G-d is departed from them." This is Rashi's language. And Rabbi Abraham ibn Ezra commented that "*tzilam* means the buckler and shield which form a shade [and protection] to people in battle, and they [Moses and Aaron] are thus saying that our fear has fallen upon them, so that they will not take buckler, shield nor helmet to arm themselves and fight against us." He has explained it well.

But it is possible that Scripture is alluding to the well-known fact that there will be no shadow over the head of a person who is [destined] to die that year, on "the night of the seal."[103] Therefore it says: "*their 'shade' is* already *removed from them,* meaning that death has been decreed upon them, *and the Eternal is with us,* for it is He Who dwells in our midst and does miracles and wonders for us in the eyes of all who behold us; therefore, *fear them not.*" Or it is possible that the verse alludes to the princes above [in heaven], for no nation falls unless its prince falls first, as it is written, *The Eternal will punish the host of the high heaven on high* etc., and afterwards, *on the kings of the earth upon the earth,*[104] and as is explained in the Book of Daniel.[105] Thus the verse is saying: "the power under whose protection the nations [in the land of Canaan] live is already removed, *and the Eternal* Who lowered them *is with us,* therefore *fear them not.*" And thus the Rabbis said in Midrash Shir Hashirim: [106] "*And the shadows*

(103) This is a term signifying the night of Hoshana Rabbah, i.e., the night of the seventh day of the Festival of Tabernacles—the twenty-first of Tishri—when the "Heavenly seal" is put upon the judgment which was decided on the New Year [and Day of Atonement] for each individual and his fate in the coming year. The subject is mentioned by R'mah [Rabbi Moshe Isserles] in Orach Chayim 664:1. However, he discourages anyone from prying into the veiled future, for it is far better to be whole-hearted with the Eternal than to pay heed to such auguries of the future. See also the learned essay on this topic in "Studies in Jewish Philosophy and Mysticism" by Israel Weinstock, pp. 249-269. (104) Isaiah 24:21. (105) Daniel 10:20. See Ramban above in *Seder Beha'alothcha,* 11:16. (106) This is not found in our editions of Shir Hashirim Rabbah. Its source is an unknown "Midrash Shir Hashirim" quoted in the commentary to Song of Songs ascribed to Ramban (see my Hebrew commentary, second edition *et seq.* Vol. II, p. 528).

flee away.[107] These are the princes of the nations and their angels," for they are the protection over the nations. I have already mentioned this in other places.[108]

13. AND THE EGYPTIANS SHALL HEAR 'KI HE'ELITHA' IN THY MIGHT. "And the Egyptians shall hear that you have killed them. *Ki he'elitha.* The word *ki* [here] means 'that,' [the meaning of the expression thus being:] 'they have seen *that Thou broughtest them up in Thy might from among them,* and when they hear that You have killed them they will not say that [it is because] they sinned against You, but [they will say] that against them [the Egyptians themselves] You were able to fight, but not against the inhabitants of this land [of Canaan].' And this is the meaning of [the phrase]: *and they will say 'el' the inhabitants of this land*[109] — what will they say concerning them? That which is stated at the end of the subject: *Because the Eternal was not able to bring this people into the Land*[110] — because the inhabitants of the land are strong and mighty, and Pharaoh [alone] is not like thirty-one kings [who ruled in the land of Canaan]." This is the language of Rashi. If so, the expression *'el' yosheiv* [literally: *'to' the inhabitants*][109] will be like *'al' yosheiv,* ("concerning" the inhabitants), and there are also many such examples.

In my opinion, [however], Moses our teacher did not mean [to say] in [presenting] this argument that [the Egyptians will say that] the Canaanites are strong and mighty in battle and that Pharaoh [alone] cannot be compared to thirty-one kings — for G-d had smitten the Egyptians with a plague and killed their firstborns in one moment, and brought upon them great punishments out of heaven, [so they knew] that it *is but a light thing in the sight of the Eternal*[111] to destroy the strong and mighty by a plague, just as [He can destroy] the feeble

(107) Song of Songs 2:17. (108) Exodus 20:3, and above 11:16. (109) Verse 14. *'El'* usually means "to", but in this context, as Rashi is pointing out, the Egyptians were not saying anything "to" the Canaanites, but "about" or "concerning" them. (110) Verse 16. (111) II Kings 3:18.

and weak, [by means of special plagues]. But the meaning of this prayer [of Moses] was as if to say: "The Egyptians will think and say that the gods of Canaan have power to save the inhabitants from Your hand, since You executed judgments on the Egyptians and their gods before You brought this people out of their midst, but You could not do the same to the Canaanites and their gods. Thus this will constitute a profanation of G-d's Name, and the hands of the idol-worshippers will be strengthened!" If so, it is possible that the expression, *and they will say 'el' the inhabitants of this land*[109] is to be understood literally, that is, the Egyptians will say "to" the people of the land of Canaan, *"Because the Eternal was not able* etc.,[110] for *surely god is in* you, *there is no other god."* [112]

14. THAT THOU, ETERNAL, 'NIR'AH' (HAST BEEN SEEN) EYE TO EYE. Rabbi Abraham ibn Ezra commented that "[this verse is to be understood in the light of what it says], *And the appearance of the Glory of the Eternal* etc. *in the eyes of the children of Israel.*[113] *Nir'ah* is a verb in the past tense,[114] and it means 'Thou hast been seen.' Similarly, *'v'neisha'ar' ani*[115] [is like *v'neisha'arti* — 'and I was

(112) See Isaiah 45:14, where foreign nations are saying this to Israel: *Surely G-d is in thee, and there is none else, there is no other G-d.* Ramban, in following his customary style throughout his commentary, uses the verse with some change and thereby puts it in the mouths of the Egyptians who are saying it to the Canaanites about their idols. (113) Exodus 24:17. (114) The Hebrew form *nir'ah* is used for both the second person feminine in the present tense ["you, a woman, are seen"], and for the third person masculine or feminine in the past tense ["he or she, a man or woman has been seen"]. The difficulty in our verse is that *nir'ah* referring to G-d [the Eternal] clearly is used here in the *third* person past tense, [since it is not a feminine word, and the context clearly refers to G-d having been seen in the past]. Yet the verse continues: [*nir'ah*] *'atah'* using the *second* person pronoun *atah* (you), with the verbal form *nir'ah*, meaning *He* has been seen! Ibn Ezra therefore explains that this is equivalent to the single word *nir'etha,* (you have been seen), and quotes other examples of such usages. (115) Ezekiel 9:8. In this case we have the same *third* person verbal form as *nir'ah,* i.e., *v'neisha'ar,* used in the *first* person, with the pronoun *ani* (I), as if it had said *v'neisha'arti* (and I remained).

left']. So also, *for 'umlal' ani*[116] [is like *umlalti* — 'I have languished away'] because the letter *lamed* is vowelled with a long *pathach.*"[116]

'A'YIN B'A'YIN' (EYE TO EYE). The double use of the word *eye* [in this phrase] has been explained by commentators[117] as indicating human [behavior], for the eyes [of a speaker] look into the eyes of the listener to whom he is speaking. A similar case is the verse, *Face to face did the Eternal speak with you.*[118] And by way of the Truth, [the mystic teachings of the Cabala], the word *a'yin* is an expression for "vision," ["appearance," as in these verses:] *'v'eino k'ein' (and the appearance thereof was as the appearance of)* *bdellium;*[119] *and I saw 'k'ein' (as the appearance of) electrum.*[120] The verse here is thus stating: "inasmuch as Thy Great Name is seen through the appearance of an appearance;" and this is also the meaning of the verse with reference to Ezekiel, *And the appearance of the vision which I saw was like the vision that I saw when I came to destroy the city; and the visions were like the vision that I saw by the river Chebar.*[121]

17. AND NOW, I PRAY THEE, LET THE POWER OF THE ETERNAL BE GREAT, ACCORDING AS THOU HAST SPOKEN, SAYING. "And what is that utterance? *The Eternal is long-suffering*[122] — both to the righteous and to the wicked. When Moses ascended to heaven [to receive the Torah], he found the Holy One, blessed be He, writing: *The Eternal is long-suffering.* Whereupon he [Moses] said to Him: 'To the righteous.' But G-d answered him, 'Also to the wicked!' Moses then said, 'The wicked — let them perish!'

(116) Psalms 6:3. Since the word *umlal* used in that verse is vowelled with a *patach* it is clearly a third person form in the past tense; for were it to be a first person form in the present tense, it would be vowelled *umlol* with a *kamatz.* Thus we have another example of a *third* person verbal form followed by the *first* person pronoun *ani* (I). Hence it must be understood as if it were *umlalti* (I have languished away). (117) Onkelos, who translated it as: "who saw with their eyes." (118) Deuteronomy 5:4. (119) Above, 11:7. (120) Ezekiel 1:27. (121) *Ibid.*, 43:3. (122) Verse 18.

Whereupon G-d said to him: 'By your life! You will [eventually] need to resort to this' [attribute — that G-d is long-suffering even with sinners]. When the Israelites had sinned because of the golden calf and spies, and Moses prayed to G-d that He be long-suffering with them, the Holy One, blessed be He, said to him, 'Did you not tell Me that this is [only] for the righteous!' Whereupon Moses answered Him, 'But did You not tell me that it is also for the wicked. *Let* then *the power of the Eternal be great* to do as You have spoken.' " These are the words of Rashi, based on the interpretation of Agadah.[123]

The way of Truth you will recognize because G-d's Name in this context is written with *Aleph Daleth* (*A-donoy*) — [a Name which alludes to the attribute of judgment], and Moses meant to say that the greatness be in the power which is mercy, since it was the attribute of judgment that was directed against them.

Now Moses mentioned among the [Divine] attributes *long-suffering, and plenteous in loving kindness,*[122] but he did not mention "truth" [although it is also one of the Thirteen Attributes],[124] for according to the attribute of truth they would have been guilty. Nor did Moses mention *keeping mercy unto the thousandth generation,*[125] because Moses did not pray [for mercy] here on the basis of the merit of the patriarchs, and [therefore] he did not mention Abraham, Isaac, and Jacob at all in this prayer. The reason [for not mentioning them] was because the Land was given to the patriarchs, and it is from them that they were to inherit it, but they rebelled against their ancestors, and did not want the gift which the patriarchs desired very much, so how could he say now, [*Remember Abraham, Isaac, and Israel, Thy servants,*] *to whom Thou didst swear by Thine own self, . . . and all this Land that I have spoken of will I give to your seed,*[126] since they were saying: "We do not want this gift!"

Moses [mentioned here the attribute of *forgiving iniquity and*

(123) Sanhedrin 111a. (124) Exodus 34:6. (125) *Ibid.*, Verse 7. (126) *Ibid.*, 32:13.

transgression but he] did not say *and sin,*[127] because these people were wilful transgressors and sinners. But I do not know why he did not mention [the attributes] *merciful and gracious.*[124] Perhaps Moses knew that judgment was directed against them and He would never forgive them; therefore he prayed only that [G-d be] long-suffering, and should not destroy them *as one man,*[128] and should not slay *them* like sheep *in the wilderness*[110] where they would die in a plague. And since Moses only prayed now for [G-d to be] long-suffering, G-d said to him, *I have pardoned according to thy word,*[129] meaning that "I will be long-suffering towards them and great in loving kindness." He [Moses] mentioned *visiting the iniquity of the fathers,*[122] meaning to say that [even] if He should see fit not to erase their iniquity, He should [at least] visit *the iniquity of the fathers upon* their *children,*[122] [thereby mitigating the severity of the punishment from upon one generation], and he should be long-suffering with them in meting out punishment upon them. It was because of this [prayer of Moses] that there was a [Divine] decree to fix a weeping for them on that night throughout their generations,[81] since He visited their sins upon their seed.

And Rabbi Abraham ibn Ezra commented that "since we find the verse, *Surely they shall not see the Land*[130] after G-d said, *I have pardoned according to thy word,*[129] we know that the expression *'s'lach na'* (*pardon, I pray Thee*) [131] [is a prayer that G-d be] long-suffering to them [but not that they be totally forgiven]. The same meaning also

(127) I.e., of *forgiving sin,* as well as *iniquity and transgression.* See the verse in Exodus 34:7, where all three are mentioned: *forgiving iniquity and transgression and sin.* The question then arises: Why did not Moses mention here *sin?* (128) Verse 15. (129) Verse 20. (130) Verse 23. (131) Verse 19. In other words, since after G-d said, *I have pardoned 'according to thy word'* (Verse 20), He yet continues to state, *Surely they shall not see the Land* (Verse 23), it follows that Moses' request, *Pardon, I pray Thee* (Verse 19) must mean only that G-d be long-suffering to them, but not that they be totally forgiven. Such is the interpretation of Ibn Ezra. Ramban will suggest another explanation of Moses' request.

applies to *'v'nislach lo'* (*and he shall be pardoned*),[132] which implies [that G-d will be long-suffering with him] until he repents sincerely."

The correct interpretation appears to me to be that the term *s'lichah* means remittance of punishment, as Onkelos rendered it: [*s'lach na* – "Let go please"]. And the offerings [which one brings for a sin committed in error] remove the punishment for the error from him [the person who brings the offering].[133] So also, *For Thou, Eternal, art good 'v'salach'*[134] [means "and are ready to remit punishment"]. And G-d said, *'salachti' according to thy word*[129] meaning [that He has remitted punishment] from the people as a whole, and will not *smite them with a pestilence and destroy them,*[135] *and make of* Moses *a nation greater and mightier than they*[135] while they and their seed will perish from the earth; instead, He will pardon them – so that their children [at least] will inherit the Land, and they [themselves] will not die in a plague, for He decreed that their carcasses perish in the wilderness[136] and that each will die when his day comes.

Now in the Book of Deuteronomy in mentioning the sin of the golden calf Moses recalled the prayer which He had prayed on their behalf, saying, *And I fell down before the Eternal, as at the first* etc.[137] and he explained there what the prayer was, *And I prayed unto the Eternal, and said* etc.,[138] and he also mentioned his prayer on behalf of Aaron. But in [recounting] the affair of the spies he did not mention at all that he had interceded on their behalf. All this is for the reason that I have mentioned, namely, that he did not pray that G-d should

(132) Leviticus 4:26. Here too the actual offering in itself does not effect atonement until the sinner repents (see Ramban in Vol. III, pp. 21, 54). Hence, says Ibn Ezra, the phrase *v'nislach lo* means that G-d will be patient and will not punish him until he has had a chance to repent. (133) Hence *v'nislach lo* (*ibid.*) stated in connection with bringing a sin-offering means that "his punishment will be remitted." (134) Psalms 86:5. The fact that the word "good" appears before *v'salach* indicates that the term *s'lichah* does not merely mean being long-suffering and patient [as Ibn Ezra has it] but expresses a complete remittance of punishment. (135) Verse 12. (136) Further, Verse 33. (137) Deuteronomy 9:18. (138) *Ibid.*, Verse 26.

forgive them [completely], but rather that He should remit their punishment and be long-suffering with them, and should visit *the iniquity of the fathers upon the children.*[122] Thus his prayer on their behalf was not a complete one [inasmuch as he was not able to intercede for total forgiveness], and therefore [when speaking to the second generation in the Book of Deuteronomy] he did not mention it to them, since they might have complained against him [for not praying for total forgiveness, without realizing that he could not do so because of the greatness of their parents' sin].

21. AS I LIVE. "This is an expression of an oath. AND ALL THE EARTH SHALL BE FILLED WITH THE GLORY OF THE ETERNAL. 23. IF THEY SHALL SEE THE LAND. This is an inverted verse [and the sense of it is as follows:] *As I live,* says the Eternal, [I swear] *that all those* [*that have seen My Glory . . . and did not listen to My voice* — Verse 22], *if they shall see the Land* [Verse 23], *and* My *Glory shall fill* [*all*] *the earth* [Verse 21], so that My Name will not become profaned through this plague, [by the nations] saying: *Because the Eternal was not able to bring* them [*into the Land*],[110] since I shall not kill them suddenly *as one man,*[128] but over a delayed period of forty years, little by little." This is Rashi's language. But it is not correct at all.[139] Rather, these verses omit the oath [itself] out of respect to Him Who is on high, [and the meaning thereof is as follows]: *"As I live and all the earth shall be filled with* My *Glory — if* all *these men* who have tested Me *shall* see the Land, this matter shall not be so!" Similarly, *As I live, saith the Eternal . . . If ye come into the Land*[140] omits the [Divine] oath [meaning: "If they shall come into the Land, it shall not be so!"] Similarly we find verses speaking of a

(139) Rashi's interpretation requires the rearrangement of the second half of Verse 21 [*and all the earth shall be filled with the Glory of the Eternal*] after Verse 23, since this second part of Verse 21 is not part of the oath of the Eternal. Ramban, however, does interpret it as part of the oath, which [as he continues to explain], starts at the beginning of Verse 21, and hence there is no need to rearrange the second half of that verse and to place it after Verse 23. See also Note 147. (140) Further, Verses 28-30.

human being which shorten the oath: *G-d do so unto me and more also,*[141] where Scripture did not want to set forth the imprecation. *G-d do so unto the enemies of David, and more also*[142] — here the verse omits the blessing.[143] Similarly we find that Caleb said to Joshua, *Thou knowest the thing that the Eternal spoke unto Moses the man of G-d concerning me and thee,*[144] and it is written there, *And Moses swore on that day, saying: Surely the land whereon thy foot hath trodden shall be an inheritance to thee and to thy children forever, because thou hast wholly followed the Eternal my G-d.*[145] This refers to that which is written here, *But My servant Caleb, because he had another spirit with him, and hath followed Me fully, him will I bring into the Land wherein he went, and his seed shall possess it.*[146] And Caleb [in the Book of Joshua, quoted above] mentioned an oath [*and Moses 'swore'*] in connection with this promise, because it is all joined to the verse, *But in very deed as I live,*[147] which is an oath, as I have explained [above]. Caleb said, *and Moses swore*[145] because Moses mentioned the oath.[148] And by way of the Truth, [the mystic teachings of the Cabala], *But in very deed as I live — and all the earth shall be filled with the Glory of the Eternal* constitutes a promise to Moses about forgiveness, the verse stating that *all the earth shall be filled with* His *Glory* through the seed of these people, but not through them [the generation of the exodus].

(141) II Samuel 3:35. See also Vol. I, pp. 273-274, where Ramban discusses this theme briefly. (142) I Samuel 25:22. (143) That is to say, David pronounced a curse against himself, but did not wish to use an actual curse; therefore he blessed his enemies, so that he would be cursed. Nonetheless he only alluded to it, but did not actually express the blessing. (144) Joshua 14:6. (145) *Ibid.*, Verse 9. (146) Verse 24 here. (147) Verse 21. According to Rashi, however, [see Note 139 above] the oath is completed at the end of Verse 23. Verse 24 promising a reward to Caleb is therefore not part of the oath. But according to Ramban, the Divine oath continues up to the end of Verse 24, and Caleb could therefore properly refer to this promised reward of his as one given by oath. Ramban continues to explain why Caleb mentioned that Moses swore. (148) Further, Verse 39: *And Moses told these words unto all the children of Israel.*

23. NEITHER SHALL ANY OF THEM THAT PROVOKED ME SEE IT. This means "for none of them that provoked Me shall see it." [149] And Rabbi Abraham ibn Ezra commented: "*any that provoked Me* of their children," but this [explanation] makes no sense. Perhaps this expression [*neither shall any of them that provoked Me see it*] alludes to the generations who were to be exiled from the Land [at the time of the destruction of the First Temple], as our Rabbis have said,[150] and it is here that He fixed that night [of the ninth of Ab] as one of weeping throughout their generations, for [on that night] He will remember their first punishment.

24. BUT MY SERVANT CALEB. He did not mention Joshua, for He explained to Caleb his reward [for his trust in G-d], namely that he would inherit *the Land wherein he went,*[146] but Joshua's reward — that he would be the successor to Moses — was not fitting to be specified at this moment [since Moses was still to be the leader for many years]. Now Scripture mentioned [Caleb's name] first, as it says, *save Caleb the son of Jephunneh, and Joshua the son of Nun,*[151] because he was the first to contradict the spies, [as it is said], *And Caleb stilled the people.*[152] But Moses said, *And Joshua the son of Nun, and Caleb the son of Jephunneh lived from the men*[153] [mentioning Joshua first], because of the great degree of Joshua's wisdom. And since [both] *Moses and Aaron fell on their faces before all the assembly of the congregation of the children of Israel*[154] to plead before Him, the communication here was addressed to Aaron[155]

(149) Since it already says in the first half of this verse: *If they shall see the Land* etc., the question arises why the same fact is repeated at the end of the same verse? Ramban answers that the second half is an explanation of the first half. (150) Taanith 29a: "You have wept without cause etc." See Ramban above in Verse 1. (151) Further, Verse 30. (152) Above, 13:30. (153) Further, Verse 38. (154) Above, Verse 5. (155) Verse 26. Since Ramban has explained (above, Verse 5) that the falling on their faces was for the purpose of Moses and Aaron pleading with the people to abandon their plan to return to Egypt, we must understand Ramban's words here as indicating that after having finished their plea with the people they proceeded to pray to G-d in their behalf.

as well, but the command was [only] to Moses, *Say unto them,*[156] since he was superior in prophecy.

28. 'IM LO' (IF NOT) AS YE HAVE SPOKEN IN MINE EARS. The meaning thereof is as an expression of wonder: "Will *I* not *do to you as ye have spoken*?" Such is the way of the [Sacred] Language: [*Thou art sent*] *not to many people of an unintelligible speech and of a slow tongue, whose words thou canst not understand. 'Im lo'* (*would they not*) *have hearkened unto thee if I sent thee to them?*[157] Similarly, *'im lo'* (*if not*) *as I have thought did it come to pass?*[158]

37. AND THOSE MEN, THAT DID BRING FORTH 'DIBATH' (AN EVIL REPORT) OF THE LAND, DIED. I have already explained[159] that their severe punishment was because of the report which they spread that *it is a Land that eateth up the inhabitants thereof,*[159] which was a complete falsehood since the Land was full with many people, as it is written in the Book of Joshua, *And they went out, they and all their hosts with them, much people, even as the sand that is upon the sea-shore in multitude, with horses and chariots very many.*[160] And in the Torah it is written, *and He shall cast out many nations before thee . . . seven nations greater and mightier than thou.*[161] The spies also emphasized the strength of the people, saying: *the people are fierce,*[162] and *they are* very *strong,*[163] and did not report back concerning the words of Moses who told them [to ascertain] *whether they are few or many,*[164] but they told the people afterwards that the *Land* is one that *eateth up the inhabitants thereof!*[159]

Now Rashi commented:[165] "Whenever Scripture uses the expression

(156) Verse 28. The Hebrew *emor* (say) is in the singular — a reference to Moses. (157) Ezekiel 3:5-6. (158) Isaiah 14:24. (159) Above, 13:32. (160) Joshua 11:4. (161) Deuteronomy 7:1. (162) Above, 13:28. (163) *Ibid.*, Verse 31: *for they are stronger than we.* (164) *Ibid.*, Verse 18. (165) On Verse 36: *And they* [the spies] *made all the congregation to murmur against him by bringing forth 'dibah' against the Land.*

'he brings forth *dibah*' it means bringing forth words which 'capture' a person so that he speaks about it, just like *'doveiv' (stirring) the lips of those that are asleep.*[166] And [the expression 'bringing forth *dibah'*] may be for good, or for evil. That is why it says [*the men . . . that did bring forth an " 'evil' dibath" (report of) the Land,*[167] because there may be a *dibah* which is good." [Thus far is the language of Rashi.] But it is written: *he that bringeth forth 'dibah' is a fool,*[168] and this cannot [refer] to a good [utterance]. Similarly, *bringing forth 'dibah' against the Land,*[169] and so also, *'v'dibathcha' (and thine utterance of 'dibah') he will not turn away*[170] — all signify speech of evil, as the term *dibah* itself connotes evil, and when Scripture uses the expression *dibah ra'ah* ["evil *dibah,*" as it does in our verse: *and those men that did bring up 'dibath ha'aretz ra'ah' (an evil report of the Land) died*] it is to emphasize the greatness of the evil that they did.

41. WHY NOW DO YE TRANSGRESS THE COMMANDMENT OF THE ETERNAL? This does not refer to the [Divine] decree which He mentioned [previously] that *your carcasses shall fall in this wilderness,*[171] but it means: "*Why do ye transgress the commandment of the Eternal:* for He has commanded me that you should not go up at all, *that ye be not smitten down before your enemies.*"[172] And similarly Moses said in the Book of Deuteronomy, *And ye deemed it a light thing to go up into the hill-country. And the Eternal said unto me: 'Say unto them: Go not up, neither fight; for I am not among you; lest ye be smitten before your enemies.'*[173]

'V'HI' (AND IT) SHALL NOT SUCCEED. "This [attempt] that you are making[174] will not succeed." This is Rashi's language. Or it

(166) Song of Songs 7:10. (167) Verse 37 here. (168) Proverbs 10:18. See Ramban above, 13:32. (169) Verse 36. (170) Proverbs 25:10. (171) Above Verse 32. (172) Verse 42. (173) Deuteronomy 1:41-42. (174) Since the verse does not contain a noun to which the feminine pronoun *v'hi* [literally: "and she"] can refer, Rashi interprets it as referring to "this attempt that you are making." Ramban suggests two other explanations.

may mean that "the violation of G-d's commandment does not carry with it success," as Rabbi Abraham ibn Ezra wrote. By way of the Truth, [the mystic teachings of the Cabala, this is like] *'hi' mithhalecheth' (she moved to and fro) between the living creatures*].[175]

15 2. WHEN YE ARE COME INTO THE LAND OF YOUR HABITATIONS. After He had assured the children [of those who had left Egypt] that they would come into the Land,[176] He completed [telling] them the laws of the offerings, and that they should bring the drink-offerings when they enter the Land. Perhaps this [section] was [told to them] now in order to console them and give them an assurance [that they would indeed take possession of the Land], for they began to give up hope, saying: "Who knows what will happen in such a long time — after forty years — for may be the children will also sin?" Therefore the Holy One, blessed be He, saw fit to comfort them, for by commanding them precepts which are applicable [only] in the Land, He thereby was assuring them that it is clearly destined by Him that they will come into and inherit the Land.

Now He commanded them concerning the drink-offerings [that they were to bring] in the Land when making burnt-offerings and peace-offerings, since in the wilderness they had no duty to bring drink-offerings except with the continual [daily] burnt-offering, concerning which it is said, *and the fourth part of a hin of wine for a drink-offering for the one sheep;*[177] for there it is said [that it be brought continually every day] *at the door of the Tent of Meeting before the Eternal, where I will meet with you, to speak there unto thee.*[178] Similarly the princes when bringing their dedication-offerings[179] did not include amongst them drink-offerings.

Now our Rabbis differed on this matter. Some of them said in the

(175) Ezekiel 1:13. The pronoun *v'hi* thus refers back to the *pi Hashem* ("the commandment of the Eternal") which, when violated cannot bring success, *for the Eternal is not among you* (Verse 42 — Abusaula). (176) Above, 14:31. (177) Exodus 29:40. (178) *Ibid.*, Verse 42. (179) Above, 7:12-83.

Sifre[180] that Scripture here teaches us that they only became obliged to bring drink-offerings from the time that they came into the Land onwards etc.; but some of them said that it is [only] the individual who was not obliged to bring drink-offerings [together with his offering] until they entered the Land [but public offerings were always accompanied by drink-offerings].

He also completed [here] the laws relating to the priests by commanding the [duty of the] dough-offering,[181] which was not applicable in the wilderness, for it was already known that the heave-offering and the tithes do not apply there, since such produce was winnowed by non-Jews and [grown] outside the Land of Israel. There is also a difference in the opinion of the Rabbis[182] concerning the [law of the] dough-offering [which is different from that of tithes etc.], namely that they became subject to the law of the dough-offering as soon as they entered the Land, but were not liable to [separate] tithes and the heave-offering until after [the fourteen years of] the conquest and settlement [of the Land].

22. AND WHEN YE SHALL ERR, AND NOT OBSERVE ALL THESE COMMANDMENTS. This section is obscure in meaning, and the commentators of the plain meaning of Scripture[183] have mistakenly explained it as referring to an offering which must be brought by one who has unwittingly failed to observe what G-d has commanded him to do. But these words are *words of wind*! [184] For if so, there would be an obligation to bring an offering for any of the positive commandments of the Torah, if a person did not fulfill them all and *unwittingly* [neglected to do] any one of them, and there would [also] be the punishment of excision[185] for anyone who does not fulfill them all, that is, who neglected *knowingly* to do [any] one of them, since Scripture states, *even all that the Eternal hath commanded him*

(180) Sifre, *Shelach* 107. (181) Further, Verses 17;21. (182) Sifre, *Shelach* 110. (183) A veiled reference to Ibn Ezra, who [in Verse 27] interprets the verse in this way. — But this is obviously not the accepted law. See Vol. III, pp. 11-13, with the respective notes. (184) Job 16:3. (185) Further, Verses 30-31.

unto you![186] Moreover, He stated here, *And it shall be if it be 'done' in error by the congregation,*[187] [clearly indicating] that the error consists of a [positive] act which they did, and not of sitting back and failing to act! Similarly, *But the soul that 'doeth' ought with a high hand*[188] [which also indicates that the sin consisted of *doing* something which the Torah prohibited]. But the meaning [of the verse before us] is: "*When ye shall err and not observe* what G-d has commanded [you to do], but you do the opposite." Or it [may be that the verse] is stating that [if] "*ye shall err and not observe* His commandments, namely those things that He has commanded you *not* to do," since matters prohibited by a negative commandment are also called "commandments," just as He said, *If any one shall sin through error against any of 'the commandments' of the Eternal concerning things which ought not to be done.*[189] Now this offering [mentioned here] which the congregation has to bring when sinning in error is different from the offering mentioned in the section of *Vayikra,* for there He commanded [the congregation] to bring *a bullock for a sin-offering,*[190] and here He commanded them to bring *a bullock for a burnt-offering and a he-goat for a sin-offering.*[191] Therefore our Rabbis had to say that this offering [mentioned here] applies only to worshipping idols in error [and hence has a stricter form of atonement].

The language of the verses [here] without being taken out of its simple meaning and implication is [to be understood as if] He were saying: "*And when ye shall err* in *all* the commandments, and transgress *all* that G-d has commanded you *by the hand of Moses,*[186] inasmuch as you will not do *anything* of that which He has commanded you, then you shall bring this offering." Therefore He does not mention here, as He does with reference to those offerings [brought] for [committing a particular] sin, *'any of all the commandments' of the Eternal*[192] [since the reference here is to transgressing *all* the commandments, and not just one of them, as is explained further on]. Thus this section according to its plain meaning

(186) Verse 23. (187) Verse 24. (188) Further, Verse 30. (189) Leviticus 4:2. (190) *Ibid.*, Verse 14. (191) Verse 24 here. (192) Leviticus 4:13.

refers to [the duty of] one who is unwittingly an "apostate" with regard to the entire Torah, [to bring] an offering, such as one who goes and becomes assimilated amongst one of the nations, and behaves as they do and does not want to be part of Israel at all. This applies if it was all done in error, such as — in the case of an individual — a child who was taken into captivity among the nations [and grew up unaware of his Jewish origin], and in the case of the community, if they [mistakenly] thought that the time of the Torah had already passed, and that it was not given for all generations; or if they say — as is mentioned in the Sifre[193] — " 'Why did G-d give [the Torah]? Was it not so that we should observe it and be rewarded for it? We will not observe it, and will take no reward!' This is similar to that which the Israelites said and asked of Ezekiel, as it is stated, *certain of the elders of Israel came to inquire of the Eternal and sat before me.*[194] They said to him: 'Our master Ezekiel: A slave that was sold by his master, does he not go out of his control?' [195] etc." Or [the section here may refer to a time] when people forget the Torah. This has already happened to us, because of our sins, for in the days of the wicked kings [of the kingdom] of Israel, such as Jeroboam, most of the people forgot the Torah and the commandments completely, as is mentioned [also] — in the Book of Ezra[196] concerning the people of the Second Temple.

(193) Sifre, *Shelach* 115. (194) Ezekiel 20:1. (195) The implication is that the Babylonian exile constituted "a sale" to another "master," and therefore they were released from the authority of the Torah. The answer was given by Isaiah: *Thus saith the Eternal: Where is the bill of your mother's divorcement, wherewith I have put her away? Or which of My creditors is it to whom I have sold you?* (50:1). The exile was thus no "sale" of Israel. Instead, it continues to be G-d's people and duty-bound to keep His commandments. (196) Nehemiah 8:14-17. *And they found written in the Torah, how that the Eternal had commanded by Moses, that the children of Israel dwell in Booths . . . And all the congregation of them that were come back out of the captivity made Booths, and dwelt in the Booths* etc. It is thus clear that the majority of the people had forgotten this commandment. See my Hebrew commentary p. 252, for a further elucidation of this point. It is important to point out that Ramban is referring only to the majority of the ordinary people, but of course even in the dark times of the kingdom of Israel, there were a significant number of individuals, who observed every commandment of the Torah. — [Ramban here calls the Book of Nehemiah "Ezra," because it was Ezra who wrote it (Baba Bathra 15a). It is generally referred to, as such by many commentators (see e.g., Rashi on Succah 12a)].

This, then, is the purport of our verse, for the "error" mentioned here refers to the totality of the Torah and the commandments. Therefore our Rabbis singled out one commandment, through the unwitting violation of which a person goes out of the community of Israel and all that they have been commanded, namely worshipping idols. The explanation of the verse is thus: "*And when ye shall err, to walk after other gods,*[197] *and not observe* one [particular] thing [which is in itself a denial] of *all the commandments* of the Eternal;" because one who acknowledges any divinity apart from Him, has already rendered meaningless *all* that *the Glorious Name*[198] has commanded, whether positive commandments or negative commandments, since if there were to be a deity other than Him, then the [duty of] fearing Him and [keeping] His commandments and all the obligations they entail are of no consequence.

This section thus comes to complete the laws of the priests with the law of one who worships idols in error, for this book [of Numbers] completes the laws of the offerings, as I have explained.[199] It was put in here because the people [after hearing the false report of the spies] rebelled against the word of G-d, and said, *Let us make a captain, and let us return into Egypt,*[200] which means to remain in Egypt as they were originally, without Torah and without the commandments. The section thus comes to inform them that even in the case of idolatry, He forgives those who are in error, but those *who do it in a high hand*[201] He will cut them off [from among their people]. I have already explained in *Seder Acharei Moth*[202] the meaning of this excision.

25. AND THEY HAVE BROUGHT THEIR OFFERING, AN OFFERING MADE BY FIRE UNTO THE ETERNAL. This refers to the *bullock* as *a burnt-offering* mentioned [in the preceding verse]. AND THEIR SIN-OFFERING, which refers to the *he-goat for a sin-*

(197) Deuteronomy 11:28. (198) *Ibid.,* 28:58. (199) In the Introduction to this book, p. 4. (200) Above, 14:4. (201) Verse 30. (202) Leviticus 18:29, see Vol. III, pp. 275-9.

offering [mentioned there]. Scripture states this on account of the greatness of the sin, involving as it does all the commandments of G-d, and is thereby saying that although the sin was exceedingly grave, since it was in error *and they have brought their offerings* for it, the burnt-offering and the sin-offering, they are worthy of atonement. And in the Sifre[203] the Rabbis interpreted this verse on the basis of its [apparent] redundancy: "Rabbi Yashiyah says: If the whole of one tribe [unwittingly] acted [committed idolatry] on the basis of a [mistaken] decision of the [chief] court of that tribe, and the other tribes did so [too, on their word], whence do we know that they [the other tribes] must also bring [these prescribed offerings] on account of them [i.e., the people of the particular tribe who acted according to the decision of its chief court]? Scripture therefore states, *'and they' have brought their offering, an offering made by fire unto the Eternal.* Rabbi Yonathan says etc." [204]

And by way of the Truth, [the mystic teachings of the Cabala], I have already informed you[205] that wherever the Tetragrammaton is mentioned it refers to the attribute of mercy, and the expression *'liphnei Hashem'* [*before the Eternal* — as here in the phrase: *and their sin-offering 'before the Eternal'*] is like *'al panai'* (*before Me*),[206] and this is similar to what the Rabbis of blessed memory have said: [207] "He and His Celestial Court." Thus the verse is stating that "*they have brought their offering* to the Proper Name of G-d [i.e., the Tetragrammaton],[208] and *their sin-offering 'l'phanai'* (*before Me*)," and thus the sin is atoned for in the attribute of mercy and in the

(203) Sifre, *Shelach* 111. (204) Rabbi Yonathan is of the opinion that if the people erred on the basis of the decision of the chief court of a particular tribe, then only the members of that tribe must bring these offerings, but not the other tribes [as is the opinion of Rabbi Yashiyah]. It is only if a wrong decision was [mistakenly] given by the Great Court of seventy-one judges — the supreme court of all Israel — and one tribe acted upon this decision, that all the other tribes must also participate in these offerings, according to Rabbi Yonathan (Malbim *ibid.*). (205) Exodus 20:3; 25:30. (206) *Ibid.*, 20:3. Literally "upon My face." (207) Bereshith Rabbah 51:3. See Vol. I, p. 260. (208) This is indicated by the first part of the verse, *and they have brought their offering, 'isheh Lashem'* (*an*

attribute of judgment. He mentioned this in the case of idolatry [due to the gravity of the sin, because of which they need to be forgiven in both attributes], but in *Seder Vayikra* where [the sin-offering for violation of] the other commandments is commanded, He mentioned many times *'liphnei Hashem'* (*before the Eternal*).[209] and the reason for this is clear.

26. AND THE STRANGER THAT SOJOURNETH AMONG THEM. He mentioned "the stranger" because they are always more liable to stumble in this sin [of idolatry] and thereby to cause Israel to stumble [with them].

31. HIS INIQUITY SHALL BE UPON HIM. "This means only as long as his iniquity is upon him, but not after he has repented." This is Rashi's language, from the words of our Rabbis.[210]

According to the plain meaning of Scripture, this expression [*his iniquity shall be upon him*] is like: *their blood shall be upon them;*[211] *they shall bear their sin; they shall die childless;*[212] *he hath uncovered his sister's nakedness; he shall bear his iniquity,*[213] [the meaning of all these verses being that the guilty have brought the punishment upon themselves]. Now I have seen in the Pirkei Derech Eretz[214] [the following text]: "What is [the meaning of the expression], *his iniquity shall be upon him?* It teaches us that the soul is cut off, and [yet] its

offering made by fire to the Eternal) where the Hebrew for *the Eternal* is the Tetragrammaton. Ramban explained at the beginning of his commentary on this verse that *their offering* refers to the burnt-offering, which was thus offered to the Tetragrammaton, the Divine Name symbolizing G-d's attribute of mercy; and the second half of the verse speaks of *sin-offering* brought *l'phanai,* i.e., to the Name symbolizing the attribute of judgment. Hence [in the concluding words of Ramban] "the sin is atoned for in the attribute of mercy and in the attribute of judgment." (209) Leviticus 4:4, 6, 7, 15, 17, 24. In all these cases only the Tetragrammaton, symbolizing the attribute of mercy, is used. See Vol. III, pp. 21-25 for fuller discussion of this theme. (210) Shebuoth 13a. (211) Leviticus 20:27. (212) *Ibid.,* Verse 20. (213) *Ibid.,* Verse 17. (214) This is also quoted therefrom by the Ricanti. I have not found it in our texts of this treatise.

iniquity is upon it." That is to say, the sin attaches to it [the soul] even after it is cut off, and it is punished in suffering forever, similar to [the verse], *for their worm shall not die, neither shall their fire be quenched.*[215]

He placed next to this section the subject of the man who gathered sticks [on the Sabbath day] because it happened at this time, after the incident of the spies — this in accordance with the plain meaning of Scripture. And this is the meaning of [the phrase], *and while the children of Israel were in the wilderness,*[216] for it was because the people tarried there on account of the above-mentioned decree, that this event happened. Afterwards He commanded the precept of *Tzitzith* (Fringes) in order that they would remember through it all the commandments, and not forget the Sabbath [as did the man who gathered the sticks], or any of the other Commandments.

Now the reason why *Tzitzith* have this [power of] reminding one of all the commandments is, as Rashi wrote,[217] because the total numerical value of the letters of the [Scriptural] word *tzitzith* is six hundred, and together with the eighth threads and five knots, you have six hundred and thirteen [corresponding to *taryag,* the six hundred and thirteen commandments]. But I have not understood this, for the word *tzitzith* in the Torah is written without a [second] *yod,*[218] so the total numerical value is only five hundred and ninety! Moreover, the number of threads [to be used for each of the Fringes] in the opinion of the school of Hillel[219] is only three [which, when passed through the hole at the corner form six threads — not eight, as Rashi mentioned], and the knots by law of the Torah [need only] be two; as the Rabbis have said: [220] "You must deduce from this that the upper knots in the Fringes are required by Scriptural law. For if you

(215) Isaiah 66:24. (216) Verse 32. (217) In Verse 39. (218) It is written with these letters: *tzade* = 90, *yod* = 10, *tzade* = 90, *tav* = 400. The sum total is thus 590 [and not 600 as Rashi wrote]. (219) Menachoth 41b. (220) *Ibid.*, 39a. See Vol. III, pp. 298-9, Notes 116-19, where this whole text of the Talmud is fully explained.

should think that they are not obligatory by Scriptural law, why then did the Torah have to state a [special] permission to use mingled stuff [of wool and linen] in Fringes! Do we not accept as the established law that if one joins two pieces together with only one stitch, it is not considered joined?"

Rather, the remembrance [of the commandments] is through the blue thread, which alludes to the all-inclusive attribute, which is *bakol*[221] and which is the aim of All. Therefore He said, *that ye may look upon it, and remember 'kol' (all)*,[222] which is *the commandments of the Eternal.* This is why the Rabbis said: [223] "[Why was blue chosen rather than any other color?] Because blue resembles the sea, the sea resembles heaven, and heaven resembles the Throne of Glory, etc." The likeness is in the name,[224] as also in the shade of the color which is the termination of all colors [and which leads one from the blue in the Fringes to the blue of the sea etc., and finally to think of Him Who is on high], for in the distance all colors appear to be that shade. That is why it is called *t'cheileth* [which is also suggestive of the word *tachlith* (termination) since this is the end of all colors]. Scripture states, *and that ye go not after your own heart,*[222] in order that one should take care concerning it and not err through it.[225] It is for this reason that our Rabbis have interpreted: [226] "*After your own heart.* This refers to scepticism. *After which ye use to go astray.* This refers to idolatry." That is to say, through the *t'cheileth* he should not think [in his heart] of any scepticism or idolatry, but it *shall* all *be unto you for 'tzitzith' — that ye may look upon it, and remember.* The Rabbis have also said: [226] "*After your own eyes.* This refers to immorality," similar to

(221) See Vol. I, pp. 290-291. (222) Verse 39 here. — And since *Kol* (All) is the all-inclusive attribute it therefore contains *all the commandments of the Eternal,* and hence the Rabbis have said that the commandment of *Tzitzith* is of equal importance to the total number of the commandments (Beiur Ha'lvush to Ricanti, quoting the text of Ramban). (223) Menachoth 43b. (224) Since the word *t'cheileth* contains in it the word *kol* (all) it alludes by its very name to that all-inclusive attribute of *Kol.* (225) I.e., by "mutilating the shoots" of faith, and thereby undermining the principle of the Unity (Tziyoni). See further my Hebrew commentary, p. 254, and see also Vol. I, p. 155. (226) Sifre, *Shelach* 115; Berachoth 12a.

that which is written, *I am He that knoweth, and am witness, saith the Eternal.*[227] The student learned [in the mysteries of the Cabala] will understand.

In the Midrash of Rabbi Nechunya the son of Hakanah[228] it is stated with reference to the verse, *and the profit of 'eretz' (earth) is 'bakol' (in all)*:[229] "And what is the *eretz*? It is that from which the heavens were hewn, and it is the Throne of the Holy One, blessed be He, and it is 'the precious stone,' and 'the sea of wisdom,'[230] and corresponding to it is the blue thread in a garment of Fringes, for Rabbi Meir has said: 'Why was blue chosen? etc.' " [as quoted above].

(227) Jeremiah 29:23. (228) Sefer Habahir, 96. (229) Ecclesiastes 5:8. (230) These are Cabalistic synonyms for the all-inclusive attribute of *Kol.* — The Ma'or V'shamesh [a commentary by Shem Tob ben Gaon on the Cabalistic passages in Ramban's commentary] continues, on this basis, to explain a basic law in the commandment of *Tzitzith,* namely, that it applies only at daytime and not at night. Thus he writes: "Hence [i.e., since the *t'cheileth* in the Fringes represents the all-inclusive attribute, and we are commanded to *look upon it, and remember* etc.] the commandment applies only at daytime and not at night, for at night physical features are indistinguishable and nothing can be seen in its entirety, while only at daytime the wholeness and perfect harmony of the *t'cheileth* can be seen and contemplated for its profound meaning]."

Korach

16 1. 'VAYIKACH KORACH' (AND KORACH TOOK). "This section is explained in a beautiful way in the Midrash of Rabbi Tanchuma.[1] *Vayikach Korach*—he betook himself[2] to one side in order to separate himself from the [rest of the] congregation so that he could contend for the priesthood [which Moses had conferred upon Aaron and his sons, and Korach claimed that it belonged to all Israel]. This is [also] Onkelos' intention in translating [the word *vayikach* as] *v'ithpleig*—'he separated himself' from the congregation to persist in his contention. Similarly, *Why 'yikachacha' thy heart?*[3] means: [Why does your heart] 'carry you away' to separate yourself from the rest of the people?"

(1) The Rabbis of the Talmud composed two great exegetical commentaries on the Bible, whose aim was to spread moral, ethical and religious teachings, as they are derived from a study of the Scriptures. These are the Midrash Rabbah and Midrash Tanchuma, both works of Palestinian Rabbis. The Midrash Rabbah is on the Five Books of Moses and the five Scrolls. As its name *Rabbah* (Great), indicates, it is the largest homiletical work of the Rabbis of the Talmud. Next in importance is the Midrash Tanchuma on the Five Books of Moses, composed by Rabbi Tanchuma ben Abba, of the fourth century of the Common Era. This Midrash was very popular, and Rashi relies upon it for a great deal of Agadic material, which he often incorporates into his commentary. On the relationship of the Midrash Tanchuma to Midrash Yelamdeinu, see Volume II, *Seder Bo,* p. 131, Note 196. (2) Since the object of the verb [*vayikach* — "and he took"] is not mentioned in the verse, Rashi explains that it is reflexive in meaning, referring to Korach himself: "Korach betook himself to one side etc." Ramban suggests a number of other possible interpretations. (3) Job 15:12. These are the words of Eliphaz the Temanite, when criticizing Job for lack of trust in G-d.

But the opinion of the Midrash [Tanchuma quoted further on] is not in accordance with the Rabbi's [i.e., Rashi's] interpretation,[4] for the Rabbis have said there: "The term *vayikach* always denotes 'division,' [and here it means] that his heart took control of him, in a similar manner to that which it says, *Why 'yikachacha' thy heart?"* [3] The verse thus does not mean to say that Korach betook himself [physically] to one side [of the camp]. Similarly, *Why 'yikachacha' thy heart?* [3] does not mean that it [your heart] takes you to one side to separate yourself [physically] from other people. Instead, the meaning of the [interpretation of the] Midrash on [the phrase] *Vayikach Korach* is that he took counsel in his heart to do that which [Scripture] relates [subsequently], for [the term] "taking" applies also to counsel and thought. Similarly, *Why 'yikachacha' thy heart?* [3] means: "What thought does your heart lead you to, that you should be thinking secretly: 'There is no justice nor Judge,' and you do not reveal it? Or, *and why do thine eyes wink?,*[3] for one can notice from your winkings that you deny G-d's justice, but you do not utter [that belief] openly, but [instead] you complain [of injustice], as one who conceals his intent." Eliphaz said this to Job before Job explained his thoughts in a clearly-expressed statement, [saying] that the Creator's concern does not extend to the individuals of the lower beings [of each species]. Therefore Eliphaz said to Job: *And thou sayest: 'What doth G-d know? Can He judge through the dark cloud?'* [5] This is the true meaning of that reply [of Eliphaz to Job: *Why 'yikachacha' thy heart? and why do thine eyes wink?* [3] — as is apparent] to one who considers it carefully. Similarly we find the term "taking" used of "thinking": *'k'chu' (take) my instruction;* [6] *nor 'kachath' (to take) instruction.* [7]

(4) Ramban understood Rashi's comment as meaning that Korach betook himself *physically* and left his tent, setting up his quarters outside the camp in order to gather people together to rally to him in his dispute with Moses. In Ramban's opinion, however, the Midrash clearly means that Korach's heart stirred him up to revolt (Mizrachi), but not that he betook himself elsewhere physically. See also my Hebrew commentary, pp. 254-255. (5) Job 22:13. (6) Proverbs. 8:10. This clearly cannot refer to taking physically, but means: "think of my instruction and guide your conduct accordingly." (7) Jeremiah 17:23.

The Rabbis have further said in the Midrash: [8] "Scripture does not state here: And Korach 'quarelled,' or 'spoke,' or 'commanded,' but it says *vayikach* (*and he took*). What did he take? He did not take anything; rather, it was his heart that took [control of] him, just as Scripture says, *Why doth thy heart take thee?*" [3] This [Midrash] coincides with what I have explained. And Onkelos who translated: [*vayikach* as] *v'ithpleig* ("and he separated himself") explained the [expression according to its] general meaning, not according to its literal sense, as is his habit in many places. Thus also he translated [the expression] *about 'd'var' (the matter of) Korach*[9] as "about 'the strife' of Korach," while *'bi'dvar' (the matter of) Balaam*[10] he translated as "through 'the counsel' of Balaam," because he mentions the [whole] subject-matter in his translation [rather than the literal meaning, as illustrated by the change in the translation of the word *d'var* in the above example].

And Rabbi Abraham ibn Ezra wrote: "*And Korach took* [means he took] 'men,' the phrase being elliptical, as in: *chamor lechem*[11] [literally: 'an ass of bread,' which means: 'an ass laden with bread']." Others[12] explain that [the word] *v'dathan* (*and Dathan*) [in the phrase: *And Korach took . . . and Dathan*] is like the verse, *And these are the children of Zibeon: 'and' Ajah, and Anah*[13] [where the letter *vav* in the word *v'ayah* is redundant, and here too the *vav* in *v'dathan* is redundant], and its correct meaning is thus: "*and Korach took* Dathan and Abiram" [*and they rose up before Moses*]. But in my opinion there is no need for [these interpretations], for it is quite correct for the [Sacred] Language to say: "and Korach took and Dathan, *and they rose,*[14] *and they assembled themselves together against Moses and against Aaron,*" [15] because the [word] "taking" always occurs at the beginning of an event, being an expression of

(8) Bamidmar Rabbah 18:13. (9) Further, 17:14. (10) *Ibid.,* 31:16. (11) I Samuel 16:20. (12) This interpretation I have found in the commentary of Chizkuni. See Genesis, Vol. I p. 298, Note 109, where the same expression "Others" also refers to Chizkuni. (13) Genesis 36:24. See Vol. I, p. 440. (14) Verse 2. (15) Verse 3.

taking action to [do] that deed. Similarly, *And Absalom in his lifetime had 'taken' and reared up for himself the pillar*[16] [which means that "he bestirred himself" to set up the pillar]. And if you prefer to explain that the term "taking" refers to the object mentioned subsequently, [so that the verse quoted means]: "and Absalom took the pillar and reared it up for himself in his lifetime" — you may likewise explain [our phrase] "and Korach took" [as referring to] the *men of the children of Israel, two hundred and fifty,*[14] *and they rose up before Moses, and they assembled themselves together against Moses and against Aaron.*[15]

Rabbi Abraham ibn Ezra wrote that this incident [of Korach's rebellion] happened in the wilderness of Sinai when the firstborns were exchanged [for the Levites] [17] and the Levites were separated [to do the Divine service in the Tent of Meeting],[18] for [some] Israelites thought that Moses our master did this of his own accord so that he could bestow greatness upon his brother [Aaron] and on the children of Kohath who were his relatives,[19] and on all the Levites, since they were of his family. The Levites [nevertheless] joined the conspiracy against him [Moses] because they were *given to Aaron and to his sons,*[20] and Dathan and Abiram [who were of the tribe of Reuben] joined in the rebellion because Moses took away the right of the firstborn from their ancestor Reuben [and gave it to Joseph].[21] Korach too was a firstborn.[22] [Thus far are Ibn Ezra's comments.] Now all this

(16) II Samuel 18:18. (17) Above, 3:44-51. (18) *Ibid.,* 8:5-22. (19) Kohath was Moses' grandfather. Since Kohath had three other sons beside Amram — namely, Itzhar, Hebron, and Uzziel (above, 3:19) — some people thought that Moses gave the Kohathites special distinction in the Tabernacle service of his own accord (see above, Chapter 4:1-20) because they were his relatives. In actual fact, of course, he did everything by Divine command (see above, 3:40, 4:1 and 8:5). (20) Above, 8:19. (21) See (Genesis), Vol. I, pp. 570-572. Here the reference is to the fact that Moses considered Joseph's sons, Ephraim and Menasheh, as two separate tribes, and Dathan and Abiram claimed that this distinction should have been conferred upon Reuben the firstborn. (22) Exodus 6:21 — *And the sons of Itzhar: Korach, and Nepheg, and Zichri.* — Now before the Tabernacle was set up, the service of the offerings was performed by any of the firstborn in Israel (Zebachim 112b), but

is based on the opinion of Rabbi Abraham ibn Ezra [himself] who has said in many places, as it pleases him, that there is no strict chronological order in the [narrative of the] Torah, but I have already written[23] that in my opinion the whole Torah follows the chronological sequence, except for those places where Scripture [itself] expressly states the "earlier" and the "later," [24] and even then it is [only changed] for a particular purpose and for good reason. But this matter [i.e., the rebellion of Korach] happened *in the wilderness of Paran,*[25] in *Kadesh-barnea,*[26] after the incident of the spies [and not, as Ibn Ezra wrote, before the sending of the spies].

A correct interpretation by way of homiletic exposition is that Korach became angry because of the status of prince [of the Kohathites] [27] bestowed [by Moses] upon Elizaphan, as our Rabbis have said,[28] and he was also jealous of Aaron, as it is said, *and seek ye the priesthood also!*[29] Dathan and Abiram [who were of the tribe of Reuben] were attracted to Korach, but not because of the [loss of their] birthright, for it was their father Jacob who had deprived Reuben of it and given it to Joseph; [30] however, they too, voiced their

afterwards it was performed only by priests. As a firstborn, Korach was thus personally amongst those deprived of his prerogative under the new order established by Moses. (23) In (Exodus), Vol. II, pp. 252, 419, and in Leviticus 8:2. Here too, Ramban's objection is that according to Ibn Ezra the rebellion of Korach took place when Israel was still encamped in the wilderness of Sinai although their departure from there has already been recorded long ago (above, 10:12)! Since then there had already been many other stages in their journey through the desert (see e.g. above, 11:35, 12:16)! (24) I.e., if the verses clearly state the dates. See, for example, the section commencing above in Chapter 9, where the date given is clearly *before* the date of the previous chapters (see Chapter 1, Verse 1). (25) Above, 12:16. (26) Deuteronomy 1:19. It is from Kadesh-barnea that they sent the spies, as related in the Book of Deuteronomy, *ibid.* (27) Above, 3:30. (28) Said Korach: "My grandfather Kohath had four sons: Amram, Itzhar, Hebron and Uzziel (Exodus 6:18). The two sons of Amram, the eldest, namely Moses and Aaron, assumed the royalty and the priesthood. Who is entitled to the next rank — the prince of the Kohathites — if not I, the eldest of the second son of Kohath, Itzhar? And yet he [i.e., Moses] went and appointed Elizaphan, whose father was Uzziel, the youngest son of my grandfather!" (Tanchuma *Korach* 1, mentioned by Rashi). (29) Further, Verse 10. (30) Genesis 48:5.

complaint [by saying that Moses had taken the people out of Egypt] *to kill us in the wilderness,*[31] and *moreover thou hast not brought us into a land flowing with milk and honey.*[32] Now as long as Israel was in the wilderness of Sinai no evil happening befell them, for even after the incident of the [golden] calf, which was a serious and well-known sin, those who died [as a punishment] were few, and the people were saved by Moses' prayer when he *fell down before the Eternal the forty days and forty nights.*[33] Thus they loved Moses as [they loved] themselves, and they obeyed him, so that had anybody rebelled against Moses at that time, the people would have stoned him. Therefore Korach endured the greatness of Aaron [when he was appointed High Priest], and the firstborns accepted [without protest] the high status of the Levites, and all [the other] acts of Moses. But when they came to *the wilderness of Paran*[25] and [some people] were burnt in Taberah,[34] and many died in Kibroth-hattaavah,[35] and when after sinning [in the matter of] the spies Moses did not pray on their behalf,[36] so that the decree against them was thus not annulled, and the princes of all the tribes *died by the plague before the Eternal*[37] and it was decreed that the whole people would be consumed in the wilderness *and there they shall die,*[38] then the mood of the whole people became embittered, and they said in their hearts that mishaps occur to them through Moses' words. Therefore Korach found it an opportune occasion to contest Moses' deeds, thinking that the people would [readily] listen to him. This was the intention of [the statement of Dathan and Abiram that Moses had taken the people out of Egypt] *to kill us in the wilderness,*[31] meaning: "Behold, you have brought us to this place and you have not fulfilled that which you promised to give us, [namely to take us to] *a land flowing with milk and honey,*[32] for you have not given us any inheritance at all; instead we will die in the wilderness and be wiped out there, for our children will also never come out of

(31) Further, Verse 13. (32) *Ibid.*, Verse 14. (33) Deuteronomy 9:25. (34) Above, 11:3. (35) *Ibid.*, Verse 34. (36) See Ramban above, 14:17 (towards the end) who explains the reason for this. (37) *Ibid.*, Verse 37. (38) *Ibid.*, Verse 35.

the wilderness, and that which you promised our children will also not be fulfilled, just as it did not come to realization with respect to their parents." This then was the reason why they murmured particularly at this juncture immediately after the [Divine] decree because of the spies. It is likely that all those who assembled [against Moses] were firstborns, and therefore they were annoyed about the priesthood [which was taken away from them],[39] and that is why Moses told them to take censers [and put incense upon them [40] as they used formerly to do, and it would become clear thereby whether G-d preferred them or the priests.

4. AND WHEN MOSES HEARD IT, HE FELL UPON HIS FACE. It does not say "and *they* fell [upon their faces]," for Aaron in his modesty and holiness did not utter a word throughout this whole controversy, *but he was as one that held his peace,*[41] and who admits that Korach's status was greater than his own, and he only acted according to Moses' behest, fulfilling the king's decree.

5. IN THE MORNING THE ETERNAL WILL MAKE KNOWN WHO ARE HIS — "for the Levitical service. AND WHO IS HOLY — for the priesthood." This is Rashi's language. He has explained it well; and the verse is thus stating that G-d will make it known if the Levites *are His,* just as it is said, *and the Levites shall be Mine,*[42] or whether the firstborns *are* still *His,* just as it is said, *for all the firstborn are Mine,*[43] so that He will not exchange them for the Levites. *And who is holy,* this refers to the priests who are sanctified for the Divine Service, just as it is said, *and Aaron was separated, that he should be sanctified as most holy.*[44] [He mentioned the Levites] because Korach, in [his attempt] to rally all the people to his side, contested also the [position of the] Levites, and tried to restore the entire service [of the offerings] to the firstborns. And then when these firstborns were burnt up,[45] it

(39) See Note 22 above. (40) Further, Verses 6-7. (41) I Samuel 10:27. (42) Above, 8:14. (43) *Ibid.,* 3:13. (44) I Chronicles 23:13. (45) Further, Verse 35.

became clear that G-d did not choose them for the service, but when Aaron's [burning of the] incense was accepted, it became known that he is the holy one [selected for the priesthood].

EVEN HIM WHOM HE HATH CHOSEN WILL HE CAUSE TO COME NEAR UNTO HIM. The meaning of this repetition [since the first half of this verse already says, *and who is holy, He will cause him to come near unto Him*] is that [at first Moses said] *the Eternal will make known who are His, and who is holy, and will cause him to come near unto Him* tomorrow, and He will have regard for his offering,[46] whereas He will not turn to the others and to their offerings. *Even him whom He hath chosen* forever *to stand to minister* before Him, *him and his* seed *forever,*[47] *will He cause to come near unto Him* tomorrow. Thus he is saying that this test will be a proof to them throughout their generations not to contest [the rights of] him who is chosen, nor those of his seed forever.

Now Rabbeinu Chananel[48] wrote that all these people who assembled [against Moses] were Levites, of the same tribe as Korach, this being the reason for the expressions [by Moses]: *ye take too much upon you, 'ye sons of Levi;'*[49] *Hear now, 'ye sons of Levi.'*[50] Perhaps they thought that their whole tribe had been chosen for the priesthood, and that it was Moses of his own accord who gave the honor to his brother. Thus far [are the words of Rabbeinu Chananel]. But G-d forbid that there should be in the tribe of the ministers of our G-d *two hundred and fifty men*[14] — of the most distinguished [of the people], and *princes* — who were *sons of rebellion,*[51] rejecting their leader, the greatest of their tribe, and murmuring against G-d! And [furthermore], if these [rebels] were only of that tribe [of Levi, as Rabbeinu Chananel wrote], then all the tribes of Israel would not have

(46) See Genesis 4:4. (47) See Deuteronomy 18:5. (48) See (Exodus), Vol. II, p. 106, Note 45, for a brief biography of this great Rabbinic scholar. See also (Leviticus), Vol. III, p. 324, Note 286. (49) Further, Verse 7. (50) *Ibid.*, Verse 8. (51) *Ibid.*, 17:25.

murmured on the next day [after the rebels were killed] *saying: 'Ye have killed the people of the Eternal,'*[52] since not one of their own tribe died, [and those who did die were] only of Moses' and Aaron's tribe. Similarly the sign of the rod[53] also proves that the controversy embraced all tribes of Israel. In addition, Scripture expressly states, [*and they rose up in the face of Moses,*] *with certain men 'of the children of Israel,'*[54] in order to point out that the men were from all the tribes, not only from the two tribes [previously] mentioned [Reuben and Levi]. But the reason why [Moses said] *ye take too much upon you, 'ye sons of Levi'*[49] is that Korach won the tribes over to his side [by persuading them] that it was because of *their* honor that he wanted to restore the service [of the offerings] to their firstborns, as he said, *seeing all the congregation are holy.*[55] But Moses in his wisdom laid bare the hidden motives of Korach's heart to the whole people, namely that he was only protesting because of his own [failure to attain the] priesthood; therefore Moses said to him that he had sufficient [honor] in the honor bestowed upon his tribe, for "you have enough honor, you sons of Levi." Then Moses continued and said, *Hear now, ye sons of Levi.*[50] [This he said] to Korach their leader — as is shown by [the first part of] that verse, *And Moses said unto Korach*[50] — but he included in his words all the Levites, since Moses in his wisdom spoke conciliatory words to Korach and all his tribe, so that none of them should be drawn after him.

Now it was Moses himself who thought of this procedure, and chose the burning of incense [as the test to show who was suitable for the priesthood] rather than any of the other offerings, because he had already seen in the case of Nadab and Abihu that when they offered strange incense before the Eternal they were burnt.[56] Therefore he

(52) *Ibid.*, Verse 6. (53) *Ibid.*, Verses 16-24. Each tribe had to deposit a rod with its name written on it in the Tent of Meeting, before the ark of the Testimony, and Moses placed another rod there with Aaron's name written on it. G-d promised that he would make the rod of the one who was chosen bud miraculously. Thus the fact that each tribe had to put a rod there shows that the controversy embraced them all. (54) Above, Verse 2. (55) *Ibid.*, Verse 3. (56) Leviticus 10:1-2.

permitted Aaron to burn the incense, because of the special needs of the time,[57] or maybe it was the [daily] incense of the morning which he used to burn when he kindled[58] the lamps, according to the ordinance, and Moses trusted that G-d *confirmeth the word of His servant, and performeth the counsel of His messengers.*[59]

And some scholars[60] say that [the meaning of the verse], *And when Moses heard it, he fell upon his face,*[61] is [that he did so] in order to inquire of G-d to know what to do, and then he was told, *In the morning the Eternal will make known* etc.;[62] but it is mentioned only in Moses' account to the people. I have already shown you[63] that in many places Scripture will sometimes deal at length with the account of G-d's communication to Moses, but mention [the matter] in brief in Moses' narration thereof, and at other times it does the opposite. At other instances [still] it does not mention one of the communications at all, such as in the story of the children of Gad and the children of Reuben, where Scripture tells the event [only] with respect to Moses himself [that he gave them the land east of the Jordan as a conditional inheritance], and [this whole matter] was [in fact] done by the commandment of the Eternal, as they said, *As the Eternal hath said unto thy servants, so will we do.*[64] And in [the Book of] Joshua it is

(57) See Exodus 30:9 (Vol. II, p. 509) that all offerings of incense are forbidden as "strange" incense, except for those especially prescribed [e.g., the daily offering of incense]. In times of emergency and special need, however, such as when the overall authority of the Torah is at stake, it is permitted to suspend temporarily the operation of a particular law or prohibition, and it was this power which Moses now made use of when he allowed Aaron to offer up this non-prescribed incense. Or it may be, as Ramban continues, that this test took place at the Service of the Morning Whole-offering, which included the burning of incense, so that there is no need to say that Moses resorted to special emergency powers. (58) In the Tur: when he "dressed" the lamps. See Vol. II, pp. 472-474, for an explanation of the Service done in connection with the lamps at the daily Morning Service. See also my Hebrew commentary here, p. 257. (59) Isaiah 44:26. (60) So quoted by Ibn Ezra in Verse 4. (61) Above Verse 4. (62) Verse 5 before us. According to this interpretation, the test of incense was declared by G-d, as is implied in Moses' falling on his face to ask for Divine guidance, and the verse only tells us what G-d told him to do when mentioning Moses' speech to *Korach and all his company*. (63) See e.g., Vol. II, pp. 101, 111. (64) Further, 32:31.

written, [*And the children of Reuben and the children of Gad and the half-tribe of Menasheh returned . . . to go*] *unto the land of Gilead, to the land of their possession, whereof they were possessed, 'according to the commandment of the Eternal by the hand of Moses'.*[65] And if we say that [Moses in fact gave these lands to the tribes of Reuben, Gad, and the half-tribe of Menasheh on his own authority, and the above-mentioned verse which says that it was done *according to the commandment of the Eternal*] refers to G-d's [subsequent] agreement to Moses' action, similar to that which it says, *This is the Land wherein ye shall receive inheritance by lot, which the Eternal hath commanded to give unto the nine tribes, and to the half-tribe,*[66] in which case this would be one of the occasions when Moses acted of his own accord and the Holy One, blessed be He, [later] approved his decision[67] — [this cannot be so because] it is not right [to say] that Moses would have done anything in connection with the division of the Land without [Divine] permission. For [in dividing the Land] he did everything at the command of G-d, as it is written, [*And the Lord spoke unto Moses saying:*] *Unto these the Land shall be divided* etc.[68]

(65) Joshua 22:9. (66) Further, 34:13. The verse thus indicates that G-d agreed that the nine and a half tribes should take their inheritance west of the Jordan, and therefore that the remaining two and a half tribes should take the land Moses gave them on the east side of the Jordan. (67) In Shabbath 87a, the Talmud mentions three occasions when Moses acted on his own authority and G-d subsequently approved his decisions. Ramban is thus saying here: "In case one should suggest that Moses' decision to grant the lands east of the Jordan as an inheritance to the two and a half tribes was in reality his own decision, which was subsequently approved by G-d — this hypothesis cannot be correct because etc.," as Ramban continues. — See also at the end of *Seder Naso* where Ramban cites cases, where man's opinion coincided with that on High. There is a marked difference though between the cases of Moses and those mentioned above. Moses according to tradition acted on his own reasoning, and G-d subsequently approved. In the cases mentioned above [such as in the section about the impure people on Passover, etc.] inquiry was first made for Divine guidance, and it happened that the opinion of those seeking guidance coincided with that on High. (68) Further, 26:53. The verse saying *And the Eternal spoke unto Moses* clearly indicates that he acted originally on Divine instruction.

My own opinion in this matter [of Moses' command to Korach and his company to take censers and burn incense], and in that which he said to Aaron [during the outbreak of the plague], *Take thy fire-pan, and put fire therein from off the altar, and lay incense thereon*[69] is that *the hand of the Eternal was upon* him[70] in these matters, and it is this which is called *Ruach Hakodesh,*[71] as happened with the books of David and Solomon which were written by *Ruach Hakodesh,*[72] and as David said, *The spirit of the Eternal spoke by me, and His word was upon my tongue.*[73] For Moses our teacher was *trusted in all* His *house,*[74] and I have explained the matter of "the house" [75] and mentioned it many times; [76] but since this was not in the usual course of Moses' prophecy, Scripture did not mention G-d's communication to him about these matters.

Now I have seen in Onkelos' translation that every time the word *k'toreth* (incense) appears in this section, he rendered it in his language [Aramaic also] as *k'toreth* and he did not translate it [as he does in all other places] as *k'toreth busmin* (aromatic incense), as he usually does.[77] From this it would appear that he was of the opinion that this was not the aromatic incense used in the Sanctuary [i.e., Tabernacle], but it [consisted of] frankincense and similar ingredients which he [Moses] made them burn for the test. Onkelos translated likewise in the case of Aaron's sons [Nadab and Abihu, who burnt *the strange incense,* for there too he did not render the Hebrew *k'toreth* as he usually does: *k'toreth busmin,* but as

(69) *Ibid.,* 17:11. (70) See Ezekiel 37:1. (71) Literally: "The Holy Spirit." See in Moreh Nebuchim, II, Chapter 45, beginning: "the second degree of prophecy." See also further, *Seder Balak* Note 63, and Ramban *ibid.* (72) Such is also the opinion of Rambam in his Moreh Nebuchim II, 45. (73) II Samuel 23:2. (74) See above, 12:7. (75) *Ibid.,* Verse 6. (76) See e.g. Exodus 32:19. (77) See e.g. Onkelos *ibid.* 30:8. — But note, however, that in our versions of Onkelos, the word *k'toreth* in this section *is* translated as *k'toreth busmin* (*aromatic incense*). In the opinion of the author of Minei Targima (Rabbi Yeshayah Pick), Ramban's version of the text of Onkelos here is the correct one, and later copyists mistakenly amended the text. See my Hebrew commentary, p. 258.

k'toreth].[78] But in the opinion of our Rabbis[79] it *was* the sacred incense, and this is the correct interpretation. Perhaps Onkelos [agrees that this was the sacred incense, but he] did not want to praise the incense by adding thereto the word *busmin* (aromatics), except when it [the incense] was used in performance of the [daily] commandment [to burn incense].

11. THEREFORE THOU AND ALL THY COMPANY. "*Therefore,* because of this [i.e., because of what I have previously said: *Hear now, ye sons of Levi: is it but a small thing* etc.] *thou and all thy company that are gathered together* [are] *against the Eternal,* for I acted as His agent in giving the priesthood to Aaron, and this controversy is [therefore] not directed against us." This is Rashi's language. And if so, the verse is saying: "thou and all thy company — it is ye that are gathered together against G-d, and not against Aaron." And Rabbi Abraham ibn Ezra commented that the letter *hei* in the word *hano'adim* (*'that' are gathered together*) is redundant [thus the verse means: "thou and all thy company 'are gathered together not against us but against G-d"]. It is possible that the verse is stating: "*Therefore thou and all thy company that are gathered together against G-d* — for it is not against Aaron [that you are gathered together] — *be ye before G-d* with *Aaron tomorrow,*"[80] and the verse is elliptic with respect to the conditions that Moses mentioned. The purport of the verses is thus as follows: At first he [Moses] spoke *unto Korach and unto all his company, saying: 'In the morning the Eternal will make known* etc.,'[81] and afterwards he

(78) Leviticus 10:1. In our version of Onkelos, again, the text there is *k'toreth busmin* (aromatic incense), which in the opinion of the author of Minei Targima is likewise a copyist's mistake. (79) Tanchuma *Korach* 5. (80) Verse 16. (81) Verses 5-7. Ramban is thus stating that all three verses (5-7) were not equally addressed by Moses to the same group. The first two verses (5-6) and first half of Verse 7 were addressed to Korach and all his company, while the concluding part of that verse [*ye take too much upon you, ye sons of Levi*] Moses spoke only to Korach. This is made necessary because, as Ramban has stated above, among the assembled were people from all tribes.

continued speaking to Korach, saying: *ye take too much upon you, ye sons of Levi,*[49] and told Korach alone, *Hear now, ye sons of Levi.*[82] Therefore he repeated himself saying, *thou and all thy company that are gathered together against G-d,*[83] meaning that the punishment would not be directed against Korach alone, but against his whole *company,* for they are all *gathered together against G-d.*

12. AND MOSES SENT TO CALL DATHAN AND ABIRAM. Now Dathan and Abiram were the instigators of this controversy as much as Korach was, as Scripture states, *Now Korach took . . . and Dathan and Abiram . . . and they rose up in the face of Moses with certain of the children of Israel* etc.,[84] meaning that they were the ones who roused them together against Moses and Aaron. Then Moses spoke [once] *to Korach and to all his company,*[80] and furthermore said to him: *thou and all thy company,*[85] for it was to him [Korach] that he spoke first, since he was the leader amongst them. Now amongst those *that* were *gathered together* were also the followers of Dathan and Abiram; therefore Moses wanted to speak to them also now, and to warn them about themselves and all those *who* were *gathered together* [with them], who were their company, and to appease them *with good words, even comforting words*[86] to Israel, since his [earlier] words to Korach were a conciliation only to the Levites.

The meaning of the expression *and Moses sent* is that Dathan and Abiram had gone away from his presence whilst he was speaking to Korach [as stated in Verses 5-7], and afterwards it again says, *And Moses said unto Korach* [Verse 8], who was still standing before him there, or maybe since Korach was a Levite he stayed in the camp of the Levites near the tent of Moses.[87] All this happened on the first day [of the rebellion], just as Moses said, *thou and they, and Aaron*

(82) Verse 8. (83) In Verse 11 before us. (84) Above, Verses 1-2. (85) Verse 11. (86) Zechariah 1:13. (87) Accordingly, the speech of Moses to Korach, which is recorded in Verses 8-11, took place near Moses' and Korach's tents, and not near the Tent of Meeting.

tomorrow,[80]— this being the "morning" he mentioned to them: *In the 'morning' the Eternal will make it known who are His.*[88]

It is possible that Dathan and Abiram, as *princes of the congregation,*[54] were more distinguished than *On the son of Peleth,*[54] and if they would have been won over to Moses, On would have followed their counsel; therefore Moses did not send for him. Thus On did not come, and was not present together with them [Dathan and Abiram], nor was he with Korach's company; since he left him when Dathan and Abiram went away, while Moses was debating with Korach, and he never returned [to Korach's company], because he changed his mind [after his original participation] on the advice of his wife who saved him, according to the words of our Rabbis.[89] For Scripture does not mention him [On] as one who was swallowed up [in the earth] together with Dathan and Abiram, nor was he *among the company of those that gathered together against the Eternal*[90] who offered the incense, since there were *two hundred and fifty men* besides the four[91] mentioned at first.

13. THAT THOU [Moses] WOULDST MAKE THYSELF A PRINCE OVER US 'GAM HISTAREIR' — [the repetition of this phrase — literally 'also to rule' means]: 'also many forms of lordship.' Or[92] [it may refer to lordship by] 'thou and thy brother Aaron.' " This is the language of Rabbi Abraham ibn Ezra. In my opinion the word *gam* (*also*) here means "even." Similarly: *There is none that doeth*

(88) Above, Verse 5. (89) Sanhedrin 109b. She said to her husband: "What benefit will you have from this controversy? Either Moses remains master and you are his disciple, or Korach becomes master and you are *his* disciple!" (90) See further, 27:3. (91) I.e., Korach, Dathan, Abiram, and On the son of Peleth. Now since Scripture mentions these four men besides the *two hundred and fifty* (Verse 2), and the fire which burnt those who offered the incense, destroyed two hundred and fifty men (further, Verse 35), it follows that On must have been saved. The death of Korach, Dathan, and Abiram, however, is expressly mentioned separately (*ibid.*, Verses 27, and 32-33). (92) In our text of Ibn Ezra's commentary the word "or" is missing, so that he is expressing only one thought: "also many forms of lordship — thou and thy brother Aaron."

good, not 'gam' (even) one; [93] *The poor is hated 'gam' (even) of his own neighbor,* [94] and similar cases. Thus Dathan and Abiram said to Moses: *"Is it a small thing* on your part that you have done us such a great evil *to kill us in the wilderness,* for which we should have stoned you, that you would rule over us even in a small measure of lordship, by sending us [a summons] to appear before you, let alone that you should play the king and be elevated over us!"

15. RESPECT NOT THOU 'MINCHATHAM' (THEIR OFFERING). "According to its plain sense [the meaning of 'their offering' is] 'the incense which they will offer up before You tomorrow — do not turn to it.' The Midrashic explanation is that Moses said: 'I know that they have a portion in the Daily Whole-offerings of the congregation; let not [their part in it] be accepted before You favorably.' " This is Rashi's language. But it does not seem to me to be correct that it is referring to the incense, because it was with reference to Dathan and Abiram that Moses said this, because he became angered by their words, and they were not amongst the company who gathered together to burn the incense. But the plain meaning [of the verse] is that because these people wanted the priesthood, to be able to perform the service of the offerings, Moses said: *"Respect not Thou their offering,* meaning: respect not the offering which they want to bring before You, nor the prayer which they will pray unto You," for all offerings, including prayer, are called *minchah* (offering) in Scripture. Onkelos also rendered [*minchatham*] as *kurbanhon* (their offering), meaning "anything that they will offer before You."

I HAVE NOT TAKEN ONE ASS FROM THEM. The meaning thereof is that Moses said: "What lordship am I exercising over them, for I have never taken from them even one ass to do my work, as is the manner of kings and princes?" For this is *the manner of the kingdom,* [95] as it is written, *and he will take your asses, and put them to his work.* [96] This is the meaning of Onkelos' rendition: ["I have not

(93) Psalms 14:3. (94) Proverbs 14:20. (95) I Samuel 10:25. (96) *Ibid.*, 8:16.

taken one ass from them] *sh'chorith* (as a levy)," for [in Aramaic] the king's levy is called *shichvur*. Thus Moses mentioned the smallest incident amongst the laws of royalty, and then he said, *Neither have I hurt one of them* by appointing him to my chariot[97] or to do my work, as is befitting for a king, or by perverting his judgment [in a lawsuit] or by treating him with disrespect, for [the phrase "hurting" in *neither have I 'hurt' one of them*] includes all kinds of injustice.

16. AND MOSES SAID UNTO KORACH: 'BE THOU AND ALL THY CONGREGATION BEFORE THE ETERNAL, THOU, AND THEY, AND AARON, TOMORROW.' Rabbi Abraham ibn Ezra wrote that "this has already been stated [above, in Verses 5-7: *And he spoke unto Korach and unto all his company, saying: 'In the morning the Eternal will make known* etc.'], but the meaning thereof here is: as Moses said to Korach, *Be ye before the Eternal, so they took every man his censer.*" [98]

The correct interpretation appears to me to be that at first Moses told them: *This do: Take you censers, Korach, and all his company . . . and it shall be that the man whom the Eternal doth choose, he shall be holy,*[99] and he did not say that Aaron would be together with them. They [also] remained silent, [so that Moses thought] perhaps they did not find this acceptable and did not agree to it, for they may have thought: "If Aaron will be together with us, either the [Heavenly] fire will come down for all of us, or it will not descend at all, so that we will all be alike; whereas if Aaron will not be together with us, and the fire will not come down, the people will say that He has not chosen us, but will think that He has already chosen him [Aaron] inasmuch as the fire came down on his offerings on the

(97) See *ibid.*, Verse 12. (98) Further, Verse 18. Thus according to Ibn Ezra, the verse here does not contain a new command heretofore not mentioned, but is the same charge mentioned already above. The reason why it is repeated here is that at the time of fulfillment Scripture records that the charge previously given to Moses was now fulfilled in deed. Ramban will offer another interpretation. (99) Above, Verses 6-7.

eighth day [of the installation of the priests].[100] But as far as that [eighth] day is concerned we have a complaint against him [Moses], namely that he should not have chosen Aaron to be the priest alone, since [the Heavenly fire] came down only in the merit of [the whole people of] Israel who made the Tabernacle, and it would have come down for any representative of the congregation, for the firstborns had not yet been exchanged at that time [for the Levites]." Therefore Korach did not want to do any sort of trial without [the participation of] Aaron. Now Dathan and Abiram were [also] present when Moses told them [these instructions], and they were thus included in what Moses said, [*This do: take you censers,*] *Korach, and all his company.*[101] But after he sent for them, *and they said: 'We will not come up,'* [102] *then Moses was very wroth,*[103] and wanted to decree that they should not *die the common death of all men.*[104] Therefore Moses returned to Korach and said, *Take ye every man his censer . . . two hundred and fifty censers; thou also, and Aaron, each his censer.*[105] Thus he excluded Dathan and Abiram from this group — this being the meaning of [the expression] *two hundred and fifty censers,* for why was it necessary to mention the number here [since the number of Korach's company had already been given above in Verse 2]? He also included Aaron amongst them. Then Korach agreed to Moses, for he thought that the matter [of the test] would be decided equally for [both] them and Aaron [as explained above].

21. SEPARATE YOURSELVES FROM AMONG THIS CONGREGATION, THAT I MAY CONSUME THEM IN A MOMENT. One may ask: If [the whole people of] Israel did not sin and did not rebel against their teacher, why was [G-d's] wrath upon them, saying, *that I may consume them in a moment*? And if [on the other hand] they also rebelled [against Moses] as did Korach and his company, how could Moses and Aaron say [on their behalf]: *shall one*

(100) Leviticus 9:24. (101) Verse 6. (102) Verse 12. (103) Verse 15. (104) Further, Verses 29-30. (105) Verse 17.

man sin, and wilt Thou be wroth with all the congregation? [106] Now Rabbeinu Chananel[48] wrote as follows: "*Separate yourselves from among this congregation* means the congregation of Korach, not the congregation of the children of Israel. [But Moses and Aaron, thinking that G-d referred to *all* the people], *said: O G-d, the G-d of the spirits of all flesh, shall one man sin* etc.[106] Immediately the Holy One, blessed be He, informed Moses that He did not want to destroy the whole congregation of the children of Israel, but only the congregation of Korach. Therefore He explained to him: 'When I said, *Separate yourselves from among this congregation,* the meaning was: *Get you up from about the dwelling of Korach, Dathan, and Abiram.*[107] He told them, *Get you up from about the dwelling* etc., because perhaps when Korach and his company would see them going away, they might repent."

These are his [Rabbeinu Chananel's] words, which are not right, for it would not be correct to say about Korach, Dathan, and Abiram — three men — *Separate yourselves from among 'this congregation,'* for they were not "a congregation," since the Israelites were not among them, and Aaron was going about[108] in the midst of the congregation that offered the incense! Besides, the expression *separate 'yourselves'* alludes only to Moses and Aaron, just like *Get you up from among the congregation.*[109] Similarly, *that I may consume them in a moment*[110] refers to a plague, which consumes a mighty and large people in a moment [and cannot therefore refer only to Korach, Dathan, and Abiram]. And [finally], far be it [from us to say] that Moses did not understand his own prophecy and made a mistake therein!

But the meaning thereof is as follows: At first the heart of the people was on the side of Moses and Aaron, but when Korach and his company took *every man his censer and laid incense thereon and stood*

(106) Verse 22. (107) Verse 24. (108) See Ezekiel 46:10. (109) Further, 17:10. Thus it is clear that Moses and Aaron were to separate themselves from the whole congregation, since they were all to be punished, and not only the congregation of Korach. (110) In Verse 21 before us.

at the door of the Tent of Meeting with Moses and Aaron,[111] *Korach* called together *all the congregation*[112] and told them that he was concerned about the honor of all of them. This was pleasing to them, so they all assembled to see *peradventure it will be right in the eyes of G-d,*[113] and the service [of the offerings] will return to their firstborn, this being the meaning of the verse, *And Korach assembled all the congregation against them.*[112] Thus they [all] became liable to destruction because they cast aspersions on their teacher, which is like casting aspersions on the Divine Presence,[114] and they [likewise] rejected in their hearts the prophecy of a prophet, for which they were liable to death by the hand of Heaven.[114] But Moses and Aaron spoke up in their defense, saying that it was only Korach who sinned in this matter, for he was the cause of it all and it was he who incited them, therefore it was right that he alone should die, in order to publicize and make known his punishment to the [whole] community.

This is indeed the way of those who plead for mercy, for they mitigate the [severity of the] people's sin, and put [the blame for] it upon the individual who caused it, because he at any rate is [certainly] guilty. And so did David say, *Lo, I have sinned, and I have done iniquitously; but these sheep, what have they done? Let Thy hand, I pray thee, be against me, and against my father's house.*[115] And the punishment [i.e., the plague in the days of David] came upon the people as well [despite David accepting the blame himself] because of their own sin, for they should have given the [half-] shekels themselves [in order to be counted] [116] — if [we say that] the punishment was on account of that sin, as our Rabbis explained it.[117] For the king had not commanded them *not* to give the [half-] shekels, as he only wanted to know their numbers,[118] therefore their guilt and his guilt in this incident was equal. Moreover, in addition to [being punished for] the

(111) Verse 18. (112) Verse 19. (113) Further, 23:27. (114) Sanhedrin 110a. See "The Commandments," Vol. I, pp. 225-226. (115) II Samuel 24:17. (116) See (Exodus), Vol. II, pp. 510-511. (117) Berachoth 62b. (118) II Samuel 24:2.

census, there was a punishment upon the people [already] at the beginning of this matter, as it is written, *And again the anger of the Eternal was kindled against Israel, and He moved David against them, [saying: 'Go, number Israel and Judah']*.[119]

Now Rashi wrote there: "I do not know why [*G-d's anger was kindled against Israel*]." And I say by way of explanation that Israel was punished because of the delay in the building of the Sanctuary,[120] since the ark *went from tent to tent*[121] *as a stranger in the Land*,[122] and none of the tribes bestirred themselves to say, "Let us seek G-d and build a house to His Name, just as it is written, *even unto His habitation shall ye seek, and thither thou shalt come.*"[123] [This situation continued] until David was roused to action in this matter after many years and a long period of time [had elapsed since he had become king], as it is said, *And it came to pass, when the king dwelt in his house, and the Eternal had given him rest from all his enemies round about, that the king said unto Nathan the prophet: 'See now, I dwell in a house of cedar, but the ark of G-d dwelleth within curtains.'*[124] Now G-d, blessed be He, prevented David [from building the Sanctuary], because He said, *for thou hast shed much blood upon the earth in My sight*,[125] and thus the building was [further] delayed until the reign of Solomon. But had Israel really desired this matter [and really wanted to build the Sanctuary], and had they bestirred themselves to action from the start, it would have been done [already] in the days of one of the Judges, or in the days of Saul, or even in the days of David. For had the tribes of Israel aroused themselves in this matter, he [David] would not have been [considered] the builder, but Israel would have been the builders. But since the people did not concern themselves about it, and David was the one who was troubled

(119) *Ibid.*, Verse 1. (120) Literally: "The Chosen House," a reference to the Temple in Jerusalem. See Deuteronomy 12:11 for the origin of this term. (121) I Chronicles 17:5. Four hundred years had already passed since the exodus up to that period in the reign of David. (122) Jeremiah 14:8. (123) Deuteronomy 12:5. (124) II Samuel 7:1-2. (125) I Chronicles 22:8.

about it and called for action, and it was he who prepared all the materials [for the House of G-d],[126] he was the builder. However, since he was a man of judgment, guided [in his actions] by the attribute of justice, he was not fit for [the task of building] the House of Mercy,[127] therefore the building [of the Sanctuary] was delayed as long as David lived due to the negligence of Israel [in not coming forth themselves to build it], and therefore the [Divine] wrath was upon them. It was for this reason that *the place which the Eternal shall choose . . . to put His Name there*[123] came to be known, as a result of their punishment through the plague.[128]

Scripture alludes to all this when it says, *For I have not dwelt in a house since the day that I brought up the children of Israel out of Egypt, even to this day, but have walked in a tent and in a tabernacle. In all places wherein I have walked among all the children of Israel, spoke I a word with any of the tribes of Israel, whom I commanded to feed My people Israel, saying: Why have ye not built Me a house of cedar?*[129] Thus Scripture is blaming [the people] because the Divine Presence was walking about among all Israel *from tent to tent, and*

(126) *Ibid.*, 29:2. (127) To my knowledge, Ramban's use of this term "the House of Mercy" as an alternative name for the Temple in Jerusalem is the first of its kind in Rabbinic literature. It is of interest to note that a generation later, the French Rabbi Estori Haparchi (1282-1357), in his classic book of itinerary on the Land of Israel, *Kaftor Va'ferach,* mentions *for the first time* that one of the gates on the eastern side of the wall surrounding Jerusalem was called by the people *Shaarei Harachamim* — the "Gates of Mercy" — a name which is still used to this day. Since no definite source is known for the name given to this gate, it is possible that it is derived from this concept of the Sanctuary as "the House of Mercy," and thus the name "Gates of Mercy" is a shortened form of "the gates of the House of Mercy." See II Chronicles 23:19 for such usage in the Scriptures: *the gates of the House of the Eternal.* (128) In II Samuel, Chapter 24, Verses 16-25 it is related that "*the angel of the Eternal was,* at the moment that the plague ceased, *by the treshing-floor of Aravnah the Jebusite,*" and on that spot David built the altar. This is the meaning of Ramban's statement that *'the place which G-d shall choose'* came to be known [i.e., identified] through the punishment and plague which came upon Israel for their indolence in the pursuit of the building of the Sanctuary. But had the people bestirred themselves to action, the place would have been identified through a more pleasant way. This is Ramban's clear intention. (129) *Ibid.*, 7:6-7.

from tabernacle[130] to tabernacle, and there was not one among all the Judges of Israel, who were their shepherds, that bestirred himself in this matter. Scripture also states that G-d too kept distant from them, and did not tell any one of them to build the House, but "now that you [David] have aroused yourself to do it, *thou didst well that it was in thy heart,*[131] and I will now command that it should be built by thy son Solomon, who will be a man of peace."

AND KORACH ASSEMBLED ALL THE CONGREGATION AGAINST THEM.[132] The meaning of [the phrase "all the congregation" is] the leading men of all tribes, who are always summoned [as the congregation's representatives] *unto the door of the Tent of Meeting,* or [it may refer to] the firstborn of all Israel who were [originally] eligible for the service [of the offerings]. Scripture does not mention [that Korach assembled] "the people," [a phrase which it uses in the incidents of the [golden] calf[133] and the spies,[134] for if all Israel were guilty [here in the rebellion of Korach] He would have said: "*that I may consume them in a moment*[135] – *and will make thee a nation.*"[136] Now all that I have mentioned [above] about the firstborn is in accordance with the explanation of our Rabbis, who say[137] that the service [of the offerings before the building of the Tabernacle] was performed by the firstborn. But according to the plain meaning of Scripture, all the Israelites [without exception] were at first eligible for the service of the offerings, for such is [indeed] always the law with respect to a High Place of an individual,[138] and

(130) I Chronicles 17:5. The continuation here by Ramban [*from tent to tent, and from tabernacle*] is clearly based on this verse in Chronicles. In II Samuel 7:6 the reading is: *in a tent and in a tabernacle.* (131) I Kings 8:18. (132) Verse 19. (133) Exodus 32:9: *I have seen 'this people'* . . . (134) Above, 14:11: *How long will 'this people' despise Me?* (135) Verse 21 before us. (136) Above, 14:12. This is the phrase used in the case of the spies, where all the people sinned, and G-d wanted to destroy them and form a new nation from Moses. Since it is *not* used here, it implies that He did not want to direct His punishment to the whole congregation. (137) Zebachim 112b. See above, Note 22. (138) In the period when it was permitted to bring offerings on High Places, i.e., during the fourteen

Aaron was chosen for the Service in the Tabernacle and Sanctuary. Korach thus was protesting against this selection [of Aaron alone], and wanted to restore the service [of the offerings] to all the Israelites, *seeing all the congregation are holy.*[139]

26. [DEPART, I PRAY YOU, FROM THE TENTS OF THESE WICKED MEN], AND TOUCH NOTHING OF THEIRS, LEST YE BE SWEPT AWAY IN ALL THEIR SINS. The correct order [in meaning] of this verse is as follows: "Depart, I pray you, from the tents of these wicked men, lest ye be swept away in all their sins and touch nothing of theirs." The meaning [therefore] is that if they do not depart from there, they will be swallowed up by the mouth of the earth, and he furthermore warned them that they should not touch [their property] and try to save any of their wealth by taking it for themselves, *for it is a doomed thing.*[140] And Rabbi Abraham ibn Ezra wrote that [the verse is to be interpreted as it reads, and it is saying] that if they attempt to save their wealth, they will go down into the pit like them [Korach and his company]. And if so, the meaning of this will be like that of the verse, *And his* [Lot's] *wife looked back from behind him, and she became a pillar of salt,*[141] as I have mentioned there in explaining the meaning of it.[142]

years of the conquest and division of the Land, [when they had not yet built the Sanctuary at Shiloh], and after the destruction of that Sanctuary until the building of the Sanctuary in Jerusalem, there were two kinds of High Places: those of a private individual, where any Israelite could perform the service, and a public one for the whole congregation of Israel — for example, the one at Nob, and later on at Gibeon. The Passover-offering could only be brought at the public High Place, and the service there was only valid if performed by a priest (Zebachim 119b-120 a-b). See also (Leviticus), Volume III, p. 123, Note 122. (139) Above, Verse 3. (140) See Deuteronomy 7:26. (141) Genesis 19:26. In other words, according to Ibn Ezra's interpretation we do not have to say that they will be swallowed up *as a punishment* for taking their wealth, but that they will automatically be affected as if it were a contagious disease. This is what happened to Lot's wife when she turned back to see Sodom, for "the plague entered her mind when she saw the brimstone and salt, and it cleaved to her" (Ramban on Genesis, Vol. I, p. 259). (142) *Ibid.,* Verse 17 (Vol. I, pp. 258-260).

29. IF THESE MEN DIE THE COMMON DEATH OF ALL MEN. Now many of the people had said to Moses many times, *Why hast thou brought us up out of Egypt?* [143] [and yet Moses did not ask for them to be especially punished]. But these people deserved punishment more than all other [previous sinners] because they said *that thou wouldst make thyself altogether a prince over us.* [144] Thus *they committed two evils:* [145] they trampled upon the honor due to a teacher, and they denied all the deeds of G-d which He did in Egypt and the wilderness, and even at the Revelation on Mount Sinai, [146] where it is said *and they will believe in thee* [Moses] *forever,* [147] by saying that Moses was not worthy to rule over them, and that nothing but evil had befallen them through him. Therefore it is said, *and Moses was very wroth.* [148] Also Korach said, *wherefore then lift ye up yourselves above the assembly of the Eternal?* [139] Therefore his tent[149] was swallowed up by the earth together with them. This was the intention of Moses' words [when he said: *if these men die the common death of all men*] *then the Eternal hath not 'sent' me,* meaning that He has not sent me at all to take the people out of Egypt, the expression being similar to: *which the Eternal 'sent' him* [Moses] *to do in the land of Egypt;* [150] *and this shall be the token unto thee, that I have 'sent' thee.* [151] Similarly, [*And Moses said*]: *"Hereby, ye shall know that the Eternal hath 'sent' me to do all these works"* [152] means the deeds which you have seen with your [own] eyes, and refers to all that he had done from the day G-d told him, *Come now therefore, and I will send thee unto Pharaoh;* [153] for the beginning of a prophet's activity is called *sh'lichuth* (being sent, a commission), similar to the expressions: *Whom shall I send, and who will go for us?;* [154] *And I sent before thee Moses, Aaron, and Miriam.* [155] And the meaning of the expression *all these works*[152] is not, as the

(143) Exodus 17:3. (144) Above, Verse 13. (145) Jeremiah 2:13. (146) See (Exodus), Vol. II, p. 251, Note 17. (147) Exodus 19:9. (148) Verse 15. (149) Further, Verse 32. See, however, in my Hebrew commentary p. 263, Note 18, on the exact fate that befell Korach and his tent. (150) Deuteronomy 34:11. (151) Exodus 3:12. (152) Verse 28. (153) Exodus 3:10. (154) Isaiah 6:8. (155) Micah 6:4.

commentators have said,[156] the appointment of the Levites instead of the firstborn, and [the appointment of] Aaron to the priesthood,[157] but it refers to the totality of the activities *which Moses wrought in the sight of all Israel,*[158] as I have explained.

30. BUT IF THE ETERNAL CREATE 'B'RIAH.' Rabbi Abraham ibn Ezra wrote: "Some scholars say that *b'riah* indicates producing something from nothing. But, [continues Ibn Ezra], many countries have already been rent [by earthquakes], and their inhabitants went down alive into the pit. Rather, the meaning of *b'riah* is 'cutting off,' from [the expression] *'u'varei'* (*and they shall cut*) *them*"[159] [thus meaning here: "if the Eternal will 'cut them' down by causing the ground to open up its mouth etc."].

The correct interpretation is that the term *b'riah* is [indeed] used [in the sense of] bringing forth something from nothing, for we have no other word in the Sacred Language denoting this concept [*creatio ex nihilo*] except for this one. The explanation of the matter is that splitting open the [crust of the] earth is [indeed] not a new creation, but that the ground should open up its mouth to swallow up [certain people] is a new event which had never occurred previously. For when the earth is split open, as happens many times during an earthquake which is called *zalzalah,*[160] it remains open and the chasm becomes filled with water, like ponds; but that it should open up and close again immediately — like a person who opens his mouth to swallow and closes it after he has swallowed — this event was a new happening which occurred [only] on that day, as if it were created out of nothing. This is the meaning of the expression, *and the earth closed upon them*[161] [that it closed up immediately after consuming them, and left no sign that it had opened]. It is for this reason that [when saying that]

(156) This is the interpretation of Ibn Ezra. (157) This is the interpretation of Rashi. (158) Deuteronomy 34:12. (159) Ezekiel 23:47. (160) The Arabic word for earthquake. See (Exodus), Vol. II, p. 324, Note 512. (161) Verse 33.

the ground did cleave asunder,[162] Scripture says: *And the earth opened her mouth, and swallowed them up.*[163] And according to the opinion of our Rabbis[164] [who say] that the opening of Gehenna came near to this spot — that phenomenon too, was a new event which occurred [only] at that moment.

32. AND ALL THE MEN THAT APPERTAINED UNTO KORACH. He [Korach] had acquired [heathen] slaves and bondmaids, and had as members of his household Egyptians, Ethiopians, and Canaanites — *the purchase of his money*[165] — and these people were punished because they were part of their goods [i.e., those of Korach's men], for they were punished both personally and in their belongings. Perhaps there were also in Korach's house Israelites as sojourners and residents, and they were influenced by his counsel and were therefore punished [with Korach]. But it [the phrase *all the men that appertained unto Korach*] cannot refer to his children, for it is written, *But the children of Korach died not,*[166] because they were adults, righteous and good men, and their [own] merit stood in their stead [so that they were not swept away with their father]. He had no minor sons and daughters, since Scripture does not mention "little ones" in the case of Korach [as it does when referring to Dathan and Abiram].[167]

33. AND THEY PERISHED FROM AMONG THE ASSEMBLY. The meaning thereof is that they [Korach and his associates] perished in their sight [that of the people], while they were standing amongst them in their midst, since the earth suddenly opened up its mouth and closed it upon them, and the place where they had been [standing] was not noticeable.[168] And Rabbi Abraham ibn Ezra commented that the meaning of the expression is: [they were blotted out from among the assembly] because of the death of their children who would have been in their stead.

(162) Verse 31. (163) Verse 32. (164) Sanhedrin 110a. Although Gehenna existed already, this movement of its opening was a "new creation." (165) Leviticus 22:11. (166) Further, 26:11. (167) Above, Verse 27. (168) See Nahum 3:17.

17 2. SPEAK UNTO ELEAZAR THE SON OF AARON THE PRIEST, THAT HE TAKE UP THE CENSERS OUT OF THE BURNING, AND SCATTER THOU THE FIRE YONDER; FOR THEY ARE BECOME HOLY. "The censers [have become holy]. And it is prohibited to have any benefit from them, since they had already made them 'vessels of service.' " This is Rashi's language. But I do not know the reason for this prohibition, since it was "strange incense" [which was not part of the daily commandment] that they offered, and if a non-priest makes a vessel of service in order to bring an offering in it outside [the prescribed place in the Tabernacle or Sanctuary], that vessel does *not* become sanctified! However, it is possible to say that since they did so at the command of Moses, the vessels did become holy, because they dedicated them to G-d, thinking that He would answer them through the [Heavenly] fire and that these censers would remain forever in the Tent of Meeting as [sacred] vessels of service. The correct interpretation, [however,], appears to me to be that Scripture is saying, *Because they were offered before the Eternal, therefore they are hallowed, and they shall be for a sign unto the children of Israel,*[169] meaning: "I [the Eternal],[169] have sanctified them [so that they may not be used], from the moment that they were offered before Me, in order that *they shall be a sign unto the children of Israel.*"

5. THAT HE BE NOT AS KORACH, AND AS HIS COMPANY, AS THE ETERNAL SPOKE BY THE HAND OF MOSES 'LO.' "The word *lo* [literally: 'to him'] is like *alav* ('about him'), that is, about Korach. And what is the meaning of *by 'the hand' of Moses,* and why is it not written 'unto Moses' [as is written elsewhere]? It is a hint to those who dispute the priesthood, that they will be stricken with leprosy, just as Moses was stricken [with it] on 'his hand.'[170] It was for this reason that Uzziah [king of Judah] was stricken with leprosy [when he attempted to usurp the function of the priests and to offer incense].[171]

(169) Verse 3. (170) Exodus 4:6. (171) II Chronicles 26:19.

And according to the plain meaning of Scripture,[172] [the interpretation is as follows: if anybody disputes the priesthood and claims it for himself, his punishment] will not be that of being swallowed up and burnt, as happened to Korach and his company; instead, [his punishment] will be like that which Moses received on his hand when it was stricken with leprosy. And some scholars[173] interpret [the verse to mean]: *that no common man, that is not of the seed of Aaron, draw near to burn incense before the Eternal*[174] — *as the Eternal spoke by the hand of Moses* with regard to Aaron, that he and his sons should be priests, and not a layman." This is Rashi's language. The correct interpretation is that [the word *lo* (to him)] refers to Eleazar who is mentioned [at the beginning of the section], when Scripture said, *Speak unto Eleazar the son of Aaron the priest* etc.,[175] and the correct order [in meaning] of the verses [before us] is as follows: *And Eleazar the priest took the copper censers wherewith they that were burnt had offered, and they beat them out for a covering of the altar*[176] — *as the Eternal spoke to him by the hand of Moses*[174] — *to be a memorial unto the children of Israel* etc.[174]

6. 'YE HAVE KILLED THE PEOPLE OF THE ETERNAL.' Onkelos rendered it: "You have caused the death of the people of the Eternal." Thus he interprets the verse [to mean that] the people accused Moses and Aaron that because they advised Korach and his company to offer up strange incense to G-d of their own accord, those who offered it up were burnt, since G-d had not told Moses to offer up this incense, nor did he tell Israel to do so in the name of G-d; thus they of their own accord proposed this matter as a result of which the

(172) This interpretation is not found in our texts of Rashi. It is mentioned, however, by Rambam in his Book of the Commandments (see my translation, "The Commandments," Vol. II, the Eighth Principle, p. 393). (173) This interpretation is brought [in our editions of Rashi], by Rashi himself in his own name at the very beginning of the verse. It is thus obvious that Ramban had a completely different text of Rashi before him here. (174) Verse 5 before us. (175) Verse 2. (176) Verse 4.

people died — when they could have [just as well] given another sign or miracle, through the rod, or [through] some other [harmless] test.

And Rabbi Abraham ibn Ezra said [that the verse means that the people said]: "What proof is this that the tribe of Levi has been chosen, and that Aaron was chosen to be the High Priest? It is possible that by your prayer or by some [secret] wisdom which you possess you burnt those that offered the incense." [All this is the language of Ibn Ezra]. And so indeed it appears, that they did not yet believe [in the Divine selection of the tribe of Levi], for when He stated afterwards, *Speak unto the children of Israel, and take of them rods, one for each fathers' house;* [177] *And it shall come to pass, that the man whom I shall choose, his rod shall bud, and I will make to cease from Me the murmurings* etc.[178] — this proves that the people did not [yet] believe, as a result of the fire, that the Levites were chosen [for service in the Sanctuary] and that the firstborn had been exchanged for them, but they thought that Moses and Aaron had caused the fire [of their own accord]. Or [it may be that the people thought] that the punishment came because they burnt the incense with *strange fire which He had not commanded them,*[179] and [that Aaron was saved because] Aaron's incense was the [daily] incense of the morning [commanded by G-d],[180] as I have explained.[181] [According to this interpretation] the complaint [of the people] was only about [those *two hundred and fifty men who offered the incense* and who were consumed by] the fire,[182] but not about those men [Korach, Dathan, and Abiram] who were swallowed up by the earth,[183] for G-d had said to Moses, *Get you up from about the dwelling of Korach, Dathan, and Abiram,*[184] and this alluded to the opening of the mouth of the earth. Moses had told this to Israel in the name of G-d. Furthermore, Dathan and Abiram were guilty to a greater extent [in this incident than the two hundred and fifty others], since *they mocked the messengers of G-d, and despised*

(177) Further, Verse 17. (178) *Ibid.,* Verse 20. (179) Leviticus 10:1. (180) Exodus 30:7. (181) Above, 16:5. (182) *Ibid.,* Verse 35. (183) *Ibid.,* Verse 32. (184) *Ibid.,* Verse 24.

His words, and scoffed at His prophets.[185] [Hence the people did not complain about the punishment meted out to Korach, Dathan, and Abiram, but only about the fire that consumed *the two hundred and fifty men who offered up the incense.*] [186]

The correct interpretation appears to me to be that the people now believed in the priesthood of Aaron [that he and his descendants were chosen by G-d to serve as priests], since *a fire* had already *come forth from before the Eternal and consumed* his offerings,[187] but they wanted the firstborn to minister in the Tabernacle instead of the Levites, and they did not like the exchange [for the Levites] which they had done to them, but they wanted all the tribes [through their firstborn] to have a share in the Service of the House of G-d. Thus they complained: "*You have killed* them, for you advised them that they should offer up incense like priests, when they were only fit to do the service of the Levites, but not to act as priests who offer up the incense." This is the meaning of the expression, *and, behold, the rod of Aaron for the house of Levi was budded*[188] [thus showing that the people's complaint was because of the appointment of the tribe of Levi to minister in the Tabernacle, and now it was confirmed that they were indeed chosen instead of the firstborn of all the tribes].

10. GET YOU UP FROM AMONG THIS CONGREGATION, THAT I MAY CONSUME THEM IN A MOMENT. I have not understood the intention of this verse, nor of its companion above, *Separate yourselves from among this congregation,*[189] for G-d has the power to kill many people in a plague around one righteous person, and he alone remains [alive], as happened during [the plague on] the firstborn of Egypt. Similarly it happened in all other plagues [throughout the generations], that three people would sleep under one blanket — two of them would die whilst the middle one would be saved! It would appear, therefore, that *the wrath went forth* to slay

(185) II Chronicles 36:16. (186) Ramban wrote all the above as a commentary on Ibn Ezra's interpretation. In the following text, he presents his own view of this matter. (187) See Leviticus 9:24. (188) Further, Verse 23. (189) Above, 16:21.

even the whole congregation with the death of these sinners [Korach and his associates], who had followed in their way, [and so became liable to death either] by the earth opening its mouth or by a consuming fire — these being general punishments which kill all those who are standing there together, unless a miracle of an unusual nature occurs [to save some individuals amongst the people].[190] Or it may be that the Holy One, blessed be He, said this [*Get you up . . .*] in honor of the righteous men, for as long as they were amongst them [the sinners], He would not stretch forth His hand against them. The intention in these and similar words is to inform them that they have to plead for mercy and forgiveness, and Moses in his zeal did so immediately.

12. TWELVE RODS. Aaron's rod was one of the twelve, since it does not say: "and you shall take a rod for the house of Levi and write Aaron's name upon it" [but instead it says in the following verse, *And thou shalt write Aaron's name upon the rod of Levi*]; for he was included in the number mentioned. Thus Joseph was counted as only one tribe [and not as two separate tribes — Ephraim and Menasheh], the reason being that the tribes of Israel are always counted as twelve, and because He counted Levi [here as one tribe], He counted Joseph as only one. I will explain this further in *Seder V'zoth Habrachah,*[191] if G-d will bless me to reach it [in my commentary].

THOU SHALT WRITE EVERY MAN'S NAME UPON HIS ROD. Some commentators[192] explain that this refers to the name of the founder of the tribe: Reuben, Simeon, Levi, and Judah. The correct interpretation is that it means the names of the [present] princes [of the tribes at that time], and He considered Aaron the prince of the

(190) The thought suggested here is as follows: Moses and Aaron would have been in no danger themselves even if they had not gone away from the midst of the congregation. But since there were some people there who had sympathized with Korach, Moses was commanded to leave that place so that all people should realize the danger involved in remaining there (Kur Zahav). (191) Deuteronomy 33:6. (192) I have not identified these sources. See Ibn Ezra.

tribe of Levi. It was necessary to explain[193] that they each had only one rod and one prince, meaning: "Even though I have divided them [the Levites] into two families, the priests separately and the Levites separately, yet they are [in fact] one tribe, and have only one prince. The reason for this is as I have explained,[194] that they only needed proof that it was that tribe [i.e., the tribe of Levi] which was chosen out of all the tribes of Israel [to minister in the Tabernacle].

25. PUT BACK THE ROD OF AARON BEFORE THE TESTIMONY, TO BE KEPT THERE, FOR A TOKEN. "As a reminder that I have chosen Aaron to be the priest, so that they should no longer murmur about the [right to the] priesthood." This is Rashi's language. But this rod was only a sign that the tribe of Levi was chosen from the rest of the tribes, but did not [serve as a sign] that Aaron should have the priesthood [since the people did not dispute his right to it ever since the Heavenly fire had descended on the eighth day of the installation of the priests and consumed Aaron's offerings, as explained above].[194] The correct interpretation is that [the expression] *to be kept there, for a token* means [that the budding of the rod of the house of Levi was to serve as a reminder to Israel that G-d had chosen] the tribe of Levi in exchange for the firstborn. This is because the burning [of Aaron's offerings by the Heavenly fire] was a sign [that Aaron had been chosen] for the priesthood, and the budding [of the rod was an indication] that the Levites [had been selected for their functions in the Tabernacle], as I have explained.[194] This is the meaning of the expression, *and, behold, the rod of Aaron 'for the house of Levi' was budded,*[195] because it budded for [the benefit of] the whole tribe of Levi, and in their merit [to confirm their appointment to do the holy service]. It is possible that since it became known through the [budding of the] rod that G-d did not desire the service of the firstborn, but preferred that of the Levites, the priesthood [automatically could be given] to Aaron without complaint [on the part of the people], since he was the most honored person in

(193) In Verses 18 and 21. (194) Above, Verse 6 (towards the end). (195) Verse 23.

the tribe, being the prince thereof, and it was befitting that he should have the authority of that tribe. But this does not appear to me to be correct, since Gershon was the firstborn of Levi.[196]

18 7. I GIVE YOU THE PRIESTHOOD AS A SERVICE OF GIFT. "[This means that] it shall be to you as a gift." This is Rashi's language, and his intention thereby is to state that it is given to you as a complete gift, [to such an extent] that [as the verse continues], *a non-priest who draws near* [to do the service] *will be* liable to be *put to death* [by the hand of Heaven]. The correct interpretation appears to me to be that He is saying: "and you shall perform the service of the priesthood, but it is not to be regarded by you as a burdensome task, like that imposed upon the servants of kings, but I have given you *the service of a* great *gift* through it, *for glory and for splendor*[197] from Me." This is similar to the interpretation of the Rabbis:[198] "*L'moshchah*[199] — as a distinction, [so that gifts given to the priests from the offerings are to be eaten by them] in the way that kings eat."[200]

10. 'B'KODESH HAKODASHIM' (IN THE MOST HOLY PLACE) SHALT THOU EAT IT. "This teaches us that the most holy offerings may only be eaten in the Sanctuary Court, and only by male priests." But I have not understood this, because the *Kodesh Hakodashim* (*Holy of Holies*) is *not* the right place for eating the offerings; for Scripture states, *in a holy place shall it be eaten, in the court of the Tent of Meeting,*[201] whereas the *Kodesh Hakodashim* is the place where the ark is, within the Veil, as it is written, *and the Veil shall*

(196) Exodus 6:16. Aaron was a grandson of Kohath, who was the *second* son of Levi. Hence the budding of the rod could only have served as a reminder that G-d had chosen the tribe of Levi to perform the service rather than the firstborn of all tribes, but it could not have confirmed Aaron's personal position as High Priest and prince of the tribe, since Gershon was the firstborn, and thereby exercised a claim to it. Therefore we must say that Aaron's personal right to authority was confirmed by the Heavenly fire which consumed his offerings, as explained above. (197) *Ibid.,* 28:2. (198) Sotah 15a. (199) Further, Verse 8. (200) I.e., roasted in fire and eaten with mustard (Chullin 132b). (201) Leviticus 6:19.

divide unto you between the holy place and the most holy.[202] It is furthermore written, *and thou shalt put the ark-cover upon the ark of the covenant in the most holy place,*[203] and there can be no eating and drinking there, since no one may enter it except for the High Priest on the Day of Atonement!

Now I have seen the following text in the Sifre: [204] "Rabbi Yehudah the son of B'theira says: Whence do we know that if the Sanctuary Court is surrounded by gentiles [besieging it], the holy offerings may be eaten even in the Sanctuary proper? From the verse, *In the most holy place thou shalt eat it.*" Thus Rabbi Yehudah the son of B'theirah noted [the implication of] this verse, and explained it as applying to a time of emergency, and [therefore] he mentioned it in trepidation, by saying: "may be eaten in *the Sanctuary,*" when he ought to have said: "may be eaten even in *'the innermost part'* " [of the Sanctuary, i.e., the Holy of Holies], if the enemy besieged the Sanctuary.

According to the plain meaning of Scripture, we must explain the verse *'b'kodesh hakodashim' thou shalt eat it* as meaning: "you shall eat it in a manner befitting the sanctity of the most holy offerings." For at first He had said, *they*[205] *are most holy for thee and for thy sons,*[206] meaning that you should not treat them[205] as you treat the lesser holy offerings, but should regard them as most holy. He then continued and explained: *in a most holy* [manner] *thou shalt eat it,* meaning that your eating thereof should be in a manner befitting the strictest degree of sanctity. And since He had already explained [in the Book of Leviticus] with reference to the meal-offering and the sin-offering what are the stricter rules concerning eating them, over and above those applying to the lesser holy offerings, in respect of place and of

(202) Exodus 26:33. Nobody could even enter therein except for the High Priest on the Day of Atonement, let alone eat the offerings there! (see Ramban further). (203) *Ibid.,* Verse 34. (204) Sifre *Korach* 117. (205) I.e., the most holy offerings which are specifically mentioned here in the first part of the verse, namely: the meal-offering, the sin-offering, and the guilt-offering. See (Leviticus), Vol. III, p. 71, Note 55 for a fuller discussion of the terms "most holy offerings," and "lesser holy offerings." See also further, Note 207. (206) Verse 9.

time,[207] He did not have to treat this subject here at length, but only said that they[205] must all be eaten as most holy offerings, meaning that the eating thereof must be with the stricter degree of holiness, not that of the lesser holy offerings. The [examples of] usage of the letter *beth* [as in the word *b'kodesh*] are many, for the prepositional *beth,* in addition to denoting place and time, can also signify manner [thus meaning here: "in a most holy manner thou shalt eat it"]. Similarly, *'b'itzavon' shalt thou eat it*[208] [means: "in a manner of toil shalt thou eat it"].

20. THOU [Aaron] SHALT HAVE NO INHERITANCE IN THEIR LAND. This means that you [Aaron] will not inherit a share amongst any one of all *the tribes of Israel.*[209] *Neither shalt thou have* [even] a small *portion* in their land at all, for the cities which were given to them [the Levites] were [also] cities of refuge, and were used by the rest of Israel. Now this admonition applies to the priests, and afterwards He mentioned with respect to the Levites: *among the children of Israel they shall have no inheritance,*[210] just as He had admonished the priests. And our Rabbis interpreted the verse:[211] "*Thou shalt have no inheritance in their land,* as referring to the time when the Land was divided up [amongst the tribes]. *Neither shalt thou have any portion among them,* that is, a portion of the spoil [taken from a defeated enemy]. *I am thy portion* — you eat at My table."[212]

(207) The most holy offerings may be eaten only in the Sanctuary Court, and only on the day that they were offered up and the following night, until midnight. These offerings may be eaten only by male priests. The lesser holy offerings may be eaten in the whole city of Jerusalem, for two days and the intervening night, and the portion given to the priests may be eaten by their wives, children, and slaves. (208) Genesis 3:17. (209) Thus they were excluded not only from having a central tribal land of their own but even from having smaller pieces of land throughout the other tribes. (210) Verse 23. (211) Sifre *Korach* 118. (212) In other words, while all Israel lives upon the yield of the land , the priests acquire their gifts directly from "the Table" of the Most High. See also "The Commandments," Vol. II, pp. 163-166.

Chukath

19 2. *This is 'chukath' (the statute of) the law.* "Since Satan[1] and the nations of the world ridicule Israel, saying, 'What is [the meaning of] this commandment [of the Red Heifer]?' therefore the Torah uses the term *chukah* (statute) in connection with it, [meaning]: 'It is a decree from before Me, and you have no permission to question it.' " This is Rashi's language, taken from the words of our Rabbis.[2] Now I have already written in connection with the goat that is sent away [to Azazel[3] the reason] why the nations of the world should taunt us about this [commandment] more than [they taunt us about] the rest of the offerings which effect atonement, and some of which bring about purification — such as the offerings of a man [or woman] who suffered a flux,[4] or of a woman after childbirth.[5] [The reason is] that since [the procedure of the Red Heifer] is performed outside [the Sanctuary], it appears to the nations that it is slaughtered *to the satyrs* which are in the open field.[6] But the truth is that [the Red Heifer] is brought to remove the spirit of impurity, and the burning thereof outside [the

(1) Here understood as "the hinderer" or "the disturber" who tries to dissuade people from keeping commandments which they do not fully understand. (2) Tanchuma, *Chukath* 7; Yoma 67b. See also Vol. II, p. 208, Note 236. (3) Leviticus 16:8. (4) *Ibid.*, 15:13-15; 25-31. (5) *Ibid.*, 12:6-8. (6) See *ibid.*, 17:5-7.

Sanctuary Court] is like the *sweet savor*[7] [of the offerings brought within the Sanctuary Court].

The reason for the impurity conveyed by a corpse is [due to man's sin committed through] the instigation of the serpent,[8] for those who die by "the Divine Kiss" do not [in fact] convey impurity according to the law, this being the [sense of the] saying of the Rabbis:[9] "The righteous do not convey impurity [when dead]." It is for this reason that Scripture states, *This is 'chukath' of the law,* meaning: [this is] that which is "hollowed out"[10] from the [Written] Torah, namely, the Oral Torah.[11] Therefore it is a [female] heifer and must be red, [symbolic] of the attribute of justice.[11] It is given to Eleazar[12] inasmuch as it must be slaughtered before him, even [though it may actually be slaughtered] by a non-priest, because the deputy High Priest [i.e., Eleazar] supervises the performance thereof, so that it should be done in accordance with his intentions, and so that they should not entertain any improper thoughts about it, as do the nations [of the world] and Satan[1] [as mentioned above].

Now this section [of the Red Heifer] completes the laws of the priests [and as such belongs in the Book of Leviticus]. However, it is written here after [the preceding section dealing with] the gifts to the priests, in order to declare that the purification of Israel must also be effected through the priest [just as atonement for sin is effected through the offerings which are offered on the altar by the priests].

THIS IS THE STATUTE OF THE LAW WHICH THE ETERNAL COMMANDED. The reason for this expression [when it should have said "that *I* commanded," since G-d is the Speaker of

(7) *Ibid.*, 1:9 etc. — In other words, as long as the observance is in accordance with the word of G-d, it does not matter if it is done within the Sanctuary Court or outside thereof, for both were equally commanded by Him. (8) See Vol. I, p. 75: "But in the opinion of our Rabbis, if Adam had not sinned he would have never died, etc." See also my Hebrew commentary, pp. 267-268. (9) Tosafoth Baba Metzia 114b. See my Hebrew commentary p. 268, for further sources of this statement. (10) From the root: *chakak* — "to engrave, hollow out." (11) See Abusaula and other Cabalistic commentators on Ramban. (12) Verse 3.

these words], is similar to the verse, *And unto Moses He said: 'Come up unto the Eternal'*[13] [where it should likewise have said: "Come up unto Me"]. Or it may be that this verse must be re-arranged [in order to be interpreted properly], its sense being: "Speak unto the children of Israel: This is the statute of the law which the Eternal hath commanded, saying etc." [14]

Scripture states *dabeir* [— in the singular — *dabeir* (*speak*) *unto the children of Israel*] and not *dabru* [in the plural, although the section begins: *And the Eternal spoke unto Moses and unto Aaron*], because Moses was the main [person who spoke to the people, "or it may mean that G-d spoke to Moses that he should tell it to Aaron, as our Rabbis have explained" (see a similar case in Leviticus 13:1) and in this sense Moses was the main person involved in the Divine communication].

THEY SHALL TAKE UNTO THEE. The reason [why the verse says] "unto thee" [Moses] is [because G-d first commanded] that they should do this in the wilderness for that particular time, and afterwards He commanded that it shall be *unto the children of Israel, and unto the stranger that sojourneth among them for a statute for ever,*[15] meaning that they should do so throughout their generations. Similarly [we find the expression *unto thee* in the following verses]: *that they bring 'unto thee' pure olive oil,*[16] and afterwards it says, *it shall be a statute for ever throughout their generations.*[17]

Scripture states: *And 'ye' shall give,*[12] and not "and 'thou' shalt give," in order to include Aaron together with Moses and thereby to

(13) Exodus 24:1. See Vol. II, pp. 422-424. (14) The order of the expressions [in Hebrew] is as follows: *And the Eternal spoke unto Moses and unto Aaron saying: This is the statute of the law which the Eternal hath commanded saying: Speak unto the children of Israel, that they bring . . .* With the sense of the verse being as Ramban transposes it, we can understand the use of the phrase *which 'the Eternal' hath commanded,* because this is part of the statement which Moses is to make to the people, when conveying G-d's command. Hence it cannot say: "which I have commanded." (15) Verse 10. (16) Exodus 27:20. (17) *Ibid.,* Verse 21. Here too, the original command was for Moses' lifetime [hence "unto thee"], and afterwards it was repeated to make it obligatory throughout the generations.

honor him [Aaron], for both of them were to command Eleazar to have it slaughtered before him. Or it may be that He said *and 'ye' shall give* [because it refers] to many [givers] — those now and those of subsequent generations, and the meaning is that Eleazar who [was in charge of it being] slaughtered [although it could actually be slaughtered by anybody, as explained above] was to take it from the possession of the court, and they were to give it to him so that it should be done properly and in accordance with their intention; in a similar manner to that which we have been taught [in a Mishnah]: [18] "And who prepared them [the ashes of the Red Heifer]? The first one was prepared by Moses our teacher; [19] the second one was prepared by Ezra, and seven were prepared after Ezra's time. And who prepared them? Simon the Just[20] and Jochanan the High Priest prepared two each etc." [21]

3. AND YE SHALL GIVE HER UNTO ELEAZAR THE PRIEST. "[The proper fulfillment of] the commandment is [only when it is done] by the deputy High Priest." This is Rashi's language. But his intention is not to say that the obligation to perform this commandment [always] devolves upon the deputy High Priest rather than devolving upon the High Priest or any ordinary priest; but that this was a [special] temporary command in the case of the first Red Heifer that it should be done by Eleazar, who [happened to be] the deputy High Priest. In the words of the Sifre: [22] " 'Scripture here

(18) Parah 3:5. (19) Moses himself did not prepare the Red Heifer, as is stated here in Scripture. But as the leader of the Sanhedrin, he directed that it should be prepared in accordance with his intention. Similarly it was prepared throughout the subsequent generations under the guidance and in accordance with the intention of the Great Court. Thus all possible vigilant care was taken to assure against anything adverse to the proper preparation of the ashes of the Red Heifer. (20) See Vol. II, p. 477, Note 52. (21) The Mishnah concludes: "And Elihu Einai the son of Hakof, and Chanamel the Egyptian, and Ishmael the son of Piabi prepared one each." — "Thus there were altogether nine Red Heifers prepared from the time [of Moses] when they were given this commandment until the destruction of the Second Temple . . . The tenth one will be prepared by the Messianic King, may he speedily reveal himself" (Rambam, Mishneh Torah, *Hilchoth Parah Adumah,* 3:4). (22) Sifre, *Chukath* 123.

teaches that the Red Heifer was to be prepared by the deputy High Priest. This is made evident [by the fact] that [although] Aaron was still living, Eleazar [who was the deputy High Priest] burnt the heifer. *And ye shall give 'her' unto Eleazar the priest.*[12] This [first heifer] was to be prepared by Eleazar,[23] but all other heifers [in subsequent generations] must be prepared by the High Priest.' These are the words of Rabbi Meir. Rabbi Yosei, Rabbi Yehudah, Rabbi Shimon and Rabbi Eliezer the son of Yaakov say: 'this one was done by Eleazar [the deputy], and all other heifers may be done either by the High Priest or an ordinary priest.' " The purport of this is to tell us that this commandment, because of its profound secret, deserved to be given to the greatest of the priests, and yet it was not given to Aaron [but to Eleazar the deputy]! Perhaps this was because of his [Aaron's] greatness, for he was *the holy one of the Eternal*[24] and His pious one, who effects atonement in His Sanctuary; therefore He did not want to give him a service which is performed outside [the Sanctuary]. Or perhaps [this was to be done by Eleazar] in order to crown him, and initiate him during the lifetime of his father by means of one of the commandments of the high priesthood. Or it may be [that the performance thereof was not given to Aaron] as a punishment for [his part in the incident of] the [golden] calf, as Rabbi Moshe the Preacher wrote.[25] Thus the Holy One, blessed be He, treated Aaron also as a prophet in this commandment, and he and Moses our teacher were to give it [the Red Heifer] to Eleazar, who was the greatest of the priests

(23) This interpretation is based upon the apparently redundant *othah* ["her" — *and you shall give 'her' unto Eleazar*]. Hence Rabbi Meir explains that it means that it was this first Red Heifer that was to be done by Eleazar, whereas all others must be done only by the High Priest. Rabbi Yosei, Rabbi Yehudah, Rabbi Shimon and Rabbi Eliezer the son of Yaakov, however, are of the opinion that the word *othah* teaches us that only *this* Red Heifer was to be done by the deputy High Priest, whereas in subsequent generations it may be done even by an ordinary priest. Ramban further on explains the deeper significance of this whole matter. (24) Psalms 106:16: *and of Aaron the holy one of the Eternal.* (25) "Since Aaron had made the [golden] calf, therefore this service was not done by him, because the prosecuting counsel cannot become the defending counsel" (Rashi on Verse 22, quoting the explanation of Rabbi Moshe the Preacher). See above, *Seder Naso,* Note 146.

after Aaron, and he was the one who had been anointed with the Oil of Anointment.[26] This is [therefore] a hint that in subsequent generations the Red Heifer was to be prepared by the greatest of the priests, namely the High Priest. Similarly we have been taught in a Mishnah: [27] "If the Heifer of Purification[28] was not slaughtered by the High Priest, it is invalid. But Rabbi Yehudah says it is valid." And in the Gemara of Tractate Yoma [it is stated]: [29] *"And ye shall give 'her' unto Eleazar the priest.* 'Her' [i.e., this first Red Heifer] you shall give to Eleazar [the deputy High Priest], but in subsequent generations it is not to be given to Eleazar. Some Rabbis say that in subsequent generations it is to be given to an ordinary priest, and some say that in subsequent generations it is to be given [only] to the High Priest." This [latter statement] is the opinion of the anonymous Mishnah [quoted above, namely that if the Red Heifer was not slaughtered by the High Priest it is invalid], and it is the correct opinion. According to the Sages who are of the opinion that during later generations it may be prepared [even] by an ordinary priest, [the reason why here] Eleazar was commanded to do it is because there was no [ordinary] priest, for it would not be fitting that his younger brother [Ithamar] should take precedence over him [and at that time there were only three priests — Aaron, and his two sons, Eleazar and Ithamar].

14. WHEN A MAN DIETH IN A TENT. The meaning thereof is: "When a man dies, and he is now [lying] in a tent" [even though he may have died outside the tent and was later on brought in]; or it may be that Scripture speaks about the usual circumstances [and people usually die inside a building], but the same law applies if he died outside and they brought him into the tent. *All that come into the tent and all that is in the tent* — this includes the vessels therein and the

(26) Exodus 30:30. See also Numbers 3:3: *the sons of Aaron, the priests that were anointed.* See further Ramban on Leviticus 10:6 (Vol. III, p. 117) where he clearly states that in a certain respect Aaron's sons were considered like the High Priest because of their anointment during the days of the consecration. (27) Parah 4:1. (28) See Rashi on Verse 9. (29) Yoma 42b.

tent itself, as He said [further on], *and he shall sprinkle upon the tent and upon all the vessels and upon the persons that were there.*[30] Scripture mentions *the tent* in order to let us know that the tent itself is rendered unclean for seven days, and [in order to become clean again] requires sprinkling [with the waters of purification]. Furthermore, the Israelites were tent-dwellers in the wilderness and Scripture spoke of the usual [circumstances at that time], because the commandment applied [both] immediately and for later generations; but the same law applies to a house and to everything that "covers" [a corpse], namely that they convey uncleanness to all the vessels and persons that are there, except that a house which is [permanently] attached to the ground cannot itself become impure [unlike a tent which is also defiled].

Now Scripture stated [that] a corpse [conveys] impurity by contact[31] and by an *'ohel,'*[32] but does not mention [that it also conveys impurity to the person who] carries it. Our Rabbis, however, deduced it by a *kal vachomer*[33] from [the law of] a dead animal,[34] and have included it in [the law of] uncleanness of seven days, just like [one who] touches [a corpse]. This is also in accordance with the plain meaning of Scripture, for He mentioned in the case of one who dies [of his own accord] or was killed that he who touches him becomes unclean for

(30) Further, Verse 18. (31) Verse 16: *And whatsoever toucheth . . . shall be unclean for seven days.* — See Vol. III, p. 129, Note 150, on the interchangeable use of the terms "clean," and "unclean," or "pure" and "impure." (32) Literally: "a tent." This refers to the law that anything "spread over" an unclean object has the same effect as "a tent." Hence if a tree shaded a corpse, the law of a dead body in a house or tent applies. (33) Literally: "a minor and major." See Vol. II, p. 133, Note 208 for a fuller explanation of this principle. (34) "If a dead animal, which only renders one impure until [the same] evening, and does not convey impurity by *ohel* (see Note 32), nonetheless does convey impurity [to one who] carries it—surely a corpse [which conveys impurity for *seven* days, and also by *ohel,* conveys impurity to one who carries it]! And just as in the case of a dead animal, touching it conveys impurity until the [same] evening and carrying it [likewise] conveys impurity until the evening, so also in the case of a corpse, where touching conveys impurity for seven days, carrying also conveys impurity for seven days" (Rambam, Mishneh Torah, *Hilchoth Tumath Hameith,* 1:2).

seven days,[31] and [requires] sprinkling [with the waters of purification]; and it is already known that [the word] "touching" in the Torah refers to actual personal contact, and to contact through another object, that is, by carrying it [in which case he is "touching" the object carried by means of the intervening object].

16. AND WHOSOEVER TOUCHETH IN THE OPEN FIELD. "Our Rabbis have said that this includes the upper board and the side board [of a coffin, when found in the open field]. And the plain meaning [of the verse] is: *in the open field* where there are no tents, a corpse conveys uncleanness [only] by contact." This is Rashi's language. But in the opinion of the Sages[35] the [law that the] upper and side boards of the coffin [convey uncleanness] is not derived from Scripture, but is a tradition [handed down by Moses who received it at Sinai]. Therefore a Nazirite [who has become impure by coming into contact with them] is not subject to [the law of] shaving his hair,[36] and likewise [one who becomes impure through contact with them] is not liable to punishment for defiling the Sanctuary [by entering it when impure] or [by eating] the hallowed offerings [in such a state of uncleanness]. Rather, [the expression] *in the open field* is to be understood according to our Rabbis in its literal sense, i.e., that he touches a person who is slain by the sword, who has fallen *in the open field,* and there is nothing covering over the corpse. And since this verse is now [seemingly] superfluous, [since it has already been stated in Verse 11 above that one who touches a corpse becomes impure], the Rabbis derived from it the following interpretation, and they said in Tractate Nazir in the Chapter "The High Priest:" [37] "*And whosoever*

(35) The reference here is to Rabbi Yishmael, whose opinion on this matter is, according to Ramban, the accepted decision of the law. Rashi's comment, however, follows the opinion of Rabbi Akiba (Chullin 72a) who does derive the principle of the upper board and the side board of the coffin from the verse before us (Mizrachi). (36) See above, 6:9. In other words, since this impurity is not derived from a Scriptural verse, although it is in fact a law of the Torah and not merely of the Rabbis, the Nazirite is not considered as having defiled himself to the extent that he must start his period as a Nazir anew. (37) Nazir 53b.

toucheth in the open field. This refers to one who 'covers over' a corpse" [and tells us that he becomes impure], since by covering over it he "touches" *the open field.* [According to this interpretation of the Rabbis the expression] *bachalal cherev* (*slain by the sword*) is lacking the [connective letter] *vav* — *u'bachalal cherev,* [meaning: "or slain by the sword"].[38] And since Scripture says *'pnei' hasadeh* [literally: "the face" of the field] and does not [just] say "the field", Rabbi Yishmael further interpreted it[39] to exclude the [case of a] foetus which died whilst still in its mother's womb [so that if the midwife put her hand inside the mother and touched it, she does not become impure], because it is impurity which is "swallowed up," and is not "upon the face" of the place.

Scripture states *slain 'by the sword'* because it speaks of the usual [way of events], but the same law applies if the person was slain by a stone or fist. It mentions those killed and those who die [naturally, stating: *one that is slain by the sword, or one that dieth of himself*] in contrast to animals for [those animals, which are permitted as food] are pure if they are slaughtered properly, but if they die of their own accord [or were not slaughtered properly] convey impurity as carrion; whereas *all* human corpses convey impurity, regardless of how the person met his death]. Since it appears superfluous, however, our Rabbis interpreted it in the following manner, namely [that the expression *one that is slain by the sword* is intended to teach us] that the sword [with which the person was slain] is exactly like the slain person himself, and the whole purpose of the verse is to equate the slain and the sword, so as to say that it [the sword] becomes an *avi avoth hatumah* (a progenitor of a primary source of impurity),[40] just

(38) Thus according to the interpretation of the Rabbis, two separate principles are enunciated in this verse: 1) *and whosoever 'touches' upon the face of the field,* i.e., who leans over a corpse or covers it with his body, because in doing so he "touches" the corpse; 2) or *whosoever touches* directly *one slain by the sword.* (39) Chullin 72a. (40) In the process of conveying impurity from one source to another, the general rule is always that the defilement of the recipient is of a lesser degree than that of the conveyor. But here in the case of a dead body there is a point of novelty. Since the corpse itself is considered an *'avi' avoth hatumah* (*a progenitor* of a primary source

like the dead person himself, and it conveys impurity of seven days' duration to people and vessels. It appears from the text of the Mishnah and Gemara[41] that it [the sword and all metal vessels] convey impurity by contact and through carrying just like the corpse, but it is unlike the corpse in [that it does not] convey impurity by *ohel*[32] [i.e., if it is in a tent or building together with a person or object, that person or object remains pure]. Perhaps the Rabbis based this exclusion on the verse dealing with the tent, which says: *when 'a man' dieth in a tent,*[42] [thus implying that the law of "the tent," i.e., that of conveying impurity by *ohel*], applies only to the dead body itself. And if a sword [or metal vessel] which became impure by [touching] a corpse were to convey impurity of *ohel,* the priests would be forbidden to enter all buildings [even after the removal of the corpse], for they all have a "sword" [i.e., some metal vessel] [43] which has become impure, and it would defile them by *ohel*[32] [and it is obviously impossible to say that priests may never enter all buildings]![44] It further appears in the Gemara[45] that a sword [or metal vessel] which touches a corpse does not render a person [who touches it] impure to the extent that he requires to be sprinkled [with the waters of purification] on the third

of impurity) the sword which touched him should have become only an *av hatumah* (a primary source of impurity), while the rule is that it becomes an *avi avoth hatumah* just like the dead itself. Hence a person that touches the sword which was so defiled becomes an *av hatumah* (a primary source of impurity), and not a *rishon l'tumah* (a first degree of impurity) as would be the ordinary rule. See further on these laws in Vol. III, p. 148, Note 252. It should also be pointed out [for the sake of the following text of Ramban] that the above principle of the sword [becoming an *avi avoth hatumah* just as the corpse] applies also to all metal vessels which have been rendered impure by a corpse. (41) See Ramban in his commentary to Baba Bathra 20a where he discusses at length these "texts of the Mishnah and Gemara" which corroborate his opinion. It is of interest to note that Ramban cites there also the varying opinion of Rabbeinu Tam [the outstanding authority among the masters of the Tosafoth] who holds that the sword is equated entirely to a corpse, even in regard to the impurity of *ohel* (see Note 32 above). — For the term *Gemara* see in Vol. II p. 132, Note 204. (42) Verse 14. (43) See Note 40 above. (44) This problem was proposed by Rabbeinu Chayim Hakohen to Rabbeinu Tam: "If so, what house would you build for them [the priests], and what place may be their resting place?" (see my Hebrew commentary p. 270). (45) Nazir 54b. See my Hebrew commentary p. 270.

and seventh days,[46] even though the person who touches [the sword or vessel] becomes a "father of impurity." This is because in the second verse where He states *and he shall sprinkle upon the tent*[47] it says, *and upon him that touched the bone, or 'the slain,' or the dead or the grave,*[47] but it does not say "or one that is slain *with a sword.*" If so, the sword [and all metal vessels] are like the corpse [in degree of impurity] only to the extent that one who touches it is rendered impure for seven days' duration, but not [to the extent that a sword conveys impurity] by *ohel*[32] [as does a corpse], nor [to the extent that one who touches it] requires sprinkling [of the waters of purification]. Likewise a Nazirite does not have to cut off his hair [on account of being in a tent together with it], nor is there any prohibition at all against a priest touching it [whereas he is prohibited from touching the corpse itself.] [48] This is the most likely and reasonable explanation, based on the words of our Rabbis. But we because of our sins are now impure in the exile, and we do not know of the purity of holiness *until the spirit be poured upon us from on High,*[49] and G-d *will sprinkle clean water upon* us[50] and we shall become pure. Amen, and may this be the will [of G-d] speedily in our days.

17. AND HE SHALL PUT UPON IT RUNNING WATER INTO A VESSEL. The meaning thereof is not that he should first put the ashes [of the Red Heifer] into the vessel and then put the water upon the ashes, for our Rabbis have taught[51] that if one places the ashes in the vessel first and then the water, it invalidates [the water, so that it may not be used as water of purification]. They derived this law from the expression, *running water into a vessel,* which implies that the running water [alone] should be put into the vessel [i.e., there should be nothing—such as the ashes—intervening between the water and the

(46) Verse 12. (47) Verse 18. The fact, that in this verse which speaks of the sprinkling of the waters of purification upon the impure, it does not mention that he became defiled by having touched "one that is slain with a sword," indicates that he is rendered impure for a seven days' duration, yet he does not require the sprinkling of the waters mentioned. (48) Leviticus 21:1. (49) Isaiah 32:15. (50) Ezekiel 36:25. (51) Sotah 16b.

vessel]. Perhaps they deduced it because He did not say: *"And for the unclean they shall take of the ashes of the burnt heifer of purification* into a vessel, and he shall put upon it running water." But [since Scripture put it in the reverse order: *And for the unclean they shall take of the ashes of the burnt heifer of purification — and running water he shall put thereto in a vessel*], the meaning of the verse is as follows: *"and he shall put* upon the ashes the *running water* which was [already] *in the vessel,"* meaning that he should mix the ashes with the water which was in the vessel until the water flows over them.[52]

20. HE HATH DEFILED THE SANCTUARY OF THE ETERNAL. Scripture mentioned this [punishment of] excision without explanation,[53] saying, *he hath defiled the Tabernacle of the Eternal,*[54] because He had already warned us against defiling the Sanctuary, just as He said, *she shall touch no hallowed thing, nor come into the Sanctuary.*[55] For since He mentioned [this prohibition] there in dealing with a lesser degree of impurity, namely, that of a woman after childbirth in the days of her purification, which is a natural event for her, it [is self-understood that it] applies equally to all impure persons. He has also mentioned the [requirement of] immersion [in a ritual pool for purposes of purification], saying, *but if he wash them not* [i.e., the garments which have become unclean], *nor bathe his flesh, then he shall bear his iniquity,*[56] that is to say, *he will bear his iniquity* if he transgresses [the law and does] that which he is admonished not to do [i.e., if he eats holy food or enters the Sanctuary whilst he is still impure, or when he is wearing impure garments]. Therefore He stated here in respect of the impurity

(52) Thus first he puts the running water into the vessel, then the ashes, and afterwards he mixes the ashes with the water so that the water which was in the vessel is on top. (53) I.e., without first saying *here* that one who is impure may not enter the Sanctuary or Tabernacle. (54) Above, Verse 13. — The Torah there uses the term *mishkan* (Tabernacle), and the same law applies of course to the *mikdash* (Sanctuary), mentioned here in Verse 20. Ramban here uses the terms interchangeably; and later on explains why the law is mentioned twice. (55) Leviticus 12:4. (56) *Ibid.*, 17:16.

[conveyed] by a corpse that *whosoever touches the dead*[54] *and purifieth not himself* [with the waters of purification], even though he washes his clothes and bathes himself in water, is [nonetheless] considered one who defiles the Tabernacle, just as if he had not immersed himself [in a ritual pool] at all. Thus it was only necessary to mention that the purification [by means of sprinkling the waters of purification] prevents him from becoming pure [if he did not sprinkle them upon himself, even if he washed his clothes and bathed himself in water], this being the meaning of the expression, *his impurity is yet upon him,*[54] that is to say, even though he has immersed himself [in a ritual pool] like all other impure people, he still remains impure, *because the water of sprinkling hath not been sprinkled upon him.*[54]

It is possible that the verse is referring to the man [mentioned above, who had become defiled by the corpse], and the meaning thereof is as follows: "*whosoever toucheth the dead, even the body of any man that is dead, and purifieth not himself* — 'he who' *hath defiled the Tabernacle of the Eternal shall be cut off from Israel.*" There are similar cases where the letter *shin* or the word *asher* [defining the nature of a relationship such as: who, which, that, etc.] is missing, [as in the following verses]: *l'chol yavo g'vurathecha*[57] [which is to be understood as: *l'chol — asher — yavo g'vurathecha — Thy might to every one 'that' is to come*]; *v'chol yesh lo* (*and all he had*) *he put into his hand*[58] [which is to be understood as: *v'chol — asher — yesh lo — and all 'that' he had he put into his hand*]; *eth haderech yeilchu bah*[59] [which is understood as: *eth haderech — asher — yeilchu bah — the way 'in which' they must walk*]. There are many such verses. And the meaning of the expression *'ki' he hath defiled the Sanctuary of the Eternal*[60] is " 'when' he has defiled the Sanctuary of the Eternal," [this usage of the word *ki* being similar to that found in the verse]: *'ki' a bird's nest chance to be before thee* [which means: " 'when' a bird's nest chance to be before thee"],[61] and [it is like] its many companion-verses.

(57) Psalms 71:18. (58) Genesis 39:4. (59) Exodus 18:20. (60) Here in Verse 20. (61) Deuteronomy 20:6.

Now Scripture mentions here [the punishment of] excision twice [once in Verse 13 in connection with defiling the Tabernacle, and again in Verse 20 in connection with the Sanctuary]. In the opinion of our Rabbis[62] this is in order to declare him liable for defiling the Tabernacle of the Tent of Meeting, and also for the Sanctuary, i.e., the Permanent House [the Temple in Jerusalem].[63] According to the plain meaning [of Scripture] it may be that *eth mikdash Hashem* [usually translated: *the Sanctuary of the Eternal*] refers to the holy offerings. For He had already declared that he *that eateth of the flesh of the sacrifice of peace-offerings, which pertain unto the Eternal, having his impurity upon him,*[64] is liable to excision; therefore He now declared furthermore that [in the case of impurity conveyed through a corpse] even if [the impure person] immerses himself [in a ritual pool] he is still liable [to that punishment], if he does not purify himself on the third and seventh day [with the waters of purification, before he eats of the holy offerings]. The meaning, then, of *mikdash Hashem* [literally: the "Sanctuary" of the Eternal] will be [as if it said]: *kod'shei Hashem* (the "holy things" of the Eternal), as in the expression *eth mik'dsho mimenu*[65] [literally: "the Sanctuary thereof," which really means: *eth kodsho mimenu* — "the hallowed part thereof"]. Thus the [punishment of] excision mentioned in [this] section refers to [entering] the Sanctuary [whilst impure, as stated above in Verse 13], and [eating] its hallowed offerings [in such a state, as mentioned in this verse here].

The correct interpretation appears to me to be that [implied] by the literal meaning [of Scripture], namely that the first [mention of] excision [in Verse 13] refers to one who [actually] touches the corpse, as He said, *Whosoever toucheth the dead, even the body of any man that is dead,*[66] and the second [mention thereof, i.e., in Verse 20 here] applies to those who were rendered impure by *ohel*[32] but did not [actually] touch *the bone* or *the grave*; for the meaning of [the expression] *but the man that shall be unclean, and shall not purify*

(62) Shebuoth 16b. (63) See Vol. II, p. 335, Note 598. (64) Leviticus 7:20. (65) Above, 18:29. (66) Verse 13.

himself [60] is: "*but the man that shall be unclean* by any of these means [mentioned in Verses 14-16] *and shall not purify himself,* [*that soul shall be cut off from the midst of the assembly*]." By way of the Truth [the mystic teachings of the Cabala], it is possible that the expression *mikdash Hashem* is alluding to the Sanctuary of the Sanctuary.[67]

20 1. AND THE CHILDREN OF ISRAEL, EVEN THE WHOLE CONGREGATION, CAME INTO THE WILDERNESS OF ZIN. "*The congregation* — an upright congregation, for those who were [punished] with death in the wilderness [on account of sinning in the matter of the spies] had already died, and these were designated to live" [i.e., they were the new generation which was to enter the Land]. This is Rashi's language, and such is also the opinion of Rabbi Abraham ibn Ezra. But if so, why was it necessary to mention this [same expression: *even the whole congregation*] when they came afterwards unto Mount Hor? [68] Now Rabbi Abraham ibn Ezra wrote [there] that Scripture mentioned it because Edom had come out to fight them,[69] therefore it mentions that none of them was missing when they came back from the city of Edom. But this is not correct, since Israel turned away from him [Edom][70] and did not wage battle with them at all.

The correct interpretation appears to me to be that it is the Scriptural style to mention ["the whole congregation"] when speaking of complaints, [just as in the following verses]: *And all the congregation of the children of Israel came unto the wilderness of Sin, which is between Elim and Sinai;* [71] *And all the congregation of the children of Israel journeyed from the wilderness of Sin, by their stages . . . and encamped in Rephidim*[72] — and Scripture thereby informs us that they all [participated] in the complaint. Similarly,

(67) A reference to the Glory of G-d (Abusaula). See my Hebrew commentary, p. 272. (68) Further, Verse 22: *And they journeyed from Kadesh,; and the children of Israel, 'even the whole congregation,' came unto Mount Hor.* (69) *Ibid.,* Verse 20. (70) *Ibid.,* Verse 21. (71) Exodus 16:1. See *ibid.,* Verses 2-3, that they murmured for food. (72) *Ibid.,* 17:1. There too it is related in Verses 2-3 that they quarrelled with Moses, saying, "Give us water."

And all the congregation lifted up their voice; [73] *And on the morrow all the congregation of the children of Israel murmured.* [74] Scripture uses that expression when they came to Mount Hor[75] in order to tell us that they all took part in the mourning for Aaron, *the holy one of the Eternal,* [76] just as it is said, *and they wept for Aaron . . . all the house of Israel,* [77] and it states [furthermore]: *in the sight of all the congregation.* [78] In Bamidbar Sinai Rabbah[79] I have seen mentioned the text [quoted above by Rashi] — "an upright congregation etc." — only in connection with the second verse [speaking] about Mount Hor [i.e., Verses 20 and 27 quoted above, which say that *'the whole congregation came'* to Mount Hor, and that Moses and Aaron *went up into Mount Hor 'in the sight of all the congregation'*], for in the case of the first verse [i.e., the present verse, the expression *all the congregation*] is used because [Scripture wants to indicate that they all joined in] the murmuring, as I have explained.

'VAYEISHEV HA'AM' (AND THE PEOPLE ABODE) IN KADESH. The intention thereof is to tell us that when they had entered the wilderness of Zin as far as Kadesh, Miriam died. Rabbi Abraham ibn Ezra erred [here] when he commented: "[Scripture states *vayeishev ha'am,* meaning 'the people dwelt,' and does not say *vayachanu* — 'and they pitched'] because they stayed there for a long time, for so it is written." [80] [This is in error] because the place called Kadesh of which it is written, *So ye abode in Kadesh many days, according unto the days that ye abode there*[80] is Kadesh-barnea,[81]

(73) Above, 14:1. In that case they were discouraged by the report of the spies, and wanted to return to Egypt. (74) *Ibid.* 17:6. There they complained about the death of Korach and his followers. (75) Further, Verse 22. (76) Psalms 106:16. (77) Further, Verse 29. (78) *Ibid.,* Verse 27. (79) Bamidbar Rabbah 19:9. (80) The verse is found in Deuteronomy 1:46: *So ye abode in Kadesh many days, according unto the days that ye abode* there. Rashi there explains that the *many days* were in fact nineteen years. See the note that follows. (81) *Ibid.*, Verse 19: *and we came to Kadesh-barnea.* From there the spies were sent to see the Land (further, 32:8). As a result of their sin, it was decreed that the people would remain in the wilderness for the following thirty-eight years, and die therein. The first half of this

which is in the wilderness of Paran[82] [and not in *the wilderness of Zin,* mentioned here]. It was from there that the spies were sent out [to see the Land] in the second year [after the exodus], and thence that they returned. But the Kadesh [mentioned] here is in *the wilderness of Zin,* and they [only] arrived there in the fortieth year [after the exodus], and there Miriam died. The verses are explicit [on this matter].

The sin of Moses and Aaron in the [matter of the] waters of Meribah[83] is not clearly expressed in Scripture. Rashi explains[84] that [their sin consisted of hitting the rock], because He had commanded them, *and speak ye unto the rock,*[85] and did not say "and ye shall strike it." For had they spoken [to the rock and it had brought forth water] the Holy One, blessed be He, would have been sanctified before the whole congregation, since the people would have said: "If [even] this rock, which does not hear and does not speak, nonetheless obeys the command of the Holy One, blessed be He, how much more so should we [obey His commands]!" These words are [in the nature of] a homiletic interpretation,[86] but they do not clarify [the matter]. For since G-d had commanded Moses: *Take the rod,*[85] it implied that he *should* smite [the rock] with it, for had He only wanted that he should speak to it, what was [the point of] this rod in his hand? Similarly, in the [case of the] plagues of Egypt where He said, *and the rod which was turned to a serpent shalt thou take in thy hand*[87] it was in order to smite with it;[88] and sometimes He said, *Stretch forth thy hand [with thy rod],*[89] when the meaning is: "to smite with the rod," since

period they spent in Kadesh, namely Kadesh-barnea. It is this Kadesh-barnea which Ibn Ezra equated with Kadesh [mentioned here], and that is an error, as explained. (82) Above, 13:26. (83) Further, Verses 7-13. I.e., the verses do not state explicitly what constituted the sin of Moses and Aaron, but it was clearly considered a grave one. Ramban proceeds to discuss various explanations at length. (84) Verses 11-12. (85) Verse 8. (86) Found in Midrash Agadah, here on Verse 8. — In other words, Ramban does not question the homiletic truth of this interpretation, for it is surely conducive to gaining the proper awe for the word of G-d. But it does not clarify the matter of the verses. (87) Exodus 7:15. (88) *Ibid.,* Verse 17: *I will smite with the rod that is in my hand upon the waters which are in the river.* (89) *Ibid.,* 8:1.

Scripture writes briefly when the subject-matter is self-understood. Moreover, the miracle [involved in the rock giving forth water] is no greater if [accomplished] by speech than by smiting, for as far as the rock is concerned both are equal. Furthermore [if the sin consisted of smiting the rock], why did He say about this: *ye* [Moses and Aaron] *trespassed against Me?*[90] [It cannot be because they failed to *speak* to the rock], for the [fulfillment of the] command to [Moses to] *speak* to the rock is indeed [also] mentioned at the occurrence [of the event]! Thus He commanded [Moses and Aaron] to say whilst the rock "listens" that G-d will bring forth water out of this rock, similar to [that which Joshua said about a stone which he put up as a witness to the covenant which he made with the people], *for 'it hath heard' all the words of the Eternal.*[91] And they [Moses and Aaron] indeed did so, as Scripture states, *And Moses and Aaron gathered the assembly together before the rock, and he said unto them* etc.[92] Thus the rock did "hear" when he [Moses] spoke these words to all the people!

Now Rabbi Abraham ibn Ezra has already refuted many claims of the commentators in [their explanations of the nature of] this sin. But the secret[93] to which he alluded is also incorrect. For if Moses lost his concentration of mind because of the strife of the people, and [therefore] did not speak to the rock, so that the water did not come forth [when he smote the rock] the first time, and only when he hit the rock again, a second time, with concentration of cleaving unto [the Creator of] all, did the water come forth [as Ibn Ezra explains] — then

(90) Deuteronomy 32:51. (91) Joshua 24:27. (92) Further, Verse 10. Thus it is obvious that Moses did utter the Divine message whilst the rock "listened." And so why did Rashi attribute to Moses the lack of speaking in this event! (93) Ibn Ezra alludes to the Cabalistic concept that when a person's mind cleaves solely to G-d, he can accomplish miracles. Now G-d told Moses to speak to the rock, and had he done so with single-minded devotion to G-d, he would have been able thereby to bring forth water. But when he began rebuking the people for their complaints, he lost that complete concentration of mind which was required for invoking G-d's miraculous intervention to bring forth water, and he then proceeded to smite the rock. When this failed to produce any water, he smote it a second time, by which time he had regained his original complete concentration of mind on G-d, so that the water then came forth. Ramban rejects this interpretation.

they [indeed] sinned the first time, but it was not such [a sin] about which He would say: *ye believed not in Me, to sanctify Me,*[94] since there was no lack of "faith" here at all!

Now Rabbeinu Rabbi Moshe [ben Maimon] advanced the following reasoning,[95] and explained "that the sin of Moses our teacher, of blessed memory, consisted of tending towards anger, when he said, *Hear now ye rebels,*[96] and G-d, blessed be He, treated this as a failing, that a man like him should show anger in front of the congregation of Israel, in a situation in which anger was not warranted. All similar actions of such a man are treated as a profanation of G-d's Name, because the people take an example from all his [Moses'] movements and words, hoping thereby to achieve successes[97] in this world and the World to Come. How could he [permit himself to] appear angry, since it [anger] is an evil trait, and is derived only from a bad characteristic of the features of the soul! But when He said of this sin: *ye trespassed against Me,*[90] [the meaning thereof] is as I shall explain. Moses was not speaking to simpletons, nor to those of insignificant status, for the least important of their women was [equal in prophetic vision] to [the prophet] Ezekiel the son of Buzi, as the Sages have mentioned.[98] Thus whatever Moses said or did the people would examine, so that when they saw him becoming angry, they said that he—may his memory be blessed — did not lack moral perfection, and therefore 'unless he knew that G-d was angry with us for demanding water, and that we have aroused His anger, blessed be He, Moses also would not have been angry with us.' But we do not find that G-d, praised be He, was angry [with the people] when He spoke to Moses on this matter. But [instead] He said: *Take the rod, and assemble the congregation, thou, and*

(94) Verse 12. (95) In his *Shemonah Perakim* (The Eight Chapters), Chapter 4. These chapters are Maimonides' introduction to the Tractate Aboth, which contains the roots of ethical and moral teachings of the Rabbis of the Mishnah. (96) Verse 10. (97) In our "Shemonah Perakim" it is in the singular: "success." The word is here indicative of achievement of those qualities of character which make one's life "a success" in the noblest sense of the word. (98) "A maidservant saw at the [splitting of the Red] Sea what the prophet Ezekiel never saw" (Mechilta, Exodus 15:25). See Vol. II, p. 228.

Aaron thy brother, and speak ye unto the rock before their eyes, that it give forth its water; and thou shalt bring forth to them water out of the rock; so thou shalt give the congregation and their cattle drink.[85] [This statement does not indicate that G-d was angry with the people for having demanded water, and hence Moses' anger was unjustified.] Thus we have solved one of the most difficult problems in the Torah, concerning which many things have been said, and which has been asked many times, namely: 'what was the sin which Moses committed?' Consider what has been said [by others] about it, and what we ourselves have explained, and let the truth prevail." These are the words of Rabbi Moshe [ben Maimon] of blessed memory.

He has added *vanity* upon *vanities*![99] For Scripture says *ye trespassed against Me,*[90] meaning that they transgressed His command, and He [further] stated, *ye believed not in Me,*[94] meaning that they lacked faith in Him, [and if so] the punishment [of Moses] was not because he showed anger! [Were this to be his sin], Moses would have deserved punishment [not so much here as] when he *was wroth with the officers of the host*[100] for no reason. Moreover, Scripture [here] does not mention anything about him being angry, for the expression *Hear now, ye rebels*[96] is [merely a form of] rebuke, similar to that which he [Moses] said: *Ye have been rebellious against the Eternal.*[101] Furthermore, Aaron never in his life became angry, for he always *walked in peace and uprightness.*[102] Besides, it is impossible [to suggest, as Rambam does], that G-d was not very angry with them [the people] for their strife with Moses! For throughout all their [previous] trials in the wilderness, their greatest sin was when they said, *wherefore hast thou brought us up out of Egypt?*[103] and they preferred to be slaves to their enemies doing rigorous work, rather than to be G-d's [people], like a son who serves his father. Thus Scripture says:

(99) See Ecclesiastes 1:2. — In other words, yet another interpretation has been added to those of the previous commentators which are not satisfactory. (100) Further, 31:14. (101) Deuteronomy 9:24. (102) Malachi 2:6. — Yet Verse 12 clearly states that Aaron too, was to be punished, although according to Rambam's explanation he had not sinned! (103) Exodus 17:3.

because that ye have rejected the Eternal Who is among you, and have troubled Him with weeping, saying: 'Why, now, came we forth out of Egypt?' [104] On the first occasion they said even less than this, [namely], *Wherefore hast thou brought us up out of Egypt, to kill us and our children and our cattle with thirst?*[103] and yet there was great [Divine] wrath against them, and [it was considered] a great sin, just as it is said, *And the name of the place was called Massah* [Trying] *and Meribah* [Strife], *because of the striving of the children of Israel* etc.[105] And here it says expressly, *These are the waters of Meribah* [Strife], *where the children of Israel strove with the Eternal!*[106] What greater transgression can there be than this! *Woe unto him that striveth with his Maker!* [107] And Moses said, *Also the Eternal was angry with me for your sakes, saying: 'Thou also shalt not go in thither.'* [108] If so, it was they [the people] who sinned and brought about all this misfortune! But according to the explanation of the Rabbi [Moshe ben Maimon], they did not commit any transgression and sin at all in this whole affair! And as for that which Rabbi Moshe said: "We do not find that G-d, praised be He, was angry [with the people when He spoke to Moses on this matter], but instead He said: *Take the rod* etc." [86] — know that whenever the people needed something for their sustenance, even though they murmured and transgressed [in asking] for it, *He, being full of compassion, forgiveth iniquity . . . and does not stir up all His wrath,*[109] nor does He hold [their sin against them], but He gives them their request.[110] Similarly in the [case of the] first [request for] water He said in a peaceful manner, *Pass on before the people* etc.,[111] even though there was *trial and strife* there,[105] such that He warned them [not to try G-d] in future generations [using it as an example].[112] So also in connection with the manna [He said], *Behold, I will cause to*

(104) Above, 11:20. (105) Exodus 17:7. (106) Further, Verse 13. Thus Scripture here emphasizes that the people's sin consisted of *striving with the Eternal,* and this is not so according to Maimonides' explanation, as Ramban continues. (107) Isaiah 45:9. (108) Deuteronomy 1:37. (109) Psalms 78:38. (110) See *ibid.*, 106:15. (111) Exodus 17:5. (112) Deuteronomy 6:16 — *Ye shall not try the Eternal your G-d, as ye tried Him in Massah.* (See also "The Commandments," Vol. II, pp. 63-64).

rain bread from heaven for you,[113] in a phrase indicating love and affection. Only at the end, in the second communication, He said, *I have heard the murmurings of the children of Israel,*[114] merely in order to tell them that they had sinned. But [it is only] when they complained for no [good] reason, that *He poured upon* them *the fury of His anger.*[115] And here there is an additional allusion to great wrath, and [the people] being liable to a plague, as it is said, *and the glory of the Eternal appeared unto them.*[116] [The expression *unto them*] refers to *the assembly* mentioned [in the first part of the verse], which indicates "the hand of the Eternal" that is present in plagues, as you may note in [incidents of] the spies,[117] the day of Korach's punishment,[118] and the following day.[119] And one must [moreover] wonder at the Rabbi [Moshe ben Maimon, who wrote that the people committed no sin in this affair] since the verse explicitly states, *They angered Him also at the waters of Meribah, and it went ill with Moses because of them!*[120] And the verse [there] counts this sin amongst the great trials with which they [the people] tested G-d in the wilderness!

The most likely explanation amongst all those that have been said about this matter, and the one best suited to answer a questioner, is that of Rabbeinu Chananel,[121] who wrote [in his commentary] that the sin consisted of their saying, *are 'we' to bring you forth water out of*

(113) Exodus 16:4. Thus G-d showed them love and affection although they sinned in murmuring and complaining. (114) *Ibid.*, Verse 12. (115) Isaiah 42:25. (116) Verse 6. (117) Above, 14:10-12: *and the glory of the Eternal appeared . . . 'I will smite them with the pestilence.'* (118) *Ibid.*, 16:19: *and the glory of the Eternal appeared . . .* The destruction of Korach and his company followed, as related *ibid.*, (Verses 31-33). (119) *Ibid.*, 17:7: *and the glory of the Eternal appeared . . .* This was followed by a plague, as related there in Verses 11-14. (120) Psalms 106:32.—See my Hebrew commentary, pp. 274-276 for various defenses of Rambam's interpretation of Moses' sin at Meribah. In his Sefer Hazikaron (see Vol. I, Preface pp. x-xi) Rabbi Yom Tov ben Abraham (Ritba) concludes his defense of Rambam's opinion as follows: "And although I know that the tradition of our master, Rabbi Moshe ben Nachman (Ramban) of blessed memory, in the matter of Moses' sin is the true tradition which one cannot criticize, yet there are seventy [different] interpretations of the Torah, and they are all the words of the living G-d." Ramban's own explanation follows now in the text. (121) See above, *Seder Korach,* Note 48.

this rock? [96] They should [not have said "are we", but] "shall the Eternal bring you forth water?" just as they had said *when 'the Eternal shall give' you in the evening flesh to eat* etc.,[122] and similarly in [the case of all the] miracles they [Moses and Aaron] informed them that the Eternal would do wonders for them. And [since they did not say so here], perhaps the people thought that Moses and Aaron brought forth the water for them out of the rock through their own wisdom [and that it was not a Divine miracle]. This is [what G-d referred to in saying], *ye sanctified Me not.*[123] Now in the case of the first episode with the rock, He said, *Behold, I will stand before thee there upon the rock in Horeb,*[124] and the seventy elders saw the pillar of the cloud[125] hovering over the rock, and thus it was made apparent to all that the miracle was the deed of the Great G-d. But here, since the people saw nothing, they misunderstood the words of Moses and Aaron [as explained above].[126]

It is possible that He said *'m'altem bi'* (*ye 'trespassed' against Me*),[123] because if one derives benefit from a sacred object, it is called *me'ilah.*[127] Similarly, He said *'m'rithem pi'* (*ye rebelled against My commandment*)[128] because He had commanded them to *speak unto the rock before their eyes,*[129] in order that I should become sanctified in their eyes. Or [it may be that *m'rithem pi*[128] means] "you have 'changed' My commandment," related to the expression *'vatemer' (and she changed) My ordinances,*[130] since I did not command you to speak in this manner [*are 'we' to bring you forth water out of this rock?*]. And [according to Rabbeinu Chananel's explanation, the criticism that] *lo he'emantem bi*[131] (*ye believed not in Me*) refers [not to Moses and Aaron *themselves* lacking in belief, but] to the children

(122) Exodus 16:8. (123) Deuteronomy 32:51. (124) Exodus 17:6. (125) *Ibid.*, 13:21. (126) See the comments of later scholars on Rabbeinu Chananel's explanation of this topic, quoted in my edition of Rabbeinu Chananel al Hatorah (Mosad Harav Kook, Jerusalem, 5732). (127) Here too, a deed which was in reality a Divine miracle came to be ascribed to Moses' and Aaron's own doing, as explained above, because they said, *are 'we' to bring you forth water out of this rock?* In a way, then, Moses and Aaron thereby "derived benefit" from a sanctified matter. (128) Further, 27:14. (129) Verse 8. (130) Ezekiel 5:6. (131) Verse 12.

of Israel [i.e., it does not mean, as it is generally translated, "ye believed not in Me," but " 'ye did not cause the children of Israel to believe in Me' because you did not attribute to Me the bringing forth of the water from the rock"]. Or [the word *he'emantem*] may mean "strengthening," as if to say: "you did not strengthen yourselves to sanctify Me in their eyes," related to these expressions: *'va'amanah' (and a 'sure' ordinance) concerning the singers;*[132] *the peg that was fastened 'bimkom ne'eman' (in a 'sure' place).*[133]

The Truth [Cabalistic explanation] is that this subject [i.e., the nature of Moses' sin in the incident of the waters of Meribah] is one of the great secrets amongst the mysteries of the Torah. For on the first [occasion with the rock] He said to Moses, *Behold, I will stand before thee there upon the rock in Horeb; and thou shalt smite the rock,*[124] meaning to say: "My Great Name will be upon the rock in Horeb," which is *the Glory of the Eternal,* the *devouring fire on the top of the mount.*[134] Therefore he only hit it there once, and a great amount of water came forth. But here He did not tell him so, and so both of them [Moses and Aaron] agreed that they would smite the rock twice — and that was their sin. Therefore He said, *lo he'emantem bi,*[131] "you did not put faith in My Name [when you should have known][135] that by faith [alone] the miracle will be done." It states, *'m'rithem pi' (ye rebelled against My commandment),*[128] because *they rebelled* against *His holy spirit,*[136] which is always called *pi Hashem (the commandment of the Eternal).*[137] Therefore He said, *'m'altem' bi,*[123] and the term *me'ilah* always denotes "untruth." [138] Thus the sin [of Moses and Aaron] is clearly expressed in Scripture. And so did the Psalmist say, [*Tremble thou earth . . .*] *at the presence of the G-d of Jacob; Who turneth the rock into a pool of water.*[139] And you can

(132) Nehemiah 11:23. Meaning: "a strong" ordinance. (133) Isaiah 22:25. Meaning "a strong" place. (134) Exodus 24:17. The verse reads: *'like' devouring fire.* (135) Abusaula. See my Hebrew commentary p. 276. (136) See Isaiah 63:10. (137) See Ramban above, 10:6. (138) In this case the "untruth" consisted of thinking that there would be no water unless they would hit the rock twice (Abusaula). (139) Psalms 114:7-8.

understand this from Moses' prayer, when he said, *O G-d Eternal, Thou hast begun,*[140] pleading before *the Glorious Name*[141] to forgive him.

And in the opinion of our Rabbis[142] who mention Moses' anger [as a factor in his sin], it is possible that he hit the rock but [only] a few drops came forth as a result of the diminution in his concentration because of his anger, and they both [Moses and Aaron] were astonished at this, and decided to hit the rock a second time, as I have mentioned, and that was the sin of both of them.

In my opinion, the meaning of the phrase, *and speak ye 'el' (unto) the rock*[129] is like *'al'* (concerning) the rock. Similarly, *Thus saith the Eternal of hosts 'el' the pillars, and concerning the sea, and concerning the bases . . . they shall be carried unto Babylon.*[143] Thus He commanded them [Moses and Aaron] to say in the presence of the congregation, when they are all gathered together, that G-d will bring them forth water out of the rock, as He indeed did. Now do not find a difficulty[144] in the verse, *and 'speak' ye unto the rock 'before their eyes,'*[129] for the meaning thereof is like "in their presence", so that they should all hear it. Similarly [we find]: *And Hananiah 'spoke before the eyes of'* [which means: "in the presence of"] *all the people, saying: 'Thus saith the Eternal: Even so will I break the yoke of Nebuchadnezzar king of Babylon* etc.' [145] There are many cases like this. Or the meaning of the word *l'eineihem* (*before their eyes*) here

(140) Deuteronomy 3:24. (141) *Ibid.*, 28:58. (142) Sifre, *Matoth* 157. (143) Jeremiah 27:19; 22. The verse clearly does not mean "unto the pillars," but "concerning the pillars." (144) The difficulty is as follows: If we explain [as we have done hitherto] that *speak ye 'el' the rock* means "to" the rock, and *the rock* will listen, then the following word *l'eineihem* (*before their eyes*) fits in perfectly. The speaking by Moses and Aaron with the rock listening, is to be done before "the eyes" of the people. But if as we now explain *speak ye 'el' the rock* as meaning *'al' the rock* ["concerning" the rock] while *the people* are to listen, how is the word *l'eineihem* in accord with the thought, since people do not listen with "their eyes?" Hence Ramban proceeds to remove this difficulty by pointing out that the word *l'eineihem* is Scripturally not always used in a literal sense and here it means "in their presence." (145) Jeremiah 28:11.

may be that [Moses'] speaking [to the rock] should be when the people are all gathered there, and the rock is *before their eyes,* as it says when the event [actually took place], *And Moses and Aaron gathered the assembly together 'before the rock'.*[96] For when they had gathered together there and saw the rock face to face, they [Moses and Aaron] said, *are we to bring you forth water out of this rock?* [96] — as the Sages have mentioned[146] — so that they should not say that there were springs [hidden at that place]. It is possible that the verse is to be [interpreted] as if it were transposed, meaning: "assemble the congregation unto the rock, and speak ye before their eyes, that it give forth water."

8. THAT IT GIVE FORTH ITS WATER. The meaning thereof is that a large amount of water should immediately spring forth, just as it is said, *and water came forth abundantly,*[147] for the term "giving" denotes abundance, as in [the verses]: *and the Land shall 'give' her produce, and the trees of the field shall 'give' their fruit;* [148] *For as the seed of peace, the vine shall 'give' her fruit, and the Land shall 'give' her increase, and the heavens shall 'give' their dew.*[149] In all these [verses] He was promising them abundance. And so, it is written, [*Behold, He smote the rock, that waters gushed out*], *and streams overflowed.*[150] Now the meaning of *'its' water* [*that it give forth 'its' water*] is not like [*the Land*] *shall give 'her' produce,* and [*the trees*] *shall give 'their' fruit,* since it is not in the nature of a rock to have water in it. But its meaning is [that it will give forth] the water which will come out of it, for when G-d turns *the flint into a fountain of waters,*[151] so that they are [contained] in it and come forth out of it, the waters may [indeed] be called *'its' water.* Similarly, *and He will bless 'thy' bread, and 'thy' water;* [152] *'his' bread shall be given, 'his' waters shall be sure.*[153] He stated it in this way [*that it give forth 'its' water*] in order to inform us that the waters will come forth from the

(146) Tanchuma, *Chukath* 6. (147) Further, Verse 11. (148) Leviticus 26:4. (149) Zechariah 8:12. (150) Psalms 78:20. (151) *Ibid.,* 114:8. (152) Exodus 23:25. (153) Isaiah 33:16.

very rock itself, not from the ground beneath it, as occurs naturally in the case of many fountains; but [these waters] will come forth from the middle of the rock. And so it is written, *Who turneth the rock into a pool of water, the flint into a fountain of waters.*[151] He repeated a second time [in this verse], *and thou shalt bring forth to them water,* meaning that "while you [Moses] are still there, you should bring them forth water from the rock, so that they should all see it gushing forth."

SO THOU SHALT GIVE THE CONGREGATION AND THEIR CATTLE DRINK. [This means] that "you should command them to drink from it in your presence." All this was for the purpose of publicizing the miracle. In the actual event, [however], it is not mentioned that "he gave the congregation and their cattle to drink;" instead, it says, *and the congregation drank, and their cattle,*[147] because owing to their great thirst, as soon as they saw water gushing out in abundance, they fell upon the river and drank.

Now according to the opinion of our Rabbis about Miriam's Well,[154] this rock [in Kadesh] is the same flint which was in Horeb;[124] therefore they explain [that the expression] *'its' water* [in *that it give forth 'its' water*] refers to the water which it used to give, for now as a result of Miriam's death the fountain ceased [and was only restored in the merit of Moses and Aaron].[155] For when our Rabbis speak of Miriam's Well, they mean that there was always a miraculous well,[156] *a fountain of living waters,*[157] flowing wherever it was His Will. Thus He caused it to come up for Ishmael in the wilderness of Beer-sheba.[158] It

(154) This was a moving well in Miriam's merit which accompanied the Israelites throughout their forty year's journeys in the desert. "When Miriam died [as mentioned here in Verse 1] the well was taken away." (Taanith 9a). Hence the crisis of the lack of water. See also Vol. II, pp. 240-241, and Note 436 *ibid.* (155) Taanith 9a. When Aaron died it continued in the merit of Moses. (156) Ramban here appears to be referring to the tradition mentioned in the Mishnah in Aboth 5:9 that ten things were created in the twilight of the eve of the first Sabbath, amongst them "the mouth of the well." It was this well which appeared wherever G-d wanted it to, as explained further on. (157) Jeremiah 2:13. (158) Genesis 21:14; 19. In Pirkei d'Rabbi Eliezer, Chapter 30 the tradition is recorded that this was the same well mentioned in connection with Miriam. See my Hebrew commentary, p. 277.

was this rock which became cleft in Horeb,[124] and throughout their travels [water] flowed from the rock wherever they encamped. But when the righteous one [Miriam] died, the fountain stopped, and now it continued through [the merit of] Moses to be *a fountain opened*[159] for him from that very same rock [which had been in Horeb], this being the meaning of the phrase, *and speak ye unto 'haselah'* (*'the' rock*) — the known rock. According to the plain meaning of Scripture, [however], there was a rock near the camp, and He commanded "*and speak ye unto the rock* which is before you" [hence the phrase *'the' rock*]. One can also explain it as "*and speak ye unto the rock* which is *before their eyes,*" meaning to say "the first rock that they will see."

10. ARE WE TO BRING YOU FORTH WATER OUT OF THIS ROCK? Far be it and [G-d] forbid that [we should explain this] as a question indicating impossibility! For Moses our teacher, who was trusted in all G-d's house,[160] [knew] that nothing is too hard for Him;[161] and he together with all Israel had seen greater and more wondrous miracles than this, and especially since this [miracle of providing water from a rock] had already been done once before through him at the rock in Horeb![124] Now the commentators[162] have said that there are certain questions which [by apparently doubting that which cannot be denied], have the force of an [impassioned or indignant] affirmation. Thus we find: *Did I reveal Myself to the house of thy father?;*[163] *The king said also unto Zadok the priest: 'Seest thou?';*[164] *Wilt thou judge?;*[165] *Hast thou eaten of the tree, whereof I commanded thee that thou shouldest not eat?*[166] But Rabbi Abraham ibn Ezra wrote [that the meaning of the verse is]: "Do we indeed have power to bring you forth water out of the rock?" He means thereby to

(159) Zechariah 13:1. (160) See above, 12:7. (161) See Genesis 18:14. (162) R'dak on I Samuel 2:27. (163) *Ibid*. The sense is: "Did I not reveal Myself, although your sons, by their actions appear to belie it!" (164) II Samuel 15:27. The sense here is: "Do you not see [that it is best that you return to the city in peace]!" (165) Ezekiel 22:2. The meaning is: "Wilt thou not judge? Of course you will judge!" (166) Genesis 3:11. The meaning is: "Have you not eaten? Of course you have eaten!"

explain that Moses said to them: *"Hear now, ye rebels* against G-d, who say, '*and why have ye brought the assembly of the Eternal*[167] *unto this evil place?*'[168] Do we have the power by natural means to bring you forth water out of this flint? You should therefore recognize that this is all from G-d, for it is He Who took you out of Egypt, and brought you to this place, and it is He Who will feed you here." This is similar to what he [Moses] told the people in the case of the manna, *and ye shall know that the Eternal hath brought you out from the land of Egypt.*[169]

In my opinion this letter *hei* [in the word *hamin* — "out of"] indicates a [real] query, [and the meaning thereof is as follows]: *"Are we to bring you forth water out of this rock* or not?" For sometimes Scripture explains a question in its positive and negative aspects, such as: *whether there are trees therein or not?*'[170] *whether thou wouldest keep His commandments, or not?*[171]—and at other times it mentions only the positive aspect, [such as in the following verses]: *Is this your youngest brother?;*[172] *Know ye Laban the son of Nachor?;*[173] *Should I weep in the fifth month, separating myself?*[174] But this question here that Moses asked of them was a probing question [to test their true intention]. He said to them: *"Hear now, ye rebels. — What do ye devise against the Eternal?*[175] — *Are we to bring you forth water out of this* strong *rock*? Will this event happen or not?" [i.e., "Do you believe that it is within His power to do it, or not?"] He thus stressed that their [behaviour was a serious] rebellion, telling them they were wanting in faith, and that the reason for their quarrelling with him was because they thought that G-d would not act wondrously for them, in a similar manner to that which it says, *And they tried G-d in their heart . . . 'Can G-d prepare a table in the wilderness . . . Can He give bread also?*'[176] Similarly the Rabbis have said:[177] "Ten times our

(167) Above, Verse 4. (168) *Ibid.*, Verse 5. (169) Exodus 16:6. (170) Above, 13:20. (171) Deuteronomy 8:2. (172) Genesis 43:29. (173) *Ibid.*, 29:5. (174) Zechariah 7:3. The reference is to the month of Ab, during which the First Temple was destroyed. When the Second Temple was built, the people asked the prophet whether they should still continue to observe the fast of the ninth of Ab. (175) Nahum 1:9. (176) Psalms 78:18-20. (177) Aboth 5:4.

ancestors in the wilderness tried the Holy One, blessed be He." [Moses' question was thus] like a query as to the belief of the person addressed, [of which we find examples] in many places in Scripture: *Must I then bring thy son back?* [178] which means: "Is that your wish?" *Shall we go to Ramoth-gilead to battle, or shall I forbear?*[179] which means, "If that is your advice." Here too, [the meaning of Moses' question is]: "Do you think that we shall bring you forth water out of this rock?" The same is also my opinion with regard to [the following verses]: *Did I reveal Myself?;* [163] *Seest thou how Ahab humbleth himself before Me?*[180] *Hast thou eaten of the tree, whereof I commanded thee that thou shouldest not eat?;* [166] *Wilt thou judge?*[165] For all these are questions, but their purpose is to ask about [the truth of] something well-known, so that the person who is asked is compelled to admit [the truth of the fact] against his will. Thus [*Did I reveal Myself*?[163] means]: "Have I revealed Myself to your father's house and chosen you? Since you know this, then *Wherefore kick ye at My sacrifice and at Mine offering?*" [181] *Do ye thus requite the Eternal*[182] with such a requital! Similarly, "*Hast thou eaten of the tree,* about which *I commanded you*[166] [not to eat], and you are ashamed [and therefore you hid yourself],[183] or [if you did not eat of the tree], why then did you hide?" And in the same way the other [verses are to be explained]. However, the expression *Seest thou?* [164] is a genuine inquiry about a matter [as to which the questioner is] in doubt, [David saying to Zadok the priest]: "If you 'advise' it, then return to the city," [and the usage of the term *'seest' thou*? means "do you see fit?"] as in the expression: "I see the words of Admon"[184] [which means: "I find the opinion of Admon correct"]. I have already explained this in *Seder Bereshith.*[185]

13. AND HE WAS SANCTIFIED IN THEM — "in that Moses and Aaron died on account of them [i.e., *the waters of Meribah*]. When the Holy One, blessed be He, executes judgment upon those who are holy [i.e., near] to Him, He becomes revered and sanctified in people's

(178) Genesis 24:5. (179) II Chronicles 18:5. (180) I Kings 21:29. (181) I Samuel 2:29. (182) Deuteronomy 32:6. (183) See Genesis 3:8. (184) Kethuboth 109a. (185) Genesis 1:4 (Vol. I, p. 30).

eyes, as it is said, *In them that are nigh unto Me I will be sanctified,*[186] and similarly it is stated, *Revered is G-d 'mimikdashecha' (out of Thy holy places)*." [187] This is Rashi's language, and it is also Rabbi Abraham ibn Ezra's interpretation. But it does not appear to me to be correct, for Moses and Aaron had not yet died and it was not commonly known amongst people that they were to die on account of this sin, so that G-d would become revered as a result of it, as happened with Nadab and Abihu,[188] and at Perez-uzzah.[189] Besides, Scripture states, *These are the waters of Meribah, where the children of Israel strove with the Eternal, and He was sanctified 'by them,'* meaning to say that He was sanctified by those who did the striving [and not through the punishment of Moses and Aaron, as Rashi and Ibn Ezra said], this being related to the expression *'In them' that are nigh unto Me I will be sanctified.*[186] And according to their explanation [i.e., that of Rashi and Ibn Ezra], it should have said, [*These are the waters of Meribah, where the children of Israel strove with the Eternal*] "and He became honored in front of them" [the children of Israel].

The correct interpretation appears to me to be that the incident with the first rock took place *in the sight of the elders of Israel*[190] alone, as it is expressly stated there. But here [in Verse 10] it is said, *And Moses and Aaron gathered the assembly together* etc. Therefore Scripture states that these *waters of Meribah* [Strife] which brought about the Divine decree against Moses and Aaron [that they would not enter the Land], *were the* same *waters of Meribah, where the children of Israel strove with the Eternal and He was sanctified in them* in the presence of all of them, similar to that which is written, *and I shall gather them out of their enemies' lands, and will be sanctified in them in the sight of many nations.*[191]

(186) Leviticus 10:3. (187) Psalms 68:36. "Read not *mimikdashecha* ('out of Thy holy places') but *mim'kudashecha* ['out of Thy sanctified ones' — out of those who are holy to His Name, upon whom He executes judgment]" (Rashi, Leviticus 10:3). (188) Leviticus 10:1-2. (189) II Samuel 6:8. (190) Exodus 17:6. (191) Ezekiel 39:27.

Know that at the first [incident with the rock] the people quarrelled with Moses — as it is said, *And the people strove with Moses,*[192] and so also did Moses say, *They are almost ready to stone me*[193] — and they [also] tried G-d, saying, *Is the Eternal among us, or not?*[194] But here they strove with Him Who is on high, but they did not test Him. Therefore [Scripture] says that these *waters of Meribah* [Strife] which were the cause of this decree [against Moses and Aaron] *are the* same *waters of Meribah, where the children of Israel strove with the Eternal, and He was sanctified in them* in their presence, and they were not the first [waters of the rock in Horeb],[124] where they tried the Eternal, and He was sanctified only *in the sight of the elders of Israel.*[190] And since there were two incidents with a rock, Scripture had to explain for which one [of these two events] these righteous men [Moses and Aaron] were punished.

14. AND MOSES SENT MESSENGERS FROM KADESH UNTO THE KING OF EDOM. Scripture did not mention the king's name, because there was no necessity to do so. It did, however, mention Sihon and Og, the kings of the Amorites, by name, because they were famous for their strength, *and* they *had a name among*[195] the nations; [therefore it stresses] that we should give thanks to Him, blessed be He, for having dealt wondrously with us, as it is said, *To Him that smote great kings; for His mercy endureth for ever . . . Sihon king of the Amorites; for His mercy endureth for ever. And Og king of Bashan; for His mercy endureth for ever.*[196] And it is customary for Scripture to mention the names of the great kings whose lands we inherited, just as it mentioned in [the Book of] Joshua *the five kings of the Amorites:*[197] *Adoni-zedek king of Jerusalem,* and *Hoham king of Hebron,* and *Piram king of Jarmuth,* and *Japhia king of Lachish,* and *Debir king of Eglon.*[198] [It mentioned also] *Jabin king of Hazor,*[199] but the rest of the kings it mentioned only by number,[200] not by name [because they were

(192) Exodus 17:2. (193) *Ibid.,* Verse 4. (194) *Ibid.,* Verse 7. (195) See II Samuel 23:18. (196) Psalms 136:17-20. (197) Joshua 10:5. (198) *Ibid.,* Verse 3. (199) *Ibid.,* 11:1. (200) *Ibid.,* 12:9-24.

not famous for their strength]. Scripture states [here], *And 'Edom' said unto him*[201] [and it does not say: "and 'the king' of Edom said"], because the whole people agreed with their ruler in his refusal [to allow the Israelites to pass through their land].

19. AND THE CHILDREN OF ISRAEL SAID UNTO HIM: 'WE WILL GO UP BY THE HIGHWAY.' At first they had said[202] that they would come into the cities, but would take care not to enter fields and vineyards as armies [consisting of] many people are wont to do, in order to plunder the threshing-floors and to invade the vineyards. Instead, they [promised] to go *along the king's highway,*[202] which is a public thoroughfare,[203] not a private road. Furthermore they said [at first] that they would not drink any of the water which they [the Edomites] have in their wells for their own needs. Afterwards the Israelites sent them a message [saying] that they would not [even] approach the cities at all, but they would go *by the highway* which leads up to the land of Canaan, which is a paved road traversed by all people, and if they or their animals drink [even] of the waters of the rivers on the way, whilst passing through the rivers, they would pay them for the benefit they derived from them. Therefore Moses said [here in Verse 19] *there is no hurt,* meaning that in [passing through their land] there would be no damage of any sort. Other scholars[204] explain [that they meant to say] *we shall not drink of the water of the wells*[202] unless we pay for it. But this is not correct, for [if so] why would he [Moses] propose to them again that which he [the king of Edom] had already refused at the beginning? [as explained in Verses

(201) Verse 18. *'Thou shalt not pass through me, lest I come out with the sword against thee.'* (202) As stated in Verse 17: *Let us pass, I pray thee, through thy land; we will not pass through field or through vineyard, neither will we drink of the water of the wells; we will go along the king's highway* . . . (203) See "The Land of Israel in Biblical Times" by Yohanan Aharoni, pp. 42-45, where the term *derech hamelech* (the king's highway) is explained as a definite official highway which followed the eastern bank of the Jordan. Ramban's interpretation is thus unlike Ibn Ezra's who explains it to mean the way which the king of Edom will specify for their passage. (204) This explanation is found in Ibn Ezra.

17-18]. The Midrashic interpretation[205] is: "We shall not drink of the waters of [our own] well,[206] but instead we will buy from you," as Rashi wrote.

Israel said to Edom, *until we have passed thy border*[207] and they did not say to him ["and we will reach] the Land which the Eternal our G-d giveth us" [as they told Sihon king of Heshbon],[208] in order that Edom should not be jealous of them [taking possession] of the Land, and [should not] claim that it would be theirs [the Edomites'], had not [Jacob] *taken* [Esau's] birthright and blessing from him *with guile.*[209] But to Sihon they did mention, *until I shall pass over the Jordan into the Land which the Eternal our G-d giveth us,*[208] as Moses stated in the Book of Deuteronomy.

21. AND ISRAEL TURNED AWAY FROM HIM. Scripture here shortened [the account, omitting to say] that it was by word of the Almighty that they were commanded, *Take ye good heed unto yourselves; contend not with them,*[210] as Moses explained to them. Thus they turned away from Edom by Divine command, since they could not do anything else because Edom did not let them pass through [his border].

26. AND STRIP AARON OF HIS GARMENTS. These are the garments [reserved only] for the High Priest, with which Eleazar his son was now appointed [High Priest in his stead]. It is likely that when Aaron came down from offering the Daily Whole-offering, and burnt the incense and kindled the lamps, Moses took him up to Mount Hor whilst he was still dressed in the garments of the [High] Priest, and [then] he stripped him of them. And according to the plain meaning of Scripture [the verse is to be interpreted: *And strip Aaron of his*

(205) Tanchuma, *Chukath* 12. According to this explanation Moses was offering to buy from the Edomites their water, although the Israelites could have drunk freely from Miriam's Well. (206) See above, Note 154. (207) Verse 17. (208) Deuteronomy 2:29. (209) Genesis 27:35. (210) Deuteronomy 2:4-5.

garments in order to] put on him the shrouds of a dead man which he had prepared for him, and then he stripped Eleazar of his ordinary clothes and put the sacred garments upon him, as he did to him on the day of initiation. And according to the Midrashic interpretation of our Rabbis,[211] various miracles occurred in connection with these garments.[212] Thus they said: "How could Moses strip Aaron of his garments in their proper order? Are not the upper ones always on top, and the lower ones always underneath? But G-d did miraculous deeds for Aaron at the time of his death, even more so than during his lifetime. Thus Moses put Aaron upon the rock and stripped him of the priestly garments, and [alternative] celestial garments clothed themselves [upon him] *underneath* them.[213] *And he put them upon Eleazar his son.*[214] But how could Moses put the garments upon Eleazar in their proper order? [215] [We must say that this was not natural], but that G-d bestowed a great honor upon Aaron at the time of his death, even more so than during his lifetime, in that celestial

(211) Sifra, *Tzav Milu'im* 1:6. (212) The miraculous nature of the event which occurred here has been explained in various ways, but from Ramban's quotation of it the explanation is as follows: Since it is obvious that Aaron would not be left naked for even one moment, we must say that as soon as the uppermost garment was removed from him, the Divine Glory wrapped him with a corresponding celestial garment. But if so, how could Moses proceed to remove the lower garments "in their proper order," since there was now a [celestial] upper garment upon them? The answer is given in the following text of the Torath Kohanim [Sifra]. See the following note. (213) "Underneath them." Thus as Aaron was stripped of his *upper* robe, he was covered with a corresponding celestial garment *underneath* his tunic [which was the lower garment directly on his body]. Moses could then proceed to remove the tunic [which was now *above* the celestial "upper" robe, thereby fulfilling the Divine command of stripping Aaron of his garments "in their proper order." As he removed the tunic, a corresponding celestial tunic likewise clothed itself *underneath* the celestial robe. This interpretation of the Torath Kohanim is based upon Malbim's commentary. (214) Verse 28. (215) For as soon as he stripped Aaron of the upper robe, Moses had to put it upon Eleazar, so that he would be clothed in the order in which the clothes are worn. If so, how could he later on put the lower garments [such as the tunic] underneath? In answer to this question the Torath Kohanim presents a second miracle, namely, that Aaron found himself arrayed in eight celestial garments and then he put on the eight garments of the high priesthood in opposite order, first

garments first [miraculously] clothed themselves underneath [the other garments], and then Moses stripped Aaron of the priestly garments in their proper order,[216] and [also] put them on Eleazar in their proper order." So it is taught in the Torath Kohanim.[211]

21 1. AND THE CANAANITE, THE KING OF ARAD, HEARD. We find [mentioned] amongst the conquests of Joshua: *the king of Arad, one.*[217] Moreover, in the section dealing with the [stages of the Israelites'] journeyings [in the wilderness], it is written, *And the Canaanite, the king of Arad, who dwelt in the south in the land of Canaan,*[218] and Scripture does not refer to [that land which is] on the eastern side of the Jordan as "the land of Canaan" without qualification, just as He said, *the land of Canaan according to the borders thereof.*[219] Furthermore, [if Arad was to the east of the river Jordan], Moses should have given the land of the king of Arad to one of the tribes of Israel [as their inheritance, in the same way that he divided up the other lands which he conquered]; but Scripture always tells[220] that it was the land of Sihon and Og, the two Amorite kings, which Moses gave to the two tribes [Reuben and Gad] and to the half-tribe [of Menasheh], whereas the nine tribes and the [other] half-tribe [of Menasheh] received their inheritance after they crossed the Jordan

the robe and finally the tunic. [Ordinarily this is not permitted, but since he was now attired already in the celestial garments underneath it was permissible for him to do it.] When Moses removed the tunic from upon Aaron and put it upon Eleazar it was thus done in proper order. See my Hebrew commentary pp. 380-381. (216) I.e., in the order he had put them on after he found himself arrayed in the eight celestial garments, which as explained above (Note 215), was in the opposite order: first the robe and finally the tunic as the uppermost garment. (217) Joshua 12:14. Ramban is to ask: since the verse in Joshua clearly indicates that Arad was in Canaan proper, to the *west* of the river Jordan: so how—as indicated in this section—could its king fight against Israel whilst they were still on the eastern bank of the Jordan: (218) Further, 33:40. (219) *Ibid.,* 34:2. Verses 10-12 *ibid.,* define the eastern boundary of Canaan as the Jordan: hence we see that the word "Canaan" does *not* include land *east* of the Jordan. So the question reappears: how come that the king of Arad, a land west of the Jordan, came to fight the children of Israel who were now encamped *east* of the Jordan? (220) *Ibid.,* Verses 13-15; Joshua 12:6, etc.

into the land of Canaan. Perhaps we may explain [that the reason for this is] that Israel utterly destroyed their land, and did not settle therein at all. But that is not [the] correct [explanation of the word *v'hacharamti* in Verse 2]. Similarly Rashi explains [that the expression: *And Israel vowed a vow unto the Eternal, and said, If Thou wilt indeed deliver this people into my hand,*] *then 'v'hacharamti' their cities*[221] means that Israel would dedicate the spoils [of those cities] to the Most High [and not that they would destroy the cities themselves].[222]

The correct interpretation appears to me to be that this king of Arad *dwelt in the south*[218] on the *western* side of the Jordan, in the land of Canaan near the Jordan, bordering onto the land of the children of Judah, near Hebron which is in the south;[223] *and he heard* from afar *of the coming of the children of Israel,*[218] so he [the king] *came by the way of Atharim*[224] to the plains of Moab to fight there against Israel. This is the meaning of the word *'vayishma'* (*and he heard*) [i.e., he heard from a distance]. Therefore Scripture relates that he *dwelt in the south in the land of Canaan,*[218] [to point out] that he came from another land, to the place where Israel was [encamped]. Then *Israel vowed a vow unto the Eternal*[221] that if He would deliver him [the king of Arad] into their hand, they would dedicate all that they had to G-d. And Scripture [further] relates[225] that G-d heard their prayer, and the vow that they had vowed unto G-d, they fulfilled,[226] for they killed them now in the days of Moses, as He had commanded, *None devoted, that may be devoted of men, shall be ransomed; he shall surely be put to death,*[227] and they gave all their spoils *into the treasury of the House of the Eternal.*[228] Scripture continued by relating *here*[225] that Israel also laid their cities waste when they came into the land of Canaan, after the death of Joshua, in

(221) Further, verse 2. (222) Hence the question would be: If Arad was on the eastern side of the Jordan, why did Moses not give it to any of the tribes? (223) Above, 13:22: *And they went up into the south, and came unto Hebron.* (224) Here in Verse 1. (225) Further, Verse 3. (226) See Isaiah 19:21: *and they shall vow a vow unto the Eternal, and shall perform it.* (227) Leviticus 27:29. See Ramban *ibid.* (228) Joshua 6:24.

order to fulfill the vow which they had made, and they called the name of the cities Hormah [Utter Destruction].[229] It is with reference to this that it is stated in the Book of Judges, *And the children of the Kenite, Moses' father-in-law, went up out of the city of palm-trees with the children of Judah into the wilderness of Judah, which is in the south of Arad*,[230] and it is [further] written, *And Judah went with Simeon his brother, and they smote the Canaanites that inhabited Zephath, and utterly destroyed it. And he called the name of the city Hormah.*[231] It was then that this vow [recorded here] was fulfilled, but Scripture, however, completed the account of the matter here, just as it did in the section speaking of the descending of the manna, [where it states]: *and Aaron laid it up before the Testimony, to be kept. And the children of Israel did eat the manna forty years, until they came to a land inhabited; they did eat the manna, until they came unto the borders of the land of Canaan*,[232] [an event which occurred] after the death of Moses, until *the morrow after the Passover.*[233] Similarly, *These are the names of the men that shall take possession of the Land for you* etc.[234] constitutes a prophecy that these men will [still] live and function [at that time]; for it is impossible [to say] that G-d would specify for them men about whom there was a doubt [as to whether they would still be living; for if so], He should rather have commanded Joshua [about them] at the time of the division of the Land. [But since the command was already given to Moses, we see that

(229) Ramban is thus saying that the account in Verse 3 of the destruction of the cities refers to an event which took place after Joshua's death, and which is recorded in detail in the Book of Judges, as will be explained further on. Thus we must say that this future event was told by G-d to Moses, who wrote it down—like the rest of the Torah—at the command and dictation of G-d. Compare Ramban's remarks in his introduction to the Commentary on the Torah, (Vol. I p. 9): "However, it is true and clear that the entire Torah — from the beginning of Genesis to *in the sight of all Israel* [the last words in Deuteronomy] — reached the ear of Moses from the mouth of the Holy One, blessed be He". Since there is no difference in time for G-d, it is written in the past tense, for past, present, and future are all the same to Him. See also Ramban Vol. II, p. 192, for the reason why the tenses are often used interchangeably in prophetic statements. (230) Judges 1:16. (231) *Ibid.*, Verse 17. (232) Exodus 16:34-35. (233) Joshua 5:11. (234) Further, 34:17.

the Torah speaks of future events, and that this constitutes a Divine promise that these specified men would live until the time of the division of the Land.]

It is also correct to say that already now in the days of Moses the Israelites destroyed this king [of Arad] *and his people with the edge of the sword,*[235] and called the place of the battle Hormah, and after they crossed the Jordan, Joshua also killed the [then] king of Arad[217] who ruled after [the one in the days of Moses], together with the [other] Canaanite kings who ruled at that time. When the children of Judah came into their cities, they destroyed them as well, and called the name of the cities Hormah,[231] because [by destroying them] they fulfilled the vow which their fathers had made, *and I will utterly destroy their cities.*[221] Therefore He stated here, *and he called the name of 'the place' Hormah,*[225] but there [in the Book of Judges] it is written, *and he called the name of 'the city' Hormah,*[231] meaning the name of every city which belonged to the king of Arad, as they fulfilled their vow, and their spoils were dedicated to the Sanctuary. Thus [according to this interpretation] everything mentioned here happened at the same time [in the days of Moses], except that He mentioned, *and their cities,*[225] [the destruction of which] occurred at a later time, when they came into their cities. It is for this reason that it says [here], *and I will utterly destroy their cities,*[221] and does not say "[I will destroy] them and their cities," because the verse [only] mentions their vow concerning the future, but they themselves [the people] died in the battle [at the time of Moses] and were destroyed there. And the language of the verse fits in well with this explanation of ours, for it should have said: "and He delivered up the Canaanites 'into their hand,' and 'they' utterly destroyed them and their cities, and 'they' called the name of the place Hormah." But Scripture omitted the pronouns[236] in order to indicate that He delivered the Canaanites into

(235) Exodus 17:13. (236) Thus it does not say that He gave the Canaanites "into their hand" [which would refer exclusively to the hand of the Israelites *of the days of Moses*]. Nor does it say *vayacharimu* (and "they" destroyed), but instead says:

the hand of whoever of the Israelites He delivered them, some of them now and some of them at a later time, for G-d hearkened to their prayer, and they fulfilled their vow.

THAT ISRAEL CAME BY WAY OF 'ATHARIM.' According to the opinion of Onkelos [who rendered the verse: "that Israel came by the way which 'the spies' had gone"], the meaning is that when the spies came and went up from the south[237] and returned, the inhabitants of the Land noticed them, and this Canaanite who dwelt in the south heard about them, and so he followed the same route which they had taken, until he reached the camp of the Israelites. Onkelos has interpreted it well. And our Rabbis have said: [238] "What was the report which he [the Canaanite] heard?" — because they found difficulty with the verse in the section [dealing with the stages] of the [Israelites'] journeyings,[239] which states, *And the Canaanite, the king of Arad, who dwelt in the south in the land of Canaan, heard of the coming of the children of Israel,*[240] since it does not mention there any war, or any other event whatsoever. Therefore they said that the report was about the death of Aaron which is mentioned there,[241] and Scripture thus states that Israel's enemies heard of the death of the righteous one, and they were consequently encouraged by that event to fight against Israel. Likewise the Rabbis have said[242] that this

'vayachareim' [literally: "and 'he' destroyed" — i.e., the one who destroyed them — now, or later on in the days of Joshua]. Similarly it does not say *vayikr'u* ("and 'they' called"), the name of the place Hormah [in the days of Moses] but *'vayikra'* ["and 'he' called" — the one who called — now or later on]. (237) Above, 13:22. (238) Rosh Hashanah 3a. (239) Ramban by implication differs here from Rashi, who quoted this text of the Rabbis on the verse before us. According to Ramban, the Rabbis made their remark with reference to the verse mentioned further on. Ramban's reason for disagreeing is apparent, because in our verse it states quite clearly the reason why the Canaanite came, namely because he had heard of the sending of the spies, as explained, and therefore he went to fight against Israel. But further on no reason is given and no war mentioned. Therefore Ramban says, the Rabbis found it necessary to give their interpretation. (240) Further, 33:40. (241) *Ibid.*, Verses 38-39. (242) Tanchuma, *Chukath* 18.

Canaanite was Amalek, and [therefore the Israelites] did not conquer his land, nor take any part of it; but they completely destroyed their cities.

AND HE TOOK SOME OF THEM CAPTIVE. "It was only one maidservant [of the Israelites that was taken captive]." This is Rashi's language, based upon the words of our Rabbis.[243] The Sages were induced to make this comment because they were of the opinion that Israel never suffered defeat at the hands of any enemy except at times when they sinned; such as at the first war with Amalek, because they had said, *Is the Eternal among us, or not?* [244] and at the second [war with Amalek][245] on account of their sin in the [matter of the] spies, when Moses had warned them not to wage war.[246] But in all wars which were by [Divine] command, not one man of them was missing[247] throughout the days of Moses. Therefore the Sages explained this verse as meaning that they [the enemy] took captive from Israel that captive whom they had in their possession, namely this maidservant whom the Israelites had [previously] captured from them. [The usage here of the term *shevi* (captive) in the sense of "servant" is] similar to the expression *'b'chor hashvi'* (*the firstborn of the captive*)[248] which means *the firstborn of 'the maidservant'*[249] [and so here too the word *shevi* denotes a maidservant], since Scripture here does not say: "and he captured men from him," or "[he captured] women and children."

According to the plain meaning of Scripture, the sense of the verse is that these Canaanites did not kill any of the Israelites, but took a few of them captive, and when G-d [later on] delivered them into their hands, they brought them all back, and not a single one of them was missing. Scripture mentioned this in order to inform us that since the Israelites saw at first that the Canaanites were winning [the war], they made this vow to dedicate all spoil which they would take to G-d, and

(243) Yalkut Shimoni, *Chukath* on this verse. (244) Exodus 17:7. (245) Above, 14:45: *Then the Amalekite . . . came down and smote them.* (246) *Ibid.*, Verses 41-42. (247) See further, 31:49. (248) Exodus 12:29. (249) *Ibid.*, 11:5.

G-d hearkened to their voice. It is possible also that we explain that G-d was angry with these Canaanites because they came from a distant land to fight against Israel, *and feared not G-d;*[250] therefore He wanted that they should be utterly destroyed, and caused them to prevail at first so that the Israelites would vow to destroy them [and dedicate the spoils] to G-d.

9. AND MOSES MADE 'NECHASH NECHOSHETH' (A SERPENT OF BRASS). "He was not told to make it of brass. But Moses said: 'The Holy One, blessed be He, called it a *nachash* (serpent); therefore I will make it of *nechosheth* (brass) — since the one word resembles the other [in sound]." This is Rashi's language, based upon the words of our Rabbis.[251] But I do not understand this, for the Holy One, blessed be He, did *not* mention to Moses [the word] *nachash,* but said to him, *Make thee 'saraf' (a fiery serpent)*![252] But the intention of the Sages is that Moses was guided by the substantive name thereof [which is *nachash*; and *saraf* is merely a particular description of a certain kind of serpent — a "fiery" serpent — hence he made the *saraf* which G-d mentioned to him from *nechosheth* (brass), corresponding with its substantive name].

It appears to me that the secret of this matter is that this is one of the ways of the Torah, every deed of which is a miracle within a miracle. Thus [the Torah] removes injury by means of the cause of the injury, and heals illness by means of the cause of the sickness, as the Rabbis have mentioned in connection with [the verse], *and the Eternal showed him a tree,*[253] and as occurred with the salt that Elisha [cast] into the water.[254] Now it is a well-known medical principle that all people bitten by poisonous creatures become dangerously ill when they see them, or [even] when they [only] see their likeness, so that if people who have been bitten by a mad dog or other mad animals look into water,[255] they see there the image of the dog or the attacker, and [this]

(250) Deuteronomy 25:19. (251) Bereshith Rabbah 31:8. (252) Verse 8. (253) Exodus 15:25. See Vol. II, p. 211. (254) II Kings 2:21. See Vol. II, p. 211, Note 259. (255) "Or any mirror." See Vol. I, p. 259.

can [cause them to] die, as is written in medical books and mentioned in the Gemara of Tractate Yoma.[256] Similarly doctors protect them from [people] mentioning in their presence the name of the animal that bit them, [and they forbid people] to mention it at all, because their minds cling to this thought and do not turn away from it altogether until it causes their death. [The doctors] have already mentioned that it is an empirical fact, amongst the wonders of reproduction, that if the urine of a person bitten by a mad dog is put in a glass receptacle after he has become rabidly sick, there will appear in that urine the likeness of the young of small dogs. And if you pass the liquid through a cloth and filter it, you will not find any trace of them at all; but if you return the liquid to the glass bottle, and it remains there for about an hour, you will again clearly see in it the small dogs. This is a true fact, and of the wonders of the powers of the soul. Now in view of all this, it would have been correct that the Israelites, who had been bitten by the fiery serpents, should *not* look upon a serpent, and should *not* mention it or bring it to mind at all. But the Holy One, blessed be He, commanded Moses to make for them the likeness of a fiery serpent, which was [the creature] that killed them. And it is well-known that these fiery serpents have red eyes and wide heads, and their bodies at their necks are like brass. Therefore Moses could not fulfill His command to make a fiery serpent except by making a serpent of brass, which appears similar to a fiery serpent. For had he made it of any other material, it would have had the likeness of a serpent, but not that of a *saraf* (a fiery serpent). And the Rabbis[251] who said [that Moses was to make a brass serpent] because "one word corresponds [in sound] to the other," [meant to imply] that the mere mention of the name [*saraf,* which is a particular form of *nachash,* as explained above] was harmful [for the people who had been bitten, and yet G-d wanted to heal them through it]. The general intention [of this section, then] is that G-d commanded that they should be healed by the harmful agent whose nature is to kill; therefore they made its likeness in form and name, and when a person concentrated

(256) Yoma 84a.

his gaze upon the brass serpent which resembled totally the offending agent, he lived. This was to make them realize that it is G-d [alone] *Who sendeth death and maketh alive.*[257]

13. FOR ARNON IS THE BORDER OF MOAB, BETWEEN MOAB AND THE AMORITES. Arnon was a city which belonged to Moab, [located] near the end of the Amorite border and the beginning of the border of Moab, and it was situated on brooks that flowed through it.[258]

The simple meaning of [the expression] *in the book of the wars of the Eternal*[259] is that there were wise men in those generations who used to write down the history of great wars, for such was [the custom] in all generations. These authors were called *moshlim* (they that speak in parables),[260] because they wrote in them [their books] by means of proverbs and figures of speech, and when there were victories which they considered wonderful, they ascribed those wars to G-d, to Whom they are in truth [to be attributed]. Now the victory of Sihon over Moab was marvellous in their eyes,[261] therefore they wrote it down in a book, speaking of it in figurative language, *Eth Vahev b'suphah* etc.,[262] and writing about it in a proverb — *Come ye to Heshbon* etc.[263] Now the name of one city of those that belonged to Moab was Vahev. *And the pouring forth of the brooks*[264] — [this refers to] the slope of the brook, because the streams [of water] flow down continuously from *the slopes of Pisgah.*[265] Similarly, *in the hill-country, and in the lowland, and in the Arabah, and in 'the slopes.'*[266] *B'suphah,*[262] [this word is] of [the root] *'b'suphah'* (*in the whirlwind*) *and in the storm.*[267] Thus when Sihon captured the cities of Moab, those who wrote in parables recorded in the book which they called "the Wars of the Eternal": *Eth Vahev b'suphah* [meaning: "The city

(257) I Samuel 2:6. (258) Verse 14: *and Arnon among the brooks.* (259) *Ibid.*: *Therefore it is said in the book of the wars of the Eternal.* (260) Further, Verse 27. (261) See Psalms 118:23. (262) Verse 14. (263) Further, Verse 27. (264) Verse 15. (265) Deuteronomy 4:49. (266) Joshua 10:40. (267) Nahum 1:3.

of Vahev He destroyed in a whirlwind"], or they wrote: "G-d warred against Vahev in a whirlwind." *And the slope of the brooks*[264] which belonged to Arnon, and the downpour of the brooks *that inclineth toward the seat of Ar,*[264] and the slope *that leaneth upon the border of Moab*[264] – all these the Eternal destroyed *in the whirlwind and in the storm,*[267] for Sihon came upon them [the Moabites] suddenly, *his horses' hoofs were counted like flint, and his wheels like a whirlwind.*[268] Similarly those [who spoke in parables] said: *For a fire is gone out from Heshbon, a flame from the city of Sihon* etc.[269] Thus Scripture is bringing a proof from the book of "the Wars [of the Eternal"] that Arnon is on the border of Moab, and was forbidden to Israel [to capture],[270] whereas the brooks and all the slopes as far as Arnon they were allowed [to take], for Sihon had captured from the king of Moab all his land until Arnon, but not Arnon itself. Thus Arnon remained part of Moab, and constituted its border, as it is written, *And unto the Reubenites and unto the Gadites I gave from Gilead even unto the valley of Arnon, the middle of the valley for a border.*[271] And so also did Jephthah say, *and they* [the Israelites] *pitched on the other side of the Arnon, but they came not within the border of Moab, for Arnon was the border of Moab.*[272]

And from thence to B'eir,[273] The meaning of this is connected with the previous [Verse 13], saying that they pitched on the other side of the Arnon, and from there they set forth on their journey and went round about B'eir since they did not enter the Arnon or any [area] beyond it, because it continued [to be] the border of Moab. Scripture called here the name of the place ["B'eir", which means "a well"] on account of the miracle[274] [which happened there], but in the [section enumerating the stages of their] journeys [in the wilderness] it is not called by that name.[275]

(268) Isaiah 5:28. (269) Further, Verse 28. (270) Deuteronomy 2:9. (271) *Ibid.,* 3:16. (272) Judges 11:18. (273) Verse 16. (274) As stated in the verse: *This is the well whereof the Eternal said unto Moses: 'Gather the people together, and I will give them water.'* (275) See further, 33:44-49. It thus shows that B'eir mentioned here was only so called on account of the miracle which happened there, but further on this place is called by a different name.

18. 'UMIMIDBAR MATANAH.' The meaning of this is as Onkelos rendered it ["and from the wilderness it was given to them"], this being an elliptical expression that is common in songs. Thus it is saying that "from the wilderness, which is a land of drought and thirst, was this gift [the well] given to us; and from this gift [of the well which descended] unto the brooks, and from these brooks [ascended] to the heights[276] until Pisgah, which looks down upon the land which is *a* complete *howling wilderness*[277] — there was no other brook, nor any other spring of water except for this one." This was the Well of Miriam in the opinion of our Rabbis,[278] or a well which came out by word of Moses at the command of the Almighty, which Israel had not asked for. For when G-d told Moses, *Gather the people together, and I will give them water,*[273] *streams overflowed*[279] from it [the well], and continued unto distant places.

21. AND ISRAEL SENT MESSENGERS UNTO SIHON, KING OF THE AMORITES, SAYING: 22. 'LET ME PASS THROUGH THY LAND.' "Although they had not been commanded to send them [a message of] peace, they nonetheless took the initiative in [offering them] peace." This is Rashi's language. I will yet explain, with the help of G-d, in its [proper] place,[280] that [unlike Rashi's explanation] they *were* commanded to offer peace [terms before beginning to fight] *all* the nations, except for Ammon and Moab. But in truth [we must say] that when Moses said to Sihon, *Let me pass through your land,* he did this of his own accord by way of conciliation, for the land of Sihon and Og was [part of the] inheritance of Israel, since it had originally belonged to the Amorite, [and was included in the territory promised to Israel]. Thus had Sihon and Og responded peaceably, and opened [their cities] to them, they would have been entitled [to take] *all the people that are found therein tributary unto* them, *and* they would

(276) Verse 19. (277) Deuteronomy 32:10. — Ramban here is thus explaining Verse 20 as well. (278) Yerushalmi, Kethuboth XII, 3. See also above, Note 154. (279) Psalms 78:20. (280) See Ramban on Deuteronomy 20:10; 23:7, and 2:24, that Ammon and Moab were excluded from terms of peace.

serve them.[281] But Moses [who only requested of Sihon, *Let me pass through your land,* and thus leave him untouched altogether] knew that Israel would not conquer now all ten nations,[282] and he wanted all their conquests to be *on the other side of the Jordan, and forward*[283] [i.e., in Canaan proper, on the western side of the Jordan] so that they should all dwell [concentrated] together, and [also because] it was *the good Land*[284] which is *flowing with milk and honey.*[285] Thus you see, had not the children of Gad and the children of Reuben requested it [the land captured east of the Jordan] from him [Moses] he would not have left anyone [to live] there, but [would have allowed it] to be a wasteland! And similarly the Rabbis have taught in the Sifre:[286] "*To give thee* [*their land*][287] — this excludes [the land] beyond the Jordan [eastward], which you took for yourself." Our Rabbis have furthermore said in connection with the ten [degrees of] holiness,[288] that the [land on the east] side of the Jordan is not suitable for [building therein] the Sanctuary and for the dwelling therein of the Divine Glory. And so it seems [also] from Scripture, for it says, *If, however, the land of your possession* [on the eastern side of the Jordan] *be unclean* etc.[289] Now they did not send to Og a message [offering] peace, because when he saw that the Israelites had defeated Sihon, he [immediately] went forth into battle against them [the Israelites].

26. FOR HESHBON WAS THE CITY OF SIHON THE KING OF THE AMORITES. That is to say, now when Israel waged battle

(281) Deuteronomy 20:11. (282) Genesis 15:18-21. (283) Further, 32:19. (284) Deuteronomy 8:7. (285) Above, 13:27. (286) Sifre, *Ki Thavo* 229. (287) Deuteronomy 4:38. In our Sifre this explanation is given on the verse *ibid.,* 26:3, and is the source of the law that the first-fruits are not brought from the land east of the Jordan. (288) Keilim 1:6-9. The text quoted by Ramban in connection with the land on the east of the Jordan is in Bamidbar Rabbah 7:8. (289) Joshua 22:19. The question there, was the building of an altar by the two and a half tribes on the east side of the Jordan near the river, which the tribes on the western side totally rejected because it was an act of rebellion against G-d. In presenting their arguments against the altar, they said, *If, however, the land of your possession be unclean, then pass ye over unto the Land of the possession of the Eternal, wherein the Eternal's Tabernacle dwelleth.* From this it is clear that the land on the east side of the Jordan is not suitable for the building of the Sanctuary etc.

against it, it was the city of Sihon the king of the Amorites, meaning to say the city of the royal residence, for *he had fought against 'melech harishon'* (*the first king*) *of Moab,* [meaning the one] who had ruled over them before any king reigned, or *harishon* [may mean] "the one before Balak," who was *the king of Moab at that time,*[290] *and* Sihon *had taken all his land out of his hand, even unto the Arnon.*[291] Now Heshbon marked the border at which this conquest [of Sihon] began; therefore it was considered the Amorites', and Israel was only prohibited [from capturing] that land of Moab and Ammon which was land that was in their possession at the time of the Divine command [not to capture any of the lands of Moab and Ammon].[292] And Scripture brings a proof that Heshbon was the city of Sihon, for *those that speak in parables* [as explained above in Verse 13] *say, come ye to Heshbon* etc.,[263] for when Sihon fought against the king of Moab, he captured at first the city of Heshbon, and the city was destroyed, and afterwards he rebuilt it as his royal abode. This is the meaning of [the phrase], *who dwelleth in Heshbon.*[293] And similarly it is said in the Book of Joshua, *Sihon king of the Amorites, who reigned in Heshbon.*[294] Thus those who spoke in parables would say to the Amorites: "*Come to Heshbon,* and settle therein; *let the city of Sihon,* over which he has become king, *be built and established*[263] after its destruction." And after Sihon had established himself in Heshbon, he assembled his army therein and captured from the border of Moab until Arnon, including Arnon itself.[295] *Therefore they that speak in parables* said, that *a fire is gone out of Heshbon, a flame from the city of Sihon* wherein he dwells; and it has *devoured Ar of Moab,* and *the lords of the high places*[296] which belong to Arnon. For Sihon has captured from Moab unto Arnon, and all the high places of the land and *the lords of the high places,*[296] this being similar [in meaning to]:

(290) Further 22:4. (291) As related in Verse 26 here. (292) Deuteronomy 2:9; 19. (293) Further, Verse 34. (294) Joshua 13:10. (295) In the Tur the phrase "*including* Arnon itself" is not found. Other scholars have also commented that the reading should be: "*excluding* Arnon itself." This is undoubtedly correct, as Ramban himself expressly states above in Verse 13. (296) Verse 28.

even the ancient high places are ours in possession.[297] He [Sihon] also took from the children of Ammon [the territory] from the Arnon to the Jabbok, as it is said in [the Book of] Joshua, *And Moses gave unto the tribe of Gad* etc. *Jazer, and all the cities of Gilead, and half the land of the children of Ammon unto Aroer,*[298] this being the land which the king of Ammon claimed from Jephthah, as he said, *Because Israel took away my land, when he came up out of Egypt, from the Arnon even unto the Jabbok, and unto the Jordan.*[299]

29. WOE TO THEE, MOAB! THOU ART PERISHED, O PEOPLE OF CHEMOSH. The meaning of this is that [the people of] Moab used to worship Chemosh their deity, and build high places [i.e., altars, to him] and trust in him more than every other people, and *in the time of their trouble they* would *say* to him: *'Arise, and save us.'*[300] Similarly Scripture refers to [this worship of theirs] in all places, as it is written, *And it shall come to pass, when it is seen that Moab hath wearied himself upon the high place, that he shall come to his sanctuary to pray; but he shall not prevail;*[301] and it is further stated [of Moab], *and Chemosh shall go forth into captivity, his priests and his princes together with him;*[302] *Moreover I will cause to cease in Moab, saith the Eternal, him that offereth in the high place, and him that offereth to his gods.*[303] Therefore those who spoke in parables said by way of mockery, that Chemosh *hath given 'his sons' as fugitives,*[304] refugees who flee [to safety] because of the sword; *and 'his daughters' into captivity;*[304] [these terms, "sons" and "daughters" are used] because those who believe in him are called "his sons" and "his daughters," in the same way that they are [here] called "his people" [*people of Chemosh*]. Similarly [we find the expression], *the daughter of a strange god.*[305] The [correct explanation is thus] not like the words of Rashi, who interpreted [the verse as follows]: "He the Giver [i.e., G-d] gave his sons [i.e., those of Moab] as fugitives from the sword."

(297) Ezekiel 36:2. (298) Joshua 13:24-25. (299) Judges 11:13. (300) See Jeremiah 2:27. (301) Isaiah 16:12. (302) Jeremiah 48:7. (303) *Ibid.*, Verse 35. (304) Here in Verse 29. (305) Malachi 2:11.

Chemosh was also worshipped by the children of Ammon, as Jephthah said [to the king of Ammon], *that which Chemosh thy god giveth thee to possess that you will possess.*[306] They also had in their country *Milcom the detestation of the Ammonites.*[307] Or [it may be that] Jephthah mentioned Chemosh to the king of Ammon because of [the land] which Israel had captured from Moab, just as he [Jephthah] mentioned to them [i.e., to the Ammonites]: *Balak king of Moab,*[308] meaning to say that neither Chemosh their god nor Balak their king had saved their land [Moab] from the hand of Israel. It is very fitting that we say, as our Rabbis explained,[309] that [the reference in the term] *'hamoshlim' (they that speak in parables)*[263] is to Balaam and those like him, the diviners who spoke in parables about future events.

34. FEAR HIM [Og] NOT. "For Moses was afraid [to wage war against Og] in case the merit of Abraham [whom Og had helped] would stand him in stead, for it is said about him, *And there came 'hapalit' (one that had escaped) and told Abram the Hebrew,*[310] this being Og who had escaped from the Rephaim whom Amraphel[311] and his allies had defeated at Ashteroth-karnaim."[312] This is Rashi's language, based on the words of our Rabbis.[313] Here too[314] the Rabbis were induced to make this comment because they knew that Moses our teacher would not have been afraid of *an arm of flesh, for with* him *was the Eternal our G-d,*[315] and *all the nations are as nothing before Him; they are accounted by Him as things of nought, and vanity.*[316] [Furthermore], it was he [Moses himself] who admonished Israel: *fear not, nor be dismayed on account of them,*[317] and who criticized them for being afraid of them, as it is said in connection with the [affair of

(306) Judges 11:24. (307) I Kings 11:5. (308) Judges 11:25. *And now art thou anything better than Balak . . .* (309) Bamidbar Rabbah 19:8. (310) Genesis 14:13. (311) In our Rashi: "Chedarlaomer." (312) Genesis 14:5. (313) Tanchuma, *Chukath* 25; Bamidbar Rabbah 19:19. (314) See Ramban above at the end of Verse 1, where he mentions a similar idea. Hence he writes now: "here too." (315) See II Chronicles 32:8. (316) Isaiah 40:17. (317) Deuteronomy 31:6.

the] spies, *Then I said unto you: 'Dread not, neither be afraid of them. The Eternal your G-d, Who goeth before you, He shall fight for you.'* [318] Therefore [we must say] that Moses was afraid [of Og] because he knew of his merit [in having helped Abraham].

In accordance with the plain meaning of Scripture, Moses had not intended now to give Israel the land of Sihon and Og as an inheritance, as I have explained.[319] But Sihon had gone out *against Israel into the wilderness,*[320] and had fought them against their will [in spite of their desire for peace]. Then G-d informed [Moses], *Behold, I have begun to deliver up Sihon and his land before thee; begin to possess his land,*[321] for here began the conquest of the seven nations [who inhabited the Land of Israel]. But Og [nonetheless] mobilized all his forces at Edrei,[322] which was a city at the end of his border, and Israel could have turned away from him just as they had turned away from Esau [i.e., Edom].[323] Therefore G-d told Moses, "*Fear him not;* go to him and contend with him in battle, *for I have delivered him into thy hand.*" And in Bamidbar Sinai Rabbah I have seen [the following text] [324] "Why was Moses afraid [of Og]? He said: Perhaps Israel committed a trespass in the war against Sihon, [by taking of the spoil for themselves], or maybe they have become defiled by sins." This is a completely homiletic exposition. And indeed all righteous people have this fear [that they might have sinned in error],[325] and this [fear] likewise occurred [in the case] of Joshua [about whom it says that G-d told him, *Fear not, neither be thou dismayed*].[326]

(318) *Ibid.*, 1:29-30. (319) Above, Verse 21. (320) *Ibid.*, Verse 23. (321) Deuteronomy 2:31. (322) Further, Verse 33. (323) Above, 20:21. (324) Bamidbar Rabbah, 19:19. (325) See Vol. I, p. 195. (326) Joshua 8:1.

Balak

22 3. AND MOAB WAS SORE AFRAID OF THE PEOPLE. The meaning of this is [that Moab stood in great fear] *because they* [the Israelites] *were many,*[1] for Moab was *small among the nations;*[2] and it was not an ancient people, like the Canaanites, the Amorites and other [nations of the] sons of Noah. Therefore they [the Moabites] were greatly afraid *of the people* who outnumbered them exceedingly, for they *were fruitful, and increased abundantly, and waxed*[3] greater than the Moabites. And they were furthermore *overcome with dread because of the children of Israel,*[4] for they had heard of the great wonders that had happened to them and their fathers. Now Moab knew that Israel would not take their land from them, since they had sent to them [offering peace][5] just as they had sent to Sihon, [asking

(1) The Hebrew text reads: *ki rav hu.* This can be interpreted as "*although* they were many," in which case the reference would be to the Moabites, [the word *ki* meaning "although"]. The meaning of the verse would thus be: "And Moab was sore afraid of the Israelites although they [the Moabites] were many, Ramban, wishing to exclude this interpretation, for the reason cited in the text, explains that the word *ki* here means "because"; hence the pronoun *hu* — "they" [they were many] refers to the Israelites. (2) See Obadiah 1:2. (3) Exodus 1:7. (4) Verse 3 here. — Hence the double expression of the verse: *And Moab was sore afraid . . . and Moab was overcome with dread.* (5) Judges 11:17: *And in like manner he sent unto the king of Moab . . .*

permission only to pass through their land], saying, *until I shall pass over the Jordan into the Land which the Eternal our G-d giveth us.*[6] Or it is also possible that they had heard of G-d's prohibition, when He said to the Israelites, *Be not at enmity with Moab.*[7] Therefore they said to the elders of Midian: "Even though the Israelites will not capture our land, *they will lick up* because of their great numbers *all that is round about us, as the ox licketh up the grass of the field,*[8] and they will capture all [the lands] that surround us, just as they did to the two Amorite kings, and they will make us *servants to do taskwork.*"[9]

7. THE ELDERS OF MIDIAN. Rabbi Abraham ibn Ezra commented that "it is possible that the five kings of Midian[10] were the elders." But if so, [the expression] *and the elders of Moab and 'the elders of Midian' departed* [further on in Verse 7] does not refer to the [same] "elders of Midian" mentioned at the beginning [here in Verse 4: *And Moab said unto 'the elders of Midian'*] since kings would not have gone to him [Balaam on such a mission] and ["the elders" mentioned in Verse 7 must perforce have been] princes, as is [expressly] written,[11] [but not "kings"]. Furthermore, according to the opinion of our Rabbis[12] who said [that the reason why Moab turned for assistance to Midian, their traditional enemy, was because they said]: "The leader of these people [the Israelites] grew up in Midian; [let us ask them about his characteristics]" — it would have been fitting for the Moabites to send [the delegation] to *the elders of Midian,* not to the kings or the people, for it was the elders who would know Moses' nature.

It appears to me that originally there were kings in Midian, but Sihon the king of the Amorites *had fought against the former king of*

(6) Deuteronomy 2:29. (7) *Ibid.,* Verse 9. (8) Verse 4 here. (9) Joshua 16:10. (10) *Evi, and Rekem, and Zur, and Hur, and Reba, the five kings of Midian* (further, 31:8). It is thus with the five "kings" of Midian [who are here in Verse 4 called "elders"] that Moab took counsel with, but not with *the elders of Midian* mentioned in Verse 7, who were lords not "kings." Ramban will refute this interpretation of Ibn Ezra. (11) Further, Verse 8: *and 'the princes' of Moab abode with Balaam.* (12) Tanchuma, *Balak* 7.

Moab, and taken all his land out of his hand, even unto the Arnon.[13] He [also] fought against the children of Ammon and took [part] of their land, just as the Ammonite king said to Jephthah, *Because Israel took away my land, when he came up out of Egypt,*[14] and Jephthah replied to him that they had taken it from Sihon.[15] In [the Book of] Joshua it is [also] written, *And their border was Jazer, and all the cities of Gilead, and half the land of the children of Ammon, unto Aroer;*[16] and Sihon furthermore fought against the kings of Midian and conquered their land, and made them *his servants bringing tribute*[17] and took the crowns off their heads, depriving them of the splendor of royalty, and he allowed them to remain as judges of the land of Midian under his authority. Therefore [although as Ibn Ezra says, they were indeed once kings of Midian], they are called *'the elders' of Midian,* similar in expression to [she shall *go up*] *to the gate unto 'the elders'*[18] [which means "the judges"]. A proof for this [that the kings of Midian were appointed judges — "elders" — by Sihon] is the verse in [the Book of] Joshua: *and all the kingdoms of Sihon king of the Amorites, who reigned in Heshbon, whom Moses smote with the chiefs of Midian, Eri, and Rekem, and Zur, and Hur, and Reba, 'the princes of Sihon,' that dwelt in the land,*[19] thus indicating that [the land of Midian and its chiefs were] under the suzerainty of Sihon. The meaning then, of [the phrase] *and the kings of Midian*[20] is "the former kings of Midian," just as it says: *the chiefs of Midian . . . the princes of Sihon.*[19] Similarly it says [of Zur, one of the five people mentioned as a king of Midian],[10] *he was the head of the people of 'a fathers' house in Midian,'*[21] but he was no longer king. Or it may be that the reason [for the use of the phrase] *the kings of Midian*[20] is that they had regained their royal status at that time.

But I do not know a reason for that which Scripture says, *and Balak the son of Zippor was king of Moab at that time,*[8] when it could have

(13) Above, 21:26. (14) Judges 11:13. (15) *Ibid.,* Verses 15-23. (16) Joshua 13:25. (17) II Samuel 8:6. (18) Deuteronomy 25:7. (19) Joshua 13:21. This verse clearly shows that the former *chiefs of Midian* had now become *the princes of Sihon.* (20) Further, 31:8: *and they slew the kings of Midian.* (21) *Ibid.,* 25:15.

said [concisely] at the beginning, *And Balak the son of Zippor,* "king of Moab," *saw all that Israel had done to the Amorites.*[22] Perhaps Balak was a mightly man of valor, very famous for *the acts of his power and of his might,*[23] and therefore Scripture mentioned that although Moab had a powerful king at that time, who was *courageous among the mighty,*[24] they nonetheless *were afraid* and *were overcome with dread because of the children of Israel.*[4] That is why Jephthah said [to the king of Ammon], *And now art thou any thing better than Balak the son of Zippor, king of Moab?,*[25] for one does not frighten a king except by [mentioning the defeat of another] king who was greatly feared.

It is possible that since Moab [at that time] did not have a king, the people stood in great fear *because of the children of Israel,*[4] therefore they did two things: they sent to the elders of Midian saying, *'Now will this people lick up* etc.,'[4] and they appointed this man [Balak] as their king on the advice of Midian, and afterwards they all sent [a deputation] to Balaam at the command of the king. This is the meaning of [the expression] *at that time* [*and Balak the son of Zippor was king of Moab 'at that time'*],[8] namely [at the time that] they took counsel about the problem of Israel, and sent the messengers to Balaam. The meaning, then, of *And Balak saw,*[22] is that he [Balak] who was one of the princes of Moab, and a mighty man of valor, took action in this matter and said to Moab, "*Come, let us deal wisely*[26] with [this] people," and they thereupon appointed him king on the advice of Midian. In the Midrash Bamidbar Sinai Rabbah I have seen [the following text, corroborating the above interpretation]:[27] "*And Balak the son of Zippor was king of Moab at that time.*[8] But was he not originally [merely] 'a prince,' as it is said, *Evi, and Rekem, and Zur, and Hur, and Reba* [*the princes of Sihon*]?[28] But [we must say] that

(22) Verse 2. (23) Esther 12:2. (24) Amos 2:16. (25) Judges 11:25. (26) Exodus 1:10. (27) Bamidbar Rabbah 20:4. (28) Joshua 13:21. And since, as the Midrash explains, Zur is a synonym for Balak, we see that Balak was merely "a prince" and not "a king"!

when Sihon was killed, at that time they appointed him king over them, the exigencies of the moment causing his [appointment as king, although he was not of the royal family]."

5. THE LAND OF THE CHILDREN OF HIS PEOPLE — "[the people] of Balak, for he [Balak] came from there [i.e., from *Pethor which is by the river*], and this man [Balaam] had prophesied and told him, 'You are destined to be king.' " This is Rashi's language, taken from an Agadic explanation.[29] But the plain meaning of Scripture is [that *the land of the children of 'his people'* is a reference to] *Balaam's* people's land [and not Balak's], for there he [Balaam] was born and there was his family background. The reason for [Scripture] mentioning this is [to indicate] that he [Balaam] was a diviner, from the land where all the people were diviners, similar to that which is written, *for they are replenished from the east, and with soothsayers like the Philistines.*[30]

6. THAT WE MAY SMITE THEM—the meaning [of the plural "we," although it is only Balaam who is speaking], is "I and Midian my ally."[31]

13. [AND BALAAM ROSE UP IN THE MORNING, AND SAID] UNTO THE PRINCES OF BALAK. According to the opinion of Rashi[32] the elders of Midian had left [Balaam] when he told them, *Lodge here this night*[33] [and therefore Scripture here only mentions *the princes of Balak*—i.e., the elders of Moab]. This is [indeed] possible, because when Balaam mentioned to them [*and I will bring you back word,*] *as the Eternal may speak unto me,*[33] they did not want to wait for Balaam's [message], for they said: "This G-d has always come to the help of Israel. It is He Who brought them out of Egypt and did signs and wonders for them." For the elders of Midian were

(29) Tanchuma, *Balak* 20. (30) Isaiah 2:6. (31) This is unlike Rashi, who explains the plural "we" as meaning "I and my people." (32) Above, in Verse 7. (33) Verse 8.

wise men, and they knew about all the words of Moses with Jethro,[34] the most distinguished of their country, although Scripture does not mention this [that Jethro informed the elders of his land what Moses had told him]. And Rabbi Abraham ibn Ezra said that "[the reason why Scripture here] did not mention them [the elders of Midian] is because Balak was the principal party [in this matter], and it was he who sent the mission." Similarly, [the verse stating] *and the princes of Moab abode with Balaam*[33] [omits "the elders of Midian"] because the main [impetus of the] mission came from their lord [the king of Moab].

The correct explanation is that the elders of Midian—who were perhaps the first kings thereof—came from their country to Balak to take counsel about the problem of Israel, and they all decided to send [a mission] to Balaam. Therefore Balak sent his princes, his judges and wise men, and they went together with the elders of Midian to the land of Midian, because from there their way led to Balaam's city; and the elders of Midian remained in their city, while the princes of Balak, who were the delegates, went on their own to Aram [Balaam's native land].[35] This is the meaning of [the expression], *and the elders of Moab and the elders of Midian departed,*[32] meaning that they all left Balak and went as far as Midian, *with the rewards of divination in their hand.*[32] *And 'they' came unto Balaam,* [*and spoke unto him the words of Balak*][32]—this refers to the elders of Moab, about whom Scripture states, *and he sent messengers,*[36] not to the elders of Midian.

[FOR THE ETERNAL REFUSETH] TO GIVE ME LEAVE TO GO WITH YOU—"but only with great princes. This teaches us that he was of a haughty spirit, and did not want to tell [them] that he was under the control of G-d. Therefore [he spoke] in arrogant language. It was because of this that *Balak sent yet again princes.*"[37] This is Rashi's language. But it is not correct, for Balaam's whole honor

(34) Exodus 18:8: *And Moses told his father-in-law all that the Eternal had done . . .* (35) Further, 23:7: *From Aram Balak bringeth me.* (36) Verse 5. (37) Verse 15.

consisted of boasting and glorifying himself in [the fact that he received] the word of G-d [and so he would not have been ashamed to tell the princes of Moab that he was awaiting G-d's word, as Rashi wrote, but on the contrary would have boasted of it]! Moreover, he did not [in fact] know that G-d would give him permission to go with other, greater, princes! Rather, the meaning [of Balaam's words] is that G-d did not want him to go at all. But Balak suspected that he was [only] saying so in order to get a greater reward; therefore he said to him, *Why camest thou not unto me? am I not able indeed to promote thee to honor?*[38] And for this reason too, *Balak sent yet again princes, more in number, and more honorable*[37] in order to show him that he wanted him very much [to come], and he promised to give him as much wealth and riches as he would demand from, and fix upon him. But Balaam answered him that even for all his money "*I cannot go beyond the word of the Eternal,* for He is *my G-d,* and *I cannot do any thing, small or great*[39] if I transgress His command, for [whatever I do] I do in His Name." Or [it may be that Balaam] is saying, "*I cannot go beyond the word of the Eternal*[39] whether [I transgress His word] in a small matter or a great matter, for He is my G-d, and I am His servant."

20. [AND G-D CAME UNTO BALAAM AT NIGHT, AND SAID UNTO HIM]: 'IF THE MEN ARE COME TO CALL THEE.' " 'If the call be 'for you' [for your benefit] and you think you will receive a reward for it, then *rise up, go with them.* But [you should realize that even] against your will, *the word which I speak unto thee, that shalt thou do'.*[40] And nevertheless *Balaam went* [as stated in the following verse], for he said: 'Perhaps I may persuade Him to agree [that I should curse']." This is Rashi's language. "*And G-d's anger was kindled because he went.*[41] [This was because] Balaam realized that the matter was not pleasing[42] in the sight of the Eternal, and [yet] he longed to go." This too, is the Rabbi's language.

(38) Further, Verse 37. (39) Further, Verse 18. (40) Verse 20. (41) Verse 22. (42) In our texts of Rashi: "that the matter was evil."

And Rabbi Abraham ibn Ezra wrote: "The Gaon [Rav Saadia][43] said: If someone wishes to argue, saying: 'Since He had told Balaam, *Thou shalt not go with them,*[44] how is it that He told him [afterwards], *Rise up, go with them?*' one may answer that G-d [indeed] did not want him to go with the first [emissaries], until more honorable princes than they would come.[45] But in my opinion [continues Ibn Ezra] there is no need for this [interpretation of the Gaon], for the meaning [of *Rise up, go with them* is not that this was a command, but] is like *Send thou men*[46] [which is not a Divine command, but permission in the nature of a concession to Israel's demand]. For G-d had said to Israel, *Go up, take possession,*[47] but they did not believe [that they would conquer it], and said instead, *Let us send men*[48]—so Moses asked G-d [and He told him, *Send thou men,*[46] meaning: 'I do not command you, but if you wish to do so, send them']. And this case [here too] is similar, for why did Balaam have to tell [Balak's servants], *tarry ye also here this night, that I may know what the Eternal will speak unto me more,*[49] [since G-d had already told him not to go with them]? It was because he harbored an evil intention in his heart [persisting in the hope that G-d would agree that he should go to Balak], and so G-d told him: '[You may] *go with them,* but be careful only to speak that which I will say to you.' And the proof for my interpretation [that G-d was angry with Balaam for his evil intention in persisting in his request to go to Balak, and that *go with them* is a concession, not a command], is the following verse, *And G-d's anger was kindled because he went.*" These are the words [of Abraham ibn Ezra].

(43) See Vol. II, p. 99, Note 230. (44) Above, Verse 12. (45) According to this explanation of Rav Saadia Gaon there was Divine consent in general terms for Balaam to go on the mission, and the meaning of G-d's words to him is: "*thou shalt not go 'with them,'* but with others, more honorable than they, you may go." The reason for this may be that since Balaam, speaking against his intention and desire, was later on to confirm G-d's love of Israel, it was fitting that this be done in the presence of more distinguished men than the former ones. (46) Above, 13:2. (47) Deuteronomy 1:21. (48) *Ibid.*, Verse 22. (49) Above, Verse 19.

Yet all this availeth me nothing.[50] For the explanation of the Gaon [Rav Saadia, that G-d wanted him to go with more honorable men] is not correct, for G-d told Balaam, *Thou shalt not go with them; thou shalt not curse the people, for they are blessed,*[44] [thus clearly indicating] that He forbade him to go in order that he should not curse the people, and he did not prohibit him from going because these princes were not sufficiently important, so how could it be permissible for him to go with other princes! And Rabbi Abraham ibn Ezra's explanation [that G-d was angry with him because of his persistence in his evil desire to go] is also not correct, [for it would mean] that G-d changed His mind and withdrew His word [in finally allowing Balaam to go], because of the persistence of the person making the request! And the matter of *Send thou men*[46] is not so [as Ibn Ezra explained it]; and I have already explained its [correct] meaning [there]. Furthermore, far be it from G-d to punish [a person for doing] something for which He had [previously] given permission! And in the Midrash the Rabbis have said:[51] "From here you learn that on whichever path a person desires to tread, he is led."

The correct interpretation of this matter appears to me to be that at first G-d forbade him to curse the people, *for they are blessed,*[44] and so there was no purpose in Balaam going with them [the elders], since he could not curse them [Israel], and they did not require him for any other reason. Therefore He said [to Balaam], "*Thou shalt not go with them,*[44] and do not curse the people, *for they are blessed.*" Now it is self-understood that Balaam informed them of G-d's words [although Scripture does not expressly say so], but [nonetheless] Balak sent him [messengers] a second time, because he did not believe him [that G-d did not allow him to go, but thought that he merely wanted a greater reward], and so he showed him greater honor by sending *princes, more in number, and more honorable than*[37] the first, and promised to increase his reward and honor. But Balaam answered them

(50) Esther 5:13. (51) Tanchuma, *Balak* 8; Bamidbar Rabbah 20:11.—From this Midrash too, it is obvious that there was no Divine concession here at all to Balaam, but that he was merely led on the path that he desired to tread.

that the matter did not depend upon money, nor upon his [own] will; but it was entirely in the hand of G-d, and he would again ask Him what He commands him [to do].[52] This [answer of Balaam] was properly given, for what could he know of *the knowledge of the Most High*[53] — and *the counsel of the Eternal* is good *forever*,[54] and *He doth instruct sinners in the way*,[55] and He would inform him *what he shall answer the messengers of the nation*,[56] or He would tell him what would happen to them [the Moabites] in the future. And G-d told him: "I have already informed you that the people *are blessed* and that you will not be able to curse them.[44] But now that they [the messengers] have come back to you, *if the men are come* merely *to call thee*, meaning that they will agree to your going with them [although it is] on condition that you shall not curse the people, as I informed you at the beginning, then *rise up, go with them; but only the word which I speak unto thee, that shalt thou do*, for even if I command you to bless them, you shall [do so and] not be afraid of Balak." This then is the meaning of [the expression], *if the men are come 'to call thee'* [i.e., if they merely ask you to go with them, despite being fully aware that you may not curse Israel—then go with them]. And this was the wish of *the Glorious Name*[57] from the [very] beginning—that he [Balaam] should go with them after telling them that he would not curse them [Israel], and that he would conduct himself towards them [entirely] as G-d would command him—because it was the Will of G-d, blessed be He, to bless Israel through the mouth of the prophet of the nations. Thus Balaam ought to have disclosed this to the princes of Balak and to say to them: "Now G-d has only permitted me to be invited by you [i.e., to accompany you], and [only] on the express condition that I do not curse the people, and that if He commands me to bless them, that I shall do so, and if they are not agreeable to these [conditions], they should leave me alone." But even on this second occasion Balak said,

(52) Verses 18-19. (53) Further, 24:16. (54) See Psalms 33:11. In other words, it is always good to seek G-d's advice. (55) *Ibid.*, 25:8. G-d is hereby described as giving instructions even to sinners [such as Balaam] in the path they should follow. (56) Isaiah 14:32. (57) Deuteronomy 28:58.

come therefore, I pray thee, curse me this people,[58] [thus indicating that] he did not want Balaam for the purpose of fortelling future events or for any other purpose, except that of cursing the people. And Balaam, because of his overriding desire to go, did not inform them of this [Divine message with the conditions mentioned above], and did not tell them anything at all; [instead], *Balaam rose up in the morning, and saddled his ass, and went with them,*[59] like someone who is eager to fulfill their wish. Therefore *G-d's anger was kindled because he went,*[41] for had he informed them [of the conditions], he would not [necessarily] have gone [because they might have refused to let him come under such conditions]. Furthermore a profanation of G-d's Name was involved in this [behavior of Balaam], for since he went with them without explanation, whereas he was in fact under the control of G-d, they thought that He had given him permission to curse the people for them. Therefore [they thought that] G-d had reneged on that which He had said originally, *thou shalt not curse the people, for they are blessed*[44] — according to what Balaam had told them — and when they saw later on that he did *not* curse them, they said that He changed [His word] yet again, or that He is mocking them *as one mocketh a man.*[60] *Far be it from* G-d *to do after this manner,*[61] for *the Eternal One of Israel will not . . . repent!*[62]

23. AND THE ASS SAW THE ANGEL OF THE ETERNAL. Angels of G-d—which are Separate Intelligences[63] — cannot be perceived by the [human] sense of sight, for they are not physical beings which can be apprehended by sight. And when they become visible to prophets or to men possessed of *Ruach Hakodesh,*[64] such as Daniel,[65] they are apprehended by them through the perception of the rational

(58) Verse 17. (59) Verse 21. (60) Job 13:9. (61) Genesis 18:25. (62) I Samuel 15:29. (63) See Vol. I, p. 59, Note 237. See also *ibid.*, pp. 228-231, where Ramban discusses at length the subject of angels in relation to prophecy. (64) Literally, "The Holy Spirit." See Rambam in Moreh Nebuchim II, 45, at the paragraph beginning: "the second degree of prophecy." See also above, *Seder Korach,* Note 71 and Ramban *ibid.* (65) Daniel 10:5. The Talmud in Megillah 3a states that Daniel did not attain the status of a prophet, but *was* worthy of receiving *Ruach Hakodesh.*

soul which reaches the degree of prophecy or some lower degree, but that they [the angels] should be perceived by the eyes of an animal—that is impossible! Therefore you could explain [the phrase] *and the ass saw [the angel of the Eternal]* to mean that she felt the presence of something which frightened her off from passing on, namely the angel that had gone forth *for an adversary.*[41] This is a similar expression [to that which says]: *yea, my heart 'ra'ah'* [literally: "had seen"] *much wisdom and knowledge,*[66] [the term "seeing" here] being used [in the sense of] perception, and not [in the sense of] physical sight [since the heart does not "see"]. Now when this miracle occurred to the ass, and the Creator gave her [the power of] speech, she said to Balaam, *Was I ever wont to do so unto thee?,*[67] but [nonetheless] she did not know why she did so now, because she was forced to do so. Therefore she did not say to him: "*Behold* the angel of G-d stands *over against* me *with his sword drawn in his hand,*"[68] since her perception did not reach this knowledge at all. [Our verse] saying: *And the ass saw the angel of the Eternal standing in the way, with his sword drawn in his hand* does not mean that she [actually] saw the sword, let alone the angel; but the verse is hinting that since the angel was ready to strike them, she *trembled very exceedingly,*[69] because she felt as if people were coming to slaughter her. [We must explain that the ass merely felt the angel's presence, but did not actually see him, because] if we were to say that those angels that appear in human form—as I have mentioned in the section of *Vayeira*[70] — *can* be seen even by the eyes of an animal, then how was it that Balaam did not see him, since he was not smitten with blindness! It is, however, possible that He Who gave the ass the power of speech, also bestowed upon her an additional power of vision, so that she saw the likeness of a human being, although Scripture does not mention it. Thus G-d opened the eyes of the ass [and she indeed saw the angel], just as Scripture mentions [later] in regard to her master, [*And the Eternal opened the eyes of Balaam, and he saw the angel of the Eternal*].[71] For the whole matter of the ass was a great miracle,

(66) Ecclesiastes 1:16. (67) Further, Verse 30. (68) See Joshua 5:13 where this expression is used of the angel who appeared to Joshua. (69) Genesis 27:33. (70) Genesis 18:1 (Vol. I, p. 231). (71) Further, Verse 31.

being a "new creation" like those that were created at twilight [on the eve of the first Sabbath],[72] and it is not merely called "an opening of eyes." However, our Rabbis have only mentioned[72] amongst the miracles the opening of the mouth [of the ass, although the whole matter—and especially her seeing the angel—was miraculous in nature]. The reason for this miracle was to show Balaam *Who hath made man's mouth, or Who maketh a man dumb?*[73] and to make him realize that it is G-d Who opens the mouth for the dumb,[74] and [since He can make the dumb speak], how much more so can He make dumb at His Will the mouth of those who can speak, and can also put words into their mouths, so that they speak in accordance with His Will, for everything is in His power. It was [thus] a warning to him [Balaam] not to follow enchantments and soothsaying, and [not] to curse Israel thereby, because he was [primarily] an enchanter and soothsayer.[75]

31. AND THE ETERNAL OPENED THE EYES OF BALAAM. From this verse we learn that Balaam was not a prophet [who habitually received Divine messages], because had he been a prophet, how could it be that he required "opening of the eyes" to see the angel, which is the term used by Scripture about someone who has *not*

(72) Aboth 5:9. Ten things are listed there, one of them being the "the mouth of the ass [of Balaam which opened and spoke]."But as Ramban clearly indicates, the *whole* matter of the ass—beginning with her seeing the angel, and culminating in her speech—were like "a new creation" similar to those things created "at twilight on the eve of the first Sabbath."—Various interpretations have been suggested on *the necessity* for these special creations. Rambam in his commentary to the Mishnah explains it as follows: Since the law of nature was established by G-d, it was His wish that it be not interfered with under any circumstance. But since He foresaw certain emergencies in the history of His people that would require special intervention in the normal operation of nature He made provision for them at the final completion of creation before the nightfall which ushered in the first Sabbath. (73) Exodus 4:11. (74) See Proverbs 31:8. (75) Ramban emphasizes this point [that Balaam was primarily an enchanter and soothsayer — see above in Verse 5] in order that his tribute to Israel's character and future should be viewed entirely as the true word of G-d which came to him in honor of Israel (see Ramban further, Verse 23:16), for on his own merit he could not possibly have risen to such heights, since he was but a mere soothsayer and enchanter.

reached the degree of prophecy, such as Elisha's young man,[76] or Hagar the Egyptian,[77] and Scripture does not speak in this manner about the prophets! And indeed Scripture calls him, *Balaam the son of Beor, the soothsayer.*[78] And when Balaam said, *as the Eternal may speak unto me,*[79] he called his [ability] to know future events by means of his soothsaying "the word of G-d," [and it does not refer to the gift of prophecy]. But for the sake of the honor of Israel G-d [indeed] came to him that night[80] [in a prophet-like vision], and afterwards he was favored with "opening of the eyes" in seeing the angel, and speaking to him, and finally he attained the degree of [seeing] *the vision of the Almighty*[81] — all this being for the sake of Israel and in their honor. But after he returned to his land, however, he [reverted to the status of a mere] soothsayer, for that is how Scripture describes him at [the time of] his death, [saying]: *And Balaam the son of Beor, the soothsayer, did the children of Israel slay with the sword,*[78] and G-d forbid that they should stretch forth a hand against a prophet of G-d! And so did the Rabbis say in the Midrash Bamidbar Sinai Rabbah: [82] "Balaam partook of the *Ruach Hakodesh,*[64] but after he associated himself with Balak, the *Ruach Hakodesh* departed from him and he became again a [mere] soothsayer, as he had been originally. Therefore he complained: "I was elevated [in prophecy], but Balak brought about my descent.' "

32. FOR THE WAY 'YARAT L'NEGDI'—for he who is going [on this journey, i.e., Balaam], has distorted his way and perverted it in front of my eyes, for *I am He that knoweth, and am witness.*[83] Or [the word] *l'negdi* [may not mean "in My presence", but] that he perverted the way [i.e., the journey] to act "against My Will," as Onkelos rendered it, ["because you wanted to go on the journey against My Will"], as in [the verse]: *for they have vexed 'l'neged' (before) the*

(76) II Kings 6:17: *And the Eternal opened the eyes of the young man.* (77) Genesis 21:19: *And G-d opened her eyes.* (78) Joshua 13:22. (79) Above, Verse 8. (80) *Ibid.,* Verse 9. (81) Further, 24:4. (82) Bamidbar Rabbah 20:16. (83) Jeremiah 29:23. In our verse the angel is speaking, of course, on behalf of G-d, Whose messenger he is.

builders.[84] The word *yarat* is an expression of "perverting." Similarly, *through the hands of the wicked 'yirteini'*[85] which means "He warps me." And the meaning of our verse is as I have explained,[86] namely that the [actual] journey had the permission of *the Glorious Name,*[57] but Balaam perverted it by going with them and apparently having them believe that he would curse the people [since he had not informed them of the conditions under which G-d had allowed him to go].

33. AND SHE TURNED ASIDE 'L'PHANAI' (BEFORE ME). Commentators[87] have explained this [word *'l'phanai'* as meaning]: *"and she turned aside* into the field when she was *before me."* But there is no need [for this interpretation and addition], for the meaning [of the word *l'phanai*] is like *mipanai* ("from" before me), for such is the usage of the letter *lamed,* as in [the verses]: *and they left off 'livnoth' (to build) the city*[88] [which is like *mivnoth* — literally: "from building" the city]; *he hath left off 'l'haskil' (to be wise), to do good*[89] [which is like *meihaskil* — literally: "from being wise"]. There are also many other cases [like this]. Similarly: *And Joab and the captains of the host went out 'liphnei'* [literally: "before," but really meaning *mipnei*— "from before," i.e. "from the presence of"] *the king, to number the people of Israel.*[90]

'ULAI'[91] SHE HAD TURNED ASIDE FROM ME. In the opinion of the commentators[92] [the word *'ulai'* here] is like *lulei* — " *'unless' she*

(84) Nehemiah 3:37. Here too, the word *l'neged* does not mean "in the presence of," but means that they have vexed the builders by speaking "against" them. (85) Job 16:11. (86) Above, in Verse 20. (87) I have not identified these sources. — The difficulty in the verse is that it should have said *and she turned aside 'mipanai' ('from' before me)* and not *l'phanai ('before' me).* (88) Genesis 11:8. (89) Psalms 36:4. (90) II Samuel 24:4. (91) The word *ulai* normally means "perhaps," which is inappropriate in the context of this verse, since there was no doubt as to whether the ass had turned aside. Hence the commentators explained it as meaning *lulei* — "unless," and the angel is thus saying, in defense of the animal, that "had she not turned aside from me, I would have killed you [Balaam]." Ramban later on offers his own interpretation of the verse and the word *ulai* actually used by Scripture. (92) Rashi and Ibn Ezra.

had turned aside from me [surely now also I had slain thee." The word *ulai*] in this context is thus used [with a meaning] different than that of all the other occasions where it is found. But in my opinion it is used here in its literal meaning ["perhaps:" — implying a doubt]; for the ass felt the presence of — or saw[93] — the angel, but did not know what it meant, and [the reason why she *turned aside*] was because of the drawn sword, as animals are wont to do [when they see a drawn sword]. Therefore the angel said to Balaam: *"And the ass saw me and turned aside from me,* [although it was only] because of a doubt that she *turned aside* from before me [not knowing my intentions], for I came to slay you, but I would have saved her life, since the sin is in you and not in the ass."

'GAM OTHCHAH HARAGTI' ("ALSO" THEE I HAD SURELY SLAIN). Rabbi Abraham ibn Ezra commented that "the word *gam* [meaning "also"] is a proof that the ass died after it had spoken. And the meaning of [the phrase] *and saved her alive* [which implies that she should have died, were it not for the angel that kept her alive] is that when [even] a human being sees an angel, he dies [straightaway, whereas the ass lived on for a while until after she had spoken to Balaam] — proof being [Jacob's statement]: *and my life is preserved*[94] — and how much more so [does it follow that] an animal, which has no common factor with an angel, as a human being has [ought to die immediately upon seeing an angel]."[95]

(93) See Ramban above, Verse 23. (94) Genesis 32:31. Since Jacob gave thanks to G-d for preserving his life after seeing the angel, one can deduce that it is usual for a person to die after having seen an angel. See this also clearly in Judges 13:22. (95) Thus according to Ibn Ezra the angel was saying: "Since even a human being, who shares with an angel the spirit of G-d, dies upon seeing an angel, how much more so the ass should have died *immediately* she saw me! But *I saved her alive* for some time after she had seen me, in order that she should speak to you." Nonetheless, *after* she had spoken to Balaam she *did* die, as implied by the angel's words: "had the ass not turned aside, 'also' you I would have killed," meaning: The ass will now have to die, because I [only] saved her life so that she should speak to you. But had she not turned aside, I would have 'also' killed you." Ramban disagrees with this interpretation, and explains that the ass did *not* die, as explained further on.

But the word *gam* cannot be interpreted as Ibn Ezra explains it, for [if so, we do not find any circumstances under which] *both* of them [Balaam and the ass] would die; because now when she did turn aside, the ass died and Balaam was saved alive, and had she not turned aside, he [the angel] would have killed Balaam and saved the ass alive![96] However, the word *gam* is [to be interpreted] as Rashi explains it, its meaning being as if [the word-order of the verse were] inverted, namely: *gam haragti othchah* ["also would I slay thee," meaning to say: "not only would I have held you up on your journey, but I would also have killed you"]. And the meaning of the expression *and saved her alive* is [not that "I would have kept her alive *temporarily,* but later on killed her," as Ibn Ezra explained, but that the angel was stressing that] "the entire [burden of] sin is upon you [Balaam], and [therefore] I would have killed you because of it, [but would have kept her alive even had she *not* turned aside], for she has done no sin for which she ought to die. Thus her act of turning aside, which she did on account of me, was for your good [only] and not for her sake at all, [because she would anyhow not have been killed], and you have therefore smitten her for no reason, and have repaid her evil for good."

Now Scripture does not say whether Balak's princes were present with Balaam at these events, or [it may be] that they were riding ahead of him and there was a [considerable] distance between them and him [so that they did not notice any of these events]. The most likely [interpretation, however] is that they were together with him, because

(96) Ramban's meaning is as follows. According to Ibn Ezra's explanation, now that the ass turned aside, she alone was killed [since she had fulfilled her purpose of arousing Balaam], but had she not turned aside, both Balaam *and* the ass would have been killed by the angel. To this Ramban replies that this cannot be so, because Scripture states explicitly here that had the ass *not* turned aside, the angel would have killed Balaam but *saved her* [the ass] *alive;* and now that she *did* turn aside, he saved Balaam, but killed the ass [according to Ibn Ezra]! Hence Ibn Ezra's statement that both Balaam *and* the ass would have been killed is not possible under any circumstances! Therefore the word *gam* must be interpreted differently. [See my Hebrew commentary p. 292, for sources in Hebrew commentaries on the elucidation of this difficult text of Ramban].

they did not become separated from him, and they saw the ass turning aside and Balaam smiting her, but thought that she was merely behaving as bad animals do, because they did not hear her speak; and they certainly [did not hear] the words of the angel, who was [visible only] *to* the *opened eyes* [97] of Balaam. But our Rabbis have said[98] that the princes of Moab were astonished, because they saw a miracle the like of which had never occurred in the world. And they [also] said[98] that as soon as the ass had finished speaking; she died, in order that the nations should not say [about her]: "This is [the ass] that spoke," and should not make her [an object of] idol-worship. Moreover, the Holy One, blessed be He, was concerned [even] about the honor of the wicked, [and therefore killed the ass so that] people should not say: "This is [the ass] that caused Balaam's downfall." All this is possible, [but is] in accordance with a tradition, for Scripture [itself] does not speak about her dying at all, as I have explained.

35. GO WITH THE MEN; BUT ONLY THE WORD THAT I SHALL SPEAK UNTO THEE, THAT THOU SHALT SPEAK. It is possible that He means to say: "*Go with the men; but only the word that I shall speak unto thee, that thou shalt speak,* and you should inform them [of this limitation of your powers]." Or it may mean that after Balaam had confessed [his evil intention, and said]: *if it displease thee, I will get me back,*[99] He said to him, "*Go with them,* for I have forgiven you your sin, but only [on condition] that you remember My warning which I have given you [only to speak that which I tell you to say]." He had to say this [again] to him, in order that Balaam should not think that He was telling him: "*Go with them* to do what they have asked you to do." It is also possible that since he who went [on the journey, i.e., Balaam] wanted to curse the people and did not want to bless them under any circumstances, therefore G-d warns him on every occasion that He speaks to him. It is for this reason that Balaam informed Balak at the very start of his speaking to him, [saying]: *Lo, I am 'come' unto thee,*[100] [meaning to say that] "I

(97) Further, 24:4. (98) Bamidbar Rabbah 20:12. (99) Verse 34. (100) Verse 38.

have only been permitted to come, but as far as [cursing] the people [of Israel] is concerned, *havė I now any power at all to speak any thing*[100] in accordance with your wish? *The word that G-d putteth in my mouth, that shall I speak* – whether it be a curse or a blessing. Decide therefore if you [Balak] want me to speak about them [despite this risk], and if you do not want it, *I will* already now *get me back.*"

41. [AND IT CAME TO PASS IN THE MORNING AND BALAK TOOK BALAAM] AND BROUGHT HIM UP INTO BAMOTH-BAAL, AND HE SAW FROM THENCE THE UTMOST PART OF THE PEOPLE. Balak took him up to a [high] place from which he could see them [the people of Israel], in order that he could concentrate his curse upon them, and his mind would not separate itself from them, for it is one of the attributes of the soul's powers that it attaches itself at the time of seeing a certain object as is known from that which the Sages tell[101] [of Rabbi Yochanan, that he said to his disciples]: " 'Lift up my eye-lids for me, because I want to see [this scholar].' They [accordingly] lifted up his eye-lids. He set his eyes upon him, and [as a result] that person died."

Now Scripture relates that Balaam did not see the whole camp [of Israel] because they were encamped in four standards [positioned in all] four directions of the heaven. On the second occasion Balak said to him, *thou shalt see but the utmost part of them, and shalt not see*

(101) Baba Kamma 117a. The story is told there of a certain Babylonian scholar [Rav Kahana] who arrived at the academy of Rabbi Yochanan in the Land of Israel and Rabbi Yochanan was informed that "a lion had come up from Babylon." When Rabbi Yochanan presented his teachings, Rav Kahana out of respect first remained silent. But when Rabbi Yochanan remarked his astonishment at his silence, Rav Kahana then successfully refuted Rabbi Yochanan's teachings. Rabbi Yochanan, who could not see properly because of his heavy eye-lids [or eyelashes] asked his disciples to lift up his eye-lids so that he could see the new great scholar. Upon doing so, Rabbi Yochanan received the impression that the scholar [owing to a malformation of his lips] was laughing for having refuted him. Thereupon hė gazed at him, and Rav Kahana died as a result. Ramban quotes this story in order to illustrate the "power of the soul" which can be transferred by a concentrated look.

them all,[102] meaning: "this time also you will not [be able to] see them all, if that is what prevents you from cursing them, but [nonetheless] *curse me them from thence*[102] if you can, for I do not have any place from where I can show you all of them." Balak thought that perhaps there was a standard in one of the sections [of the camp of the Israelites] consisting of righteous and good people whom *it pleased* not *the Eternal to crush,*[103] [and therefore Balak took Balaam to other places from which Balaam could see other parts of the camp, in order to curse them effectively].

It is also possible to explain that on the first occasion [referred to in this verse] Balaam did see the whole camp, for Bamoth-baal is a high place, and from there both of them [Balak and Balaam] saw part of the people, and built the altars there; [104] then Balaam ascended to the peak of the hill on that mountain, and saw the whole people, this being the meaning of [the expression] *and he* [Balaam] *went 'shephi,'*[105] which means he went to "the height" thereof, as Rabbi Abraham ibn Ezra has explained.

23 1. SEVEN ALTARS. Rabbi Abraham ibn Ezra alluded here to a profound secret.[106] Now Balaam wanted that the Will of G-d should cleave to him through these sacrifices, and therefore he *offered burnt-offerings according to the number of them all,*[107] and wanted that Balak should occupy himself personally in [offering] them. Therefore Scripture states, *and Balak and Balaam offered on every altar a bullock and a ram,*[108] the one slaughtering [them], and the other sprinkling the blood [upon the altar]. And the meaning of [Balaam's words], *I have prepared the seven altars*[109] is by way of prayer, as if he

(102) Further, 23:13. (103) Isaiah 53:10. (104) Further, Verses 1-2. (105) *Ibid.,* Verse 3. (106) "There are profound secrets which are understood by few in number. There is a unit of seven, in days [making a week] etc." Ibn Ezra continues to show the mystic power of the number seven, which is a major factor in time and also in the worship of G-d through offerings, an allusion to which is seen here in the "seven altars" which Balaam asked Balak to build. These allude to the seven [lower] Emanations. — See also my Hebrew commentary, p. 293, and p. 294, Note 12. (107) Job 1:5. (108) Verse 2. (109) Verse 4.

were saying: "I have prepared for You the perfect [number of] altars with the perfect [number of] sacrifices;[110] *may they come up with acceptance on* Your *altar*,"[111] this being similar to that which Scripture says: *Receive the memorial of all thy meal-offerings, and accept the fat of thy burnt-offering*,[112] and it also states, *I will offer unto Thee burnt-offerings of fatlings, with the sweet smoke of rams; I will offer bullocks with goats. Selah*,[113] and so also in many places. And the meaning of the definite article [in *'hamizbechoth'* — *'the' seven altars*] — Rabbi Abraham ibn Ezra has already mentioned.[106] Now in the end when Balaam no longer wanted *to meet with enchantments*,[114] he did not want Balak to participate in the bringing of the sacrifices, in order that he should not cause them to be rejected on account of his [improper] intention; and therefore Scripture said: *and 'he' offered up a bullock and a ram*,[115] [the singular pronoun] referring to Balaam mentioned [previously at the end of that verse: *And Balak did as Balaam had said, and he offered up a bullock and a ram*].[115] It is possible, however, that Balak [and not Balaam] offered them up, for he [Balak] did it to appease his [own] mind, while he [Balaam] no longer desired these sacrifices.

4. AND G-D HAPPENED TO MEET BALAAM. Because this man had not reached the status of prophecy, therefore Scripture speaks of him in this way, [meaning to say] that now the [Divine] communication came to him by way of chance, and in honor of Israel. Hence it says concerning him, *and G-d 'came' unto Balaam*,[116] for this expression is not used in connection with [true] prophets, but only about a person who has not attained this status. Similarly [we find]: *and G-d 'came' to Abimelech; and G-d 'came' to Laban*.[117] It is possible that [the term "coming" in these verses] means the "coming" through speech of the Will from the Most High to the [Separate] Intelligences[63] that cause one to dream, for Balaam also *would fall*

(110) This refers to the seven altars and the seven sacrifices, which allude to the seven Emanations. (111) Isaiah 60:7. (112) Psalms 20:4. (113) *Ibid.*, 66:15. (114) Further, 24:1. (115) Chapter 23, Verse 30. (116) Above, 22:9. (117) Genesis 20:3 — *Ibid.*, 31:24.

down at daytime, and a deep sleep would fall upon him while he was *yet with opened eyes.*[97]

AND G-D HAPPENED TO MEET BALAAM AND HE SAID UNTO HIM. The meaning [of this verse] is that when an occurrence happened to Balaam in the nature of those experiences which occur to men of *Ruach Hakodesh*[64] when dwelling alone and *a spirit passed before* his *face that made the hair of* his *flesh to stand up,*[118] *fear came upon* him, *and trembling, and all* his *bones were made to shake,*[119] *and his vigor turned into weakness*[120] and he fell upon his face to the ground—and then Balaam said, *I have prepared the seven altars,*[109] this being by way of prayer, as I have explained.[121] But G-d did not hearken to him and his intention, but told him: *Thus shalt thou speak.*[122]

5. AND THE ETERNAL PUT A WORD IN BALAAM'S MOUTH. Some commentators[123] explain that Balaam did not understand the words [he said], but G-d filled him with words and said to him: "*Return unto Balak, and thus thou shalt speak,*[122] for the words will come forth [automatically] from your mouth." Perhaps this is also the opinion of our Rabbis, who have said: [124] "He shaped his mouth and formed it [so that he would speak as He desired], like a person who fixes a nail onto a board. Rabbi Eleazar says: It was an angel that spoke: Rabbi Yehoshua says: etc."[125] But it does not appear to me to be correct [that Balaam did not know what he was saying], because he said [that he] *heareth the words of G-d; seeth the vision of the Almighty.*[97] But the meaning of [the word] *'vayasem'* (*and He put*) is "instruction," signifying He taught him the words so that he should recite them with his mouth, and he should not forget or omit any part of it, similar to [the expression], *teach thou it the*

(118) Job 4:15. (119) *Ibid.,* Verse 14. (120) Daniel 10:8. (121) Above in Verse 1. (122) Verse 5. (123) I have not identified these commentators. See, however, my Hebrew commentary, p. 294, Note 22, for a similar opinion found in the Zohar. (124) Tanchuma, *Balak* 12; Bamidbar Rabbah 20:16. (125) "It was the Holy One, blessed be He, that spoke through the mouth of Balaam" (*ibid.*).

children of Israel; 'simah' (put it) in their mouths.[126] Similarly, *for by the appointment of Absalom this hath been 'sumah' ('put; determined').*[127]

9. FOR FROM THE TOP OF THE ROCKS I SEE HIM. The meaning of this is that since Balak had brought him up to Bamoth-baal[128] [which was a high place] to see Israel, Balaam said: *"From the top of the rocks and from the hills* I look and I see him, for he [*is a people that*] *shall dwell alone,* and there is no other nation with him that can be counted together with him, in the way that many [different] peoples and various nations gather together to become one camp—for these [people of Israel] all have *one law and one ordinance,*[129] and are one nation, dwelling alone by the name of Jacob and Israel." Therefore he [Balaam] mentioned, *Come, curse me Jacob, and come defy Israel,*[130] referring to them [both] by their name of honor [Israel] and by the name of their ancestor [Jacob], meaning to say that they are *a people alone,* and have names befitting them from their ancestors. For Balak did not tell him [Balaam] the name "Israel," but merely said, *Behold, there is a people come out from Egypt,*[131] as if he was a stranger to them and did not know them, and he was not grateful for the favor that their father had done.[132] And the meaning of Balaam's words is that "just as I see him now dwelling alone, so will he forever *dwell in safety, the fountain of Jacob alone,*[133] and he will always be at the head, for no nation will [ever] prevail over him [and cause him to perish], and he will never become assimilated to them [i.e., other nations].

10. WHO HATH COUNTED THE DUST OF JACOB? Balaam is saying: "I see them from *the top of the rocks* dwelling alone, and I

(126) Deuteronomy 31:19. This means: let them know the words of this song by heart (Ibn Ezra). (127) II Samuel 13:32. (128) Above, 22:41. (129) *Ibid.*, 15:16. (130) Above, Verse 7. (131) Above, 22:5. (132) This refers to Abraham risking his life in order to save his nephew Lot — who was the ancestor of the Moabites (Genesis 14:12-16; 19:36-37). (133) Deuteronomy 33:28.

cannot count them for they alone are like the dust of the earth, and no *man can number the dust of the earth;* [134] nor can I count even *rova Yisrael* (*one fourth of Israel*) when they are encamped under four standards." Thus he prophesied that they would increase in number *and they shall not be diminished,* [135] and the seed of Jacob will always be alone *as the sand of the sea, which cannot be measured nor numbered.* [136] This is Onkelos' opinion [as to the meaning] of *rova Yisrael* [that it means "one fourth" of the total population of Israel, i.e., one standard of the four in which the people encamped].

It is also correct that the term *rova* be [interpreted as in the expression], *Thou dost measure my going about 'v'riv'i' (and my lying down),* [137] of [the same root as in]: *Thou shalt not let thy cattle 'tharbia' (gender) with a diverse kind,* [138] and similar in expression to: *and are come forth out of the fountain of Jacob.* [139]

Balaam said [in this verse]: *Let me die the death of 'yesharim' (the righteous), and let mine end be like his,* meaning that they are those who are inheritors of the Garden of Eden [i.e., they are assured of eternal life after death]. For since the end of man is death, therefore he wanted to *die the death of 'yesharim' (the righteous),* these being Israel, who are called *Yeshurun,* [140] because *they spend their days in goodness.* [141] *And let mine end be like his*—like that of Israel *whose portion is in* [eternal] *life,* [142] and who do not go to Gehenna and destruction. Thus the general tenor of Balaam's prophecy this time was that G-d does not want us to be cursed, and that we are *a people* [dwelling] *alone,* His portion and His people; we shall not mix with the [other] nations, nor be counted amongst them, and our end will be good, according to the way of the righteous.

16. AND THE ETERNAL HAPPENED TO MEET BALAAM. Now, in honor of Israel, this man ascended to [the level of]

(134) See Genesis 13:16. (135) Jeremiah 30:19. (136) Hosea 2:1. (137) Psalms 139:3. (138) Leviticus 19:19. (139) Isaiah 48:1. (140) Deuteronomy 33:5: *And there was a King in Jeshurun . . .* (141) Job 21:13. (142) Psalms 17:14.

prophesying through the Divine attribute of mercy, by the Great Name [i.e., the Tetragrammaton—here translated as "the Eternal"] that had been revealed to Moses,[143] for until now it says about Balaam: *and G-d 'happened to meet' Balaam,*[144] *and G-d 'came' unto Balaam.*[145] But now he knew that he would not be able to curse them under any circumstances, seeing that He [wanted] to deal graciously with them through the attribute of mercy. For until now, since he [Balaam] heard [the words of G-d] through the attribute of justice, [the Divine Name of *Elokim,* symbolizing the attribute of justice, is used in all the previous verses], he thought that he might find some pretext [to curse] them because of some sin that they had committed—so that G-d would consent to the curse falling upon them], as we find in [the verse saying]: *Therefore He was to be their enemy, Himself fought against them;*[146] or [he hoped] that some evil would befall them from G-d, from which they would not be able to save themselves because of the attribute of justice [but now when G-d spoke to him through the attribute of mercy, he knew that he would not succeed in cursing the people under any circumstances]. This is the meaning of [the verse], *And Balaam saw that it pleased the Eternal to bless Israel,*[147] for *Yea, the Eternal will give that which is good*[148] in the blessing. The student learned [in the mysteries of the Cabala] will understand.

21. HE HATH NOT BEHELD 'AVEN' (INIQUITY) IN JACOB. It [the pronoun "he"] refers to "G-d" mentioned [in Verse 19. *G-d is not a man, that He should lie,* and not to Balaam, who is referred to in Verse 20: *Behold, I am bidden to bless*], the verse stating that G-d has *not beheld iniquity* and falsehood in Jacob, *nor* has He *seen* in them *anything perverse* or any provocation that they have committed before Him, and therefore He is with them, and *the shout of* His *Kingdom is among them,* for *He will cry, yea, He will shout aloud, He will prove*

(143) See Vol. II, pp. 34-39. (144) Above, Verse 4. (145) *Ibid.,* 22:9. (146) Isaiah 63:10. (147) Further, 24:1. (148) Psalms 85:13.

Himself mighty against their *enemies.*[149] This is the opinion of Rabbi Abraham ibn Ezra, and it is correct.

It is also possible to explain that the usage of the word *aven* here is like [that in the verse], *I see the tents of Cushan under 'aven' (falsehood).*[150] So also the word *amal* [in the verse before us: *neither hath He seen 'amal' in Israel*—denotes "deception"]. Similarly, *under his tongue is 'amal v'aven'*[151]—meaning "deception and falsehood," for a thing which will not happen and will not come to pass because it is false, is called *aven v'amal* [meaning: "trouble and toil"], because a person will only derive from it toil. Balaam is thus stating: "*Behold, I am bidden to bless; and when He hath blessed, I cannot call it back,*[152] for no man *hath beheld in Jacob nor hath* anyone *seen in Israel* any deceit or falsehood. Their Trust is not false. And their hope of Him is not in vain[153] for all their blessings and their confidence will exist forever." [The usage of the word *hibit* in the verse before us: *lo 'hibit' aven b'Ya'akov*] is similar in expression to: *behold, such is 'mabateinu' (our expectation)*;[154] *and they shall be dismayed and ashamed, because of Ethiopia 'mabatam' (their expectation)*[155] — [thus making the meaning of the verse here to be: "the trust and expectation of Jacob will not end in trouble and sorrow"]. So also *'v'lo hibatetem' (but ye looked not) unto Him that hath done this, neither had ye respect unto Him that fashioned it long ago,*[156] [where the word *hibatetem* is] an expression of trust and hope [thus the verse is saying: "you trusted not in Him, nor did you hope in Him"].

Balaam states the reason for this, saying: because *the Eternal his G-d is with him,* Who does not lie nor repent, *and the shout of a* mighty *King is among them,* Who will never be vanquished. For by bringing them *forth out of Egypt* He has [shown] His great might, *like the lofty horns of the wild-ox*[157] which are above all animals. And so it is not possible that all their blessings should not be fulfilled, seeing that there is *no enchantment* or *divination in Israel!*[158]

(149) Isaiah 42:13. (150) Habakkuk 3:7. (151) Psalms 10:7. (152) Verse 20. (153) See Job 41:1. (154) Isaiah 20:6. (155) *Ibid.*, Verse 5. (156) *Ibid.*, 22:11. (157) Verse 22. (158) Verse 23.

23. FOR THERE IS NO ENCHANTMENT IN JACOB. "They do not need an enchanter or a diviner to tell *Jacob and Israel what hath G-d wrought* and what are His decrees on high. They practice neither enchantment nor divination [in order to know such matters], because they are told through the word of the prophets the decree of G-d, or the Urim and Thummim[159] declare it to them." This is Rashi's language.

The correct interpretation appears to me to be that since Balaam [himself] was a diviner, and Balak sent to him saying, *for I know that he whom thou blessest* through thy means of divination *is blessed, and he whom thou cursest* through them *is cursed,*[160] and he sent him the tools of divination,[161] therefore Balaam said to Balak: "*There is no enchantment in Jacob* which can do them evil or good, *neither is there any divination in Israel* to harm them or to benefit them, for at all times *it shall be said to Jacob and to Israel: 'What hath G-d wrought* for them?' " For *out of the mouth of the Most High proceedeth* to them *evil and good,*[162] meaning to say that *the portion of the Eternal is His people,*[163] and they are not under the rule of the [celestial] princes and *the stars of heaven and the constellations thereof,*[164] so that one should be able to harm them by means of divination and enchantment, as [one can harm] other nations. This is similar to that which Moses said: [. . . *all the host of heaven* . . .] *which the Eternal thy G-d hath allotted unto all the peoples under the whole heaven. But you hath the Eternal taken and brought forth out of the iron furnace, out of Egypt, to be unto Him a people of inheritance,*[165] as I have explained in *Seder Acharei Moth.*[166] Balaam prophesied also about them [Israel] that *he will rise up 'k'lavi,'* which is the lion's whelp, *and* afterwards *he will lift himself up like a* [fully-grown] *lion,*

(159) See Vol. II, pp. 480-484. (160) Above, 22:6. (161) *Ibid.,* Verse 7: *And the elders of Moab and the elders of Midian departed 'u'ksamim' (and the implements of magic) in their hand.* (162) Lamentations 3:38. It should be noted that the verse is actually stated in the negative: "proceedeth *not.*" But it is actually a rhetorical question — (see J.P.S. translation), and Ramban therefore quotes it in paraphrase, in a positive form. (163) Deuteronomy 32:9. (164) Isaiah 13:10. (165) Deuteronomy 4:19-20. (166) Leviticus 18:25. See Vol. III, pp. 268-270.

and he will not rest in his Land *until he eat of the prey, and drink the blood of* the kings of Canaan,[167] as Onkelos explained it.

Thus Balaam added now in this second prophecy [to the words of his first prophecy], telling Balak that they [the Israelites] would conquer the Land and kill mighty kings. Now Balak knew that the Israelites would not receive his land as an inheritance,[168] and therefore although Balaam told them now that the Israelites would ultimately conquer the kings of Canaan, Balak still wanted [Balaam] to curse them so that [Balak] would be victorious [over them], and that he would be able to overcome them, and possibly he could fight against them and inflict losses on them. Therefore he still said, [*Come now*], *I will take thee unto another place; peradventure it will please G-d that thou mayest curse me them from thence.*[169] Balak did not [ask Balaam] to withdraw the blessing [which he had previously given Israel], since he had already informed him, *G-d is not a man, that He should lie, neither the son of man, that He should repent,*[170] but he thought: "Indeed the Israelites are destined to conquer the land of Canaan, which is their inheritance, and to kill their kings; but it is still possible that I will prevail over them and inflict losses on them, as did *the Amalekite and the Canaanite who dwelt in that hill-country,* who *smote them even unto Hormah.*"[171] Balak intended to do this because of his fear of them, as he mentioned to the elders of Midian,[172] or it may be that his purpose was that he should be able to reconquer all [that land] which the Israelites had captured from the possession of Sihon which originally belonged to Moab, as is stated explicitly in the words of Jephthah.[173] I have already mentioned this.[174]

24 1. AND HE WENT NOT, AS AT OTHER TIMES, TO SEEK FOR ENCHANTMENTS. [This means] that on the previous [two] occasions Balaam acted as an enchanter, and wanted to curse them by means of enchantment, and G-d came to him as if by chance, and not

(167) Verse 24. (168) As explained by Ramban above, 22:3. (169) Verse 27. (170) Verse 19. (171) Above, 14:45. (172) *Ibid.*, 22:3-4. (173) Judges 11:13. (174) Above, 21:29; 22:4.

because he [Balaam] had concentrated on [attaining] prophecy, nor because of any superior status that he had achieved [because he was in fact *not* worthy of prophecy]. But now when he was told, *For there is no enchantment in Jacob, neither is there any divination in Israel,*[158] whether to do them evil or good, Balaam abandoned his enchantments, and *he went not* [any more] *as at* [the] *other times to seek* them. Instead, *he set his face toward the wilderness* where Israel was [encamped], so that he would see them and prepare his soul towards them, so that the Divine communication would come unto him, as had happened to him twice [previous], and so indeed it happened to him now. Therefore Scripture states, *and 'the spirit of G-d' came upon him,* [175] for now *the hand of the Eternal was upon* him as it was upon the prophets,[176] and just as Moses said, *would that all the Eternal's people were prophets, that the Eternal would put 'His spirit' upon them!*[177] — and it is further said: *'The spirit of the Eternal G-d' is upon me.*[178] Therefore Balaam now referred to himself as *him who heareth the words of G-d,*[179] *for he* was [for that particular moment] *a prophet.*[180] Now Rashi commented: *"And he set his face toward the wilderness.* This is to be understood as the Targum [Onkelos] rendered it." For the Rabbi's [Rashi's] Targum contained [the following text]: "He directed his face toward the wilderness in which the children of Israel had made the [golden] calf." But this is not found in accurate editions of Onkelos' Targum,[181] and is [only] written in some of the texts [of Onkelos], which were emended on the basis of the Targum Yerushalmi,[182] but the correct interpretation is as we have explained [above, that Balaam turned to the wilderness in order to receive Divine communication as he had previously, and not because that was the place where they had made the golden calf].

(175) Verse 2. (176) Ezekiel 37:1: *The hand of the Eternal was upon me.* (177) Above, 11:29. (178) Isaiah 61:1. (179) Verse 4. (180) Genesis 20:7. (181) Nor is it found in our texts of Onkelos. (182) It is also found in our texts of the Targum of Yonathan ben Uziel. — There are three traditional *Targumim* (translations) of the Pentateuch: *Onkelos, Yonathan,* and *Yerushalmi.* The latter was lost for many centuries, and only parts of it have reached us. Recently, however, a copy of this Jerusalem Targum has been found in its full version, and the text quoted here by Ramban appears in it.

Scripture says [in describing Balaam]: *Who seeth the vision of the Almighty,*[179] meaning that he now saw through a lucid spectrum, as did the early prophets of whom it is said, *And I appeared unto Abraham, unto Isaac, and unto Jacob by the Name 'E-il Sha-dai' (G-d Almighty).*[183] Or it may be that Balaam [only] received [the Divine communication] through a degree [of vision] less than theirs, since *'the vision of' the Almighty*[179] is not the same as *the Almighty.*[183] Thus the patriarchs saw by *'E-il Sha-dai' (G-d Almighty)*, [a double expression], whereas Balaam saw only by *'the vision of' the Almighty*—two degrees lower than them [because only one Name of G-d is used, and he only saw a *vision of* it]. Therefore Balaam described himself as [one who saw *the vision of the Almighty*] *with opened eyes,* which is the degree of prophecy attained by the sons [i.e., the disciples] of the prophets, as it is said, *Eternal, open the eyes of these men* etc.,[184] and in connection with Balaam himself it says, upon his seeing the angel, *And the Eternal opened the eyes of Balaam.*[185] Now do not [be induced to] think otherwise than that which we have explained in this matter, because of the statement of our Rabbis who said in the Sifre:[186] "*And there hath not arisen a prophet since in Israel like unto Moses.*[187] *In Israel there hath not arisen,* but in the [other] nations of the world there has arisen. And who was he? It was Balaam. But there was a difference between the prophecy of Moses and that of Balaam, because Moses did not know about what G-d was going to speak to him [as will be explained further on], and Balaam knew about what He was going to speak to him, as it is said, *The saying of him who heareth the words of G-d.*[179] Moses did not know when He would speak to him, as it is said, [*then he heard the Voice*] *speaking unto him,*[188] and Balaam knew when He would speak to him, as it is said, *and knoweth the knowledge of the Most High.*[189] He spoke to Moses while he was standing, as it is said, *But as for thee* [Moses], *'stand' thou here by Me,*[190] and to Balaam He spoke when he was fallen down, as it is said,

(183) Exodus 6:3. (184) II Kings 6:20. (185) Above, 22:31. (186) Sifre, *Berachah,* 357. (187) Deuteronomy 34:10. (188) Above, 7:89. (189) Further, Verse 16. (190) Deuteronomy 5:28.

fallen down, yet with opened eyes.[179] [The prophecy of Balaam may be] compared to the cook of a king, who knows what expenses the king has for [the food on] his table."

The explanation of the meaning of this *Beraitha*[191] is as follows: Scripture stated, *And there hath not arisen a prophet since in Israel like unto Moses,*[187] and our Rabbis explained that this verse does not come to declare the superiority of Moses' prophecy over that of the other prophets, since Scripture has already informed us of his superiority over them in two places—in the verse, *And I appeared unto Abraham, unto Isaac, and unto Jacob by the Name 'E-il Sha-dai' (G-d Almighty), but by My Name, the Eternal, was I not known unto them,*[183] and in the verse, *If there be a prophet among you* etc.[192] But now [in speaking of Moses' prophecy][187] He did not say about Moses that he knew G-d, as Moses had requested, *Show me now Thy ways, that I may know Thee,*[193] for the verse there[187] does not say that "he knew G-d face to face," but says: *whom 'the Eternal' knew face to face,*[187] because it is telling us an explanation of [the nature of] Moses' prophecy. It is thus saying that to Moses our teacher [the Divine communication] used to come clearly, like one who speaks to his friend *face to face,*[187] and tells him his words and his meaning until he sees from [the expression on] his face that he understands his words and his intention, and [indicates this] by saying so and by showing on his face that he recognizes what [his friend] wants. Thus the Rabbis [in the Sifre quoted above] said that Balaam had this [degree of prophecy only] when he prophesied in honor of Israel, for he fully understood the words of G-d and His intention and wish in all that was destined to happen to Israel. And even so there was still a difference between the prophecy of Moses and that of Balaam! For Moses did not know what He would tell him, and about what topic or which commandment He would speak to him, but he was ready at any time for the Divine communication, and the Holy One, blessed be He, would command

(191) The teachings of the Sifre are considered *Beraithoth.* See in Vol. II, p. 133, Note 209, for fuller explanation of this term. (192) Above, 12:6. (193) Exodus 33:13.

him as He so desired. But Balaam had to concentrate and think about the [particular] matter which he wanted [G-d to speak to him about], and he would retire into solitude and prepare himself spiritually so that the [Divine] Spirit[63] would come upon him, *peradventure the Eternal will come to meet* him, as is explicitly stated here [in our verse]. He knew [also] that if the Spirit *were* to come upon him, it would speak to him [only] about that subject which he had thought of, and not about any other matter. Furthermore, Moses did not know when He would speak to him, because he did not have any fixed time for the [Divine] communication, but whenever Moses wanted it and directed his mind towards [receiving] a Divine communication, He would speak to him; as Moses said, *Stay ye, that I may hear what the Eternal will command concerning you,*[194] and similarly whenever G-d wanted to command him *from the Tent of Meeting,*[195] *then he* [Moses] *heard the Voice speaking unto him.*[188] But Balaam knew how to determine the [exact] moment when he would have the [Divine] communication, and the Spirit would only rest upon him at that moment. Perhaps this is "the moment" that our Rabbis speak of in Tractate Berachoth[196] and in Tractate Sanhedrin,[197] and at that moment he [thought he] would utter the curse, and it was [only] at that moment that the Spirit would rest upon him, and never at any other time. Similarly the fact that Moses remained standing [during the Divine communication] indicates his superiority, whereas Balaam's falling down denoted his inferiority, [implying] that he could not endure the prophecy, just as it says, *if we hear the voice of the*

(194) Above, 9:8. Although Moses had not been told in advance that G-d would speak to him, he knew that if he concentrated on receiving a Divine communication, he would surely receive one. (195) Leviticus 1:1. (196) Berachoth 7a. The Gemara there states that there is "one moment" every day when G-d, is angry, and Balaam knew precisely when that moment was. The anger is occasioned when the sun begins to shine "and the kings of the world put on their crowns and prostrate themselves to the sun." — It is the Rabbis' way of saying that the deification of nature by man occasions the displeasure of the Creator, for how could they change His glory for that which is His creation and tool! (197) Sanhedrin 105b. The same text as in Berachoth 7a is also quoted there.

Eternal our G-d any more, then we shall die;[198] *Go thou near, and hear.*[199] The Rabbis further said [in the Sifre quoted above]: "[The prophecy of Balaam may be] compared to the cook of a king, who knows etc." [This comparison refers] to the first distinction [between Moses' prophecy and that of Balaam, namely, that Moses did not know in advance about what G-d would speak to him, whereas Balaam did know], and the intention of the Rabbis thereby is to say that the cook knows what are the expenses of the [upkeep of the] king's table, but his minister who *is trusted in all* his *house*[200] and knows his secrets, does not know the expenses of the household. This example indicates that the Sages' intention was to say that Balaam himself knew, after concentrating [his intention on receiving a Divine communication], that G-d would tell him [to say]: *How shall I curse, whom G-d hath not cursed?*[201] and the whole of the blessing [mentioned in the verses], and that afterwards he would hear the communication in [precisely] those words which he had thought of in his heart. This is, as I have mentioned,[202] because he was a diviner, and thus future [events which would befall the people of Israel] would come into his heart [through divination]; but now on account of Israel he also heard the [Divine] utterance about them, and therefore he now prided himself, saying, *The saying of him who heareth the words of G-d.*[179]

Now I have seen this same subject which is taught in the Sifre [quoted above] said in another form in the homiletics of Bamidbar Sinai Rabbah,[203] but there is no need for me to prolong [this subject]. The general idea is that the Sages intended to say that Balaam's prophecy came to him in words which he clearly understood, and the reason for this was, as the Sages have said,[203] so that the nations of the world should not have an excuse to say: "If we had had a prophet like Moses, we would have served the Holy One, blessed be He." But the degree of Balaam's prophecy was [nonetheless] lower than that of the other prophets, because it was [only] by *the 'vision' of the Almighty,*[179]

(198) Deuteronomy 5:22. (199) *Ibid.*, Verse 24. (200) A reference to Moses. See above, 12:7. (201) Above, 23:8. (202) *Ibid.*, 22:5; 31. (203) Bamidbar Rabbah 20:1.

as we have explained. And so also the Rabbis have said in Vayikra Rabbah:[204] "The Holy One, blessed be He, only revealed Himself to the prophets of the [other] nations of the world with a half-communication,' as it is said: *'Vayikar Elokim' (And G-d 'happened to meet' Balaam*[205] [instead of saying *'vayikra' Elokim* — and G-d 'called' to Balaam], but to the prophets of Israel [He revealed Himself] with a complete communication, as it is said: *'Vayikra' (And He called) unto Moses."*[195] The meaning of [the expression] "a half-communication" you will understand from what we have explained [above].

3. 'SHETHUM HA'AYIN.' The commentators have not found the root of this word [*shethum*] anywhere else in Scripture. Onkelos translated it: "who sees well," as [if to say] "open-eyed," and in the language of the Sages we find:[206] "sufficient time *sheyishtom* and to close it up"—meaning to say: [enough time to open a hole in the barrel of wine] — and to stop it up again. Perhaps the word [*shethum*] is a composite one [consisting of the two words *shethui mah* — "whatever is put" before the eye], from the root *'shithi' (My setting) these My signs,*[207] [and here it means] that Balaam is a person [of whom one can use the phrase] "whatever is put" [before him] — because he understands everything that he puts his eye upon.

7. AND HIS KING SHALL BE HIGHER THAN AGAG. "Their first king [Saul] will conquer Agag[208] king of the Amalekites. Agag is here called by his name before he was born.[209] Similar cases are [the expressions]: *to Cyrus, whose right hand I have holden;*[210] *Behold, a son shall be born unto the house of David, Josiah by name.*[211] So also were the names of Isaac,[212] Ishmael,[213] and Solomon[214] [given before

(204) Vayikra Rabbah 1:13. (205) Above, 23:4. (206) Abodah Zarah 69a. (207) Exodus 10:1. Thus, unlike Rashi and R'dak who explain the word *shethum* on the basis of the root *shatham* found in the Mishnah, Ramban explains it on the basis of Biblical language. (208) I Samuel 15:8. (209) This whole paragraph — from "Agag is here called" until ". . . before they were born" — is not found in our texts of Rashi. (210) Isaiah 45:1. (211) I Kings 13:2. (212) Genesis 17:19. (213) *Ibid.,* 16:11. (214) I Chronicles 22:9.

they were born]. AND HIS KINGDOM — that is, Jacob's — SHALL BE EXALTED more and more, because David and his son Solomon will come after him [Saul]." This is Rashi's language, and he has explained it well.

It is possible that every king of the Amalekite people was called Agag, because the first king whom they set up over them was so called [Agag], and thus all his descendants who occupied his throne were called by his name,[215] as are most kings even nowadays, who are called by the name of those who [originally] seized the kingdom. So also *Haman the Agagite*[216] [was so called] because he was a descendant of that royal family. For it is unlikely that the prophet [Balaam] would cite the name of a wicked man [Agag] even before he was *formed in the womb.*[217] So also [the name] *Gog*[218] was one by which all the princes of Magog were called.

Thus Balaam added with this third prophecy of his [to his previous two prophecies] by telling Balak that Jacob's tents *are goodly,*[219] referring to the period from the time that they were dwellers in tents until they would inherit the land [of Canaan], and the *dwellings* of *Israel*[219] after the conquest and division of the Land will also be good, meaning that they will dwell therein in safe habitations. And [Balaam further informed Balak that] Israel's land will be full of all goodly things, *like a watered garden, and like a spring of water, whose waters fail not,*[220] and that Israel will conquer Amalek because he attacked him, and will destroy his memory; and that the *kingdom* of Israel *will be* even more *exalted,*[221] because they will have afterwards mighty kings, who will be exceedingly elevated. And he further told him that Israel would *eat up his adversaries and break their bones in pieces,*[222] referring to their wealth and all their belongings. And [finally, in Verse 9] he told him that Israel would dwell in the Land safely, fearing

(215) Thus there is no need to say, as Rashi did, that Agag here refers to the specific Amalekite king of King Saul's days, and that his name is foretold a few hundred years before he was born, as Scripture would not foretell the birth of a wicked man. (216) Esther 3:1. (217) See Jeremiah 1:5. (218) Ezekiel 39:1. (219) Verse 5. (220) Isaiah 58:11. (221) Verse 7. (222) Verse 8.

no people, *as a lion, and as a lioness* that does not fear *any ravenous beast.*[223] And so now Balak despaired of [ever fighting] Israel, for [he realized that] if he would fight against him, he would be truly destroyed, for Israel would *eat up* all *his adversaries*[222] in the same way that he would destroy Amalek because he attacked him. Therefore Balak now told Balaam to *flee to* his *place,*[224] for he has no more desire for him [and his counsel].

12. [AND BALAAM SAID UNTO BALAK]: 'SPOKE I NOT ALSO TO THY MESSENGERS ETC.?' Balaam was now defending himself on the basis of what he had told Balak's messengers when they came back to him, before he knew *what the Eternal* would *speak unto* him *more;*[225] but afterwards [i.e., after G-d had told him that he may only go with them, but must not curse the people] he still made out that he was ready to come and curse [the people], until the angel warned him on the road, as I have explained.[226]

14. COME AND I WILL COUNSEL THEE. Since Balaam wanted to tell [Balak] about the punishment [that would befall] his people, as it is written, *and he shall smite through the corners of Moab,*[227] therefore he told him, *I will counsel thee,* that is to say: " I will tell you 'on the side' an advice, so that others should not hear it." "*Come and I will counsel thee* what you have to do [to revenge yourself upon Israel]. And what was the advice [that he gave him]? [He told him]: 'The G-d of these [Israelites] hates immorality, etc., [therefore I advise you to seduce Israel into sin by means of the lure of the Moabite women],' as is narrated in the Chapter *Cheilek.*[228] You may know that

(223) Isaiah 35:9. (224) Verse 11. (225) Above, 22:19. In other words, in Verse 18 *ibid.*, we are told that he said to Balak's servants that he *cannot go beyond the word of G-d* even if *Balak would give* him *a house full of silver and gold.* It is on the basis of these remarks that he is now defending himself. But, as Ramban continues, in actual fact he misled Balak, because he still made out that he was prepared to curse the people even after the Eternal spoke to him further, and he did not tell Balak of G-d's true message then. (226) *Ibid.,* Verse 20. (227) Further Verse 17. (228) Literally: "Portion" — "All Israel have 'a portion' in the World to Come." Sanhedrin 106a. The story of the Israelites committing immorality with the

it was Balaam who gave them this counsel [to lead Israel astray] through immorality, for it is said, *Behold, these* [women] *caused the children of Israel, through the counsel of Balaam,* [*to revolt so as to break faith with the Eternal*].[229] WHAT THIS PEOPLE SHALL DO TO THY PEOPLE. This is an elliptical verse [which means as follows]: '*I will counsel thee* how to corrupt them, and I will [also] tell you what evil they are destined to do to Moab *in the end of days.*' " This is Rashi's language.

The correct interpretation [of the word *i'atzcha,* normally translated: *I will counsel thee*] seems to me to be that Balaam told Balak: "I will tell you the purpose that G-d has planned that *this people shall do to thy people in the end of days,*" this being similar to the expressions: *This is the 'eitzah' (purpose) that is 'y'utzah' (purposed) upon the whole earth;*[230] *Hear ye the 'atzath' (design) of the Eternal, that He hath 'ya'atz' (purposed) against Edom.*[231] Balaam said *i'atzcha* [which literally means "I will give you counsel"], because one who hears counsel, [as Balaam heard G-d's counsel], is called a *no'atz* [he with whom counsel is taken].[232]

And this prophecy [in the following verses], refers to Messianic times, for all of Balaam's prophecies added [to the previous ones] in [speaking of more] distant events. Thus at first[233] he said that Israel is [now] *the portion of the Eternal* and *His inheritance;*[234] in the second prophecy[235] he added that they would [later on] conquer the Land and kill its kings. In the third [prophecy][236] he saw them dwelling in the Land and increasing and multiplying therein, and that they would appoint a king [Saul] who would defeat Agag, and that the *kingdom* [of Israel] would *be* further *exalted*; for he saw David [whose kingdom]

Moabite women is related in the following chapter of the Torah, and tradition has it that this plan was suggested by Balaam in his parting words to Balak. This, as Rashi explains, is the reason why he used the phrase "*I will 'counsel thee' what this people shall do*", meaning: "*I will counsel thee* how to lead the people astray, and I will tell you *what this people shall do . . .*" Ramban explains the phrase "*I will counsel thee*" differently. (229) Further, 31:16. (230) Isaiah 14:26. (231) Jeremiah 49:20. (232) See Isaiah 40:14: *'Eth mi no'atz'* (with whom took He counsel). (233) Above, 23:7-10. (234) Deuteronomy 32:9. (235) Above, Chapter 23, Verses 18-24. (236) Above, Verses 3-9.

was exalted exceedingly,[237] as it is said, *And David perceived that the Eternal had established him king over Israel, and that He hath exalted his kingdom for His people Israel's sake,*[238] that is to say, because He had promised them that their *kingdom* would *be exalted.* And now in this fourth prophecy Balaam continued [on the future] and saw the Messianic era; therefore he spoke of it as a very distant event, saying, *I see him, but not now; I behold him, but not nigh,*[227] [a phrase] which he did not use in his first [three] prophecies. He stated that this is the purpose of G-d which He had planned, to come to pass *in the end of days.*[239] He referred to himself now as one *who heareth the words of G-d,*[240] and as one *who seeth the vision of the Almighty,*[240] as he had done in the third prophecy,[179] but he added now [the phrase] *and knoweth the knowledge of the Most High.*[240] Now one who speaks in this manner, saying "I know the knowledge of a certain person" means to say that he understands him, and what is in his heart, [even] those matters which he does not utter verbally, and similarly this [man Balaam] intended to say that he knows and will now say what is in the "mind" [i.e., intention] of G-d the Most High to do in His world at *the end of* all *days.*[239] This is similar to that which it says, *for the day of vengeance is in My heart,*[241] and the Rabbis have said[242] [with reference to that day, that its precise timing is a matter which "His] heart has not divulged to the mouth." Now Scripture states here, *And 'he took up his parable,' and said*[243] and it does not mention that this was [said] by prophecy, as it says about the [previous] three occasions, for since he said, *The saying of him who heareth the words of G-d . . . who seeth the vision of the Almighty*[240] it is self-understood that *the hand of G-d was upon*[176] him, just as at the third time, where it says: *and the spirit of G-d came upon him;*[244] and he himself said so.[245]

(237) I Chronicles 14:2. (238) II Samuel 5:12. (239) Verse 14. (240) Verse 16. (241) Isaiah 63:4. (242) Midrash Tehillim 89:2. (243) Verse 15. (244) Verse 2. (245) For in his third prophecy, Balaam said of himself, *who heareth the words of G-d, who seeth the vision of the Almighty* (Verse 4) and it says there, *and the spirit of G-d came upon him* (Verse 2). So here too, in his fourth prophecy, where it says *who heareth the words of G-d, who seeth the vision of the Almighty,* it was also through the *spirit of G-d* which came upon him, even though it

17. THERE SHALL STEP FORTH A STAR OUT OF JACOB. Because the Messiah will gather together the dispersed of Israel from all the corners of the earth, Balaam compares him [metaphorically] to *a star* that passes through the firmament from the ends of heaven, just as it is said about [the Messiah]: *and behold, there came with the clouds of heaven, one like unto a son of man* etc.[246] Balaam thus said that he saw that at a distant time *a star* would pass from the ends of heaven, and there would rise out of it the sceptre of a ruler, *and he shall smite through the corners of Moab, and break down all the sons of Seth,* the son of Adam,[247] who was the father of all the nations.[248] He mentioned *the corners of Moab* in order to inform Balak that his people would not fall into the hand of Israel now, but *in the end of days*[239] Moab will not be saved from the hand of the ruling king [in Israel]. And the meaning of *'the corners' of Moab* is that this ruler [in Israel] *will break down all the sons of Seth,* and they [Moab] will not be saved, even though they are *cut off on 'the corner,'*[249] and have no name among the nations, and will not fight against Israel.

18. AND EDOM SHALL BE A POSSESSION, SEIR ALSO, EVEN HIS ENEMIES SHALL BE A POSSESSION. The downfall of Edom[250] will be by the hand of the Messiah, because our present exile under the hand of Rome is considered Edom's [exile], just as it is said: *The punishment of thine iniquity is absolved, O daughter of Zion, He will no more carry thee away into captivity; He will punish thine iniquity, O 'daughter of Edom,' He will uncover thy sins*[251] — for G-d will not punish Edom until the sins of Zion are absolved, at the time when *He will no more* keep them *in captivity.*[251] Therefore Balaam mentioned Edom, for it is he who disputes our [right to] kingdom, and about him

does not say so expressly. (246) Daniel 7:13. (247) Genesis 5:3. (248) See Ramban *ibid.,* Vol. I, p. 98. (249) Jeremiah 9:25. This is an epithet for certain Arabian tribes, who had the corners of their hair clipped. Ramban here uses this term metaphorically, in its literal sense of "cut off in the corner", to refer to a people who live in the remotest corners of the world. (250) See Vol. I, pp. 444-445, and 568-569, for an explanation why this term is used about Rome. (251) Lamentations 4:22.

it has been said, *and the one people shall be stronger than the other.*[252] Balaam was thus prophesying that Edom will not completely fall until the time of the end [of the exile] by the hand of *'the star'* [i.e., the Messiah] who will *step forth out of Jacob* [as stated in the previous verse].

Seir also, even his enemies shall be a possession. This means that Seir will become a possession of his enemies [i.e., of Israel].[253] Or [the term] *his enemies* may refer to [Jacob's enemies, i.e.,] Edom and Seir mentioned [previously in the verse], who are the enemies of Jacob, [and the meaning of the verse would thus be: "Edom, and Seir also, who are the enemies of Israel] will become a possession [of Israel]."[254] And the meaning of the verse, *and he shall destroy the remnant from 'the' city,*[255] is "from *'every'* city," for there will not be left a remnant of any city in the world [i.e. of those belonging to the Roman Empire, here referred to by the names Edom and Seir]. Thus at first [in Verse 17] Balaam said that [the Messiah] will *break down all the sons of Seth,* and now he is saying that he will not leave any remnant or survivor [of them]. Thus was completed Balaam's counsel to Balak.

20. 'VAYAR' (AND HE SAW) AMALEK. "He contemplated the punishment of Amalek and he said, *Amalek was the first of the nations* — he was the first of them all to wage war against Israel. And so did Onkelos translate it. *But his end* will be to be destroyed by their hands, [as it is said], *thou shalt blot out the remembrance of Amalek.*"[256] This is Rashi's language.

It is possible that the word *vayar* is to be understood in its literal meaning ["and he saw," and not, as Rashi explained it, "and he contemplated"], since Balaam was on *the top of Peor, that looketh down upon the desert*[257] and so he looked towards the land of Amalek

(252) Genesis 25:23. "They will never be equally great at the same time; when one rises, the other will fall" (Rashi *ibid.*). (253) This is Rashi's interpretation, according to which the phrase *his enemies* is to be interpreted as *to his enemies.* (254) See my Hebrew commentary p. 301 for a quote from the Zohar, which interprets the verse in this way. (255) Verse 19. (256) Deuteronomy 25:19. (257) Above, 23:28.

who dwelt in that hill-country.[258] Thus he said that *Amalek is* now *'the first' of the nations,* meaning that he is considered a leader of the nations, because they were *mighty men, and valiant men for the war;*[259] for were it not so, it would not have occurred to them to come and attack Israel, and Moses would not have had to choose a select number of men [to fight them],[260] or to pray and lift up his hands [towards heaven] until he was weakened.[261] He [Moses] also built an altar and called its name *'Ado-nai nissi'* (*the Eternal is my banner*),[262] because he considered [the defeat of Amalek] a great miracle. Therefore this [man Balaam] said that *Amalek is the first of the nations, but his end shall come to destruction* more than all the others, as He said, *For I will utterly blot out the remembrance of Amalek from under heaven.*[263] Similarly, *'the first' oils*[264] means "the best" of them, which are counted first [in quality].[265] The same [usage is also found in these expressions]: *'the first'* [i.e., "the best"] *of the devoted things;*[266] *'head' and chief over them;*[267] *'the chief' spices.*[268]

And the meaning of the verse, *And 'he saw' the Kenite*[269] is also that Balaam [actually] saw their land, for he [*the Kenite*] dwelt with Amalek. *And he took up his parable, and said*[269] to them by way of counsel, *Firm is thy dwelling-place, and thou puttest thy nest in a rock,*[269] meaning: "Make thy dwelling in a firm place, and [set] thy nest in a rock, that is, depart and go away from the Amalekites, lest *thou be swept away*[270] with them, *and put in a* firm *rock thy dwelling,* with Israel," just as it is said, *And the children of the Kenite, Moses' father-in-law, went up out of the city of palm-trees with the children of Judah* etc.[271] And Balaam continued: *For if the Kenite will be wasted,*[272] meaning to say: "Do not be afraid of coming [to settle] in Israel, because even if you *will be wasted* together with them, because when the enemy will exile Israel they will destroy all inhabitants from

(258) *Ibid.*, 14:45. (259) Jeremiah 48:14. (260) Exodus 17:9. (261) *Ibid.*, Verses 11-12. (262) *Ibid.*, Verse 15. (263) *Ibid.*, Verse 14. (264) Amos 6:6. (265) Of the quality used for lighting the lamps in the candelabrum (see Menachoth 86a). (266) I Samuel 15:21. (267) Judges 11:11. Literally: *'first' and chief.* (268) Exodus 30:23. Literally: *'the first spices.'* See Ramban, Vol. II, p. 528. (269) Verse 21. (270) Genesis 19:15. See also I Samuel 15:6. (271) Judges 1:16. (272) Verse 22.

the Land, — *'ad mah' (for how long) will Ashur* [Assyria] *carry thee away captive?* [272] He will not hold you captive forever, because you shall be redeemed from his hand together with Israel, but if you will remain with the Amalekites, *your end* will be to perish with them forever." Similarly we find [this usage of *ad mah* in the following verses]: *'ad mah' O Eternal, wilt Thou be angry forever?*; [273] *'ad meh' shall my glory be put to shame?* [274] — which [in both cases] means "for how long." Or [it may be that the phrase *ad mah*] comes to emphasize the magnitude of something, such as: *'mah' (how) weak is thy heart!;* [275] *'mah' (how) was thy mother a lioness!* [276] and [here it means] to say: "To what extent can the captivity which Assyria will take captive of you reach, and how great [can it be]? It should be of no significance at all to you, because you will not [ultimately] be destroyed, as you would be if you were together with Amalek." Therefore Balaam continued and *took up his parable* about Assyria, [saying] that *the time of his own land* [277] will come for him too, and nobody will be saved from *the great and terrible day of the Eternal* [278] [which will come] upon all the nations; for *ships shall come from the coast of Kittim,* which refers to the Romans, *and they shall afflict* [the] *Ashur* [who is] mentioned [later on in that verse], *and shall afflict Eber,* [279] which means Israel. He is thus stating that [the Romans] will oppress both the captors [i.e., the Assyrians] and their captives [the Hebrews]; *but he also* — the people of *Kittim* [namely the Romans, as explained above] — *shall come to destruction* [279] in the end.

Thus Balaam completed his words [by foretelling] the destruction of the *Kittim,* who are the *fourth beast* [280] which will be destroyed by the hand of the Messiah, as it is said, *I beheld even till the beast was slain, and its body destroyed, and it was given to be burned with fire,* [281] [and the phrase here] *shall come to destruction* [is used] because their memory will be completely extirpated. Now it is well-known in the

(273) Psalms 79:5. (274) *Ibid.,* 4:3. (275) Ezekiel 16:30. (276) *Ibid.,* 19:2. (277) Jeremiah 27:7. (278) Malachi 3:23. (279) Verse 24. (280) In Daniel's vision of the four kingdoms [symbolized by four beasts], the fourth beast represents Rome (see Daniel 7:7). See an important note on this subject in Genesis, Vol. I, p. 350, Note 8. (281) Daniel 7:11.

sayings of our Rabbis[282] that the *fourth beast* which Daniel saw[280] represents Rome who exiled us, and it is this ["beast"] which will be destroyed by the hand of the Messiah.

Now do not be astonished at this [explanation we have given above, that *Kittim* means Rome, and do not refute it] because the *third* kingdom [mentioned in Daniel] [280] was Greece, as is stated explicitly in the Book of Daniel,[283] and the Kittim are of the seed of Javan [who was the ancestor of the Greeks], as it is said, *And the sons of Javan: Elishah, and Tarshish, Kittim, and Dodanim*[284] [and therefore one might think that the Romans, who are the *fourth beast*, i.e., the fourth kingdom, could not be the *Kittim*]! For it is indeed true [that *Kittim* are the Greeks, as is stated in the verse quoted above,[284] but nonetheless here it refers to the Romans, who were descendants of the Greeks]. And our Rabbis admit this [that the Greeks and Romans were related], as they have said: [285] "Italy of *Greece* — this is the great city of *Rome*," and it is well-known that the name of the land of which [the city of] Rome forms a part, is called in their books and in their language "Italy." [Thus it is clear that Greece and Rome are related, and therefore the *Kittim*, who in the Book of Genesis are described[284] as descendants of the *Greeks*, refer here in the prophecy of Balaam to *Rome*.] But the history [of the *Kittim*] is similar to that of Canaan; for the Jebusite, and the Amorite, and the Girgashite, and the Hivite, they and their children and their fathers, are each of them considered an independent nation, just as it says: *the Hittite, and the Girgashite, and the Amorite, and the Canaanite, and the Perizzite, and the Hivite, and the Jebusite, seven nations greater and mightier than thou.*[286] The reason for this [i.e., for considering each one a separate nation], is because each one of these [seven] sons [of Canaan] became a mighty nation, and these [individual] nations were called by the names of their ancestors. But the other sons of Canaan[287] who did not become strong as did their brothers, considered themselves a part of

(282) Abodah Zarah 2b. (283) Daniel 7:6. See also Ramban further on for a fuller explanation. (284) Genesis 10:4. (285) Megillah 6b. See my Hebrew commentary, p. 302, Note 86. (286) Deuteronomy 7:1. (287) Genesis 10:17-18: *the Arkite, and the Sinite,* etc.

him [i.e., of Canaan].[288] So also the "land of Canaan" is so called because of [Canaan] the father [and not because of that particular son of his who founded the Canaanite people—since all his seven sons lived there with their peoples.[286]]. And *the Philistines* and *Caphtorim,* the sons of [Mitzraim][289] also became separate nations[whereas the other sons of Mitzraim: *Ludim, Anamin* etc. were known merely as descendants of Mitzraim].[290] Similarly we find in the families mentioned in the section of *Pinchas: [The sons of Menasheh]: of Machir, the family of the Machirites — and Machir begot Gilead; of Gilead, the family of the Gileadites.*[291] There are many such cases [in Scripture]. Here too: *The sons of Javan: Elishah and Tarshish*[284] are considered part of Javan [Greece], and they constitute the third kingdom [in the vision of Daniel], but the *Kittim* [who were also amongst the sons of Javan][284] became a mighty nation, and are [therefore] counted as the fourth kingdom [i.e., that of Rome], and it is this kingdom which will continue until the [times of the] Messiah, and it will be destroyed by him.

But Rabbi Abraham ibn Ezra has confused this matter,[292] and introduced into it the kingdom of Ishmael [i.e., the Arabic kingdoms of his times] *for* their *fear was fallen upon* him,[293] and he argued: "How can one not count such a great and powerful empire [as the Arabic empire, amongst those seen in Daniel's visions]!" This argument stems from a lack of knowledge, for each of the four kingdoms which Daniel saw, gained power one after another, and

(288) See Vol. I, p. 151, for an explanation why the verse in Deuteronomy 7:1 [quoted above] counts *the Canaanite* as one of Canaan's seven children, since, as we have explained, each of his seven sons founded a nation in his own right. (289) Genesis 10:13-14. (290) *Ibid.,* Verse 13. (291) Further, 26:29. Here *the Gileadites* — descended from Gilead the son of Machir — are counted by Scripture as a separate family, although it first mentioned *the family of the Machirites.* This is because Gilead increased more than the other sons of Machir, and became a large family in his own right. (292) Ibn Ezra in his commentary to Daniel 7:14. To include all the empires in the "four kingdoms" that will rule the world, as symbolized by the *four beasts,* Ibn Ezra suggested that both Greece and Rome should be counted as the "third beast," and the "fourth beast" will then be the Islamic empires of his times. Ramban totally rejects this interpretation. (293) Esther 8:17.

each one prevailed over its predecessor and seized the kingdom [of the world] from it. [Likewise] each one continued the enslavement and exile of Israel during the period that it ruled. Therefore Daniel saw in his dream that the Chaldeans [i.e., the Babylonians] would [be the first] to enslave us [i.e., the Jewish people], and that after them the Persians would seize the kingdom, and would [continue] to enslave us, and after them in their stead would come the Greeks; and after them the Romans would become powerful and seize the kingdom, and subjugate us *until the time of the end*[294] [of the exile], for their kingdom would only come to an end by the hand of the redeemer [i.e., the Messiah]. Thus [the extent of] our exile is the duration of [rule of] the four kingdoms [Babylon, Persia, Greece, and Rome], and even if there will be other empires in the world contemporaneously with these four kingdoms, Scripture does not count them and Daniel did not see them [in his visions], since he did not have to see them at all in order to know the [date of the final] redemption. And indeed in the days of [the kingdoms of] Persia and Greece, and today also, there are great empires in the world, besides those of Rome and Ishmael, such as the peoples of India, Ethiopia, Rumania, the Tartars, and others. And if so, [Ibn Ezra] should have counted many kingdoms! And [another reason why Ibn Ezra is mistaken is that] it is well-known that it was the Romans who exiled us in the days of Vespasian and Titus, and not the Ishmaelites [the Arabs]; therefore wherever we are, whether under Ishmael, or [anywhere] *from India, even unto Ethiopia,*[295] we are in the exile of Rome, until her memory will be destroyed and we shall be redeemed from it. Who knows, perhaps the kingdom of Ishmael will still be destroyed before the coming of the Messiah! But the *fourth beast* is the one which exiled us, as is said with reference to it, *I beheld, and the same horn made war with the saints and prevailed against them.*[296] We shall remain in this exile until the coming of the Messiah, as it is written, *until the Ancient of days came, and judgment was given for the saints of the Most High; and the time came, and the*

(294) Daniel 12:9. (295) Esther 1:1. This is a term which refers to anywhere in the known world. (296) Daniel 7:21.

saints possessed the kingdom.[297] And anyone who understands the visions of Daniel will find this interpretation clearly indicated there. For in the second vision Daniel saw *the pushing ram,*[298] which was explained to him as [representing the] kingdom of Persia,[299] *and the rough he-goat is the king of Greece, and the great horn is the first king*[300] Alexander [of Greece], who prevailed over Persia. And when *he was strong,* his kingdom *was broken,*[301] *in the place whereof four stood up,*[302] these being his four generals [Ptolemy, Seleucus, Antigonus and Lysimachus] who reigned in his stead after his death. And Scripture mentions: *And 'out of one of them' came forth a little horn, which waxed exceeding great, toward the south, and toward the east, and toward the beauteous Land*[303] and it says concerning it, *Yea, it magnified itself, even to the prince of the host, and from him the continual burnt-offering was taken away.*[304] Thus it clearly refers to the kingdom of Rome, which came "out of Greece" since [the *Kittim* referred to by Balaam, which means, as explained above, Rome] were of his sons [i.e., Javan's,[284] who is the ancestor of the Greeks], and it is that kingdom [Rome] which removed *the continual burnt-offering*[304] [through destroying the Second Temple]. Therefore [Daniel] calls both of them [Greece and Rome] one beast, this being *the rough he-goat,*[300] one of whose [four] horns *waxed great*[303] and removed *the continual burnt-offering.*[304] There are further such proofs there [in the Book of Daniel, that the fourth kingdom means the Romans]; however the tradition of our Rabbis, of blessed memory, [that the "fourth beast" is the kingdom of Rome] is true [in its own right] and needs no other support.

25 1. AND ISRAEL ABODE IN SHITTIM, AND THE PEOPLE BEGAN TO COMMIT HARLOTRY WITH THE DAUGHTERS OF MOAB — "because of the advice of Balaam, as is related in [the Chapter of] *Cheilek.*"[228] This is Rashi's language. And indeed this

(297) *Ibid.,* Verse 22. "The Ancient of Days" is a synonym for G-d the Eternal. (298) *Ibid.,* 8:4. (299) *Ibid.,* Verse 20. (300) *Ibid.,* Verse 21. (301) *Ibid.,* Verse 8. (302) *Ibid.,* Verse 22. (303) *Ibid.,* Verse 9. (304) *Ibid.,* Verse 11.

[seduction to] immorality was not instigated as a plan of the [Moabite] women, but was done upon the advice of their men and their leaders. [The idea] came to them from the elders of Midian, as it says of the Midianites, *for they harass you, by their wiles wherewith they have beguiled you in the matter of Peor,*[305] for *they beguiled* them by means of immorality in order to draw them astray [to worship] Baal-peor. Therefore it is [indeed] possible that Balaam was behind this counsel, since he was considered by them [the Moabites] *great in counsel,*[306] and his intention was to bring evil upon Israel, and therefore he did everything in his power to this end, as it is said, *And the Eternal thy G-d would not hearken unto Balaam,*[307] and therefore *they slew* him *with the sword.*[308]

But according to the simple meaning of Scripture, it is not alluding here to the counsel of Balaam, but only [alludes to it] when it says afterwards, *Behold, these* [women] *caused the children of Israel, through the counsel of Balaam* etc.,[309] just as it does not mention here the counsel of the elders of Midian, and only [mentions it] when it says, *for they harass you.*[305] Thus [it is only] after the event [had happened], at the time of [describing] their punishment, that He mentions what was the source of the evil that befell them. He is [thus] saying that what happened [to them] as a result of the desire for sexual pleasure which exists naturally in men and women from [the time of] their youth, was only [the result] of an evil plan [whose purpose was] to lead them astray [into worshipping Baal-peor]; therefore [the instigators of this plan] deserve a severe punishment. The interpretation of the verse, *Come and I will counsel thee what this people shall do to thy people in the end of days*[310] is thus indeed as I have explained [there].

It is also possible according to the simple meaning of Scripture that Balak at first wanted to curse them [the Israelites] and to wage war against them, and he did not want to give them permission to enter his

(305) Further, 25:18. (306) Jeremiah 32:19. (307) Deuteronomy 23:6. (308) Further, 31:8. (309) *Ibid.*, Verse 16. (310) Above, 24:14.

borders at all. But when Balaam told him[311] that he would not prevail over them, and informed him that they would only destroy his land and his people *in the end of days,*[310] then he [Balak] *brought forth bread and wine*[312] in the plains of Moab [i.e., *in Shittim*], and enticed them [with the daughters of Moab] as if he were their friend. This is [the meaning of the phrase] *'bidvar' (through 'the word' of) Balaam,*[309] for it was because of his words [i.e., his prophecy that the Israelites would not conquer their land now, that the Moabites] did so [i.e., that they did not fight them, but tried to seduce them and lead them astray through their women]. But because it was Balaam's desire to curse them, and he allowed Balak to hire him [and would indeed have cursed them] were it not for *the righteous acts of the Eternal*[313] *Who turned the curse into a blessing,*[307] therefore *they slew* him *with the sword,*[308] for both the hirer [Moab] and the hired one [Balaam] were punished, just as He said, *and because he hired against thee Balaam the son of Beor* etc.[314]

5. [AND MOSES SAID UNTO THE JUDGES OF ISRAEL]: 'SLAY YE EVERY ONE HIS MEN [THAT HAVE JOINED THEMSELVES UNTO BAAL-PEOR].' "Each one of the judges of Israel killed two [men, as the word *anashav* — his 'men,' in the plural, indicates], and the judges of Israel were seventy-eight thousand,[315] as is stated in Tractate Sanhedrin."[316] This is Rashi's language. But I cannot

(311) See Ramban above, Verse 17. (312) Genesis 14:18. See Ramban to Deuteronomy 23:5, that the Moabites did meet the Israelites with bread and water when they were near their country; only the Ammonites failed to do so. — Ramban introduces here the element of "wine," as a clear reference to what the Rabbis in the Sifre here have stated: "[The Israelite] entered; a gourd of wine lay near her. Said she to him, 'Wouldst thou like to drink?' etc." (313) See Micah 6:5. (314) Deuteronomy 23:5. (315) Our texts of Rashi have the figure 88,000, but 78,000 [the number found in a Ramban manuscript] is correct [to the nearest thousand] — and this is also the figure quoted in Tractate Sanhedrin. The exact figure for the 600,000 Israelites is 78,600 judges, as follows: Captains of thousands, 600; captains of hundreds, 6,000; captains of fifties, 12,000; captains of tens, 60,000 — which total 78,600. It should be noted that in the first edition of Rashi (Reggio 1475) this whole text is missing. (316) Sanhedrin 18a.

understand this, that [we should say that] those *who joined themselves* [*to Baal-peor*] who were judged [liable to death] were more than a hundred and fifty thousand — a quarter [of the total population] of Israel![317] Heaven forbid! [Moreover], cases punishable by death [cannot be decided] by [only] one judge, but [require] a court of twenty-three judges. And [even if we were to say that two people were killed by each court of twenty-three judges], they would still be very many people! And the difference between the [two] censuses is not so great,[318] although all those *who joined themselves to Baal-peor* died, as it is written, *for all the men that followed Baal-peor, the Eternal thy G-d hath destroyed them from the midst of thee.*[319]

But the meaning of *every one his men* is that the judges should kill all those *who joined themselves* [*to Baal-peor*], that is to say, each court should judge [the men of] its own tribe and its [groups of] thousands, as it is written, *So I took the heads of your tribes, wise men, and full of knowledge, and made them heads over you, captains of thousands, and captains of hundreds . . . and officers, 'tribe by tribe'.*[320] And afterwards I found in the Gemara Yerushalmi [the following statement] in the Chapter *Cheilek:* [321] "And how many were the judges of Israel? Seventy-eight thousand and six hundred. Moses said to them: 'Each one of you should kill two.' Thus you find that those killed were one hundred and fifty-seven thousand and two hundred." [317] If so, we must say that according to their opinion [that of these Rabbis] the Israelites increased very remarkably between the

(317) For if the judges of Israel who numbered 78,600, each killed two men, a total of 157,200 men is reached! This is more than a quarter of the total population of the people! (318) In the census taken in the second year after the exodus, the people totalled 603,550 (above 1:46) and now after the incident of Baal-peor, they totalled 601,730 (further 26:51), the decrease being only 1,820! That figure is nowhere near the total number of people killed according to Rashi, for even if two people were killed by each court of twenty-three judges, over 7,000 people were killed. Ramban further on, explains that in actual fact none of the people were put to death. (319) Deuteronomy 4:3. (320) *Ibid.,* 1:15. The phrase *tribe by tribe* indicates that each tribe had its own judges who dealt with offenses committed by men of this tribe. (321) Yerushalmi Sanhedrin X, 2. For the term *Cheilek,* see above, Note 228.

[time of the first] census and the [second] census [in order to make up the loss of the many people killed because of this sin of Baal-peor]!

The correct interpretation of the meaning of this section [of the Torah] appears to me to be that at first it says, *And Israel joined himself unto Baal-peor; and the anger of the Eternal was kindled against Israel,*[322] [meaning] *that there is wrath gone out from the Eternal; the plague is begun;*[323] and G-d in His mercy told Moses that the judges should [first] try and then hang those *who joined themselves* [*to Baal-peor*], so that the wrath will not *indeed sweep away the righteous with the wicked.*[324] And Moses gave this command to the judges; and when all the congregation was assembled *at the door of the Tent of Meeting*[325] to do as Moses commanded, and the plague was still raging amongst them, this Simeonite [*Zimri the son of Salu*][326] brazenly *brought unto his brethren a Midianite woman*[325] to rebel against Moses and the judges, and to do so publicly, because he was *a prince*[326] and a great man and [knew that] many would come to his help. Or it may be [that he dared to do this publicly] because, as our Rabbis have said,[327] [the people of] his tribe complained to him: "We are being sentenced to death, and you keep quiet!" Then [when Zimri came forth] Moses and the judges began weeping,[325] *and Phinehas stood up, and wrought judgment, and so the plague was stayed.*[328] Thus none of the people was [actually] sentenced by the judges, for G-d had said, *and hang them up unto the Eternal in face of the sun, that the fierce anger of the Eternal may turn away from Israel,*[329] and His anger had already turned away [by the action of Phinehas, so that the judges no longer had to proceed with the execution of the judgment]. It is for this reason that Scripture does not say: "and the judges of Israel did so [as they had been commanded]."

It is possible that the intention of the text mentioned [above as to the number of men slain in this episode is not that they were *actually*

(322) Verse 3. (323) Above, 17:11. (324) See Genesis 18:23. (325) Verse 6. (326) Further, Verse 14. (327) Sanhedrin 82a. (328) Psalms 106:30. (329) Verse 4.

killed, but means, as explained above], that according to [the strict] command [of G-d] there ought to have been more than one hundred and fifty thousand killed, meaning to say that there were many sinners, but the act of Phinehas protected them. Thus there remained [many of those] *who* had *joined themselves* [*to Baal-peor*], and the Holy One, blessed be He, destroyed them later on before they crossed over the [river] Jordan. This is [the meaning of] the verse which says, *for all the men that followed after Baal-peor, the Eternal thy G-d hath destroyed them from the midst of thee. But ye that did cleave unto the Eternal your G-d are alive every one of you this day.*[330]

(330) Deuteronomy 4:3-4.

Pinchas

11. PHINEHAS, THE SON OF ELEAZAR. The Holy One, blessed be He, [here] informed Moses that He would give Phinehas a good reward for his zeal, *because he was zealous for his G-d,*[1] and *for the righteousness*[2] which he did for Israel by bringing about atonement for them, so that they did not all die in the plague. He [also] commanded Moses to tell Israel that he [Phinehas] would be *a priest forever,*[3] and this is the sense of the phrase, *Therefore say,*[4] that Moses was to tell this to Israel. Now Scripture does not say: *"and it shall be unto him, and to his seed after him 'an everlasting priesthood,' "* as He said about Aaron,[5] but instead it says: *'the covenant' of an everlasting*

(1) Verse 13. (2) Psalms 107:31: *And that was accounted to him* [Phinehas] *for righteousness.* (3) The promise is expressed here in Verse 13; Ramban's language though is taken from Psalms 110:4. (4) Ramban's intent is that Verse 11 [*Phinehas, the son of Eleazar, the son of Aaron . . .*] was G-d's communication exclusively to Moses, telling him that He is desirous of rewarding Phinehas for the reasons stated in that verse, but He did not tell him what was to constitute the reward. Verse 12 then continues with the thought: "Since it is My desire to reward Phinehas, *Therefore say to the children of Israel . . .* " Thus the contents of Verse 11 was not to be told to Israel (Aboab). This interpretation of Ramban is unlike that of Rashi from whose words it may be implied that even the contents of Verse 11 was to be told to the people, the object being that they were not to speak disparagingly of Phinehas for having killed a prince of Israel, for G-d testified that he is a descendant of Aaron, who was a lover of peace, and what Phinehas did was to save the honor of Israel. (5) Exodus 29:9: *and they shall have the priesthood by a perpetual statute.*

priesthood,[1] and it [also] says, *I give unto him 'My covenant' of peace,* meaning that He will give him a covenant with peace cleaving to it, whereas in the case of Aaron it says *for splendor and for beauty.*[6] Therefore it says [here concerning Phinehas]: *because he was zealous for his G-d.* The student learned [in the mysteries of the Cabala] will understand.

Scripture mentions, *Now the name of the man of Israel that was slain;*[7] *And the name of the Midianite woman that was slain,*[8] in order to indicate that [Phinehas] deserved this great reward because he killed a prince of Israel, and the daughter of a heathen king and [nonetheless] he feared them not in his zeal *for his G-d.* And after He had requited His good reward to the righteous one [Phinehas], He commanded Moses to punish the wicked ones, and He told him, *Harass the Midianites,*[9] but first He commanded him to count the people. This is the intent of [the phrase] *And it came to pass after the plague [that the Eternal spoke unto Moses . . . 'Take the sum* etc.'],[10] meaning that the taking of the census should be done first [before the punishment of the Midianites].

18. FOR THEY [the Midianites] HARASS YOU BY THEIR WILES. The meaning [of the expression *by their wiles*] is, as I have explained,[11] that this evil plan [to lead the Israelites astray through their seduction by the Moabite women] was contrived by the elders of Midian, as it is said, *And Moab said unto the elders of Midian,*[12] [thus showing] that it was with them [the elders of Midian]

(6) Exodus 28:2. Since this indicates the very high spiritual status achieved by Aaron [as alluded to in the words of *kavod* and *tiphereth,* which represent certain Emanations], it was not necessary to mention *'the covenant of' an everlasting priesthood,* indicating the perfect Unity. But in the case of Phinehas it does not say that his priesthood was *for splendor and for beauty;* therefore the verse had to mention *'the covenant of' an everlasting priesthood,* indicating that Phinehas' priesthood was also in the perfect Unity, *because he was zealous for his G-d* (Abusaula). See also my Hebrew commentary, p. 305. (7) Verse 14. (8) Verse 15. (9) Verse 17. (10) Verse 19 of this chapter, and Verses 1-2 of Chapter 26. (11) Above, 25:1. (12) *Ibid.*, 22:4.

that the Moabites originally took counsel. And they gave this advice [later on] to Moab, to encourage their daughters to prostitute themselves with them [the Israelites], and thereby cause them to join Baal-peor, and to draw them away from G-d, even though this advice is not [explicitly] mentioned there. Moreover, [a proof that the Midianites gave this idea to the Moabites is] that they even sent them their own king's daughter to commit harlotry with them, this being the meaning of the expression, *and in the matter of Cozbi, the daughter of the prince of Midian, their sister.*[13] For were this not done with the knowledge [and encouragement] of the counsellors of the [Midianite] kingdom, what was the distinguished Midianite princess seeking in Shittim, in the plains of Moab, that she should come to the camp of a foreign people, for Israel was in the plains of Moab, in Shittim, and how did this [important] Midianite woman come to be there? But [the only reasonable explanation of this is that] she was very beautiful, and therefore the elders of Midian sent her there, because they said: "Through the figure of a beautiful woman many people become corrupted."[14] It is probable that Balaam was also involved in [giving] this counsel, for on his return from the land of Moab [after he departed from Balak][15] he passed through Midian, from where he had come, and he deliberated with the counsellors of the kingdom. Perhaps Balaam stayed there a while in order to know what would [ultimately] happen to them [i.e., the Israelites], and that is why the Israelites found him in Midian and killed him.[16] In that case the meaning [of the verse], *And Balaam rose up, and went and returned to his place*[15] is that Balaam "went on his way [with the intention] of returning to his land" [but he did not actually get there, since he stayed on the way in Midian]. And it indeed appears so [that Balaam participated in giving this evil advice], for the Israelites would not have killed one who had prophesied except after [receiving a special] permission of the Torah [to do so, and we do not find any mention of such permission]. But after they had been told [that they were to

(13) Verse 18 here. (14) This saying is quoted in Tractate Yebamoth 63b, from the book Ben Sira. (15) Above, 24:25. (16) Further, 31:8.

punish the Midianites because] *they harass you by their wiles wherewith they have beguiled you* etc.,[17] [it is self-understood] that all those who took part in this beguilment were liable to the death penalty, and therefore they killed Balaam as well, since they knew that he was the one who had proposed this evil design.

Now the Holy One, blessed be He, commanded [the Israelites] to avenge themselves of them [the Midianites], but as for the Moabites, He had already warned them, *Be not at enmity with Moab.*[18] For Israel had at first come to the border of Edom, and He had warned them [against fighting] them, [as it is said], *and take ye good heed unto yourselves;*[19] and afterwards they arrived at the border of Moab, and He told Moses, *Be not at enmity with Moab.*[18] He said furthermore, *Thou art this day to pass over the border of Moab, even Ar; and when thou comest nigh over against the children of Ammon, harass them not,*[20] and He [further] stated, *Rise ye up, take your journey, and pass over the valley of Arnon; behold, I have given into thy hand Sihon.*[21] And after all this Balak *saw all that Israel had done to the Amorites,*[22] that is, to the two Amorite kings, Sihon and Og, and then this whole episode [of the blessings of Balaam, and the seduction at Shittim by the Moabite women] took place. If so, [we must perforce say] that the warning *Be not at enmity with Moab*[18] was declared before the command *Harass the Midianites.*[9] And therefore I am astonished at the expression of the Agadah [homiletic exposition], where the Rabbis say in Tractate Baba Kamma:[23] "*Be not at enmity with Moab, [neither contend with them in battle].*[18] But would it have entered Moses' mind to wage war [against Moab] without the permission [of G-d, so that he had to be especially told to refrain from doing so]! But Moses of his own accord reasoned by [the syllogism of] a *kal vachomer,*[24] saying: 'If, in the case of the Midianites, who only came to assist the Moabites, the Torah said, *Harass the Midianites, and smite them,*[9] surely [this duty applies] even more so to the

(17) Verse 18 here. (18) Deuteronomy 2:9. (19) *Ibid.*, Verse 4. (20) *Ibid.*, Verses 18-19. (21) *Ibid.*, Verse 24. (22) Above, 22:2. (23) Baba Kamma 38 a-b. (24) "Minor and major." See Vol. II, p. 133, Note 208 for a full explanation of this term.

Moabites!' But the Holy One, blessed be He, said to Moses: 'It is not so as it has entered your mind! I have two [good] doves who are to come forth from them—Ruth the Moabitess, and Naamah the Ammonitess.' "[25] But He had already warned Moses [against waging war on Moab] long before the *kal vachomer* [could have occurred to Moses, since He had, as explained above, given the command not to harass Moab *before* the incident with the women, and thus before the command to punish Midian for their share in that incident]! Moreover, if [it was only to negate] Moses' *kal vachomer* [that he had to be warned against fighting Moab], why did He have to warn him [also] not to fight the children of Ammon[20] [since they played no part at all in the incident at Shittim]! Perhaps the Rabbis were not so particular in their language in the Agadah [about the actual chronological order of events]; since their main [intention] was to say that it was known [beforehand] to Him, blessed be He, that when He would command Moses, *Harass the Midianites,*[9] Moses would have [an opportunity to argue by the syllogism of] a *kal vachomer*[24] that he ought to wage war against Moab, without any other [special] permission, therefore He warned him in advance not to do so. And because He warned him about Moab, therefore He also admonished him with respect to the children of Ammon, so that Moses should not think that [the fact that] He only forbade him [not to fight] Moab was [tantamount to an implied] permission to [wage war] against the children of Ammon who had also dealt evil to the Israelites *because they met* them *not with bread and with water.*[26] According to another Midrash[27] [the reason why Israel was commanded to punish Midian but not to attack Moab], was because the Moabites acted out of fear that they [the Israelites] would plunder them, but the Midianites

(25) See Ruth 1:4; Kings 14:21. Naamah was the mother of Rehoboam, who was one of the righteous kings of the kingdom of Judah. (26) Deuteronomy 23:5. Ramban there explains that it was only the Ammonites mentioned in Verse 4 *ibid.,* who were guilty of this, whereas the Moabites [also mentioned there] did meet the Israelites with bread and water. They are excluded, however, from the assembly of the Eternal because they hired Balaam to curse the Israelites. (27) Also quoted by the Rabbis in Baba Kamma 38b.

meddled with a *strife not* their *own,*[28] as Rashi wrote in the section of *Eileh Mas'ei.*[29]

According to the plain meaning of Scripture, a further reason [for the different treatment that G-d commanded with respect to the Midianites and with respect to the Moabites] is that the lands of Ammon and Moab G-d *had given unto the children of Lot for a possession,*[30] because of Lot their father who ministered to the righteous one [Abraham] and went into exile with him to that Land; therefore He did not allow [anyone] to do them evil in their countries. However, because of their sin in showing hostility to Israel and not treating them in a friendly manner, He punished them by excluding them from [the possibility of joining] His people, by commanding, *An Ammonite or a Moabite shall not enter into the assembly of the Eternal,*[31] measure for measure.

26 5. [REUBEN, THE FIRSTBORN OF ISRAEL: THE SONS OF REUBEN]: HANOCH, THE FAMILY OF THE HANOCHITES. Perhaps [the reason why the individual families of each tribe are mentioned here is that] when the Land was divided among the tribes [in equal parts] according to the opinion of our Rabbis,[32] so that Simeon, the smallest of the tribes,[33] took [a share] equal to that of Judah, the most populous of the tribes,[34] it was also divided up [amongst each tribe itself] according to the number of families that went down to Egypt. Thus they made out of Reuben's inheritance four [equal] parts [because it consisted of four main families: Hanoch, Pallu, Hezron, and Carmi], and the Hanochites received a share equal to that allotted to the Palluites, the Hezronites, and the Carmites, even though these [four families] were not all equal in *the number of names . . . by their polls*[35] This is the reason here for counting [the

(28) See Proverbs 26:17. (29) In our text of Rashi this explanation is found in the section of *Matoth* — further, 31:2. (30) Deuteronomy 2:19. (31) *Ibid.*, 23:4. (32) Baba Bathra 122a. See Vol. I, pp. 570-572. (33) The tribe of Simeon numbered 22,200 men (further, Verse 14). (34) The tribe of Judah numbered 76,500 (Verse 22). (35) Above, 1:18.

people] in this manner, [namely] by counting the family according to those who went down to Egypt, and it does not mention [here] *by their polls,* even though it mentions the numbers [of each tribe] as a whole. And when Scripture states [here]: *To the more thou shalt give the more inheritance,* [*and to the fewer thou shalt give the less inheritance,*[36] which seems to indicate that the Land *was* divided according to population,[37] it refers to the [division amongst the] members of each [small] family,[38] for each [of these minor families] received a share according to their numbers *by their polls.*[35] It is for this reason that in the Book of Joshua [when speaking of] the division of the Land, it says *according to their families,* as is stated in the verse, *And the lot for the tribe of the children of Judah 'according to their families,'*[39] and similarly in the case of all the other [tribes]. Or the meaning of [the phrase there] *according to their families* may be: "to 'all' the families of the tribe" [meaning that each minor family of each tribe was taken into account, according to the numbers of its individual members, as explained above]; or that they divided the Land *according to their families,* so that each family received its share in one place, so that it did not become mixed up with [that of] another family. This [latter interpretation] appears to me to be the correct one.

9. AND THE SONS OF ELIAB: NEMUEL, AND DATHAN, AND ABIRAM. THESE ARE DATHAN AND ABIRAM WHO [QUARRELLED AGAINST MOSES] etc. Scripture mentions this

(36) Further, Verse 54. (37) As is indeed Rashi's opinion. See further, Verse 54, for a complete discussion. Ramban also touches briefly on this subject in Genesis 48:6 (Vol. I, pp. 571-572). (38) Thus when, for example, the family-group of Hanochites received their quarter-share of Reuben's overall inheritance, they further subdivided it amongst their members according to the number of individuals in each family. However, they themselves received a share — [one quarter] — of the total inheritance of Reuben, equal to that received by the three other *main* families of Reuben, despite differences in their respective populations. Likewise each of the twelve tribes, whether large in population, like Judah, or small like Simeon, received an equal share of the whole Land [that is, equal in value, although not in area] (Baba Bathra 122a).

[episode leading to the death of Dathan and Abiram] in order to indicate that the whole inheritance of the Palluite family remained for *Nemuel* alone, because *Dathan and Abiram* [the other sons of Eliab] and all their belongings were swallowed up [in the earth, and hence Nemuel was the only surviving son of Eliab, who was in turn the only son of Pallu]. Or it may be, as our Rabbis have said,[40] that [Dathan and Abiram's death is mentioned here] to allude [to the fact] that they lost their share in the Land even though they were amongst those who came out of Egypt, and were therefore eligible to [receive] an inheritance.

13. 'L'ZERACH' (OF ZERAH). "He is [identical with] *'Tzochar'* [Zohar — mentioned in Genesis 46: 10 as one of the sons of Simeon who went down to Egypt], and it [the name *Zerach* (Zerah)] is an expression meaning *tzohar* ['shining,' which is also the meaning of *Zerach*]. But the family of Ohad [the other son of Simeon mentioned *ibid.*, in Genesis] became extinct. Similarly five families of the tribe of Benjamin [had by now ceased to exist], for he [Benjamin] went down to Egypt with ten sons,[41] and here[42] Scripture only counts five." This is Rashi's language.

And Rashi has furthermore written: [43] "All the families were called by the names of those [of their ancestors] who went down to Egypt, but those who were born after that time were not called families [in their own right and their own names], except for the families of Ephraim and Menasheh, both of whom were born in Egypt, and Ard and Naaman, the sons of Bela the son of Benjamin.[44] And I have found [it

(39) Joshua 15: 1. (40) Baba Bathra 118 b. (41) Genesis 46:21. (42) Further, Verses 38-39. (43) In Verse 24. (44) Further, Verse 40. The meaning of Rashi is as follows: Since Ard and Naaman are mentioned in Genesis 46:21 among the sons of *Benjamin* who went down to Egypt, and here in Verse 40 they are referred to as sons of *Bela,* who was himself a son of Benjamin, we must perforce say that the ones referred to here were not the same as those mentioned there [but had the same names]. Furthermore we must perforce say that the Ard and Naaman mentioned here were not amongst those who went down to Egypt, for otherwise Scripture would have mentioned them there in Genesis, in the same way that it counts the grandchildren of

written] in the work of Rabbi Moshe the Preacher[45] that their mother [that of Ard and Naaman — i.e., the wife of Bela] went down to Egypt when she was already pregnant with them [and therefore they formed separate families, since they are also included amongst 'those who went down' to Egypt]. Now if this is a tradition, well and good. But if not, I say that Bela had many children, but from each of these two, Ard and Naaman, there came forth a large family, [and therefore they formed families in their own right and in their own names], whereas the descendants of the other sons were called by Bela's name, and [only] the descendants of these two [Ard and Naaman] were called after their [own] names." All this is the language of the Rabbi [Rashi], of blessed memory.

But I am astonished at [the words of] Rashi. For the difficulty [raised by Rabbi Moshe the Preacher] is not that Scripture counts the family of the Belaites by itself,[46] and [nonetheless counts also] the families of the Ardites and the Naamites his sons, by themselves,[47] for that was [indeed] because they became [large] families, as the Rabbi [Rashi] has said. This is the way of Scripture, as in the case of the children of Judah [where it counts Hezron and Hamul, who were *grandchildren* of Judah, as forming families by themselves],[48] and [likewise] the children of Menasheh and Ephraim,[49] and likewise the children of Asher.[50] However, if we say that Ard and Naaman were born to Bela, the son of Benjamin, *after* they went down to Egypt, they

Judah and Asher. This is the meaning of Rashi when he wrote: "except for the families of Ephraim and Menasheh, both of whom were born in Egypt, and Ard and Naaman, the sons of Bela the son of Benjamin." However, the question then arises: why are Ard and Naaman, the sons of Bela, counted here, since they were not amongst those who went down to Egypt? In other words, why were they an exception to the rule? To answer this question Rashi quotes the statement which he found in the work of Rabbi Moshe the Preacher. (45) See above in *Seder Naso,* Note 146. (46) Further, Verse 38. (47) *Ibid.,* Verse 40. (48) Verse 21. Hezron and Hamul were the sons of Perez, who was the son of Judah. Although Perez himself formed a family (Verse 20), the verse nonetheless counts independently the two families formed by his sons Hezron and Hamul. (49) Verses 29-32; 36. There too, the grandchildren [and even great-grandchildren] are counted as separate families. (50) Verses 44-45. Asher's grandchildren are counted as separate families.

should not have been counted here as [separate] families![51] And should we say that [Ard and Naaman, the sons of Bela] were born to him *before* [he went down to Egypt], then [the family of Jacob] would consist of more than seventy souls, for then the sons of Benjamin were ten[41] apart from these two sons of Bela [thus the overall total of people who went down to Egypt would be seventy-two, whereas Scripture there only mentions a total of seventy]![52] It was for this reason [and not for the reason implied by Rashi's explanation] that Rabbi Moshe the Preacher explained that their mother [the wife of Bela] was already pregnant with them [Ard and Naaman, when the family of Jacob went down to Egypt], and [since they were not yet born] they are not

(51) Ramban's meaning is as follows. Rashi seems to have understood that Rabbi Moshe the Preacher found it difficult to understand why *Ard and Naaman* are mentioned as forming separate families, since their father Bela is also mentioned as forming a separate family. To answer this, Rabbi Moshe gave the explanation that their mother was already pregnant with them when she went down to Egypt; and Rashi himself [because he questioned the authenticity of that tradition] gave a different reason, i.e., that they formed large families in their own right. Ramban is saying that Rabbi Moshe's difficulty was *not* why Scripture mentions them as forming separate families, because the answer to that question is clearly that they had large families, which were worthy of constituting separate families and hence were not included in Bela's family. That this is so we see clearly from the examples of Judah, Menasheh, Ephraim and Asher, as Ramban points out. Yet Rabbi Moshe did not ask about the children of these people, but only about *Ard and Naaman,* the children of Bela! Clearly this is because Scripture only counts as separate families the children of those who went down to Egypt, [e.g. Judah and Asher] or who were already there when Jacob went down [e.g. Menasheh and Ephraim]. But in the case of Ard and Naamán, there is a difficulty, whether we say that they went down to Egypt with Jacob or not, [as explained further on in Ramban], and it is *this* difficulty which Rabbi Moshe the Preacher was trying to answer. The question whether they went down to Egypt with Jacob depends, of course, on when they were born. For if we say that they were born to Bela *after* he went down to Egypt, the question arises: Why are they counted *here* as separate families, since only those who were among the *seventy souls* who went down to Egypt with Jacob are counted here as separate families? And if they were born *before* Jacob's family went down to Egypt, then since they are not mentioned in Genesis, the total number of people who went down must have been seventy-two, so why does Scripture omit them and count only seventy? In brief it was *this* difficulty that Rabbi Moshe the Preacher had in understanding the verses, a difficulty which applies only to *Ard and Naaman,* and not as Rashi assumed his question to be, which would apply to other cases as well. (52) Genesis 46:27.

counted there [in the Book of Genesis], but here they are included[47] among those born [*before* the descent into Egypt, because their mother was already pregnant with them when they went into Egypt].

Now if this is a tradition [of the Rabbis, that Bela's wife was pregnant with Ard and Naaman when she went down into Egypt], we will force ourselves to accept it despite its difficulty.[53] We will also have to say that Jochebed[54] was born [whilst they passed] through the walls [of the border-city of Egypt], on the very day that they entered into [Egypt], and therefore she *is* included amongst the *seventy souls* [*that came into Egypt*], whereas these [Ard and Naaman, the sons of Bela] were born some months [after Jacob's family had come to Egypt, and therefore they are not included amongst the *seventy souls that came into Egypt with Jacob*]! But if it is not a tradition of our Rabbis [but merely a personal opinion of Rabbi Moshe the Preacher] we will reject this theory of his with all our might. But we can say that Ard and Naaman, the sons of Benjamin [as mentioned in Genesis 46: 21], died without children, and Bela [their brother] wanted *to raise up unto his brother a name in Israel,*[55] and therefore he gave his sons the names of his brothers who had died. Perhaps Bela [actually] performed the rite of marriage with their wives, since he was the firstborn,[56] and Ard and Naaman, the sons of Bela [from these marriages] became heads of families *to raise up a name*[55] for Ard and Naaman the sons of Benjamin, who were amongst those that went down to Egypt.[41]

(53) The difficulty is that in Genesis 46:8-27 the verses do *not* mention Ard and Naaman amongst the *seventy souls that came into Egypt,* because although their mother came into Egypt when she was pregnant with them, they were not yet born and thus one cannot say that *they* "came into Egypt." Yet here they *are* counted as forming separate families, although only the families of those *that came into Egypt* are counted as separate families, and the reason is because they "came into Egypt" since their mother was pregnant with them! Thus there is an apparent contradition! Furthermore, we will have to differentiate between the case of Jochebed and that of Ard and Naaman, as will be explained further on. (54) See Genesis 46:15 (Vol. I, pp. 554-558.) (55) Deuteronomy 25:7. (56) Genesis 46:21: *And the sons of Benjamin: Bela* etc. — The duty of marrying a childless brother's wife falls primarily on the eldest of the remaining brothers; if he refuses the duty devolves upon any other surviving brother (Yebamoth 39a).

The correct interpretation appears to me to be that the Naaman and Ard[57] who are counted amongst *the sons of Benjamin* in the section of *And these are the names* etc.,[58] were in fact [not the real *sons of Benjamin* at all, but they were] *the sons of* his firstborn son *Bela,* as is stated explicitly here,[47] and similarly Scripture counts them [as the sons of Bela] in the Book of Chronicles.[59] Such is the custom of Scripture to speak of grandchildren as children [and therefore in Genesis 46:21 the verse describes them as *the 'sons' of Benjamin*], just as it says, *Laban the son of Nahor,*[60] and in the Book of Chronicles it is written, *The sons of Shem: Elam, and Asshur, and Arpachshad, and Lud, and Aram, and Uz, and Hul, and Gether and Meshech,*[61] although the last four were in fact his grandchildren![62] And even though Scripture did not treat the sons of Perez [as the "sons" of Judah, their grandfather,[63] as it did in the case of Ard and Naaman], likewise [it did not treat] the sons of Beriah [as the "sons" of Asher, their grandfather,[64] as it did in the case of Ard and Naaman],— this may be because they [Ard and Naaman, the sons of Bela], *were born upon* Benjamin's *knees*[65] [i.e., he brought them up], and therefore

(57) In Genesis 46:21 they are listed in the following order: *And the sons of Benjamin: Bela . . . and Naaman . . . and Ard.* Ramban now suggests that these two people who are mentioned there in Genesis as the "sons" of *Benjamin,* are in fact identical with the *Ard and Naaman* mentioned here in Verse 40, who are described as the sons of *Bela,* who was the son of Benjamin. Naaman and Ard were thus in fact the *grandchildren* of Benjamin, and it is the style of Scripture to describe grandchildren as children, as Ramban shows. This explains why Ard and Naaman are counted here as separate families in their own right, since they *were* amongst those who went down to Egypt [as stated explicitly in Genesis 46:21], and there is thus also no problem about how we reach the number of *seventy souls* who went down there. In other words, the Ard and Naaman mentioned there in Genesis [as the sons of Benjamin] and here in Verse 40 [as Benjamin's grandsons] are identical persons. (58) Genesis 46:8-27. (59) I Chronicles 8:3-4: *And Bela had sons, Addar . . . and Naaman. Addar* mentioned is synonymous with *Ard.* (60) Genesis 29:5. Nahor was actually his grandfather, for Bethuel was his father. See Ramban *ibid.,* Vol. I, p. 360. (61) I Chronicles 1:17. (62) Their father was Aram, the son of Shem — see Genesis 10:22-23. (63) The verse there (46:12) mentions that Perez was the son of Judah; and Hezron and Hamul, the sons of Perez. (64) The verse there (46:17) mentions that Beriah was the son of Asher, and Heber and Malchiel the sons of Beriah. (65) See Genesis 50:23.

they are considered his sons. This is then similar to [the verse], *And these are the generations of Aaron and Moses,*[66] [where the verse proceeds to mention only the sons of Aaron! The explanation given is that they were in actual fact only the sons of Aaron, but since Moses brought them up and taught them Torah, they are also called his children]. Or it may be that because Benjamin had many sons — for he had eight — therefore Scripture included the few [i.e., his two grandsons, Ard and Naaman] amongst the many [real sons, and therefore spoke of all ten as Benjamin's sons].

And it is possible also that we suggest as a hypothesis that Scripture here does not count only the families of those who went down to Egypt, [as Rashi explained above], because [we see] that even those who were born in Egypt from that time onwards are also counted as families, such as Scripture does here in the case of [the families of] Ephraim and Menasheh [whose families are counted separately, even though they did not go down to Egypt with Jacob].[67] It is not a [satisfactory] reason for Scripture to do so [as exceptions in their cases only], on the grounds that they were [already] in Egypt [and therefore are included as separate families together with all those who came down afterwards with Jacob], because it is at the time of the [actual] descent [into Egypt] that one ought to count them all in one number, and to make families out of the *seventy souls* [who actually went down with Jacob, and it is not correct to include Ephraim and Menasheh who were there but did not go down with the others]![68] Similarly Scripture always

(66) Above, 3:1. The explanation of this verse quoted now by Ramban is found in Rashi *ibid.* (67) Verses 29 and 35 here. Ephraim and Menasheh of course were not amongst those who went down to Egypt with Jacob, but were born to Joseph beforehand (see Genesis 48:5). (68) Ramban's meaning is that since Scripture's main purpose is to list the seventy people who "went down" to Egypt with Jacob, it ought to include only those who actually went down at that time. But in actual fact only sixty-eight went down, since Ephraim and Menasheh were already there! And one cannot suggest that an exception is made in their case, since Scripture always stresses the factor of actual descent, referring to the seventy souls *who went down* to Egypt. Hence we must say that in fact Scripture includes in its list not only those who actually went down to Egypt with Jacob, but also those who did not go down then, and even

counts them [Ephraim and Menasheh] together with those who went down to Egypt, [such as in the verse]: *Thy fathers went down into Egypt with threescore and ten persons*[69] So also the sons of Bela [Ard and Naaman] were born afterwards [i.e., after the descent into Egypt, and they are nonetheless counted here as separate families! This proves that the determining factor whether to count a family here separately, is not the criterion of whether its founder was amongst those who went down to Egypt with Jacob, as Rashi said, but must have been some other reason, as will now be explained].

But [we must say that] this matter was [as follows]. It was the custom in Israel [for people] to appoint over themselves "heads of fathers' houses," and all the descendants of that man would always trace their lineage back to him, and be called by his name in his honor; just as all the Arabs do to this very day, and as do all the Jews who live in their [the Arabs'] countries, calling themselves by family [names, such as] "Ibn Ezra," or "Ibn Shushan." This is the meaning of the verse which says, *These are the heads of their fathers' houses,*[70] for from the time that they *were fruitful and multiplied*[71] in Egypt, they established heads of families over themselves, to whom they would trace their lineage. Perhaps they initiated this practice in Egypt in order not *to mingle themselves with the nations*[72] and so that they would be recognized and distinguishable among their tribes, [for it is there in Egypt] *whither the tribes went up, even the tribes of the Eternal, as a testimony unto Israel,*[73] *and it* became *a custom in Israel.*[74] Thus [all] those mentioned here [in this section] were, every one of them, heads of their fathers' house in Egypt, from whom the family traced its descent. That is why Scripture counts in the house of Machir [the son of Menasheh]: *the family of the Machirites* and *the family of the Gileadites* his son,[75] and *the family of the Iezerites* and that *of the*

some who were born later, as explained further on. In that case we can understand that Ard and Naaman are included in the list, even though they were born later. (69) Deuteronomy 10:22. This includes Joseph and his two sons, Menasheh and Ephraim (see Genesis 46:19-20), although they did not go down to Egypt with Jacob. (70) Exodus 6:14. (71) *Ibid.,* 1:7. (72) Psalms 106:35. (73) *Ibid.,* 122:4. (74) Judges 11:39. (75) Further, Verse 29.

Helekites,[76] the sons of Gilead and their [other] brothers.[77] In a similar way [Scripture records] the children of Judah [and also counts Hezron and Hamul, who were the sons of Perez and grandsons of Judah, as separate families][78] and those of Ephraim,[79] for these children mentioned were great and distinguished people, and became heads [of their families]. But [the reason for them being counted as separate families] is not because they [each] gave birth to a large family, as the Rabbi [Rashi] wrote, because they *all* begot large families [even those who are not mentioned individually], since *they were fruitful, and increased abundantly, and multiplied, and waxed exceedingly mighty.*[71] But [Scripture named separate families here] as a mark of honor, meaning that [the members of that particular family] had appointed [that person] as their head. Now most of the families when they were in Egypt traced their descent from those who went down to Egypt [with Jacob], because they considered them distinguished ancestors, and the others appointed for themselves heads of houses from those who were born there shortly after [Jacob's descent to Egypt]. Therefore most of the [people] mentioned here [in this census as forming families] were [amongst] those who went down to Egypt [with Jacob], and therefore these families trace themselves back to those who came down [originally] to Egypt, because it was there that they established them [these people, as the heads of their family-groups].

42. THESE ARE THE SONS OF DAN AFTER THEIR FAMILIES: [OF SHUHAM, THE FAMILY OF THE SHUHAMITES. THESE ARE THE FAMILIES OF DAN AFTER THEIR FAMILIES]. The meaning of this[80] is that Shuham had

(76) *Ibid.,* Verse 30. (77) I.e., Asriel, Shechem, Shemida, Hepher (Verses 31-32) — brothers of Iezer and Helek, and sons of Gilead. (78) Further, Verse 21. (79) Verse 36. There Eran, who was the son of Shuthelach and the grandson of Ephraim, is counted as forming a separate family, although his father Shuthelach is also mentioned there as founding a separate family. (80) The difficulty here is that Scripture speaks of an individual [Shuham — the only son of Dan] in the plural, saying: *these are 'the families' of Dan.*

children who formed families which were called by the name of the [respective] fathers of the family, but they all traced back their lineage to Shuham the head [of them all], and [therefore] they were called by his name, so that one would say [for example]: "Of Daniel, the family of Daniel the Shuhamite; of Ezekiel, the family of Ezekiel the Shuhamite." Thus [the sons of Shuham] consisted of many families, but [all identified themselves] as the one Shuhamite family, and therefore they are all ascribed to him. And according to those who say[81] that the people traced their lineage [only] to those who went down to Egypt [with Jacob, we must say that] there were many families [descended from Dan] who were called by the name of their ancestor, and who were born in Egypt, and here Scripture described them [i.e., all the families of Dan's descendants] as Shuhamites, because he [Shuham] alone [as the only son of Dan] went down to Egypt.[82]

46. AND THE NAME OF THE DAUGHTER OF ASHER WAS SERACH. "Because she was still alive [at the end of Israel's period of bondage in Egypt, and after forty years in the desert, and was one of the seventy people mentioned in Genesis 46 who went down to Egypt with Jacob], Scripture mentions her here." This is Rashi's language. And Onkelos translated [the verse as follows]: "and the name of the daughter of Asher's *wife,* was Serach." By this he intended to say that she was a *daughter that possesseth an inheritance*[83] [in the Land in her own right], and therefore Scripture mentions her here just as it mentions the daughters of Zelophehad,[84] for she [Serach] is included amongst [those referred to in the verse], *Unto these the Land shall be divided.*[85] Now had she been the daughter of Asher himself, she would not have inherited [a portion in the Land], since he had male children [as stated in Verse 44]. But she [Serach] was the daughter of his [Asher's] wife from another man [namely Asher's wife's first husband], who did not have a son; therefore his inheritance [in the Land] passed to his daughter. In that case, the reason [why Scripture uses the

(81) I.e., Rashi — see Ramban above, Verse 13, at length. (82) Genesis 46:8; 23. (83) Further, 36:8. (84) Further, 27:7. (85) Verse 53.

phrase] *and Serach their sister*[86] is because she was a [half-]sister to Asher's sons, but was not his daughter. And therefore it says [here], *And the name of the daughter of Asher was Serach,* and it does not say "and Asher's daughter [was Serach]," because [the intention of the verse] is to say that her name was [i.e., she was known as] "Asher's daughter," and she was [actually] called Serach.[87] Now if she were still alive [at the end of the period of Israel's sojourn in the desert], as Rashi explained, then she was like the daughters of Zelophehad as regards [receiving] an inheritance [in the Land in her own right], but if she had died [by then, Scripture mentions her here to indicate that] her family received [a portion in the Land] because of her [since she was amongst those who went down to Egypt].

According to the simple meaning of Scripture, Serach had a large family which was called by her name, and she is included in the phrase, *These are the families of the sons of Asher according to those that were numbered.*[88] Scripture, however, did not want to trace their ancestry to a woman, by saying: "Of Serach, the family of the Serachites," but instead alluded to this matter [briefly].

54. TO THE MORE THOU SHALT GIVE THE MORE INHERITANCE. "To a tribe which was larger in population they gave a larger portion [of the Land than that given to the smaller tribes]. And although the portions were [thus] not equal, since they divided [the Land] according to the size of the tribe, they did so only by means of the lot [as commanded in Verse 55], and the lot [assigned the portions] by means of *Ruach Hakodesh.*"[89] This is Rashi's language.

(86) Genesis 46:17. The verse reads: *And the sons of Asher: Imnah and Ishvah and Ishvi and Beriah and Serach their sister.* Ramban here is pointing out that the verse avoids calling her Asher's daughter, and describes her especially as the sister of his sons, because she was in actual fact not his daughter at all, but only their half-sister. (87) The meaning of the verse is thus: "*And the name of* the person known as *'the daughter of Asher' was Serach.*" (88) Verse 47. (89) "The Holy Spirit." See above in *Seder Chukath,* Note 64.

But the interpretation of our Rabbis about this verse is not so. Instead, they said in the Sifre: [90] "*To the more thou shalt give the more inheritance.* Supposing somebody came out of Egypt with ten sons, and when they entered the Land they were [only] five etc. [we apply to this case the verse, *To the more thou shalt give the more inheritance;* if on the other hand he had five sons when he came out of Egypt, and when they entered the Land they were ten, we apply to them the verse, *and to the fewer thou shalt give the less inheritance*]."[91] And likewise it is explicitly stated in the Gemara[92] that the meaning of [this section] according to the Sages was not to distinguish in any way between [the portion given to] each particular tribe [since they each received an equal portion], just as they have said: [92] "It is well-understood according to the Sage who says [that the Land was divided] according to [the numbers of] those who came out of Egypt, why Scripture states, *To the more thou shalt give the more inheritance* etc."[93] Furthermore, I have already written in *Seder Vayechi Yaakov*[94] that in the Gemara of the Chapter *Yesh Nochalin*[95] the Rabbis expressly came to the conclusion that the Land was *not* divided according to the heads of men, [i.e., according to the overall population], but it was divided among [all] the tribes [equally]. Thus they divided it into twelve equal parts, and each tribe took that part which was assigned to it by the lot.

(90) Sifre *Pinchas* 132. (91) In other words, the division of the Land depended not on the number of people in each family *upon entering the Land,* but upon the number that the family had *when they left Egypt* — hence if they became fewer, we still apply the verse: *To the more . . .* since they were more when they left Egypt, and vice versa. It is thus obvious that the Sifre applied these verses to the division of the Land *among the fathers' houses,* and not, as Rashi explained it, to the division between the twelve tribes as a whole. (92) Baba Bathra 117b. (93) "For if a person came out of Egypt with ten sons, and by the time they entered the Land he only had five sons, we apply to him the verse, *To the more* etc.; whereas if he had originally five sons etc. [as explained by Ramban above in the text]. But according to the Sage who says that the Land was divided according to the number of people at the time that they entered the Land, what is the meaning of the phrases: *to the more* and *to the fewer,* since each family received a share equal to its numbers at that time?" From this text, too, it is obvious that the Sages were not referring to differences between the portions of larger or smaller *tribes,* but instead applied this verse to the subsequent allocation of the land among the various families of each tribe. (94) Genesis 48:6 (Vol. I, pp. 570-572). (95) "There are some [near of kin] who inherit." The text quoted here is in Baba Bathra 122a.

It was for this [reason] that the sons of Joseph complained about it, saying [to Joshua], *'Why hast thou given me but one lot and one part for an inheritance, seeing I am a great people?'*[96] However, Joshua did not give them any additional [land] at all [since each tribe received an equal share], but he told them, '[*If thou be a great people*], *get thee up to the forest, and cut down for thyself there in the land of the Perizzites and of the Rephaim; since the hill-country of Ephraim is too narrow for thee,'*[97] meaning to say that they should conquer for themselves that land [which had been assigned to them and] which they had not yet taken, and thereby they should extend their border.

This is [also the meaning of] that which Scripture says, *according to the names of the tribes of their fathers they shall inherit.* [*According to the lot shall their inheritance be divided*] *between the more and the fewer.*[98] [That is to say], each of the tribes should take equally, whether it has a large population or a small one. And then the meaning of [the verse which says], *To the more thou shalt give the more inheritance, and the fewer thou shalt give the less inheritance,* [is not "to the *tribe* that is more populous you shall give more etc. but] to the members of the tribe itself [for each tribe received an equal portion; and therefore Scripture is saying here that when the tribe divides its portion amongst its individual families, it should give a larger portion to a family with more members etc.]. Or [the meaning of this phrase may be] according to its interpretation [by the Rabbis, as mentioned above],[91] that it [the Land] was divided according to [the numbers of] those who left Egypt. Thus supposing somebody came out of Egypt with ten sons, and when they entered the Land they were [only] five, we apply to this case the verse, *To the more thou shalt give the more inheritance.*" That is to say, if those ten sons who were twenty years old [or more] at the time that they left Egypt died, and they had five sons [born to them] in the desert, or if [five of the children] were minors [at the time of the exodus],[99] and became

(96) Joshua 17:14. (97) *Ibid.,* Verse 15. (98) Further, Verses 55-56. (99) The Divine decree that the generation of the wilderness was not to enter the Land (see above, 14:29-31) did not apply to those who were minors at the time of the exodus. Hence it was possible for those born in the desert, or were minors at the time of the exodus, to actually take possession of the Land.

twenty years of age [in the desert], we apply to such a case the verse, *To the more thou shalt give the more,* meaning: *to* those who were *more* at the time of leaving Egypt, *thou shalt give the more* [land], even though they are now fewer. "And supposing a person came out of Egypt with five sons, and at the time that they entered the Land they were ten, in that case we apply to him [the verse], *and to the fewer thou shalt give the less,*"[100] as is stated in the Sifre [mentioned above].

However, I have seen there [in the Sifre[90] a text explaining our verse] which states [as follows]: "*To each one according to those that were numbered of it* [*shall its inheritance be given*]. This teaches us that the Land was only allocated amongst each tribe according to what it was [in population]. Thus it is said, *And the children of Joseph spoke unto Joshua, saying: 'Why hast thou given me but one lot and one part for an inheritance, seeing I am a great people, forasmuch as the Eternal hath blessed me thus?'*[96] What does it say [further]? *And Joshua said unto them: 'If thou be a great people, get thee up to the forest, and cut down for thyself there in the land of the Perizzites and of the Rephaim; since the hill-country of Ephraim is too narrow for thee.'* "[97] This is the language of this Beraitha.[101] And it appears from it that the Land was indeed divided [amongst the twelve tribes themselves] according to the number of heads [i.e., according to their population], as the Rabbi [Rashi] has said! But according to the Gemara this [Beraitha] is rejected [as the final interpretation]. Furthermore, if it is so [as the Beraitha implies, that the Land was divided amongst the tribes themselves according to their relative populations], what did the children of Joseph complain about? Surely he [Joshua] gave them [a greater share] in proportion to their larger numbers, as [he gave] the other tribes [according to their relative sizes]!

In my opinion this Beraitha is a shortened text, and it is [in fact based] upon that which the Rabbis said in the Gemara[102] that

(100) Meaning: "*and to those who were fewer* at the time of the exodus from Egypt, *thou shalt give less* land, even though they are now, at the time of entering the Land, greater in population." (101) See Vol. II, p. 133, Note 209. (102) Baba Bathra 118a.

the children of Joseph complained because of their many [young] children. The explanation of the matter is [thus as follows]: The children of Joseph took [the amount of land which they deserved] as two tribes, the children of Ephraim one share, and the children of Menasheh another share, for so it is written,[103] and neither of their [two] tribes was larger in population than any of the other tribes. Indeed, some of the other tribes were more numerous than they were, for the tribes of Judah, Issachar, Zebulun, and Dan were [all] more populous than they were,[104] so why [therefore] should they have complained whilst the more numerous ones remained quiet? This [question] applies with even greater force if the Land was divided according to [the number of] those who came out of Egypt, according to the interpretation [of the Sifre quoted above], because the sons of Judah at the [time of the] first census were more numerous than these two tribes [Ephraim and Menasheh] put together![105] Therefore [we must rather say that] they complained because of their children, for the sons of Menasheh in the [first] census [taken at the time] of the exodus from Egypt totalled thirty-two thousand [and two hundred],[106] whereas they had increased by the [time of the] second census [taken] in the desert to fifty-two thousand [and seven hundred]![107] None of the [other] tribes increased to such an extent. And they [the tribe of Menasheh] continued to increase in population until the [time of the] division of the Land [in the days of Joshua],[108] and this also happened

(103) Genesis 48:5: *As Reuben and Simeon, shall Ephraim and Menasheh be mine.* (104) Judah numbered 76,500 (Verse 22); Issacher 64,300 (Verse 25); Zebulun 60,500 (Verse 27); Dan 64,400 (Verse 43). Thus they were each larger than the tribe of Ephraim, who were only 32,500 (Verse 37), or that of Menasheh, who were 52,700. It is therefore evident that the tribe of Ephraim did not complain merely because they were a large tribe. (105) At the time of the first census, Judah numbered 74,600 (above, 1:27), whereas Ephraim and Menasheh together were only 72,700 (*ibid.,* Verses 33 and 35). Thus the tribe of Judah had far greater cause to complain than Ephraim or Menasheh. (106) Above, 1:35. (107) Verse 34 here. Thus they increased by 20,500. (108) From the time of this second census [taken in the fortieth year of Israel's stay in the desert] until the actual *beginning* of the division of the Land by Joshua, there was a period of something over seven years, since tradition assigns a period of seven years for the conquest of the Land, and seven years for its division. In the meantime, naturally, the sons of Menasheh continued to increase.

in the case of the children of Ephraim.[109] Now since these children received no share [in the Land], therefore [the children of Joseph] complained, but *there* was *no man to hear* them,[110] for such was the law—that only those who were above twenty years of age received a share in the Land.[111] Therefore the Beraitha [quoted above] is saying: "*According to those that were numbered* — who were twenty years old and over. This teaches us that the Land was only allocated amongst each tribe according to what it was [in population] at the time of the census, meaning that they were not to give anything to the children, even if they had grown up and reached the age of twenty at the time that they divided [the Land].

Now the verse stating [that the children of Joseph complained to Joshua, saying]: *Why hast thou given me but one lot and one part for an inheritance, seeing I am a great people,*[96] cannot, as all must agree, be understood as would appear from its literal meaning. For if he [Joshua] divided the Land amongst them [the twelve tribes] according to the number of people [in each tribe], as Rashi explained, then they [the children of Joseph] must have taken their fair share, for according to their greater population, [in the same proportion] they took a larger portion [in the Land]. And if [the Land was divided] according to the [number of] tribes [so that each tribe received an equal part], it is impossible that Joshua should not have given them their share of the birthright, for he would not have transgressed the testament of

(109) This text is difficult to understand, because in fact the children of Ephraim *decreased* in numbers between the first census at the time of the exodus from Egypt and the second census here! [In the first census they totalled 40,500 (Above, 1:33), and in the second census 32,500 (Verse 37 here)]. A suggestion has been made [by Kur Zahav] that Ramban's meaning is as follows: Since Scripture says that it were *the children of 'Joseph'* who complained [a term which of course comprises the tribes of both Ephraim and Menasheh], it shows that the children of Ephraim also had increased between the time of the second census and the division of the Land, although they had decreased between the time of the first census at the exodus and the second census now. This interpretation is supported by a close reading of the text of Ramban here, who wrote: "[the tribe of Menasheh] continued to increase in population until the [time of the] division of the Land," and *then* added: "and this also happened in the case of the children of Ephraim." See also my Hebrew commentary, p. 312. (110) See II Samuel 15:3. (111) See above, Verses 2 and 53.

Jacob![112] And the Holy One, blessed be He, also commanded likewise in the Torah, [mentioning] the tribes of Ephraim and Menasheh [separately, amongst those who were to take possession of the Land].[113] Moreover, it is expressly written that he [Joshua] gave them [the children of Joseph] two lots, as it is said, *And the border of the children of Ephraim according to their families was thus;*[114] *This is the inheritance of the tribe of the children of Ephraim.*[114] And [with reference to] the children of Menasheh [it is said], *And this was the lot for the tribe of Menasheh;*[115] *And the border of Menasheh was* etc.,[116] just as it is said in the case of [all] the other tribes. But in saying: [*Why hast thou given me but*] *one lot and one part*[96] they meant to say: "All that you [Joshua] have given the two of us together, each one [of us] deserves to get as his [own] lot." They used this expression because Joshua at first cast [only] one lot for both of them, as it is said, *And the lot for 'the children of Joseph' went out from the Jordan at Jericho* etc.[117] until: *the goings out thereof were at the sea.*[118] And there it is stated, *And the children of Joseph, Menasheh and Ephraim, took their inheritance,*[119] meaning to say that they both *took their inheritance* by means of this [one] lot, and afterwards he divided this portion amongst the two of them by [a further] lot, as it is said there, *And the border of the children of Ephraim according to their families was thus,*[120] and it is [further] written, *And this was the lot for the tribe of Menasheh.*[115] Therefore they [the children of Joseph] said to Joshua: "Behold, this single first lot [which you drew for the two of us before you further subdivided it], each one of us deserves to get, since we are *a great people,*[96] and why [therefore] did you subdivide it afterwards into two

(112) Genesis 48:5. In other words, it is inconceivable that Joshua should violate Jacob's command that Joseph's two sons, Ephraim and Menasheh, should be treated as separate tribes and each receive the same share in the Land that all the other tribes received, instead of treating them as merely one tribe [of Joseph], so that they would together receive only one share. Since this is inconceivable, why then did the children of Joseph complain, for they must have received the extra portion due to them as the birthright which had been taken away from Reuben! (113) Further, 34:23-24. (114) Joshua 16:5 and 8. (115) *Ibid.*, 17:1. (116) *Ibid.*, Verse 7. (117) *Ibid.*, 16:1. (118) *Ibid.*, Verse 3. (119) *Ibid.*, Verse 4. (120) *Ibid.*, Verse 5.

parts?" And the [reason for this] complaint, according to the explanation of the Gemara,[102] was because of their children who increased greatly amongst them.

And according to the simple meaning of Scripture, it seems to me that this complaint [to Joshua by the children of Joseph] was that of the children of Menasheh [only, and not that of the children of Ephraim], but the two tribes came to him together. Similarly, *Then the children of Judah drew nigh unto Joshua in Gilgal, and Caleb the son of Jephunneh the Kenizite said unto him* etc.,[121] for that case [affected only] one person, and yet the whole tribe came to join him in his complaint. And the [particular] grievance of the children of Menasheh was because none of the other tribes had left many great cities in the hands of the Canaanites, as had Menasheh, who left [unconquered] *the three regions,*[122] [which Yonathan translated] "three districts." A proof for this [explanation of the cause of their grievance] is that it is after it says, *And the children of Menasheh could not drive out the inhabitants of those cities,*[123] that it is written: *And the children of Joseph spoke,*[96] for at first they did not complain, until they had waged war against them and they were not able to prevail over them. It is possible that this is the meaning of [the expression] *one lot and one part.*[96] They said: "Because you cast originally one lot for both of us [Ephraim and Menasheh], our portion [in the Land] came together, and so it happened that both of our portions were [allocated] in this place which is difficult to capture but had you cast two lots for us, as was done for all other [separate] tribes, our portion might have been allocated in a place which is easier to conquer." And Joshua replied [to this claim by saying] that if they go up to the forest *of the Perizzites and the Rephaim,*[97] they will be able to select for themselves from there whatever they want, and thus extend their borders.[97] Then they [the children of Joseph] spoke up and explained their [original] grievance, saying, "*The hill-country will* also *not be enough for us,* for *all the Canaanites* that you have given us *in the land of the valley have chariots of iron.*"[124] Then Joshua told

(121) *Ibid.*, 14:6. (122) *Ibid.*, 17:11. (123) *Ibid.*, Verse 12. (124) *Ibid.*, Verse 16.

them that he would not give them in the mountain *one lot only,*[125] *but the* whole of the *hill-country shall be* theirs together with the large *forest* which is there,[126] and they should choose for themselves as much as they need from those [lands], and they shall have all *the goings out* of the borders of the hill-country. And [he further told them that] they would *drive out the Canaanites* from there *though they have chariots of iron, and though they be strong,*[126] as a result of which none of the other tribes wanted it [that land], but they, the two brothers, who are *a numerous people and have great power*[125] will [be able to] help each other to *drive* them [the Canaanites] *out.* The end of the matter was that Joshua did not listen to them and did not add anything to their portion, for such was the law [that they get in the same proportion as all the other tribes]. We have written at length on this subject, because of the necessity [to clarify this matter fully] and we have furthermore written about it, with proofs, in the section of *Vayechi Yaakov.*[94]

The general principle thus is that the law which [the Rabbis] reached as a conclusion in the Gemara[95] [that the Land was divided amongst the twelve tribes into twelve equal parts] is true, and that is the proper basis on which to explain the verses. Thus the meaning of the section [before us] is as follows: *Unto these*[127] who are mentioned according to their families *the Land shall be divided [for an inheritance] according to the number of names,*[127] giving each male person, according to their number, his share. *To the more* ye *shall give the more inheritance* — thus for example they are to divide the land of Reuben into four parts [because the tribe consisted of four main families],[128] and "we will give to *the family of the Hanochites,* for example, who were the largest [in population], a greater *inheritance,* and to *the family of the Palluites,* [for example], who were the least populous, we will give a smaller share, for *to each one according to those that were numbered of* the [particular] family *shall its inheritance be given,* and the whole family shall receive its share in one place." It was for this reason that He [commanded here] that they

(125) *Ibid.,* Verse 17. (126) *Ibid.,* Verse 18. (127) Verse 53. (128) Hanoch, Pallu, Hezron, and Carmi (above, Verses 5-6).

should be counted according to their families. Therefore the Sages mentioned [with reference to the law of the Seventh year]: [129] "If they divided the land [of a tribe] amongst its [main] families, but did not [yet] subdivide it amongst the houses of the families, and each individual does not yet know what his share is . . . etc."[130]

55. HOWEVER, THE LAND SHALL BE DIVIDED BY LOT amongst the tribes of Israel, and ACCORDING TO THE NAMES OF THE TRIBES OF THEIR FATHERS who constituted twelve tribes THEY SHALL INHERIT them [i.e., the twelve equal portions of the Land]. And then He repeated: 56. ACCORDING TO THE LOT SHALL THE INHERITANCE of the tribe BE DIVIDED BETWEEN THE MORE AND THE FEWER, meaning that they should also cast lots amongst the [individual] families, so that [for instance] the portion of the Hanochites should be in the direction and place which the lot chooses for him, and the portion of the Palluites should be in the place which the lot chooses for him, but we are to allot more[of the land] to the larger [families], and give less to the smaller families. This is the meaning of that which it says in the section[131] of *Eileh Mas'ei: And ye shall inherit the land by lot according to your families—to the more ye shall give the more inheritance, and to the fewer thou shalt give the less inheritance; wheresoever the lot falleth to any man, that shall be his; according to the tribes of your fathers shall ye inherit.*[132] Thus He explained that the inheritance should be allotted to families by the lot, and in whichever direction the lot chooses for him [any individual family], there we shall give a larger [portion] to the larger of the families and a smaller [portion] to the smaller [families]. He [furthermore] said that it [the division of the Land] should be *according to the tribes of your fathers,* meaning to say twelve tribes.[133]

(129) Torath Kohanim, beginning of *Seder Behar.* (130) " . . . I might think that the law of the Seventh year applies. For this reason Scripture states, *thou shalt not sow 'thy' field* (Leviticus 25:4) [using the singular, to indicate that] the law applies only when each person recognizes his own field." (131) Literally: "In the book of " *Eileh Mas'ei.* (132) Further, 33:54. (133) Thus it is clear that the Land was initially divided into twelve equal parts, so that each tribe was allocated an equal share

Now that which Rashi said — "*According to the names of 'matoth' of their fathers,* this means those who came out of Egypt" — is not correct, for the term *matoth* always means "the tribes" of Israel, just as it is written, *So shall no inheritance remove 'mimateh' (from one tribe) 'l'mateih acheir' (to another tribe); for 'matoth' (the tribes of) the children of Israel shall cleave each one to its own inheritance.*[134] Similarly [it is written], *a thousand 'l'mateh' (of every tribe) throughout all 'matoth' (tribes of) Israel,*[135] and so also in the case of the spies,[136] and likewise in all other places — for the terms *sheivet* and *mateh* are identical. And when the Rabbis said in the Gemara:[137] "Rabbi Yashiyah says: The Land was divided amongst those that came out of Egypt, for it is said, *according to the names of 'matoth' of their fathers they shall inherit*"—this interpretation [is not based, as Rashi understood, on the meaning of the word *matoth* itself, but] is deduced because of the [seeming] redundancy of the verse, for it would have been enough for Scripture to say: *However, the Land shall be divided by lot according to the names of the tribes* [and to omit the concluding phrase . . . *of their fathers they shall inherit*]. But since He did mention . . . *of their fathers they shall inherit,* the Rabbis interpreted that it is *'the fathers'* — namely those who are mentioned [as having left] Egypt, [as it says]: *These are the heads of their fathers' houses.*[138] It is they who are to inherit the Land, and it is through them that the Land is to come to those who [actually] divided it.

57. AND THESE ARE THEY THAT WERE NUMBERED OF THE LEVITES. I do not know why He [commanded] that the Levites should be counted [here], and what purpose [is served] now by counting them [since they did not receive any portion in the Land].

of the Land, and the lot also determined the location of each tribe's portion. Subsequently each tribe subdivided the land which it had received, amongst its individual families, and this division was made in proportion to the number of members of each particular family. This division too, was by means of a lot which determined the direction and location of each family's inheritance. (134) Further, 36:9. (135) *Ibid.,* 31:4. (136) Above, 13:2: *'l'mateih' (of every tribe) of their fathers.* (137) Baba Bathra 117a. (138) Exodus 6:14.

Perhaps [they were counted because] it was only to these [Levites] that they gave the [forty-eight] *cities to dwell in and their open land for their cattle,*[139] and not to those who were born afterwards. Or [it may be that this census] was done as an expression of honor for them before G-d, so that "the legion of the King"[140] should not be treated as less important [than the other people], by not bothering to count them like the rest of the people. Scripture mentions *Amram* and his wife [*Jochebed,* with the children she bore — *Aaron, Moses and Miriam their sister,* although it does not do so in connection with any other Levite families], because the sons of [that] Levite [Amram] were counted as two [groups], as priests and as Levites,[141] and it was fitting that Aaron and his sons [who were originally Levites but later on became priests] should be counted separately [therefore Scripture mentions especially the names of the parents and of their children].

Now Rashi commented: "*And these are they that were numbered of the Levites.* The families of the Shimeites[142] and the Uzzielites[143] and part of the Itzharites, namely Nepheg and Zichri, are missing here."[144] And I [further] wonder! Why did Scripture count here in [Verse 57, speaking of] the Levites, the families of the three ancestors [Gershon, Kohath, and Merari — the three sons of the Levites mentioned above, 3: 17], and then again count [in Verse 58] the families of their sons [mentioning amongst them: *the family of the Machlites, the family of the Mushites,* who were both sons of Merari],[145] since Merari had no other children except Machli and Mushi,[145] and for what then *is the family of the Merarites* [mentioned here in Verse 57, seeing that both his children, Machli and Mushi, are counted in Verse 58 as separate families], and there were no other [children of Merari] apart from them! But [we must say that Scripture mentioned each of the three

(139) Further, 35:2-7. (140) Bamidbar Rabbah 1:10. (141) In other words, since one son of Amram, i.e., Moses, was counted amongst the Levites, and the other son, Aaron, was counted amongst the priests, therefore Scripture pointed out especially that Amram had two sons. (142) Above, 3:21. (143) *Ibid.,* Verse 27. (144) Exodus 6:21: *And the sons of Itzhar: Korach, and Nepheg, and Zichri.* Now *the family of the Korachites* is mentioned here in Verse 58, but *Nepheg and Zichri* are omitted. This is the meaning of Rashi's statement that "part of the Itzharites are missing here." (145) *Ibid.,* Verse 19.

families of the three sons of Levi here in Verse 57] as [a sign of] honor, since all three sons of Levi were great men in Israel, and their memories were a blessing. Therefore all the descendants of Gershon [the first son of Levi] were called *the family of the Gershonites* in his honor, and similarly all the children of Merari [his third son] were called *the family of the Merarites* in his honor [as mentioned here in Verse 57]. And afterwards they appointed for themselves paternal families, and became divided up into [smaller] families as did the other tribes, and were called by particular names, [such as] *the family of the Machlites* and *the family of the Mushites* [in Verse 58]. Similarly in the case of Kohath [the second son of Levi] all his children were included in [the term] *the family of the Kohathites* [in Verse 57], and continued to divide themselves up further into [smaller] families of [his] children — *the family of the Hebronites,* and *the family of the Korachites* [in Verse 58]. And Scripture did not mention here [in Verse 58] "the family of the Amramites,"[146] because it was divided up into priests and Levites, and it mentioned their [individual] names [Aaron and Moses — in Verse 59] in [their] honor. However, it did not mention [in that verse Aaron's] priesthood, because of the honor of Moses [i.e., since Moses was *not* the High Priest, but remained a Levite, Scripture in his honor did not want here to emphasize that Aaron was "the priest"]. Similarly you will see in the first census [taken in the second year after the exodus] when counting [the Levites], that Scripture states, *And these were the sons of Levi, by their names: Gershon, and Kohath, and Merari,* [stating all their names] because of their individual distinction, for in [the case of] the other tribes it does not mention them in this way [i.e., it does not mention any individual names].

And the reason [why Scripture mentions in Verse 58] *the family of the Korachites* [and does not mention *'the family of the Itzharites,'*[143] which would have included the other two sons of Itzhar apart from Korach, i.e., Nepheg, and Zichri][144] is because it was originally called *the family of the Itzharites*[143] since at [the time of] that [first] census

(146) As it did above, 3:27: *And of Kohath was the family of the Amramites . . .*

Nepheg and Zichri also had children, [hence *the family of the Itzharites* included Itzhar's three sons, *Korach, and Nepheg, and Zichri*[144] and their descendants]. Now, however, [at the time of this second census] only Korach had children, and therefore they were called after his name [*the family of the Korachites,* here in Verse 58]. However, in my opinion, it was not right that the name of *the Itzharites* should be completely removed from his offspring, even though some of his [Itzhar's] children had died; but they did this after the incident of [the rebellion of] Korach because of the honor of Korach's sons[who originally joined their father's revolt against Moses, but subsequently repented], in order to publicize in Israel their name and their memory in all future generations. For likewise [we see that] Scripture makes a point of saying, *But the children of Korach died not*[147] [in order to emphasize that they turned aside from their father's evil ways]. And since Nepheg and Zichri had come to an end [because all their children died], and all the descendants of Itzhar [that] remained [were] Korach's, they called them *the family of the Korachites* [here in Verse 58], in order to publicize [the fact] that this [Korach's] children were *more righteous and better than he.*[148] And the Midrash of Rabbi Moshe the Preacher on the verse, *ye are 'hame'at' (the fewest) of all peoples*[149] — that [you are] less [than all peoples] by *'hei,'* is not true — because Scripture counts [here] eight

(147) Above, Verse 11. (148) I Kings 2:32. (149) Deuteronomy 7:7. Since it could have said: *"ye are 'me'at' of all peoples"* instead of *'hame'at',* Rabbi Moshe the Preacher explained it as an allusion to the fact that the Israelites numbered sixty-five families, five less than the families of the traditional seventy nations of the world. The verse thus means: "you are *'hei* [which is the Hebrew number five] less' than all the peoples." Now Rabbi Moshe the Preacher arrived at this figure of sixty-five by counting fifty-seven families amongst all the other tribes [as mentioned here in Verses 5-49], and eight families of Levites [as mentioned here in Verses 57-58]. — To this Ramban objects, since, as explained above, the three mentioned in Verse 57 are *not* separate families, but are merely mentioned as a sign of honor to the three distinguished sons of Levi. Hence there are only *five* separate families of the Levites [as mentioned in Verse 58], so that the total together with the fifty-seven of the Israelites is only sixty-three! Consequently the whole interpretation of the verse, *ye are 'hame'at' of all the peoples* by Rabbi Moshe the Preacher, is not true — since there were not sixty-five families, but only sixty-three.

[families] for the children of Levi [in Verses 57-58], but they were only five — [those mentioned in Verse 58], for the three mentioned [in Verse 57] were the fathers [of these five, and thus cannot be counted as separate families], as we have explained.

59. [JOCHEBED, THE DAUGHTER OF LEVI], WHO WAS BORN TO LEVI IN EGYPT. The meaning of this according to the simple sense of Scripture is [to point out] that because all the [other] sons of Jacob went down to Egypt with their sons and daughters, and none of them bore children there afterwards, except for Levi who begot this *joyful mother of children;*[150] for G-d delayed her birth [since He wanted to redeem Israel through her children], and the time of the redemption had not yet come, as I have already explained.[151]

63. THESE ARE THEY THAT WERE NUMBERED BY MOSES AND ELEAZAR. [This phrase refers] to *they that were numbered of the children of Israel* [mentioned further on in this verse], but does not refer to *they that were numbered of the Levites* [Verse 57], because of them it could not be said [as is said in the following verse]: *But among them there was not a man [of them that were numbered by Moses and Aaron the priest in the wilderness of Sinai],*[152] since that decree [that they must perish in the wilderness] did not apply to the tribe of Levi, as our Rabbis have said.[153] And a proof [of this is] Eleazar, and also Phinehas [who were born in Egypt[154] and yet are both mentioned here, and came into the Land].[155]

64. BUT AMONG THESE THERE WAS NOT A MAN OF THEM THAT WERE NUMBERED BY MOSES AND AARON THE PRIEST. For Joshua and Caleb [who *were* amongst those who were

(150) Psalms 113:9. Jochebed here is described by Ramban as a *joyful mother* because she gave birth to three such distinguished children, Aaron, Moses and Miriam. — The reference is based upon Sotah 12a, where it is said that at the time of marriage of Amram and Jochebed the angels of G-d chanted a *joyful mother of children.* (151) Genesis 46:15 (Vol. I, p. 559). (152) Verse 64. (153) Baba Bathra 121b. (154) Exodus 6:23; 25. (155) Joshua 14:1; 22:13.

numbered at the first census] were not [included] now in this census, because they were over sixty years old, and the census was only of [people] aged between twenty and sixty, which [years] are the principal ones of a man's life, similar to that which is stated in [the law of] Valuations,[156] and it is then [in those years] that he *goes forth to war in Israel,*[157] and not after the age of sixty, as our Rabbis have said.[153] But when Scripture says [in the following verse], *And there was not left a man 'of them,' save Caleb the son of Jephunneh, and Joshua the son of Nun* [the words "of them" do not refer to those who *were numbered* now *in the wilderness of Sinai,* but to] *them that were numbered* at the first [census] and did not die [in the wilderness, since Caleb and Joshua, being over sixty years old, were not numbered now in this second census].

27 3. [OUR FATHER DIED IN THE WILDERNESS], AND HE [Zelophehad] WAS NOT [AMONG THE COMPANY OF THEM THAT GATHERED THEMSELVES TOGETHER AGAINST THE ETERNAL IN THE COMPANY OF KORACH]. "Since they came to say, *but he died in his own sin,* they had to say [that he did] not [die because of participating] in the sin of those who murmured,[158] nor [because he was] amongst *the company of Korach* who incited [the people] against the Holy One, blessed be He; but [he died] in his own sin, and did not cause others to sin with him." This is Rashi's language. But he did not explain why they [the daughters of Zelophehad] came to say that *he died in his own sin,* when they should [only] have said: *'Our father died in the wilderness, and he had no sons!'* For that was the fitting thing to say [since the cause of his death was not relevant, and it is not right for children to stress their father's sin]! But in the opinion of our Rabbis[159] they had to say that *he was not among the company of Korach,* because the company of Korach did not receive a portion in the Land, and likewise the murmurers in the company of Korach, [and *the daughters of Zelophehad* knew this]

(156) Leviticus 27:3. (157) Above, Verse 2. (158) *Ibid.,* 11:1. (159) Baba Bathra 118b.

because it had become known amongst the people from the court of Moses. And Rabbi Abraham ibn Ezra explained it in a similar manner, saying that the daughters thought that those who had *gathered together against the Eternal*[160] would not inherit in the Land.

In my opinion, according to the simple meaning of Scripture, they spoke in this way because they thought that Moses our teacher hated *the company of Korach* more than all other sinners who died in the desert, because they had rebelled against him and had denied [the Divine approval of] all his deeds; therefore they thought that perhaps *because he hated them*[161] [the company of Korach] he would say: *Let there be none to extend kindness unto him; neither let there be any to be gracious unto his fatherless children.*[162] Therefore they informed him that he [their father] was not one of them, and they furthermore hinted that he was not amongst those who died in one of the plagues [which came as a punishment for the sin of the people], but that he died [a natural death] in the wilderness in his bed. And the meaning of [the expression] *but he died in his own sin* is that they said that he had died in the wilderness *in his sin*, because he was not worthy to enter the Land [and this in itself is considered the punishment for a sin]. Or it may be as the poet Rabbi Yehudah Halevi, of blessed memory,[163] explained, that it is connected [in meaning] with [the phrase following it]: *and he had no sons,* as people say nowadays: "Such-and-such an event happened because of [certain] sins."

9. AND IF HE HAVE NO DAUGHTER, THEN YE SHALL GIVE HIS INHERITANCE UNTO HIS BRETHREN. Our Rabbis have

(160) Above, 16:11. (161) See Deuteronomy 9:28. (162) Psalms 109:12. (163) This is the great Hebrew poet and philosopher of the Spanish Golden Era (1085-1142 Common Era). According to his interpretation, the daughters of Zelophehad were saying that "because of his sins, he died without any sons" and hence the problem arose what to do with his inheritance. This therefore answers Ramban's question above, "why the daughters of Zelophehad found it necessary to mention their father's death because of his sin." — This explanation is mentioned by Ibn Ezra, who remarks: "It is not remote, [it is indeed probable]."

received a tradition[164] that a father inherits his son if he [the son] dies without any children, but Scripture, however, did not mention this. The reason [for this omission] is that in the laws of inheritance [the rule is]: "Whoever can bequeath an inheritance to his relations can inherit [from them]," since their relationship is mutual. Now since Scripture stated that a son inherits his father, [it is self-understood that] the father also inherits his son [if the son died without direct descendants, but left, for example, brothers]. And furthermore, the [primary law of] inheritance is [that it follows the direct] line of [descent of] successors [of the progenitor] according to his [direct] descendants, and does not go by means of a side-succession [such as to a brother; hence the father gets it back from his son].[164] If so [the meaning of the verse] *then ye shall give his inheritance unto his brethren* is the inheritance which the father inherits in the grave [in a direct line back from his son]; and from him [the father, who is already dead], it comes [again in a direct line] to the brothers [who survive the deceased son]. But [although according to the tradition of our Rabbis, a father inherits his son who dies without any children, even if the son has surviving brothers], Scripture yet did *not* want to say: *"And if he have no daughter, then ye shall give his inheritance unto* 'his [surviving] father,' " [but instead states that you shall give his inheritance *'to his brothers'*] since the Torah speaks "in a way of blessing" [and therefore mentions only the children or brothers who inherit], for it does not [want to speak about] those who are "cut off" [i.e., a case where the dead man is "cut off" in his youth, during the lifetime of his father]. And perhaps [the reason why Scripture does not mention it explicitly is] because it did not happen to any of those who entered the Land, that a father [outlived and] inherited his son, but the sons always had direct descendants to inherit them; for it is about them [those who entered the Land] that Scripture speaks.

11. AND IT SHALL BE UNTO THE CHILDREN OF ISRAEL A STATUTE OF JUDGMENT. The meaning thereof is that this *judgment* should be for all [future] generations, and not only for now when they inherited the Land [hence the expression *"a statute,* i.e., a

(164) Baba Bathra 115a.

permanent one, for all *the children of Israel* in all future generations"].

AS THE ETERNAL COMMANDED MOSES. This means: "as I have commanded you," and the usage here is similar to [that in the verse], *This is the statute of the law which the Eternal hath commanded.*[165] There are many similar cases.

12. GET THEE UP INTO THIS MOUNTAIN OF ABARIM. The name of this mountain was Mount Nebo, as is stated explicitly in the sections of *Ha'azinu,*[166] and *'V'zoth Habrachah;*[167] but it is [here] called *the mountain of Abarim* [meaning "fords"] because it is situated by the fords of the Jordan, from which one passes over into the land of Canaan, as it says here, *that is over against Jericho,*[168] and it was from there that they [actually] crossed over the Jordan, as it is said, *And the people came up out of the Jordan . . . and encamped in Gilgal, on the east border of Jericho.*[169] Now this [statement *get thee up*] is not a commandment which the Holy One, blessed be He, commanded Moses to fulfill now, for if so he would have had to go up there at once [and we do not find that he did so], but it means: "you shall go up into the mountain of Abarim and shall behold the Land [but you shall not enter it]." For since He had commanded Moses, *Unto these the Land shall be divided,*[170] He informed him that "it will not be divided by you, but you shall go *up into* the top of the *mountain of Abarim* before Israel journeys away from the land of Moab, and you will die therein, and all you will have of the Land will be the sight thereof ." Similarly [Verse 18 which says] *Take thee Joshua the son of Nun,* means that "when your time [to die] comes, you shall take Joshua," [but is not a command to do so now]. And Scripture completed [this episode] by saying that Moses did so whole-

(165) Above, 19:2. Since G-d Himself is speaking, one would have expected the verse to say: "This is the statute which I have commanded." (166) Deuteronomy 32:49. (167) *Ibid.,* 34:1. (168) *Ibid.,* (32:49; 34:1). The word "here" in Ramban cannot be explained literally, since in this section here, the phrase *over against Jericho* is *not* found. It must therefore refer to the verse in *Ha'azinu* and *V'zoth Habracha* which Ramban has just referred to. (169) Joshua 4:19. (170) Above, 26:53.

heartedly,[171] and this is the [same] act which is mentioned at [the time of] Moses' departure [from the world],[172] when *he and Hoshea the son of Nun spoke* [*the words of*] the *Song.*[173]

19. AND THOU SHALT COMMAND HIM [Joshua] – "concerning Israel, [saying to him]: 'Know that they are troublesome, that they are stubborn. [Accept this position of leadership over them with full awareness of this and] on condition that you take upon yourself [all this].' " This is the language of Rashi. But it is not correct in my opinion, because it says [*and thou shalt command him*] *before their eyes* [and Moses would not have told Joshua to say such words in their presence], for this matter ought rather to have been told to him [Joshua] between the two of them [Moses and Joshua]; for if he would say it in their presence, it would [only] have caused them to break off all restraint. And it would have been more fitting that he [Moses] should chastise the people, warning them separately [and not in Joshua's presence] not to be troublesome and stubborn any more [rather than to tell Joshua, in their presence, that they were a troublesome and stubborn people]! But [the meaning of] *and thou shalt command him before their eyes* is that you should instruct him in the duties of a prince and judge, since it was because he [Joshua] was to be their leader that he entrusted them to his care. [Therefore] he should [indeed] have warned him to exert himself exceedingly on their behalf, and to fight the battles of the Eternal, and that he should be the one to *go out before them* [in battle] and to *bring them in,*[174] and that he should be careful in matters of judgment. These [instructions] indeed ought to be said in their presence, in order that they should trust him and listen to him, for they would then know that he will treat their affairs in a truthful manner, since his master had so commanded him. And this is what Moses [actually] did, as it is said there, *And Moses called unto Joshua, and said unto him in the sight of all Israel: 'Be strong and of good courage* etc. *fear not, neither be dismayed.'*[172]

(171) *Ibid.,* Verses 22-23. This refers to the fact that although Moses was only commanded (in Verse 18) to lay "his [single] hand upon him," *he laid his 'hands' upon him,* which shows that he appointed his successor whole-heartedly, although he knew that he was now to die. (172) Deuteronomy 31:7-8. (173) *Ibid.,* 32:44. Thus Scripture points out there that Moses and Joshua said the Song together, with equal enthusiasm and equally whole-heartedly. (174) Above, Verse 17.

And in the Sifre [we find the following text]:[175] *"And command Joshua*[176] – concerning instruction [learning and teaching Torah].[177] *And encourage 'him,' and strengthen 'him.'*[176] This teaches us that there cannot be two leaders in one generation." Now these are duties of the prince, to be firm and not to be afraid of the people.

In my opinion the plain meaning of Scripture is that the explanation of [the expression] *'v'tzav' (and thou shalt command) him before their eyes* is [that it refers to] appointing [him officially as their leader], for Moses was to appoint Joshua in the presence of the people to be the ruler over them. This is similar to [the expression], *from the time 'tzivah othi' (I was appointed) to be their governor* etc.[178] So also: *'vayetzaveihu' (and the Eternal hath appointed him) to be the prince over His people.*[179] Similarly, *Even from the day that 'tzivithi' ('I commanded') judges to be over My people Israel,*[180] which means "I appointed" [and likewise all these expressions of *'tzav,'* which literally mean "command," here mean "appoint"].

28 2. COMMAND THE CHILDREN OF ISRAEL, AND SAY UNTO THEM: MY OFFERING, MY BREAD FOR MY FIRE-OFFERINGS. The reason [for stating this command here] is that after He had said, *Unto these the Land shall be divided,*[170] He completed the commands relating to the laws of the offerings which they are to observe in the Land, since they did not bring any Additional Offerings [of Sabbaths and festivals] in the desert, as I have mentioned in Seder *Emor El Hakohanim.*[181] Likewise they were not obliged to bring drink-offerings in the wilderness, as I have explained in Seder *Shelach Lecha.*[182] But now He charged those who were to come into the Land with the duty of bringing all [these offerings] there – the Daily Whole-offerings, the Additional Offerings, *and their meal-offerings and their drink-offerings.* And although He did not say expressly here:

(175) I have not found this exact text in our editions of Sifre. For the closest approximation, see my Hebrew commentary, p. 316, Note 93. (176) Deuteronomy 3:28. (177) Moses is hereby told to transmit the Torah to Joshua, and to command him to teach it further to Israel. See Aboth 1:1 – "Moses received the Torah on Sinai, and handed it down to Joshua, and Joshua to the elders, etc." (178) Nehemiah 5:14. (179) I Samuel 13:14. (180) II Samuel 7:11. (181) Leviticus 23:2. (182) Above, 15:2, in the verse: *when ye are come into the Land . . .*

"when you come into the Land," He has already mentioned it in the section of drink-offerings,[182] and He hinted at it in the first section dealing with the festivals.[183] Now He started here with the [laws of the] Daily Whole-offering, [for] although it has already been mentioned in the section of *V'atah Tetzaveh,*[184] He repeated it in order that it should all be arranged in one section. And Rashi wrote [in Verse 4]: "That one [i.e., the section in *V'atah Tetzaveh*] was an instruction [only] for the days of the installation [of the priests], and here He [repeated it] as a commandment for [all future] generations." But this is not correct, since there it says, *It shall be a continual burnt-offering 'throughout your generations.'*[185]

And according to the interpretation [of the Rabbis][186] many new teachings are added here [in this repetition of the section of *V'atah Tetzaveh;* namely]: "*My offering* — this is the blood. *My bread* — this refers to [those parts of the offering] that are to be burnt on the altar. *My fire-offerings* — these are the handfuls [of flour] and the frankincense [of the meal-offering]. *For a pleasing odor unto Me* — these are the [two] bowls [of frankincense that were brought as a memorial] with the showbread.[187] *Ye shall observe* — that it should only be brought from [animals which have been] kept [for a number of days, and examined so that no blemish occurs to them]. *Ye shall observe* — that one may only bring [the offering] from that [money] which was donated to the treasury [of the Sanctuary]. *Ye shall observe* — that priests, Levites and Israelites should stand over it. *Ye shall observe* — Scripture uses here the term *shmirah* ['keeping,' or 'observing'], and elsewhere it [also] uses the term *shmirah;*[188] just as there the offering requires observation [so that no blemish should be

(183) Leviticus 23:10: *when ye are come into the Land . . .* (184) Exodus 29:38-42. (185) *Ibid.,* 29:42. Hence the commandment to offer this in future generations has already been stated there. (186) Sifre, *Pinchas* 142. (187) Leviticus 24:7. (188) I.e., in the case of the Paschal-lamb where it says: *And it shall be to you 'l'mishmereth' (in your keeping) until the fourteenth day of the same month* (Exodus 12:6). Since the lamb had to be bought on the tenth of that month (*ibid.,* Verse 3), the verse implies that it has to be carefully examined for a blemish for four days before it is slaughtered. Since here, in speaking of the Daily Whole-offering, Scripture likewise uses the term *shmirah* [— *'tishmeru' (ye shall keep)*], we deduce that it also has to be examined for four days before it is slaughtered

found in it] for [a period of] four days before it is slaughtered, so here too etc." [See] the whole interpretation, as it is stated in the Sifre.[186]

By way of the Truth, [the mystic teachings of the Cabala], the verse also hints to the following: It states *My offering, My bread 'l'ishai'* — of *'ishai'* (My Divine powers) — *ye shall keep* and be careful *to offer unto Me* to My Name, *in its due season. And thou shalt say unto them*[189] further, *This is the fire-offering which ye shall offer unto the Eternal,*[189] "so that the offering should bring about [the desired unity and harmony on high]."[190] Now there is no sin-offering amongst the Additional Offerings of the Sabbath, as there is in all the other Additional Offerings [i.e., those brought on the New Moon and the festivals], because the congregation of Israel is its partner [that of the Sabbath],[191] and all is [therefore] peace [and harmony]. The student [learned in the teachings of the Cabala] will understand. Similarly He mentioned [here for the purpose of arranging all offerings in one section] *And in the first month, on the fourteenth day of the month, is the Eternal's Passover,*[192] meaning that they should offer the Paschal-offering, in order to command them about it together with the other [additional] offerings of the Festival of Unleavened Bread. And He dealt with it [the Paschal-offering] briefly, referring to it only by its name, since He had already explained [all] its laws, *according to all the statutes of it, and according to all the ordinances thereof.*[193]

7. AND THE DRINK-OFFERING THEREOF — "of wine. IN THE HOLY PLACE THOU SHALT POUR — upon the altar they shall be poured out. A POURING FORTH OF STRONG DRINK — wine which has an intoxicating power. This excludes wine straight from the [wine-]press." This is the language of Rashi. But it is not correct, for the Rabbis have already said:[194] "Wine straight from the wine-press one may not bring [for the drink-offering, since it is non-intoxicating], but if one did bring [such wine], it is valid" [and there is no need to bring other wine]. Thus [we see that] wine straight from the wine-press is *not* excluded on the basis of a [Scriptural] verse [for in

(189) Verse 3. (190) See *L'vush Ha'orah* on Ricanti. (191) See Vol. I, p. 60. The allusions here are Cabalistic. (192) Further, Verse 16. (193) Above, 9:3. (194) Baba Bathra 97a.

that case, he *would* have to bring other wine instead of it], but it is merely a prohibition of the Rabbis to be observed as a rule directly [but if not observed, it does not invalidate the drink-offering]. However, [the correct interpretation is]: [195] "*Strong drink,* to exclude wine which is diluted [with water]," which is invalid even if already brought [so that one must bring other wine which is undiluted]. And this is how it is interpreted in the Sifre.[195] And there they [furthermore] said: "*In the holy place thou shalt pour* — it was to be poured *in the holy place,* and *in the holy place* it was absorbed."[196]

Now Scripture mentions in the [case of the] Daily Whole-offering and [the Additional Offerings of] *your New Moons* the amount of fine flour in the meal-offering [which accompanied them],[197] and the amount of wine in the drink-offerings [which accompanied them],[198] but in the [case of the Additional Offerings of the] Sabbath, the Festival[s] of Unleavened Bread, Weeks, the New Year, the Day of Atonement, and the first day of the Festival of Tabernacles, He mentioned the amount of the meal-offering, but did *not* specify the amount of the drink-offerings. The reason for this is that although in the section [dealing with] the drink-offerings[199] He commanded how much the meal-offerings and the drink-offerings should be *for the bullocks, for the rams, and for the lambs,*[200] in vow-offerings, freewill offerings, and [the offerings of] the festivals,[201] we find a double meal-offering for the lamb brought with the sheaf [of barley],[202] and on the day of *Atzereth*[203] [they brought] *two tenth-parts of an ephah* [*baked*] *with leaven,*[203] and so also we find [*unleavened cakes, wafers, and cakes of leavened bread*] in a thanks-offering, which were a meal-offering.[204] Therefore Scripture had to specify [here] in the case of all the festivals that their meal-offering does not change, as it changed in these [above-mentioned cases]. But the drink-offerings never varied;

(195) Sifre, *Pinchas* 143. (196) This is a reference to the cavity at the side of the altar, into which the libations were poured. It was a natural cavity in the ground which had existed since the six days of creation, and the wine went down and was absorbed therein. See my Hebrew commentary, p. 317. (197) Verses 5, 13. (198) Verses 7, 14. (199) Above, 15:4-12. (200) Further, 29:33. (201) Above, 15:3. (202) Leviticus 23:13. (203) I.e., the Festival of Weeks. See in Vol. III, p. 393, why this festival is called by the name *Atzereth.* — *Ibid.,* Verse 17. (204) *Ibid.,* 7:12-13.

therefore He mentioned them at first in [the case of the] Daily Whole-offering, and did not refer to them afterwards in the case of [the Additional Offering of] the Sabbath. He did refer to them again [when speaking] of the New Moon,[205] in order to mention also the drink-offerings of the bullocks and the rams, but afterwards He did not have to mention them at all. [Likewise] He mentioned on the first day of Tabernacles the amount of the meal-offering,[206] and it was [therefore] no longer necessary to mention it in connection with the other days of the festival, except [to state], *and their meal-offering and their drink-offerings . . . according to their number, after their ordinance,*[200] meaning to say: "*after their ordinance* on the first day [of the festival] as mentioned [previously]."

20. THREE TENTH-PARTS SHALL YE OFFER FOR 'A BULLOCK' — that is, for each of the [two] bullocks, [mentioned in the preceding verse]. Similarly, *three tenth-parts for 'the one bullock'*[206] means for each one of the [thirteen] bullocks [mentioned in the preceding verse]. And [the expression in the following Verse 21] *for the one lamb* shows us [the meaning of] this [phrase — *for 'a bullock,'* in Verse 20 before us], since it says [there in Verse 21], *'isaron isaron'* [literally: *'a tenth-part, a tenth-part' shalt thou offer for 'the one lamb'* — thus indicating clearly that this amount of the meal-offering is for *each* of the lambs; and here too the amount stated is for *each* of the bullocks and rams]. Scripture further states explicitly [in Verse 21]: *for every lamb of the seven lambs.* So here too, *for 'a bullock'* means for [each of] the two bullocks. Scripture, however, sometimes speaks briefly in a matter which is self-understood, for it is obvious that there are not *three tenth-parts* [of an ephah offered up] *for one bullock,* whilst the second one has none [at all]. And [the reason why] He stated explicitly [in the following Verse 21] in connection with the lambs [that the meal-offering specified is for *each* one of the lambs], is because they are many [i.e., seven], and it follows all the more so in the [case of the] bullocks [mentioned here in Verse 20 that the meal-offering specified there is to be offered up for each of the two bullocks]. And in [speaking about the first day of] the Festival

(205) Further, Verse 14. (206) *Ibid.,* 29:14.

of Tabernacles, when the bullocks were more [than on any other festival], He explains *three tenth-parts for the one bullock of the thirteen bullocks.*[206]

29 6. He mentioned [with reference to the Additional Offerings of] *the first day of the seventh month* [i.e., the New Year], *beside the burnt-offering of the New Moon and the meal-offering thereof,* but He did not mention the sin-offering of the New Moon,[207] while [with reference to] the Day of Atonement He *did* mention *beside the sin-offering of atonement,*[208] but did not mention the burnt-offering of atonement.[209] The reason for this is that concerning the Day of Atonement, it is obvious that the burnt-offering which He commanded here to be brought on that day][210] is *beside the* burnt-offering which He commanded there,[209] for both of them are commanded with reference to the same day, and they are not equal; for there [in the Book of Leviticus] the Israelites were only commanded [to bring on the Day of Atonement] *one ram for a burnt-offering,*[209] and here He commanded as a burnt-offering [that they bring] a *bullock,* a *ram,* and *seven he-lambs.*[210] If so, it is quite clear that these [offerings mentioned here] are in addition to those mentioned there. But [in the case of] the sin-offering, which is the same [both] here[208] and there,[209] one might possibly have made a mistake in connection with it, and think that [the one commanded here] is the same sin-offering which is mentioned there, since [we do not find] two sin-offerings [brought] on one day. Therefore when mentioning it [here] He expressly stated: [*one he-goat for a sin-offering*] *'beside the sin-offering of atonement,'*[208] for that sin-offering [mentioned in the Book of Leviticus] is *the sin-offering of atonement,* that is to say, it is the inner sin-offering[211] that is burnt [outside the camp, or outside the city of Jerusalem], and atones *for the holy place, because of the uncleanness of the children of Israel, and because of their transgressions, even all their sins;*[212] whereas this outer sin-offering[211] is like other sin-offerings, which come together with the Additional Offerings.[213] Similarly [when speaking about] *the day of*

(207) Above, 28:15. (208) Further, Verse 11. (209) Leviticus 16:5. (210) Verse 8 here. (211) See Vol. III, p. 70, Note 52. (212) Leviticus 16:16. (213) These sin-offerings were eaten by male priests in the Sanctuary Court

the first-fruits [the Festival of Weeks], it was not necessary to say that what is commanded here is "beside what has been said about it in the section of the festivals,"[214] since the two sections are said about the same day, and the offerings are not the same [and therefore it is self-understood that the offerings mentioned here are in addition to those mentioned there]. Nor was it necessary to state [here when speaking about the offerings of the Festival of Weeks, i.e., Shavuoth, that they are beside] the sin-offering [mentioned in the section of the festivals],[215] because Scripture said there explicitly, *And ye shall present with the bread* [*seven lambs* etc. *And ye shall offer one he-goat for a sin-offering* etc.],[216] and it is quite clear [therefore] that all [the offerings] mentioned there come because of the [two] loaves and must be brought with them, and that these mentioned here are in addition to them. But in the case of the New Moon of this seventh month, one might have thought that when Scripture says, *And in your New Moons ye shall present* etc.[217] it applies to all the other months [of the year], but that [on the New Moon of] *the seventh month* the total offering is to be only this [group of] offerings which He especially commanded for it; therefore it was necessary to say, *beside the burnt-offering of the New Moon, and the meal-offering thereof.*[218] And having mentioned this, we can already deduce that *everything* that is mentioned in the section of *And in your New Moons*[217] is an obligation for all months, including the sin-offering [of the New Moon], and therefore it was not necessary to say [here in the case of the New Year]: "*beside the burnt-offering of the New Moon, and the meal-offering thereof,* 'and the sin-offering thereof.' "

30 1. AND MOSES TOLD THE CHILDREN OF ISRAEL [ACCORDING TO ALL THAT THE ETERNAL COMMANDED MOSES]. " 'This is [stated] in order to separate the subject [of the offerings from that of the following chapter, dealing with vows and

on the same day that they were slaughtered, and on the evening of that day until midnight. In the case of the sin-offering of the Day of Atonement, however, since eating is forbidden on the actual Day of Atonement, the sin-offering could of course only be eaten in the evening after the fast until midnight. (214) Leviticus, 23:18. (215) *Ibid.,* Verse 19. (216) *Ibid.,* Verses 18-19. (217) Above, 28:11. (218) Verse 6 here.

oaths].' These are the words of Rabbi Yishmael. [The meaning thereof is as follows:] Since up till this point [we have] the words of G-d [to Moses],[219] and the [following] section of vows begins with the statement of Moses,[220] it was necessary to separate the subject [of the offerings] by stating that Moses repeated it and told this section to Israel; for if this were not stated, one might have thought that he did not tell them this [section dealing with the offerings], but began his words with the section of vows." These are the words of Rashi. But I do not understand them, for [we find] similarly that it says — at the end of the section [dealing with] blemishes [in priests], *And Moses spoke unto Aaron, and to his sons, and unto all the children of Israel;* [221] and it says at the end of the section of the festivals, *And Moses declared unto the children of Israel the appointed seasons of the Eternal*[222] [and in both these cases the subsequent chapters also begin with G-d's utterance to Moses; so why was it necessary, according to Rashi, to separate here the sections by saying that Moses declared those laws *to the children of Israel*]!

But according to its plain meaning, the verse here comes to say that although this section deals with the laws of the offerings, G-d did not single out Aaron and his sons in connection with it, as in the sections of [the book] "the Law of the Priests" [i.e. the Book of Leviticus]. Instead Moses said it *to* all *the children of Israel* together, *according to all that the Eternal commanded Moses,* including the laws of refraining from work on the festivals,[223] and [the laws of] the Daily Whole-offerings, the Additional Offerings, the vow-offerings and the freewill offerings, for thus it was told to Moses, *Command the children of Israel.*[224] And the reason [for this] is because this commandment applies after they enter the Land, and it is a commandment to all Israel to observe [the laws of] the Daily Whole-offerings and the Additional Offerings [of the Sabbath and festivals] in their appointed times, and to bring their vow-offerings and freewill offerings. Furthermore, the main intention of the commandment [to offer up offerings] is that *these days should be remembered and kept,*[225] and to

(219) See above, 28:1: *And the Eternal spoke unto Moses, saying . . .* (220) Further, Verse 2: *And Moses spoke unto the heads of the tribes . . .* (221) Leviticus 21:24. (222) *Ibid.,* 23:44. (223) Above, 28:18, 26. etc. (224) *Ibid.,* Verse 2. (225) Esther 9:28.

refrain on them from all servile work [and therefore it was told *to* all *the children of Israel*]. Now this section is like the section of the festivals in "the Law of the Priests" [i.e. the Book of Leviticus]. For it says there at the beginning, *Speak unto the children of Israel, and say unto them,*[226] and at the end it says, *And Moses declared unto the children of Israel the appointed seasons of the Eternal,*[222] and here likewise at the beginning [of the section it says], *Command the children of Israel, and say unto them,*[224] and at the end [in the verse before us] it says, *And Moses told the children of Israel according to all that the Eternal commanded.* It did not mention [here in this verse that Moses told] "the appointed seasons of the Eternal," because in this section here other matters are mentioned [as well] which do not apply to "the appointed seasons of the Eternal," such as the Daily Whole-offerings of weekdays, and the Additional Offerings of the Sabbath and the New Moons.

The interpretation given by Rabbi Yishmael [quoted above by Rashi] is because Scripture never has to say of Moses that he told the children of Israel all that G-d commanded him, [because it is self-understood that he always did so], and it is not usual for the Torah to say so at each and every section. Therefore the Rabbis [similarly] explained[227] the verse, "*And Moses spoke unto Aaron, and to his sons, and unto all the children of Israel*[221] — [as implying that] he warned Aaron about his sons [i.e., that Aaron as High Priest should preserve the sanctity of the Sanctuary, and prevent priests with a bodily blemish from performing the Divine Service], and [he warned] the sons concerning the Israelites [that they should prevent the Israelites from entering those parts of the Sanctuary which are forbidden to them], and [he warned] the Israelites about each other" [that they should each prevent the other from violating the sanctity of the Sanctuary]. And in the section of the festivals they explained [the verse, *And Moses declared unto the children of Israel the appointed seasons of the Eternal*][222] in many ways. [Thus they said]:[228] "This teaches us that Moses used to tell Israel the laws of the Passover on Passover, the laws of Shavuoth [the Festival of Weeks] on Shavuoth, and the laws of Tabernacles on Tabernacles. [It further teaches us that] in the very

(226) Leviticus 23:2. (227) Torath Kohanim, *Emor* 3:12. (228) *Ibid.,* 17:12-13.

language that he heard it [from G-d], he told it to Israel. And all the sections [mentioned here] are subject to the same law.[229] Rabbi Yosei the Galilean says: It states [*and Moses declared unto the children of Israel*] *the appointed seasons of the Eternal,*[222] but the Sabbath of Creation [i.e., the weekly Sabbath] was not said together with them.'[230] Ben Azai says: It is said, [*And Moses declared unto the children of Israel*] *the appointed seasons of the Eternal,*[222] but the section of vows was not said together with them [as will be explained further on]. Rabbi[231] says: What does this verse — *And Moses declared unto the children of Israel the appointed seasons of the Eternal*[222] — come to tell us? Since [hitherto] we have only learnt that the Paschal-lamb and the Daily Whole-offering override the Sabbath [i.e., are brought on the Sabbath although they entail doing work which is normally forbidden], because it says about them *in its appointed season*[232] [which includes even the Sabbath]; but we have not [yet] been taught that [the same applies to] the other public offerings. Therefore Scripture says: *These ye shall offer unto the Eternal 'in your appointed seasons'*[233] thus indicating that all public offerings mentioned in this section of the Additional Offerings of the festivals, override the Sabbath. [But we still do not know that the sheaf [of new barley brought on the second day of Passover], and the offerings brought with it,[234] and the two loaves [brought on the Festival of Shavuoth] and the offerings that come with them[235] [override the Sabbath, since they are not mentioned in this section of the offerings, and hence are not included in the phrase *in your*

(229) This means, as explained further, that just as fixing the days of the festivals [through the sanctification of the New Moon] can only be performed by a qualified court (see Vol. II, p. 116) so the adjudication of vows [mentioned in the following section] requires a court of qualified experts. Hence the statement: "All sections [mentioned here—namely the preceding one dealing with the festivals, and the following one treating of vows], are subject to the same law." (230) This means that the Sabbath, unlike the festivals, does not require "sanctification" by the court, since its sanctity is permanent and endures forever, being based on its original sanctification by G-d at the creation of the world (Genesis 2:3). (231) This is Rabbi Yehudah Hanasi, the redactor of the Mishnah. Because of his great status, he is known simply as "Rabbi." See also Vol. II, p. 349, Note 64. (232) Above, 9:2 (Paschal-lamb). *Ibid.,* 28:2 (Daily Whole-offering). (233) Above, 29:39. (234) Leviticus 23:12-13. (235) *Ibid.,* Verses 17-18.

appointed seasons.[233] But when Scripture says [there], *And Moses declared unto the children of Israel 'the appointed seasons of the Eternal,'*[222] it established 'an appointed season' for all [public offerings, so that they all override the Sabbath]." Thus far is the text of the Torath Kohanim.[228]

Now it is possible to say that the interpretation of Rabbi Yishmael who said that [the verse before us: *And Moses told the children of Israel . . .* is said] in order to separate the subject [of the offerings from that of the vows, as Rashi mentioned], is identical with that of Ben Azai, who said: "It says *the appointed seasons of the Eternal,*[222] but the section of vows was not said together with them," meaning that the law of the festivals is not like the law of the section of vows, which was told *to the heads of the tribes*[236] in order to say that a single person who is expert [in the laws] can release a vow, and so can three ordinary people, for the festivals require the sanctification [of the New Moon] by a court of [at least] three experts, as is explained in [Tractate] Baba Bathra.[237] Ben Azai thus derived this distinction between them [the festivals and vows] from the limiting phrase: [*And Moses declared*] *the appointed seasons of the Eternal,* and Rabbi Yishmael derived this [same] principle from the [apparent] redundancy of this verse [before us], and [hence he explained] that it only comes to separate the subject of the festivals from that of the vows. Thus both of them [Ben Azai and Rabbi Yishmael] are saying the same thing, differing only as to the text from which this law is derived.

The correct interpretation [of the words of Rabbi Yishmael who said that our verse comes only to separate the subjects] appears to me to be that he only intended to say [as follows]: Had He finished the section [here] of the festivals with [the verse]: *These ye shall offer unto the Eternal in your appointed seasons,*[233] and begun [immediately with the verse] *And Moses spoke unto the heads of the tribes of the children of Israel, saying: This is the thing which the Eternal hath commanded,*[236] it would have been possible [to explain] that the verse refers to the previous [subject], meaning that *Moses spoke unto the heads of the tribes: "This is the thing which G-d commanded* concerning the Daily Whole-offerings and the Additional Offerings"

(236) Further, 30:2. (237) Baba Bathra 121a.

mentioned [previously], and the phrase *unto the heads of the tribes* would not be interpreted as referring to the following section of the vows. Therefore He divided [the subjects] and finished the section of the festivals [with the verse before us], *And Moses told the children of Israel according to all that the Eternal commanded Moses,* and then began the section of vows [with the statement] that Moses *spoke unto the heads of the tribes, This is the thing that the Eternal hath commanded.*[236] This is the truth, for such is the explanation of [the expression] "to separate the subject" in many places in the Sifra and Sifre. And Rashi himself has already mentioned[238] what the Rabbis have said in the Sifre: [239] "[*Now therefore kill every male among the little ones,*] *'and kill'* [*every woman that hath known man by lying with him*]. [238] Why is [the expression]*and kill* used [since it has already been said once at the beginning of the verse]? It is to separate the subject. These are the words of Rabbi Yishmael. For if I were to read [the verse without the repetition of the expression 'and kill,' namely]: *'Now therefore kill every male among the little ones, and every woman that hath known man by lying with him. And all the women-children . . .* [*keep alive*], I would not know what the verse is saying [about *the women* who *have known man by lying with him* — whether they are to be killed together with *every male* mentioned in the beginning of the verse, or to be kept alive together with *all the women-children* mentioned in the following verse]. Therefore it says [again], *and kill,* in order to separate the subject [from the following verse].' These are the words of Rabbi Yishmael." Similarly we find [such a usage of the expression "to separate the subject"] in other places in the Torath Kohanim [i.e., the Sifra].

(238) Further, 31:17. (239) Sifre, *Matoth* 157.

Matoth

2. AND MOSES SPOKE UNTO THE HEADS OF THE TRIBES. Scripture did not precede this section with [the statement]: "And the Eternal spoke unto Moses, saying: Speak unto the heads of the tribes, and say unto them: This is the thing which the Eternal hath commanded," as He stated in the section [dealing with] slaughtering [offerings] outside the Sanctuary Court,[1] and in other sections. Instead, He mentioned it as the *end* of this section, saying, *These are the statutes, which the Eternal commanded Moses.*[2] And in the section of *Vayehi Bayom Ha'shemini*[3] it says: *And Moses said: 'This is the thing which the Eternal commanded that ye should do,'*[4] but did not mention the [actual] command [given by G-d to Moses] at all. Similarly, in the section about the manna [it is said], *And Moses said: 'This is the thing which the Eternal hath commanded: Let an omerful of it be kept* etc.'[5] [although the Divine command about it to Moses is not expressly stated].

Now *the heads of the tribes of the children of Israel* are the princes of the standards, whom the tribes had appointed over their standards

(1) Leviticus 17:2. (2) Further, Verse 17. (3) Leviticus 9:1. (4) *Ibid.*, Verse 6. See also Ramban *ibid.* Verse 2. (5) Exodus 16:32.

after Nachshon the son of Amminadab [prince of the children of Judah][6] and his colleagues had died. It is possible that they [*the heads of the tribes* referred to here] were those who are mentioned in the section [dealing with] the inheritance [of the Land]: *These are the names of the men that shall take possession of the Land for you;* [7] or it may be that those [referred to here] were others, for there Scripture speaks about [the leaders of] the future [saying] that when they come to divide up the Land [in the time of Joshua] all those mentioned will be living, and they will represent them [in the apportionment of the Land].

And Moses spoke unto the heads of the tribes. The reason [why he did not address this section to the entire people] is because it was not necessary to teach all the children of Israel that the father and husband [of a woman] can declare void those vows [of their daughter or wife, respectively] which involve affliction of the soul, and perhaps it is [even] necessary to conceal these [rights] from them, so that they should not treat vows lightly. But it was to the Sages of Israel, the heads of their tribes, that he taught the ordinance [of vows]. The verse also alludes to the interpretation of our Rabbis[8] [who said] that the *heads of the tribes* have a special function and power in vows over and above the rest of the people, namely, that a single person who is an expert in the laws can release a person from a vow [and therefore, this section was addressed to the heads of the tribes, i.e., the Sages].

Now the [power of] release from vows [by a Sage] is not expressly stated in the Torah, but it is a law declared to Moses on Sinai, and Scripture "hung it on a hair's-breadth," just as the Rabbis have said: [9] "[The rules concerning] the release from vows [by a Sage] hover in the air, and have nothing [in Scripture itself] on which they can be based." But Scripture did allude to it [by saying]: *'lo yacheil'* (*he shall not*

(6) Above, 2:3. (7) Further, 34:17. (8) Nedarim 78a. (9) Chagigah 10a. — Now although these rules concerning the release from vows by a Sage "have nothing [in Scripture itself] on which they can be based," they are yet on an absolute par with those laws which do have support in Scripture, as "they are all the essentials of the Torah" (*ibid.*, 11b).

profane) his word.[10] For it did not say: "he shall not *transgress* his word." but commanded that he should not make "profane" his word, meaning that he should not treat the vow as a hollow [and irreverent] thing; and when he comes to the court and they find him a cause for absolution[11] and he regrets [having made the vow], and they release him thereof, he is not profaning it.[9] And the reason for this [law being indicated in this manner of allusion] is as I have said [above], that Scripture treated absolution from a vow or oath as if it were one of the secrets of the Torah which are only to be revealed to those who are fit to [hear] them, and therefore they are written [in the Torah] in allusion. And this section [of vows] is placed here [in the Torah] because since [in the section above] He mentioned vows to the Sanctuary, [as it is said], *beside your vows, and your freewill offerings, whether they be your burnt-offerings, or your meal-offerings, or your drink-offerings, or your peace-offerings,*[12] therefore He said furthermore: "Apart from these above-mentioned vows, there are also vows of a secular nature. [In the case of these vows, too], *according to all that proceedeth out of* a man's *mouth*[10] he is obliged to fulfill, and to do all with which he bound his soul; for in [the case of] all vows [whether of a holy or secular nature] *he shall not profane his word,*[10] but others may absolve it for him" [by finding him a cause for absolution, as explained above].

3. IF A MAN 'YIDOR NEDER' (VOWETH A VOW). "[This means if] a person says: 'May there be *konam*[13] upon me that I shall

(10) Verse 3. (11) Thus, for example, if a man vows or swears that he will divorce his wife, the court may say to him: "Had you known that people would say about you: 'Such is the nature of this person to divorce his wife,' and that they will say about your daughters: 'They are the daughters of a divorced woman! What did her mother do that she was divorced?' [Had you known all this], would you then have made your vow?" If he says, "Had I known this I would not have made my vow," they may release him from his vow (Nedarim 66a). See also Note 44 further on. (12) Above, 29:39. (13) The word *konam* is a substitute for *korban* (offering), and is used for a vow of abstinence, meaning, "May this object be forbidden to me in the same way as it is forbidden to have any benefit from a holy offering."

not eat, or that I shall not do such-and-such a thing.' I might think that even [if he vowed] that he would eat *n'veilah*[14] [which is forbidden by the Torah to be eaten] I apply to him [the verse], *he shall do according to all that proceedeth out of his mouth.*[10] Scripture therefore says, *to bind his soul with a bond,*[10] which means [that he has the power] to forbid [upon himself] that which was [hitherto] permitted to him, but not to allow himself to do that which is forbidden [by means of vowing to do it]." This is Rashi's language. But the text of the Sifre[15] is not so. Instead the Rabbis taught there [the following explanation] of [the expression] *to bind his soul with a bond:*[10] "I might think that even if 'he swore'[16] to eat *n'veiloth* and *treifoth,*[14] abominable things and reptiles, I apply to him [the verse], *he shall do according to all that proceedeth out of his mouth.*[10] Scripture therefore says, *to bind his soul with a bond,*[10] which means [that he has the power] to forbid [upon himself] that which was [hitherto] permitted to him, but not to bind himself to do that which is forbidden [by means of vowing to do that which is prohibited by the Torah]." Thus the Rabbis [in the Sifre] mentioned this matter in connection with *shevuoth* (oaths), and the Rabbi [Rashi] changed it to apply to *nedarim* (vows).[17] And in my opinion he was not mindful [about this],[18] for the Rabbis have said[19] that in the case of vows one

(14) *N'veilah* is an animal that has died a natural death, or was not properly slaughtered. *Treifah* is an animal suffering from a certain serious organic disease, even if it is properly slaughtered. Both are forbidden to be eaten by law of the Torah. See Vol. III, p. 343, Note 96. (15) Sifre, *Matoth* 153. (16) The words "he swore" show clearly that the Sifre is speaking about an oath, while Rashi applied it to a vow. (17) The language of the verse before us is as follows: *If a man 'voweth a vow' unto the Eternal, or 'sweareth an oath' to bind his soul with a bond.* Ramban's intent is to point out that Rashi, who made his comment on the phrase *if a man voweth a vow,* and speaks of *konam* [a term used *only* in *vows*], is diverging from the Sifre who gives this explanation on the phrase *or sweareth an oath.* Since, as will be explained further on, there are important legal differences between vows and oaths, Rashi's application of the Sifre to the case of a vow [instead of to *an oath*] is thus incorrect. (18) In my "Kuntros on Variant Readings in Rashi according to the first print, Reggio 1475," p. 27 (printed in Berliner's Rashi, Feldheim, Jerusalem, 5730) I have shown that on the basis of a minor emendation in the text of Rashi [as found in the Reggio edition], Ramban's criticism of Rashi disappears. (19) Nedarim 2b.

makes the [actual] object [referred to in the vow] forbidden to oneself [as when one says: "May this bread be *konam*[13] upon me"], and therefore [vows] do not take effect upon non-tangible matters,[20] such as when one says, "A vow be upon me that I shall not speak to you, or that I shall not walk, or that I shall not sleep," and similar expressions [affecting non-tangible matters]. Now this being so, it would appear that even in the case of a permitted object, if one said: "A vow be upon me that I shall eat today," or "that I shall eat this loaf," it is not a [valid] vow since this vow does not have any object at all on which to take effect, but [was expressed in such a way as to impose] a duty upon him [*personally*] to do it.[21] And we do not find mentioned anywhere in the Gemara *vows* about [matters which require one] to "get up and do" [a particular action, but only about matters which require one to *abstain* from certain things, such as when he says, "May this loaf be *konam* upon me," in which case he must fulfill the vow by *not* eating it]. And although we find in the case of vows [to G-d Who is] on high [that they *are* valid if uttered in the following manner]: "I undertake upon myself [to bring] a burnt-offering,"[22] or "I undertake upon myself [to bring] a peace-offering" [which would seem to indicate that vows *do* take effect when expressed as an obligation resting upon a person, and not, as explained above, that they only take effect upon a specific *object* which itself becomes forbidden], this [vow is valid]

(20) *Ibid.*, 13b. (21) In other words, there is no question as to when a person "vows" to eat *n'veilah* [which is forbidden] that it is invalid, but even if he "vowed" to eat a permissible thing it is also invalid, since we do not find anywhere in the Gemara *vows* about matters which require one "to get up and do," but only matters which require one to *abstain* from certain things. On the other hand, in the case of an "oath," as where one says "I *swear* to eat this loaf," the oath would indeed be valid. Since Rashi applied it to "vows," it is therefore incorrect, as explained above. — The reason for this distinction between oaths and vows is as follows: An oath takes effect upon the person himself. Hence if he says, "*I swear* to eat the loaf," he is obliged to do so. But a vow takes effect upon the object. Hence if he says, "*This bread is 'konam'* to me," it is a valid vow and he may not eat it. But if he were to say, "A *vow* be upon me that I shall eat this loaf," it would be invalid, since it is a contradiction in terms [the statement begins with a reference to a *vow*, but concludes with — "I shall eat . . ." — which is appropriate only for an *oath*]. (22) Kinim 1:1.

because [there is a general principle that] dedicating something [verbally] to the Sanctuary creates an obligation on one's property exactly as if it had been handed over to an ordinary person.[23] Or [it may be that] this is a stringency[24] applicable [only] to vows to the Sanctuary, because they [such vows] involve an object which becomes forbidden to an ordinary person and invested [with sanctity] for the Sanctuary when [the object is actually] set aside [as an offering]; therefore right from the start [when he merely bound himself verbally to separate an animal as an offering at some future date], the obligation created by the vow takes effect upon his property. But the case of [ordinary] vows of utterance [about a secular matter] we have no such rule, because there is no [tangible] object existing at all, neither at the beginning [i.e., at the time of uttering the vow], nor at the end [i.e., at the time that the vow is to be fulfilled]. Similarly, [the expression of the Sifre mentioned by Rashi that] he can "forbid [upon himself] that which was [hitherto] permitted to him, but cannot allow himself to do that which is forbidden [by vowing to do that which is prohibited by the Torah]" is a statement which is not correct to make in connection with *vows* [as Rashi did], because they *do* take effect on matters of [religious] commandments, just as they do on secular matters [i.e., on matters which do not come within the scope of the commandments]. Thus someone who says in the form of a *vow* "I will not make a Booth [for the Festival of Tabernacles]" or "I will not put on phylacteries" is indeed forbidden [to make the Booth, or to put on the phylacteries] although he thereby violates a positive

(23) Therefore when he says, "I undertake upon myself [to bring] a burnt-offering," it is as if he had actually separated a specific animal to be an offering. Thus his vow attaches to a definite object, and therefore it is valid. (24) In other words, even if we are not to resort to the preceding explanation that a verbal promise to the Sanctuary is tantamount to *actual delivery* of the object, we may yet explain the reason why vows to the Sanctuary are valid, because of a stringency ordained by the Rabbis based on the fact that since *ultimately* he will set aside a specific animal for his offering, therefore the effect of the vow takes place immediately upon his utterance thereof, and all his property becomes mortgaged to the fulfillment of the vow.

commandment.[25] Similarly a man who *vowed* not to have [sexual] intercourse with his wife is forbidden [to have such intercourse with her] although he thereby violates a negative commandment.[26] Similarly, *vows* take effect to oblige one to observe a negative commandment [although, of course, he already is bound not to transgress it], such as if he vowed not to eat *n'veilah*[14] — [so that if he does it he violates two prohibitions: against eating *n'veilah,* and against breaking his vow, this principle being deduced] from the words of the Mishnah:[27] "A vow may take effect upon a vow etc."

Thus a vow takes effect to forbid [not only that which was previously permitted, but also to forbid] that which was [already] forbidden [such as when he vows not to eat *n'veilah*][14], and [a vow takes effect] not to do [something] which he is [commanded to do and] forbidden to transgress [such as the duty to have sexual intercourse with his wife,[26] as mentioned above], except that vows do not take effect to allow him to *actively* transgress a negative commandment.[28] But oaths are *only* able to render forbidden that which was [hitherto] permitted, and they do not apply at all to matters involving commandments, neither to transgress [the prohibition of] a negative commandment

(25) The reason for this is that since a vow takes effect upon a particular object (see Note 21), he may forbid the use of the particular Booth or of the phylacteries in the fulfillment of the commandment. But he cannot prohibit their use by means of an oath, swearing not to use them, since the oath creates a prohibition on the person, and that is invalid for him to do, since "he has already sworn on Sinai" to fulfill the commandment, and an oath does not take effect upon another oath, as will be explained. (26) Exodus 21:10: *her food, her raiment, and 'her conjugal rights' he shall not diminish.* See Vol. II, pp. 356-357, where Ramban discusses at length the nature of this prohibition. (27) Nedarim 17a. The Mishnah there establishes the distinction that a vow may take effect upon another vow, but one oath may not take effect upon another. From this Ramban deduces the teaching that if *an object* is prohibited to a person for some reason, such as *n'veilah* or *treifah* (see Note 14 above), or indeed any other prohibition, another vow — *not* to eat it — can still take effect upon that object doubly prohibiting the person from eating it, so that if he does eat it, he violates two prohibitions: one for having eaten *n'veilah,* and one for having violated his vow. (28) Thus if he vowed *to eat* the flesh of *n'veilah* which is prohibited by a negative commandment, the vow takes no effect whatever, so that if he does not eat it he is not punishable for having violated his word.

[even passively, such as by swearing not to have intercourse with his wife], nor to strengthen its observance [such as by swearing not to eat *n'veilah*],[14] nor to neglect [the performance of] a positive commandment, such as [by saying]: "I swear that I will not make a Booth," or "[I swear] that I will not put on phylacteries." Even to strengthen the performance of a positive commandment [an oath] cannot take effect, so that if a person swears to fulfill a commandment and does not fulfill it, he is not liable for [breaking his] oath either to [the punishment of] stripes [if he deliberately neglects it] or to [bring] an offering [if he neglects it accidentally].[29] But it is permitted for a person to encourage himself [to fulfill a commandment by swearing to do so], for it is written, *I have sworn, and have confirmed it, to observe Thy righteous ordinances.*[30] Therefore it is only with reference to swearing [and *not,* as implied by Rashi, to vows] that one can interpret [the expression] *to bind his soul with a bond*[10] [as the Sifre does, that he may forbid upon himself that which was hitherto permitted to him, but may not allow himself to do that which is forbidden, by means of swearing to do it]. These are great [i.e., complex and important] laws, and the scholar will find them [explained in the Talmud] in their [proper] places.

YIDOR NEDER LA'SHEM (VOWETH A VOW 'UNTO' THE ETERNAL). The meaning of [the expression] *'yidor neder la'shem'* is not like that of *'asher nishba la'shem* (*how he*—David — *swore 'unto' the Eternal*),[31] for that [expression mentioned by David] is like

(29) The punishment for breaking an oath in optional matters deliberately is the same as for transgressing any negative commandment; i.e., stripes (Deuteronomy 25:1-3), and for accidentally breaking it, there is a duty to bring an offering (Leviticus 5:4-13). But if one swears to fulfill a positive commandment [e.g. "I swear to wear phylacteries"] the oath is invalid, because "he has already sworn at Mount Sinai" [to perform all the commandments of the Torah], and an oath does not take effect upon another oath (see Note 27). Therefore if he does *not* fulfill the commandment, he is responsible for neglect of a positive commandment, but is not subject to stripes or an offering for failure of fulfilling the additional oath, since his oath never took effect. (30) Psalms 119:106. See Nedarim 8a. (31) *Ibid.,* 132:2.

'vayishava lo' (and he swore 'to him')[32] which means that he swore to him for his [the recipient's] benefit. But [the use of the prepositional *lamed* in the case of vows is equivalent to the use of the preposition *beth* ("by")[33] in the case of oaths, for] in the case of oaths Scripture says: *'u'vishmo' (and 'by' His Name) shalt thou swear;*[34] *v'ashbiacha 'ba'shem' (and I will make thee swear 'by' the Eternal)*;[35] *as I swore 'lecha' (unto thee) 'ba'shem' ('by' the Eternal), the G-d of Israel, saying: Assuredly Solomon thy son shall reign after me;*[36] *swear 'li' (unto me) here 'bei'Elokim' ('by' G-d).*[37] But in the case of a vow Scripture does not say: "he vows *'ba'shem'* ('by' G-d)" but *la'shem* ('to' G-d). The Sages in the Sifre have already alluded to the reason for this matter [the different terminology], saying: [38] "What is the difference between vows and oaths? Vows are like vowing[39] 'by the life of the King;' oaths are like swearing 'by the King Himself.' Although there is

(32) This is in reference either to Genesis 24:9, where Eliezer swore to Abraham to find a wife for Isaac from the country of his birthplace, or to Genesis 47:31, Joseph swearing to Jacob that he would bury him together with his fathers. In both cases the meaning of the prepositional *lamed* [*'lo'*] is its literal meaning — "unto him," and the intention is to say that the oath was "for his benefit." Likewise the prepositional *lamed* [in the word *la'shem*] used by David has its literal meaning — "for 'the benefit' [so to say] and glory of G-d," since the oath concerned his determination to build the House of G-d. (33) The gist of Ramban's reasoning is as follows: The prepositional *lamed* in the case of *oaths* [in the examples cited above] has the meaning of "to" — to the benefit of the recipient, as is the case of Eliezer where the oath was for the benefit of Abraham. This principle, however, cannot be made to apply to vows, since in our verse it says *if a man vows a vow 'la'shem,'* and the verse is *not* speaking exclusively about vows to the benefit of the Sanctuary but refers to vows of all sorts, even of secular matters. Hence we must say that the prepositional *lamed* in *vows* has the same meaning as the *beth* [not the *lamed*] in *oaths,* which in both cases means "by" — by G-d. In other words, the prepositional *lamed* in *vows* and the *beth* in *oaths* are identical in meaning. Finally, Ramban will conclude that the Cabala does offer an explanation why a different preposition is used in each case. Thus it is shown that the mystic character of the Sacred Language is deeply embedded in the text of the Torah. (34) Deuteronomy 6:13. (35) Genesis 24:3. (36) I Kings 1:30. (37) Genesis 21:23. (38) Sifre, *Matoth* 153. See Vol. I, p. 66, where Ramban quotes this Sifre. (39) This is the text in the Sifre and in Ramban here. In Genesis, however, Ramban has "swearing" (Vol. I, p. 66). The intent of the texts in both places is equivalent.

no [clear] proof for this explanation [in Scripture], there is an allusion to it: *By the living G-d, and by the life of your soul. I will not leave thee.*"[40] And the secret thereof is that the *shevuah* (oath) is derived from the word *shivah* ["seven" — alluding to the seven Emanations], for *she* [wisdom] *hath builded her house, she hath hewn out her seven pillars,*[41] whereas the vow is on [the level of] understanding, *the beginning of His way, the first of His works of old.*[42] Thus you find that vows take precedence over the Torah, and therefore they apply to commandments just as to optional matters [as explained above]. Thus all vows are *la'shem* ("to" the Eternal), whereas all who swear [do so] "by" Him.

4. AND IF A WOMAN VOWETH A VOW UNTO THE ETERNAL . . . 5. AND HER FATHER HEARETH HER VOW. Scripture wanted to mention the [case of] prohibition first [in Verses 4-5, namely that if she makes a vow and her father is quiet about it or confirms it, *then all her vows shall stand* . .] in order to tell us that a young girl [in her father's house] is also subject to the negative commandment mentioned [previously], that *he shall not break his word,*[10] and therefore if her father confirms her vow [expressly or tacitly] the vow shall *stand,* but if he disallowed her, it *shall not stand.*[43] And Scripture states [in conclusion], *and the Eternal will forgive her, because her father disallowed her,*[43] in order to tell us that G-d *will* only *forgive her* if she acted [in disregard of her vow] *after* her father had disallowed it, but not [if she broke it] at the beginning, that is, if she [first] transgressed her vow and later on her father disallowed it, just as the Rabbis have said: "[The father or husband] 'cuts off' [the vow from the moment that he disallows it], but [unlike a Sage] he does not uproot it retrospectively."[44]

(40) II Kings 4:30. See Vol. I, p. 66, Note 290 where this text is explained in detail. (41) Proverbs 9:1. (42) *Ibid.,* 8:22. (43) Verse 6. (44) Nedarim 68a. The intention of this statement is to contrast the law, of a Sage who "releases" a vow, with that of a father or husband who "annuls" it. In order that a vow or oath should be valid, the person who makes it must at the time of the utterance thereof have been

7. AND IF SHE WERE AT ALL [BETROTHED] TO A MAN, AND THERE ARE VOWS UPON HER. In the opinion of our Rabbis[45] Scripture [here] is saying: *"and if she,* this woman [mentioned above in Verses 4-6] *were at all [betrothed] to a man, and bound herself by a bond, being in her father's house, in her youth*[46] — *and there are vows upon her,* meaning that her father had not heard them, so that they were neither annulled nor confirmed, *and her [betrothed] husband hears* them as well [as her father who hears them now when she is betrothed], then *he makes void her vow,*[47] signifying that he also joins [now] with the father in annulling her vows [that *are upon her*]." And the phrase *she were at all 'to a man'* means that she is [promised] unto him but [still] is in her father's house, and has not yet come to his [the man's] house, and [hence] this must refer to a betrothed girl, for Scripture calls her too, *the wife of his fellow.*[48] Now our Rabbis did not explain [that this verse refers to a fully-married wife, and teaches] that a husband himself can annul the vows of his *married* wife which she "brought along" from her father's house to his house, as would seem the simple meaning of the verse, for if that were so, why would Scripture have to repeat itself and say [in Verse 11], *And if a woman vowed in her husband's house,* for if he can annul [even] those vows which preceded [his marriage to her], surely [he can

fully aware of its consequences. If at that time he did not fully understand all that his vow or oath entailed, the Sage points this out to him and affords him an opportunity to regret having made it. If he so declares that he regrets it, the Sage "releases" him from the vow or oath. This release "uproots it" from the very start, since it has now been shown that he made it under a misapprehension. The father or husband, on the other hand, is empowered by the Torah to "annul" the vow or oath, even if made under no misapprehension and the daughter or wife does not regret it. Therefore there is no power of retroactive effect; instead, the "annulment" only "cuts off" in the future. One of the differences between these two procedures is here referred to by Ramban, and that is namely, if the person who made the vow or oath violates it *before* the time of "release" or "annulment." In the case of the release by the Sage, since it takes effect retrospectively, there is no sin. In the case of the father or the husband, however, there is a sin entailed. (45) Nedarim 71a. (46) Verse 4. (47) Verse 9. (48) Deuteronomy 22:23. Thus she is already called the *wife* of the man to whom she is betrothed, in the same way that here he is described as her *ish* (man) — literally "husband."

annul] those vows which [she makes whilst she is] in his house![49] And [even without resorting to this reasoning], it is the tradition [of the Rabbis] which decides [the true meaning of the verses].

14. EVERY VOW, AND EVERY BINDING OATH TO AFFLICT THE SOUL, [HER HUSBAND MAY ESTABLISH IT, AND HER HUSBAND MAY MAKE IT VOID]. "Since He had said [in the preceding verses] that a husband may annul [his wife's vows], I might think that this includes all her vows! Scripture therefore says, *to afflict the soul,* meaning that he can only annul vows which afflict the soul, and they are explained in Tractate Nedarim." These are the words of Rashi. But his language here is [too] concise, because a husband annuls vows which afflict the soul, such as [if she vows] "The fruits of the world be forbidden to me," or even if she [only] vowed that she would not taste one of all the kinds [of fruits]; and likewise he may annul matters [which concern the relationship] between himself and his wife, even if they do not involve affliction of the soul, such as [if she swore] "I will not paint [my eyes]" or "I will not put powder on my face," or "I will not have sexual intercourse," these being matters about which He said, *between a man and his wife,*[50] as is explained in the last chapter of Tractate Nedarim.[51] Such is also the law with respect to the father himself, as we have been taught in the Sifre: [52] "I only know that a husband may annul vows [which concern the relationship] between himself and his wife, and vows which afflict the soul, [to the exclusion of other vows which he may not annul]. Whence

(49) So why, then would the Torah state the obvious (in Verse 11): *And if* a woman *vowed in her husband's house* etc.? It must be because Verses 7-9 speak about a *betrothed* woman, in which case both the father and the betrothed do jointly annul her vow. "If the father revoked the vow but not the betrothed, or if the betrothed revoked it but not the father, the vow is not revoked. Still less need it be said if one of them explicitly confirmed the vow" (Nedarim 67a). — It should be noted that the term "betrothed" in this connection has reference to the actual "betrothal" of a man to a woman to be his wife [not a mere "engagement"]. In the eyes of the Jewish law she is then considered his wife, except that the consummation of the marriage takes place some time after the betrothal. (50) Further, Verse 17. (51) Nedarim 79b. (52) Sifre, *Matoth* 155.

do I know that the father [is similarly limited in his rights]? You can reason [in the following manner] etc. . . But I have not succeeded in establishing [the father's law] by reason. Therefore Scripture says: *These are the statutes, which the Eternal commanded Moses, between a man and his wife, between a father and his daughter.*[50] [This teaches us that] we must of necessity compare the father to the husband, so that just as the husband may only annul vows [which concern the relationship] between himself and his wife, and matters which involve affliction of the soul, so also the father may only annul matters [which concern the laws] between him and her,[53] and matters which involve affliction of the soul." It is also taught in this way in the Gemara Yerushalmi of Tractate Nedarim.[54]

16. [BUT IF HE SHALL MAKE THEM NULL AFTER THAT HE HATH HEARD THEM], THEN HE SHALL BEAR HER INIQUITY — "he [the husband] takes her place.[55] Thus we learn that one who causes somebody else to commit an offense takes the place of that person with respect to all punishments [which that person would otherwise incur]." This is Rashi's language, taken from the Sifre.[56] It would appear that this woman [broke her vow] in error or was misled, for Scripture speaks [here] of a husband who heard [his wife's vow and did *not* annul it on that day], and the wife does not know about this, and after some time he "annulled" [the vow, although he in fact no longer had the power to do so], and told her that [he annulled it] *in the day he heard it.*[57] Thus Scripture teaches us two things: that the husband *bears her iniquity* as if he had made a vow and profaned his word, and that she is totally free and not liable to any of the punishments [found elsewhere] for errors.[58] But if the wife knows that he [her husband] did not annul it *in the day he heard it,*[57] and she is

(53) Such as if she vows not to give him the wages for her work. (54) Yerushalmi Nedarim XI, 1. For "Yerushalmi" see Vol. III, p. 192, Note 44. (55) According to Rashi the verse speaks about a case where the husband confirmed his wife's vow, and then on the same day annulled it, which he can no longer do. If she only heard about the annulment but not about the confirmation, and therefore unknowingly violated her oath — he *bears her iniquity.* Ramban presents another interpretation. (56) Sifre, *Matoth* 156. (57) Above, Verse 15. (58) See Ramban on Leviticus 1:4, (towards the end).

versed in this law [that he only has a right to annul her vows on the day that he hears it, and not later, and nonetheless she breaks her vow], then she is the guilty one, and [since] the husband did not cause the offense, therefore his punishment is [only] like that of someone who can protest [at another person committing a sin] and does not protest.

Now Scripture mentions this case with reference to a husband [misleading his wife to think that he annulled her vow *in the day he heard it,*[57] when in actual fact he "annulled" it only afterwards when he no longer had the right to], although the same law applies to a father [and his daughter's vows], because Scripture speaks of normal circumstances, that a father usually guards himself against doing this because of his love for his daughter, whereas a husband might perhaps hate his wife and think that he will make her guilty [by misleading her to break her vow]. Now Rabbi Abraham ibn Ezra wrote: "*Then he shall bear her iniquity,* because she is under his control." If so, the verse is speaking of a case where he forces her to do that *which she has bound herself*[47] [not to do, and it is then that *he shall bear her iniquity*]. But it is not correct [since the same laws obviously apply when he misleads her without actually forcing her].

31 2. AVENGE THE CHILDREN OF ISRAEL OF THE MIDIANITES; AFTERWARD SHALT THOU BE GATHERED UNTO THY PEOPLE. It was decreed upon our teacher Moses not to cross over the Jordan, but on the other [eastern] side of the Jordan he fulfilled all the commandments [that were necessary] for Israel. Thus he conquered the two great Amorite kings, and divided their land up as an inheritance [amongst the tribes of Reuben, Gad, and half of the tribe of Menasheh], and it was he who was worthy of executing vengeance upon the enemies of the Eternal, leaving Joshua only the commandment of [conquering and dividing] the Land. Furthermore [this commandment was given to Moses because] the Holy One, blessed be He, gave him honor so that *the righteous shall rejoice when he seeth the vengeance,*[59] this being the meaning of *afterward shalt*

(59) Psalms 58:11 — Since the Midianites had enticed the people of Israel to immorality and the worship of Baal-peor (see Ramban above *Balak* 25:1, and *Pinchas*

thou be gathered unto thy people. And Moses showed honor to Phinehas[60] because he had begun the meritorious task [of punishing the Midianites, by killing Cozbi][61] and it was up to him to finish it, and therefore he appointed him the anointed priest for this war.[62] It was not fitting that Eleazar should go [as the anointed priest of the war], because he was the High Priest [after the death of Aaron].[63]

6. AND MOSES SENT THEM, A THOUSAND OF EVERY TRIBE. He did not send all the members of the army there, although the Midianites were a large people, *and their cities were fortified, and very large.*[64] The reason for this is that those who had sinned with the Moabite women were many, and they were not fit *to execute the vengeance of the Eternal;*[65] therefore they chose those men who were known amongst their tribes as righteous men.[66] Now Moses did not command them what to do, but merely told them *to execute the vengeance of the Eternal on Midian,*[65] and he thought that they would *let none of them remain or escape,*[67] but [would *execute the vengeance of the Eternal*] like the vengeance [they were commanded] in connection with Amalek or the vengeance [they were commanded] in connection with the seven nations [of the land of Canaan]. And therefore when Moses saw that they had spared the women and children and the cattle, he was angry about [the fact that they had left alive] the women who had had sexual intercourse, because the officers of the army should have killed them as the very first thing, both as execution of the vengeance [which they were now commanded to do], and in performance of the general law of the Torah [that a living thing which causes a man to sin must be killed, as it is said], *and ye shall slay*

25:11) the triumph of right over evil was thus a source of rejoicing to *the righteous* one [Moses]. (60) Verse 6. (61) Above, 25:15. (62) See Deuteronomy 20:2. (63) Above, 20:28 — The position of the anointed priest of the war was always distinct from that of the High Priest (see Rambam, Hilchoth Klei Hamikdash, Chapter 3). Hence "it was not fitting," as Ramban expresses it, that Eleazar the High Priest should go with the army and function in the role of the anointed priest of the war. (64) *Ibid.,* 13:28. (65) Verse 3. (66) See Deuteronomy 1:13. (67) Joshua 8:22.

the beast.[68] And when he saw that the people wanted [to keep] the spoil, he remitted [and allowed them to keep] the female children[69] and the spoil.[70]

It is also possible to explain that Moses was [only] commanded to *Harass the Midianites,* and *Avenge the children of Israel of the Midianites,*[71] [but was not commanded to destroy them all like Amalek and the seven nations]. Therefore he sent only a small contingent [twelve thousand men] to strike at *the unwalled towns*[72] *and fell every good tree, and stop all fountains of water, and mar every good piece of land with stones*[73] as spoilers usually do, and he did not give them any specific commands except that they should execute whatever vengeance they were able to do — and G-d, blessed be He, Who controls [the course of all] battles, gave the Midianites and their [five] kings and cities into their hands. Therefore Moses was only angry about [their sparing] the women who had had sexual intercourse, and [he was] not angry about anything else,[74] and his command [to kill] the male children[75] was an [additional measure of] retributive punishment.

Now *Moses was wroth with the officers of the host*[76] but showed honor to Phinehas [by not criticizing him, too], because G-d had given *unto him* His *covenant of peace.*[77] And in the Sifre we are taught:[78] "Phinehas said to Moses: As you have commanded us, so have we done." But I do not know what this statement means, since according to the Scriptural verses [here] Moses did not command them anything specific, for had he commanded them something which [as Phinehas said] they fulfilled, how could he [Moses] have been angry with them? [We cannot say that he was angry because they did not do *everything*

(68) Leviticus 20:15. (69) Further, Verse 18. (70) *Ibid.,* Verse 20. (71) Above, 25:17, and Verse 2 of this Chapter. (72) Deuteronomy 3:5. (73) II Kings 3:19. (74) Thus, according to this second explanation, Moses originally did not command them to destroy everything, but only to *harass the Midianites* as a form of vengeance. Hence we understand why he was not angry about their sparing the children and spoil, but only about their sparing the grown-up women who had caused the sin. (75) Verse 17. (76) Verse 14. (77) Above, 25:12.. (78) Sifre, *Matoth* 157.

that he told them to,] because had he commanded them, Heaven forbid that [we say that] Phinehas would transgress his command! Saul lost his kingdom on account of such disobedience![79] But the [explanation of the matter] is as I have said, that Moses [merely] commanded them *to execute the vengeance of the Eternal on Midian,*[65] and Phinehas told him: "We have executed great vengeance on them." It is also possible to explain that Phinehas told Moses: "Just as you charged us with the law of the Torah given at Mount Sinai, namely, *When thou shalt besiege a city* etc.[80] so have we done to them." And Moses was angry about [their sparing] the adult women, because, *Behold, these caused the children of Israel* etc.,[81] and he added [the command to kill] *every male among the little ones*[75] in order to complete the retribution.

19. WHOSOEVER HATH KILLED ANY PERSON, AND WHOSOEVER HATH TOUCHED ANY SLAIN, [PURIFY YOURSELVES ON THE THIRD DAY AND ON THE SEVENTH DAY]. "Rabbi Meir says: Scripture is speaking about someone who killed with an object which is susceptible of impurity, and the verse [here] teaches you that the object [i.e., the weapon] renders the person impure through [indirect] contact with the corpse as if he had touched the corpse itself.[82] I might think that even if he shot an arrow at him and killed him [the same law applies]; Scripture therefore says, *and whosoever hath killed any person [and whosoever hath touched any slain]*.[83] Thus it compares a person who kills to a person who touches. Just as he who touches [is rendered impure] by virtue of that contact [with the corpse], so is the person who kills [rendered impure] by virtue of his contact [with the corpse, effected through the weapon he holds

(79) I Samuel 13:14. (80) Deuteronomy 20:19. In the context of Ramban's remarks here, it would seem that the reference is to Verses 10-14 *ibid: When thou drawest nigh unto a city to fight against it . . . but the women, and the little ones, and the cattle . . . thou shalt take.* It was this law which was Phinehas' defense. (81) Verse 16. (82) The implication is that the sword is itself "a progenitor of fathers of impurity" like the corpse, and the person who touches the sword becomes a "father of impurity," who is rendered impure and may not enter the Divine camp for seven days. See above, *Seder Chukath,* Note 40. (83) Verse 19.

in his hand, which contact is non-existent when he shoots an arrow and kills him]." Thus far is the language of Rashi.

But his words are not clear to me. For if he killed with an object which is susceptible to impurity but can be [made pure] by immersion,[84] then the person touching it does *not* contract the seven-day period of impurity, nor does he require the sprinkling [of the waters of purification], since the object [with which he killed] becomes "a father of impurity,"[85] and the person who becomes impure through it, becomes a "first degree of impurity" [who is only required to immerse himself in a ritual pool and he becomes pure the evening of that same day; and since the verse here requires a seven-day period of impurity, it cannot be referring to such a case]. And if [he killed him] with a *metal* instrument, we have already been taught[86] that a sword [or any metal object with which a person is killed] is exactly the same degree of impurity as the dead person himself,[82] and therefore conveys a seven-days' impurity [to anyone who touches it, so there is no need for our verse to repeat this principle]. And if the Rabbi [Rashi] is of the opinion that since he [the killer] touched the instrument *whilst* it was itself still in contact with the corpse [then even if it was *not* a metal object] it renders him impure for a seven-day period just as [if he had touched] the corpse itself — such [conveyance of a stricter degree of] impurity through [indirect] contact is only a law of the Rabbis when the contact is that of objects with a corpse, as is explained in Tractate Neziruth, Chapter *Shloshah Minim*.[87]

(84) This term includes all vessels except those made of earthenware, which, once rendered impure, cannot be purified by immersion in a ritual pool or by any other means. All other vessels can be so purified. (85) See above, *Seder Chukath,* Note 40, for an explanation of this subject. (86) Above 19:16. See Ramban there. (87) Literally: "Three things" [the opening words of that particular chapter of the Tractate]. The text referred to here is found in Nazir 42b: "But is [the law that the corpse conveys] impurity [to a human being] by contact [with an object which touches the corpse at the same time as touching the human being] a Scriptural law? [It is only a law of the Rabbis!] "It is obvious, therefore, that the *Scriptural* verses here cannot be speaking of such a case. Hence Rashi's comment "that the verse [here] teaches you that the object renders the person impure through contact etc." cannot be the correct explanation of this verse.

But the language of the Rabbis in the Sifre is as follows: [88] "Rabbi Meir says: Scripture is speaking about someone who killed with an object which is susceptible to impurity, and [teaches us that] it conveys impurity by moving [the corpse, as will be explained further on]. Or I might think that even if he shot an arrow at him and killed him [the same law applies]; Scripture therefore says etc."[89] And the meaning of [this Sifre] is that Rabbi Meir came to deduce from here [the principle] that a human corpse conveys impurity when carried. Thus if he killed him with a walking-stick or a spear, even if it did not consist of metal, and he was "carried," [i.e., the slain person was moved] through them,[90] at the time of death, the corpse conveys impurity of seven-days' duration to the person who "carried" [i.e., moved] it. And when [using the phrase] "an object which is susceptible to impurity," Rabbi Meir was not referring to a vessel which forms a receptacle [and is therefore susceptible to impurity] but to an object through which the person receives impurity [directly] from the corpse itself,[91] such as by "carrying" [i.e., moving it]. And the beginning of this Beraitha there [in the Sifre] states as follows: [88] "Whence do we know that it [a corpse] conveys impurity by shaking it? You make use of a *kal vachomer:* [92] If a

(88) Sifre, *Chukath* 127. (89) "*And whosoever hath killed any person, and whosoever hath touched any slain.* Thus it compares etc. "[as quoted by Ramban from Rashi's commentary]. (90) This is known as *tumath heset* — "the impurity caused by shaking" an impure object [such as *n'veilah,* or a human corpse] so as to move it from its place. Such movement, even if done in an indirect manner, is sufficient to convey impurity, just as if it had been carried directly. (91) In other words, Rabbi Meir's statement [quoted by Rashi] does not refer to *a vessel* forming a receptacle but to an object through which *the person* becomes impure from the corpse itself by shifting or shaking it, even if the person did not touch or carry the corpse at all, since causing an impure object to move or to shake is subject to the same law as carrying it. This interpretation of Rabbi Meir's meaning is made clear by the first part of the Beraitha, which Ramban now brings, and which Rashi did not quote. Ramban in conclusion proceeds to explain that although the anonymous opinion in the first part of the Beraitha agrees with Rabbi Meir on the main principle referred to here, that causing a corpse to move also conveys impurity of seven-days' duration — they disagree on the process of reasoning which establishes this principle, as Ramban explains. (92) The syllogism of "a minor and major" [*a fortiori* argument]. See Ramban, Vol. II, p. 133, Note 208.

dead animal that conveys a non-stringent form of impurity [since it conveys impurity only until the evening of the same day] nonetheless conveys impurity by being moved, is it not logical that a human corpse that conveys a stringent form of impurity [i.e., an impurity of seven-days' duration] should convey impurity by being moved! But if so [you might argue] that just as there, the impurity conveyed [by moving the dead animal] is only until the evening, so here also [in the case of the human corpse], the impurity conveyed [by moving or shaking it] is only until the evening [of that day]! You must say that this cannot be so. Rather,] you must say that the law of moving it is the same as touching it. Where touching [the source of impurity] renders one impure for a seven-days' duration [as does touching a corpse], so also does moving it render one impure for a seven-days' duration, and where touching renders one only impure until the evening [as does touching a dead animal], moving it also renders one impure only until the evening. Rabbi Meir says etc." From here then, the meaning of the Beraitha becomes apparent, as we have explained it above: [91] Thus the First Sage [i.e., the anonymous Sage of the first part of the Sifre] deduced from a *kal vachomer*[92] the principle that carrying [or moving] a corpse [without touching it] conveys impurity even for a seven-days' duration, because he does not adopt [the principle of] *dayo*,[93] whereas

(93) Literally: "It is sufficient." This means that it is "sufficient" for a law to be derived by logical conclusion from another law to be only *as strict* as that law, but it cannot be *stricter* than the law from which it is derived. Thus, in the case before us, the law that causing *a corpse* to move conveys impurity, is derived — according to the First Sage of the Beraitha — from the law causing *a dead animal* to move. Hence if we apply the principle of *dayo* we must conclude that the impurity conveyed to one by causing a corpse to move is *only as strict* as causing a dead animal to move, namely, until the same evening. But since the anonymous First Sage recorded in the first half of the Beraitha clearly states that causing a corpse to move conveys a seven-days' duration of impurity, it is clear that he does *not* accept the principle of *dayo*. On the other hand, Rabbi Meir who accepts this principle of *dayo*, cannot therefore derive the law that causing a corpse to move conveys a seven-days' duration of impurity from the *kal vachomer* of the law of causing a dead animal to move. Hence he derives it from our verse which expressly likens the law of causing a corpse to move with that of touching it, in which latter case the impurity conveyed is that of a seven-days' duration. This is the gist of Ramban's explanation.

Rabbi Meir derived it from this verse [before us], because since he follows the principle of *dayo,*[93] therefore he cannot derive it by a *kal vachomer*[92] [from dead animals], as is stated in Tractate Baba Kamma, Chapter *Keitzad Haregel.*[94]

YE AND YOUR CAPTIVES. [This means that] the captives also have to purify their garments[95] which touched the slain, *and every garment and every vessel of skin*[96] which were in their possession, just as was the law with regard to the Israelites, in order that they would not defile the people with their garments and their vessels.

23. EVERY THING THAT MAY COME INTO THE FIRE YE SHALL PASS THROUGH THE FIRE AND IT SHALL BE CLEAN. A vessel which touched a human corpse or dead animal does *not* become purified by fire, since the immersion mentioned in the Torah is always in water. Therefore our Rabbis had to explain[97] that this purification [mentioned here by Scripture] refers to remove from them [the traces of] the forbidden foods which they had absorbed whilst they were in the possession of the non-Jews. This is the true [explanation] without any doubt.

AND ALL THAT COMETH NOT INTO THE FIRE — "anything which is not [normally] used on fire, such as cups, flasks, and pitchers which are used [to contain] cold substances, and [therefore] have not absorbed [any of the traces of forbidden foods] *ye shall pass through the water,* meaning that it is sufficient to immerse them." This is Rashi's language. But it does not appear to me to be correct, for the term *ta'aviru* (*ye shall pass through*) does not refer to immersion; for

(94) Baba Kamma 25a. — The heading of the chapter means literally: "How is the leg" of a beast an attested danger. The Gemara there records a difference of opinion among the Sages of the Mishnah whether we accept the principle of *dayo,* although Rabbi Meir's name is not specifically mentioned. (95) Since the captives were non-Jews to whom the laws of ritual impurity do not apply, the question arises: why Moses said: *purify yourselves . . . ye 'and your captives?'* Ramban therefore explains that this refers to their garments, as explained in the text. (96) Verse 20. (97) Abodah Zarah 75b.

[had this been the case], it would have said *"tavi'u* (ye shall put it) into water," which is the expression used in connection with immersion, just as it says, *it 'yuva' (must be put into) water, and it shall be unclean until the even, and then it shall be clean.*[98] Furthermore, even those vessels, which are only used for *cold* things [of forbidden foods] need purification from [the traces of] their forbidden foods in addition to this immersion [which Rashi mentioned], and how can it be that Scripture [here] does not mention the [method] of purification [for such vessels] as it did with reference to those vessels *that come into the fire*? And when the Sages deduced [the necessity for] this immersion they did not mention that the source for it was this [part of the] verse [quoted here by Rashi], but interpreted it[97] [on the basis of that part of the verse which says]: *"Nevertheless it shall be purified with the waters of 'niddah'*[99]—waters which are fit for a *niddah* (a menstruant woman) to immerse herself in."

But the meaning of *ye shall pass through the water* is that you should wash them and rub them thoroughly in water until you remove the deposit of forbidden foods which has formed on the vessels by being used for such foods, and this [process] constitutes their purification from the forbidden foods. Scripture is thus saying that [in order to purify a vessel from the forbidden food which it has absorbed] you must put into fire those [vessels] which are used on the fire, in exactly the same way that they were used for [cooking] the forbidden foods. Hence if it was used on the flame itself — such as [a vessel of] iron or copper, and also silver or gold — he must make it white-hot in a flame, and if it was used to contain hot substances, such as [a vessel made of] tin or lead, he cleanses it with boiling-hot water; and if it was not used on fire [or for hot substances] but only for cold foodstuffs, he scours it with water until it is properly cleansed, and then it becomes pure. And similarly the Sages said: [97] "He scours them, and immerses them, and they are then pure." In the language of the Sifre: [100] *"Ye*

(98) Leviticus 11:32. (99) Here in Verse 23. (100) Sifre, *Matoth* 158. This language shows that the "passing through water" referred to here, means cleansing of the food deposits, and not, as Rashi explained, merely immersion.

shall pass through the fire—such as knives, because they are [used as spits and] burned by the non-Jews. *And all that cometh not into the fire,* such as cups, *ye shall pass through the water* in order to remove the deposits of [the food of] the non-Jews." And Scripture did not need to mention again [at this second part of the verse, i.e., *and all that cometh 'not' into the fire*], the necessity of immersion [in a ritual pool, which is required after cleansing the vessel before it can be used], because He had already mentioned [in the first part of the verse, concerning vessels that are used in the fire, stating]: *nevertheless it shall be purified with the waters of 'niddah'* [meaning, as explained above, "waters which are fit for 'a menstruant' woman to immerse herself in"], and [it is self-understood that] after the traces of forbidden foods have been removed from the vessels they are all alike with respect to the law [requiring] immersion [whether they were used in the fire or not].

And I further take into consideration[101] that this immersion [of all vessels obtained from non-Jews, after they have been cleansed from the traces and absorption of forbidden foods prepared in them], is a law of the Rabbis, and they quoted the verse merely as a Scriptural support [for the Rabbinic ordinance]. And similarly Onkelos translated [the phrase, *the waters of 'niddah'*] as meaning "the purification of 'sprinkling' of [the water containing] the ashes of the [Red] Heifer" [which was required in order to purify those who had come into contact with a dead body, and thus it does not refer at all to the requirement of immersion. The Rabbis [according to this explanation] only required immersion of *metal* vessels, because some of them are used on fire, either as a "first vessel" [used directly on the flame], or as a "second vessel" [i.e., those which are not actually used for cooking but into which a boiling substance has been put or

(101) Literally: "And my heart further thinks" on this matter to say etc. — See Rambam in Mishneh Torah, *Hilchoth Ma'achaloth Assuroth* 17:5, who is also of the opinion that the requirement of immersion of vessels is an ordinance of the Rabbis. See also Shulchan Aruch, *Yoreh Deiah* Chapter 120, for the application of this law nowadays.

poured], and [some metal vessels are used] for cold foodstuffs. But this matter needs further investigation.

Now He warned them here to remove from the vessels of the Midianites the [traces and absorptions of the] forbidden foods [which they had absorbed when they were in the possession] of the non-Jews, but He did not tell them this [law] at the beginning—in connection with the vessels of [the Amorite peoples ruled by] Sihon and Og which they also took as spoil, as it is said, *Only the cattle we took for a prey unto ourselves, with the spoil of the cities which we had taken.*[102] The reason for this is that Sihon and Og were Amorite kings, and their land was part of Israel's inheritance, and therefore all spoil taken from them was allowed for the Israelites, including foods [usually] forbidden; for it is written, *and houses full of all good things, which thou didst not fill,*[103] and our Rabbis have said: [104] "*kadlei*[105] of swine was [hereby especially] permitted for them." But Midian was not part of their [inheritance], and they [the Israelites] did not capture their land from them; it was only to execute vengeance on them [as they were commanded to do as a punishment for causing the Israelites to sin] that they killed them and took their spoil, and therefore the [usual] prohibition of using their vessels [without removing from them the traces and absorptions of the forbidden foods] applied. Similarly, He [only] commanded them [now] about the law of impurity [conveyed by the dead, saying], *And abide ye without the camp seven days* etc.[106] [and did not command them about it in the earlier war against Sihon and Og], because in the war against Sihon and Og *all* Israel participated, and when the [entire] public is involved, impurity is permitted,[107] [whereas, as explained above in Verse 6, only

(102) Deuteronomy 2:35. (103) *Ibid.,* 6:11. (104) Chullin 17a. (105) The hind part of the head, together with the neck. In our Gemara *ibid.,* the reading is "*katlei* of swine," which Rashi interprets as "dried swine." See also Ramban on Deuteronomy 6:10. (106) Above, Verse 19. (107) This principle refers primarily to the Divine Service in the Sanctuary, and the gist of it is that if all the priests and people became defiled, the public offerings may nonetheless be brought in this state of impurity, because "impurity is permitted when the [entire]

a select few, and not the whole people, were sent to execute vengeance on Midian.] But according to the plain meaning of Scripture, He warned them [the twelve thousand men who fought against Midian], "*And abide ye without the camp seven days*[106] and purify yourselves," in order that they should not defile [the rest of] the people, but there [in the case of the wars against Sihon and Og] they were all equally impure [since they all went to fight; hence there was no point commanding them to *abide without the camp,* since they all required purification anyhow].

28. AND THOU SHALT LEVY A TRIBUTE UNTO THE ETERNAL. The reason for this tribute [given to the priests and Levites] was also because this spoil was taken from [a war constituting] *the vengeance of the Eternal*[108] on a land that was not theirs. But [from the spoil taken] in the lands of Sihon and Og they did not give any part at all to the priests and Levites; [on the contrary], they were even warned against [taking of] it, as it is said, *neither shalt thou* [Aaron] *have 'any' portion among them,* even in the spoil.[109]

31. AND MOSES AND ELEAZAR THE PRIEST DID AS THE ETERNAL COMMANDED MOSES. The reason why it does not mention the princes [i.e., *the heads of the fathers' houses of the congregation,* although in Verse 26 it said that they were to be present at the counting and division of the spoils] is because it is self-understood that they did as Moses commanded them, since he was their ruler, although in the matter of counting the people it does say, *These are those that were numbered, which Moses and Aaron numbered, 'and the princes of Israel.'*"[110] Perhaps the reason [for not using such an expression] here is that G-d commanded that [*the heads*

public is involved." Ramban's application of this principle to the problem before us [namely why the people were not commanded in the wars against Sihon and Og that all who had come into contact with the dead must *abide without the camp for seven days*], has engendered much discussion among later scholars. See my Hebrew commentary, p. 328. (108) Above, Verse 3. (109) *Ibid.,* 18:20, according to the explanation of the Sifre, *Korach* 119. (110) Above, 1:44.

of] the fathers' houses of the congregation[111] should be present [at the counting and distributing of the spoils] because it involved monetary matters, so that the people would not suspect Eleazar of taking for himself more than he was entitled to; therefore this commandment [to include the heads of the congregation] was an optional matter [for their benefit], and they said: "Far be it from us! *For he* [Eleazar] *is the messenger of the Eternal,*[112] and there is no need for us to be there."

36. AND THE HALF, WHICH WAS THE PORTION OF THEM THAT WENT OUT TO WAR, WAS IN NUMBER etc. Scripture had to enumerate [the spoil] in such detail, mentioning how much was the half [of these who went to war] and how much was the tribute [given to the priests and Levites, although both these figures can be worked out from the total figures mentioned], in order to inform us that from the day that they took this booty until they counted and halved it, set aside the tribute and gave it to Eleazar the priest, not one of all this great herd died. This was a miracle. This is also [the reason why Scripture mentions] the half [given] to the congregation [of Israel who did not fight, and the amount that they gave] to the Levites.[113]

49. THY SERVANTS HAVE TAKEN THE SUM OF THE MEN OF WAR THAT ARE UNDER OUR CHARGE, AND THERE LACKETH NOT ONE MAN OF US. [The meaning of this is]: "G-d has wrought a great salvation through us, for not one of all those *men of war that were under our charge* died, or was wounded by the sword so that he would be missing from the host; and therefore we want to bring *the Eternal's offering*[114] [to Him] Who saved us, to give before Him the *atonement for our souls*[114] because He *redeemed* [us] *from death, and in war from the power of the sword.*"[115] And our Rabbis have interpreted [the verse as follows]: [116] *"And there lacketh not one man* — [going off] to commit a sin." That is to say, they were continually under our charge, and not a single one of our brothers who

(111) Verse 26. (112) See Malachi 2:7. (113) Verses 42-47. (114) Verse 50. (115) Job 5:20. (116) Shabbath 64a.

were in the host went off to another place to commit a sin." And Moses said to them: "If so, what is this offering for?" They replied, "*To make atonement for our souls*[114] — sinful "thoughts of the heart."

54. AND THEY BROUGHT IT INTO THE TENT OF MEETING, FOR A MEMORIAL FOR THE CHILDREN OF ISRAEL BEFORE THE ETERNAL. It would appear from this verse that they made them [the ornaments they had captured] into vessels to be used for the Service [in the Sanctuary], and handed them over to the public *for a memorial for* all *the children of Israel* with which to perform the Service of G-d throughout their generations. For had these vessels [merely] gone to the treasury of the House of G-d [rather than actually being used for the Divine Service], the verse should rather have said, "a memorial 'for them' before the Eternal," but [the phrase] *the children of Israel* [*a memorial for 'the children of Israel'*] includes all the people, and [it means] that the memorial consists of something permanent.[117]

32 2. AND THE CHILDREN OF GAD AND THE CHILDREN OF REUBEN CAME AND SPOKE UNTO MOSES. In the preceding verse Scripture mentioned the children of Reuben first, [saying], *Now the children of Reuben and the children of Gad had a very great multitude of cattle,* as is the correct way [of referring to them], for he [Reuben] was the firstborn and he was the son of the principal wife [of Jacob, i.e., Leah, whereas Gad was the son of Leah's handmaid, Zilpah]. Similarly also when Scripture tells of [the occurrence of] this event it says, *And unto the Reubenites and unto the Gadites I gave* etc.[118] However, in the whole of this section He mentions the children of Gad first, because it was they who suggested this idea, and it was

(117) For had the donations gone to the general treasury of the Sanctuary they would have only been *a memorial* to the donors, whereas now that they themselves were used as vessels in the Divine Service, they served as *a memorial for* all *the children of Israel* for all times, as the Service in the Sanctuary is designated for all generations (see e.g. Exodus 29:42). (118) Deuteronomy 3:16.

they who first spoke to Moses about this inheritance; and they were also stronger than the children of Reuben, as it is said [of the Gadites], *and he teareth the arm, yea, the crown of the head,*[119] and therefore they were not afraid of living alone amongst the inhabitants of that land. Now Moses suspected that they were only suggesting this [plan of settling on the east side of the Jordan] because they were afraid of the people in the land of Canaan, concerning whom the spies had said, *We are not able to go up against the people; for they are stronger than we*[120] — therefore he told them that they did not trust in G-d, just like their fathers [who did not trust in Him] and therefore He would again punish them like their fathers, by *leaving them in the wilderness.*[121] Therefore they answered him: "Far be it from us to fear them! For we shall pass over [the Jordan] armed for battle, and we shall be the most eager and the first amongst the people to fight against the enemies of the Eternal, *for they are bread for us.*"[122]

19. FOR OUR INHERITANCE HAS COME TO US — "we have already received it on the eastern side [of the Jordan]." This is Rashi's language. But it would not be correct for them to speak in this manner in front of Moses, saying, "we have already received it," for it was not up to them, but on his will that the matter depended, and they did not receive it until he [decided to] give it to them. Instead, [the explanation of their words is that] they said to Moses: "For you do not have to give us an inheritance with them, thereby making their inheritance in their good Land smaller, *for* an *inheritance* which is suitable for us *has come to us,* since it is a land [fit] for cattle, and we have more cattle than the other tribes." This they said in the nature of a request, not by way of contention. Or perhaps they said: "*For we will not inherit with them,* because even if you do not want to give us the land [on the east side of the Jordan] now, we will cross over together with them [the rest of the children of Israel], we and all that we have, but *we will not inherit with them,* for we will return to this land which

(119) *Ibid.,* 33:20. (120) Above, 13:31. (121) Further, Verse 15. (122) Above, 14:9.

is the inheritance that is suitable for us, and which we want, and which none of the other tribes want at all."

29. [AND MOSES SAID UNTO THEM]: 'IF THE CHILDREN OF GAD AND THE CHILDREN OF REUBEN WILL PASS WITH YOU etc. THEN YE [Joshua and the princes] SHALL GIVE THEM THE LAND OF GILEAD FOR A POSSESSION.' The reason for this [command that *then ye shall give them . . .*] is that Moses did not give them now all the land of Sihon and Og, but only a few cities in the land of Gilead which was a place fit for cattle, namely *Ataroth, and Dibon,* etc.[123] and those mentioned here,[124] in which they built fortifications to settle their children and cattle therein, but the rest of the land they left waste. Therefore [Moses] commanded Joshua and the princes: *"If* they *will pass over* [the Jordan] *with you, you shall give them* all *the land* as a perpetual inheritance. *But if they will not* want to *pass over with you,*[125] you should take away from them all this land and drive out from it their wives and children, and give them an inheritance fitting for them in the land of Canaan, which they shall conquer for themselves when they cross over [the Jordan]." And Rabbi Abraham ibn Ezra commented: *"But if they will not pass over*[125] of their own free will, you shall take them with you against their will, and they shall take their possession there [in the land of Canaan] together with you."

31. AND THE CHILDREN OF GAD AND THE CHILDREN OF REUBEN ANSWERED, SAYING: [AS THE ETERNAL HATH SAID UNTO THY SERVANTS, SO WILL WE DO]. 32. WE WILL PASS OVER ARMED. They said to Moses: "Our lord need not command us with a double condition[126] [to cross over the Jordan]. Far be it from your servants to transgress that which my lord commands! For they [i.e., your words] are the words of G-d, and we will not

(123) Verse 3 here. (124) Further, Verses 34-38. (125) Verse 30. (126) *If they will pass over the Jordan . . . then ye shall give them the land of Gilead . . . But if they will not pass over, they shall have possessions among you* (Verses 29-30).

transgress His commandment!" And this is the meaning of the expression, *as the Eternal hath said,* for at the beginning [i.e., *before* Moses had made the double condition] they had [already] said that they would do *as my lord commanded*[127] [hence we must say that here in Verse 31 they were telling Moses there was no need for the double condition, for the reason explained above].

33. V'LACHATZI (AND UNTO A PART OF THE) TRIBE OF MENASHEH THE SON OF JOSEPH. At the beginning the tribe of Menasheh did not come to Moses [to ask for their inheritance to be on the east side of the Jordan], but when Moses apportioned the land to the two tribes [of Gad and Reuben], he saw that the land was larger than they required, and therefore he asked for people who were prepared to take their inheritance with them. And there were people of the tribe of Menasheh who wanted that land — perhaps they were [also] owners of cattle — and therefore he gave them their portion [in that land].

Now the meaning of *v'lachatzi* [literally "and unto the half"] is "unto one part" of them [as will be explained]. Similarly, *Then were the people of Israel divided "lacheitzi" (into two parts): 'chatzi' (part of) the people followed Tibni the son of Ginath, to make him king, 'v'hachatzi' (and the other part) followed Omri.*[128] And the explanation [here is as follows]: The children of Menasheh consisted of eight paternal families as is written in the section dealing with the census,[129] and [only] the families of the Machirites and of the Gileadites took their inheritance in this land [on the east of the Jordan], because they were men of valor and they conquered it for themselves, and Moses gave them a large part of it. The [other] six families, however, crossed over the Jordan [to take their inheritance in Canaan proper], as it is written in [the Book of] Joshua, *And the lot was for the rest of the children of Menasheh according to their families; for the children of Abiezer, and for the children of Helek, and for the children of Asriel, and for the children of Shechem, and for the children of Hepher, and*

(127) Above, Verse 25. (128) I Kings 16:21. (129) Above, 26:29-32.

for the children of Shemida.[130] And this is the meaning of what is written there, *And there fell ten parts to Menasheh, beside the land of Gilead and Bashan, which is beyond the Jordan,*[131] the interpretation thereof being as follows: They divided the [whole] Land into nine equal parts[132] for the nine tribes, but they could not give to the remaining [part of the] tribe of Menasheh a whole portion [because two of their families had settled on the east side of the Jordan], nor could they give them [only] half a portion, because most of them had remained [in the land of Canaan]. Therefore they divided the whole tribe into parts and they found that only a tenth[133] of [the total population of] the tribe took their inheritance in the land of Bashan [on the east side of the Jordan] and ten parts remained [and settled in the Land of Israel]. These were then given *ten parts*[131] [of the amount] given to a whole tribe,[133] while one part remained [on the east side of the Jordan for the families of the Machirites and the Gileadites]. Perhaps it was because these two families — the Machirites and the Gileadites — were the smallest of their tribe [and would therefore have received only a small portion of the land allotted to their tribe] that they wanted to separate themselves from their tribe, in order that they should have a greater inheritance [proportionally] than the rest of them, for they could conquer it by their sword, as it is said, *because he* [Machir] *was a man of war, therefore he had Gilead and Bashan.*[134] This is why Scripture mentioned *'parts'* with reference to this tribe [of Menasheh, saying, *And there fell ten 'parts' to Menasheh,*[131] a term] which it does not use in connection with any of the other tribes. This

(130) Joshua 17:2. (131) *Ibid.,* Verse 5. (132) As Ramban explained at length above, 26:54. (133) Ramban is thus saying that in calculating their population they found that the two families on the east of the Jordan constituted *one-eleventh* of the total population of Menasheh, and the remainder consisted of ten-elevenths. The one-eleventh part of the whole is expressed as "one tenth," because after separating it from the whole, it is one-tenth of the remainder. Thus out of the total inheritance given to the whole tribe of Menasheh, ten-elevenths were allotted to the families that settled in the Land of Israel proper — they are the *ten parts* referred to in Joshua 17:5 — while the remaining eleventh part was assigned to the families of Menasheh on the east side of the Jordan. (134) Joshua 17:1.

appears to me to be the explanation of this verse [*And there fell ten parts* . . .] according to the simple meaning of Scripture.

Now Moses did not mention in the Torah that he [Joshua] was to apportion this land amongst them [the tribes of Gad and Reuben], giving each one of these two tribes his own portion, but instead Scripture says [in Verse 33] that he [Moses] promised them and the part of the tribe of Menasheh the kingdoms of these two kings [Sihon and Og]; and in the Book of Deuteronomy he explained that he gave the part of the tribe of Menasheh a portion for itself, *all the region of Argob,* and *all the Bashan.*[135] Thus the Torah dealt briefly [with this matter], because He did not want to mention therein the [details of the] allocation of the land between these two [tribes], just as the allocation amongst the other tribes is also not mentioned. But in the Book of Joshua it is clearly stated that Moses gave them their [specific] portions, as it is written, *And Moses gave unto the tribe of the children of Reuben according to their families. And their border was* etc.,[136] and it is further written, *And Moses gave unto the tribe of Gad, according to their families. And their border was* etc.,[137] and again it says, *And Moses gave inheritance unto part of the tribe of Menasheh; and it was for the part-tribe of the children of Menasheh according to their families. And their border was* etc.[138]

38. AND NEBO, AND BAAL-MEON — THEIR NAMES BEING CHANGED. "Nebo and Baal-meon were names of idols, and the Amorites used to call their cities by the names of their idols, therefore the children of Reuben changed [the names of these cities and gave them] different names, this being the meaning of the expression *their names being changed,* which means that Nebo and Baal-meon were changed to other names." This is Rashi's language. But the [concluding part of this] verse which says, *and they called their names*

(135) Deuteronomy 3:13. Likewise we can deduce [although it is not stated so clearly] that Moses assigned the rest of the land of Sihon and Og between the tribes of Reuben and Gad. (136) Joshua 13:15-16. (137) *Ibid.,* Verses 24-25. (138) *Ibid.,* Verses 29-30.

unto the cities which they builded refers to *all* the cities [mentioned there], and not only to Nebo and Baal-meon [and therefore the phrase *their names being changed* cannot be understood as Rashi explained it]. Furthermore, what sense would there be in Scripture mentioning the cities [only] by the names of their idols, and saying that the children of Reuben built them and changed their names, without mentioning the good names which they were [now] given! And indeed it is quite usual for Scripture when speaking about [any] captured cities to mention always the new names [given them, as in the following cases]: *and they called Leshem, Dan, after the name of Dan their father;* [139] *and he called them the hamlets of Jair;* [140] *and he called it Nobach.* [141] And likewise wherever the name [of a city] was changed [for any reason] Scripture mentions [the new name as well, as it is said], *Now the name of Hebron beforetime was Kiryath-arba;* [142] *now the name of Debir beforetime was Kiryath-sepher.* [143]

The most likely explanation seems to me to be that these names [Nebo, Baal-meon, etc.] were the names of the cities when they were in the possession of Moab, and Sihon captured all these cities from *the former king of Moab,* [144] for thus it is written about Heshbon, Dibon and Medeba, as it is said, *We have shot at them; Heshbon is perished, even unto Dibon* etc. [145] This also appears to me to be the [meaning of the] words of Jephthah, when he said, *While Israel dwelt in Heshbon and its towns, and in Aroer and its towns, and in all the cities that are along by the side of the Arnon,* [146] this being the same Aroer [mentioned here in Verse 34] which they took from Sihon. Now when Tiglath-pileser the king of Assyria[147] exiled the Reubenites and the Gadites, the Moabites returned and settled in their lands and cities, for we find in the Book of Jeremiah that when Nebuchadnezzar [king of Babylon] destroyed Moab, he conquered from them all these cities. And [the Book of Jeremiah] mentions by name *Heshbon* and

(139) Joshua 19:47. (140) Further, Verse 41. (141) *Ibid.*, Verse 42. (142) Joshua 14:15. (143) *Ibid.*, 15:15. (144) Above, 21:26. (145) *Ibid.*, Verse 30. (146) Judges 11:26. (147) II Kings 15:29.

Elealeh,[148] *Kiryathaim,*[149] *Dibon* and *Nebo,*[150] *Jazer,*[151] *Aroer,*[152] and *Baal-meon*[153] which is [there] called *Beth-meon,*[149] and *Beth nimrah*[154] which is [there] called *Nimrim,*[148] and *Jahza.*[155] Thus you see that all these cities mentioned [in these verses] belonged [originally] to Moab, [and Sihon, king of the Amorites captured them from Moab]. Similarly in [the Book of] Isaiah most of these cities are mentioned[156] when Sennacherib [king of Assyria] overran Moab, for he first exiled the Reubenites and the Gadites, and afterwards he overran Ammon and Moab.

Therefore it appears that the meaning of [the phrase] *their names being changed* is that all these cities had [previously] had their names changed, because the Amorites changed their original names when they captured them [from Moab] and these [names] were their original names which they had when they still belonged to Moab. But the children of Reuben and f Gad still called them by [these Moabite] names when they rebuilt them. [This explanation is borne out by the fact that] the verse does not say, "and they gave names to the cities which they built," but it says, *and they called by names the names of the cities* [*which they builded*], meaning that they called them by name with the same names which they originally had [when they were still under the rule of Moab. This was] because they wanted to refer to them by the names with which they had previously been known, either in order to shame Moab, or, as our Rabbis have mentioned,[157] because

(148) Jeremiah 48:34. (149) *Ibid.,* Verse 23. (150) *Ibid.,* Verse 22. (151) *Ibid.,* Verse 32. (152) *Ibid.,* Verse 19. (153) Of Verse 38 here. (154) Verse 36 here. (155) *Ibid.,* Verse 21. (156) Isaiah 15:2-9. (157) In the Midrash Agadah on our verse, quoted by Rashi at the beginning of the section. Thus Rashi and Ramban still differ as to the meaning of the verse here that the names of the cities were changed. According to Rashi, the phrase *their names being changed* means that they were changed *by the children of Reuben and Gad,* because their [Amorite] names were the names of idols. According to Ramban, the phrase refers to *the Amorites,* who changed the original Moabite names in an attempt to erase the Moabite origin of these cities. Since the Amorites gave them the names of their idols, therefore the children of Reuben and Gad reverted to the original Moabite names in order not to have to mention the names of idols, or, as Ramban suggests, in order to shame the Moabites.

[they did not want to use the Amorite names since] the Amorites used to call their cities by the names of their idols. However, we do not find that Joshua changed the names of the cities which he captured.

AND SIBMAH. The meaning of this is that "they built Sibmah," but it was not [a city] whose name was changed.

41. AND JAIR THE SON OF MENASHEH. This man [who was in fact from the tribe of Judah, as will be explained] is [here] traced back by genealogy to his mother's family [Menasheh], because he took his inheritance together with them [i.e., the children of Menasheh]. And in the Book of Chronicles[158] it says explicitly that he was a son[159] of Hezron, the son of Perez, the son of Judah, and his mother was the daughter of Machir the son of Menasheh, as it says, *And afterward Hezron went in to the daughter of Machir the father of Gilead; whom he took to wife when he was threeescore years old, and she bore him Segub. And Segub begot Jair, who had three and twenty cities in the land of Gilead;* [158] and it is [further] written, *And Geshur and Aram took the hamlets of Jair from them, Kenath, and the villages thereof, even threescore cities. All these were the sons of Machir the father of Gilead.*[160] From this [fact that Kenath is here described as being amongst *'the hamlets of Jair'*] it would appear that Nobach [mentioned here in Verse 42] who *conquered Kenath and the villages thereof* was a son of Jair, [although it is not mentioned here], and therefore these cities were also called *'the hamlets of Jair.'*[161]

And the meaning of the verse, *And Moses gave Gilead unto Machir the son of Menasheh*[162] is [not "unto Machir" himself, but unto] his

(158) I Chronicles 2:21-22. (159) Actually "a grandson," for his father was Segub, the son of Hezron (*ibid.,* Verse 22). (160) *Ibid.,* Verse 23. (161) Ramban here means that the explanation of the phrase at the end of Verse 42, *vayikra lah Nobach bi'shmo* is: "Nobach called it [i.e., *Kenath and the villages thereof*] by *his* name" [i.e., by the name of Jair — his father — mentioned in the previous verse]; hence these towns also came to be called *'the hamlets of Jair,'* as they are described in I Chronicles *ibid.* (162) Verse 40 here.

family, for it was his sons who conquered it.[163] Similarly, *And unto Machir I gave Gilead*[164] means "unto the Machirites," for since Machir was an honored man and the chief of all his descendants, therefore his children were called by his name, and in the same way the verses refer to the heads of the tribes in connection with the inheritance [given to their children]: *southward it was Ephraim's, and northward it was Menasheh's.*[165] So also: *The land of Tappuah belonged to Menasheh* etc.[166] And when Scripture says in the Book of Joshua, *And this was the lot for the tribe of Menasheh; for he was the firstborn of Joseph. As for Machir the firstborn of Menasheh, the father of Gilead, because he was a man of war, therefore he had Gilead and Bashan,*[167] it also refers to his sons, who were men of war, for it was they who went to Gilead and conquered it, and therefore Moses gave them a great part of these lands. Perhaps Machir was still alive [at the time of the division of the Land in the days of Joshua], for the decree [against the generation] of the wilderness [resulting from the incident of the spies, that they were to die in the desert] had not been decreed upon him, as he was not amongst those counted by Moses and Aaron, being he was more than sixty years old [at the time of the first census after the exodus],[168] and he enjoyed longevity as did the earlier generations.[169]

42. 'VAYIKRA LAH NOBACH' (AND HE CALLED IT NOBACH). "[The word *lah*] has no dot in the [letter] *hei* [as it usually has when it means "to it"]. And I have seen in the work of Rabbi Moshe the Preacher[170] that because it did not keep this name permanently, therefore [the letter *hei* in the word *lah*] is pronounced softly [without the dot], and the interpretation implied is [as if it said] *lo* [meaning "not"]. But I am astonished at this, for what interpretation will he [Rabbi Moshe the Preacher] give in the case of two other similar words: *'Vayomer lah Boaz'* (*And Boaz said to*

(163) Verse 39: *And the children of Machir the son of Menasheh went to Gilead and conquered it.* (164) Deuteronomy 3:15. (165) Joshua 17:10. (166) *Ibid.,* Verse 8. (167) *Ibid.,* Verse 1. (168) Baba Bathra 121b. (169) See Vol. I, pp. 98-99. (170) See above in *Seder Naso,* Note 146.

her);[171] *'livnoth lah bayith'* (*to build her a house*)[172] [in both of which places the word *lah* is also written without a dot in the letter *hei*]!" This is the language of Rashi.

Now although the Rabbi [Rashi] is "like a filled treasury of knowledge"[173] of Torah, Halachoth and Agadoth, yet the explanation of the Rabbis in Midrash Ruth escaped his attention, [for they remarked[174] on the verse: "*Though I* [Ruth] *be not as one of thy handmaids.*[175] Said Boaz to Ruth: Far be it from me [to consider you like one of the handmaids!] You are not like one of the handmaids, but like one of the matriarchs![176] Similarly, *And Nobach went and conquered Kenath, and the villages thereof, 'vayikra lah Nobach bi'shmo'* (*and he called it Nobach, after his own name*) — this [lack of the dot in the letter *hei*] indicates that this name did not remain. So also, *And he said unto me: To build 'lah'* (*for her*) *a house in the land of Shinar*[172] — this teaches us that falsehood does not lead to any salvation."[177] Thus far is the Agadah. And similarly in the Gemara of Tractate Sanhedrin[178] the Rabbis said [with reference to the measure seen by the prophet Zechariah]:[177] "This was the measure of flattery and conceit which came down to Babylon;" [Whereupon the Gemara asked that we find elsewhere that conceit settled in Elam, and the

(171) Ruth 2:14. (172) Zecharia 5:11. (173) Gittin 67a. (174) Ruth Rabbah 5:5. (175) Ruth 2:13. (176) Thus the phrase *'Vayomer lah Boaz'* (*and Boaz said to her*), which follows Ruth's remark [*though I be not as one of thy handmaids*] is written without the dot in the letter *hei*, the idea being, as Rabbi Moshe the Preacher explained, to convey the thought of *lo*, meaning a negation. Boaz is therefore saying to Ruth: " *'Lo'* — it is *not* as you say that you are like one of the handmaids in my eyes; on the contrary, you are like one of the matriarchs, and you are destined to be the ancestress of kings." (177) The point here is that the prophet Zechariah saw a measure of falsehood being flown to a certain country. When he asked the angel, *Whither do these* [messengers] *bear the measure?* (Zechariah 5:10) he received the answer: *'livnoth lah bayith'* (*to build her a house*) *in Shinar* [which is another name for Babylon]. Now since the word *lah* is written without the dot in the letter *hei*, the Rabbis interpreted that this is a negation, as if it said *lo*, conveying the idea that one may build a house of falsehood, but it will not last. — Thus the Midrash explains both the verses which Rashi found difficult. (178) Sanhedrin 24a.

answer was:] "It indeed came down [originally] to Babylon, and became dragged along to Elam. You may deduce this also from the verse, *'livnoth lah bayith'* (*to build her a house*),"[172] [which is written without the usual dot in the letter *hei*]. Thus the interpretation is based upon the absence of this dot [in the letter *hei* of the word *lah,* which indicates] that the house [of flattery and conceit] did not last in the land of Shinar [but was dragged along the Elam].

Mas'ei

33 1. THESE ARE THE JOURNEYS. After the vengeance [executed] upon Midian, concerning which the Holy One, blessed be He, told Moses, *afterwards shalt thou be gathered unto thy people,*[1] and after Moses had apportioned the land of Sihon and Og [to the tribes of Reuben, Gad, and half of the tribe of Menasheh] and they had built the [previously] mentioned cities,[2] he set his mind to write down [the various stages of] the journeyings [in the desert]. His intention in so doing was to inform [future generations] of the loving kindnesses of the Holy One, blessed be He, towards them, for even though He had decreed upon them that they had to move about and wander around in the wilderness, you should not think that they were continually wandering and moving around from place to place without any rest; for throughout all this long [period of] time they only went on forty-two journeys as the Rabbi — Rashi — wrote, [citing] the words of Rabbi Moshe the Preacher.[3]

(1) Above, 31:2. (2) *Ibid.*, 32:34-38. (3) See above in *Seder Naso,* Note 146.

And the Rabbi [Moshe ben Maimon] added in the Moreh Nebuchim[4] another [explanation as to the] benefit [that we derive] from knowledge [of these stages], saying: "There was a very great necessity in mentioning the [stages of the] journeyings. For [although] the miracles and wonders that were done were [recognized as] true ones by all who saw them, in later times these events would be matters of hearsay, and those who hear about them [then] might deny them altogether. Now among the greatest miracles and wonders [related] in the Torah is Israel's survival in the wilderness for forty years, and finding the manna every day, although these places [where they stayed] are very far from cultivated settlements, and are not natural habitat for human beings, not being a *place of seed, or of figs, or of vines, or of pomegranates,*[5] and the Torah states, *Ye have not eaten bread, neither have ye drunk wine or strong drink.*[6] All these [matters] are signs of events of a miraculous nature which were seen by [the human] eye. But the Creator blessed be He, knew that these wonders will be subject to the process which occurs to [all] historical events — that those who hear them will not believe them; and they will think [about these events] that the sojourn of the Israelites in the wilderness was [in a place] near the cultivated settlement, where people can live there, such as the deserts in which the Arabs live today, or [that they stayed in] places where there was plowing and harvesting, or where there were grasses and plants suitable for human consumption, and that there were wells of water in those places. Therefore in order to remove from people's hearts all such thoughts, and to firmly establish [the truth of] all these miracles, [He recorded] as a [permanent] memorial the [stages of their] journeyings [in the wilderness], so that the future generations would see them and acknowledge the great wonders [entailed] in keeping people alive in such places for forty years." All these are his words [i.e., the words of Rabbi Moshe ben Maimon].

(4) Guide of the Perplexed III, 50. Ramban is using Al Charizi's Hebrew translation from the Arabic [rather than Ibn Tibbon's]. (5) Above, 20:5. (6) Deuteronomy 29:5.

Thus the writing down [the stages of] the journeyings was a commandment of G-d, either for the reasons mentioned above or for some other reasons, [for] a purpose the secret of which has not been revealed to us. For [the expression] *by the commandment of the Eternal*[7] is connected with [the beginning of that verse], *And Moses wrote,*[7] unlike the opinion of Rabbi Abraham ibn Ezra who wrote that it is connected with *according to their journeys,*[8] for Scripture has already informed us of this [fact, saying]: *according to the commandment of the Eternal they remained encamped, and according to the commandment of the Eternal they journeyed.*[9]

14. AND THEY PITCHED IN REPHIDIM, AND THERE WAS NO WATER FOR THE PEOPLE TO DRINK. Scripture [here] does not mention the miracle [that occurred] with the water in Marah,[10] nor the [daily] wonder of manna [which took place] in the wilderness of Sin.[11] But [it mentioned the giving of water at Rephidim] because this episode at Rephidim was an important event, since they tried G-d [there], and that place was therefore called Massah (Trying) and Meribah (Strife),[12] wherein He was sanctified in their presence by bringing forth water for them out of the rock,[13] and it was there that they were attacked by the Amalekites.[14] Therefore He [only] described it here in brief, [saying], *and there was no water for the people to drink,* since it was the place which was recognized and known by this [fact].

(7) Verse 2. (8) Verse 2 reads: *And Moses wrote their goings forth according to their journeys by the commandment of the Eternal.* Ibn Ezra explains that the phrase *by the commandment of the Eternal* is connected with *according to their journeys,* meaning that all *their journeys were by the commandment of G-d.* Ramban objects to this explanation because this fact has already been expressed elsewhere in Scripture, and therefore he explains that the phrase refers to the beginning of the verse, *And Moses wrote,* and the intention is to say that Moses wrote down the various stages of the journeys by G-d's command, and not of his own accord. (9) Above, 9:20. (10) Exodus 15:23-25. (11) *Ibid.,* Chapter 16. (12) *Ibid.,* 17:7. (13) *Ibid.,* Verse 6. (14) *Ibid.,* Verse 8.

41. AND THEY JOURNEYED FROM MOUNT HOR, AND PITCHED IN ZALMONAH. These places — Zalmonah and Punon[15] — were *by the way of the Red Sea* circling *the land of Edom, and the soul of the people became impatient because of the way,*[16] and they [therefore] *spoke against G-d, and Moses*[17] on the way, and G-d sent against them the fiery serpents whilst they were travelling and when they rested in camp. Then Moses made the serpent of brass, which they carried upon a pole[18] all the way, and [kept it] when they encamped in Zalmonah and Punon, and it was not removed from them until they pitched in Oboth.[19] Therefore Scripture there, in narrating this episode [of the fiery serpents, above in Chapter 21], did not mention the name of the place [from which they set forth again, i.e., Zalmonah and Punon] and [merely] stated, *And the children of Israel journeyed, and pitched in Oboth,*[20] without saying "and they journeyed from such-and-such a place and pitched in Oboth," as it does with all the [other stages of their] journeyings. This is because the matter [of the brass serpent] continued throughout this way — from the time that they journeyed from Mount Hor until they pitched in Oboth, *and they journeyed from Oboth and pitched in Ije-abarim.*[21] From there they journeyed *and they pitched in Divon-gad,* and then *in Almon-diblathaim,* and [finally] *in the mountains of Abarim,*[22] [all these] being places *in the valley of Zered.*[23]

53. AND YE SHALL DRIVE OUT THE INHABITANTS OF THE LAND, AND DWELL THEREIN; FOR UNTO YOU HAVE I GIVEN THE LAND TO POSSESS IT. In my opinion this is a positive commandment,[24] in which He is commanding them to dwell in the

(15) Verse 42 here. (16) Above, 21:10. (17) *Ibid.,* Verse 5. (18) *Ibid.,* Verse 9. (19) Verse 43 here. (20) Above, 21:10. (21) *Ibid.,* Verse 11.—Verse 44 here. (22) Verses 45-47 here. (23) Above, 21:12. (24) Among the great scholars who enumerate the individual 613 Commandments, Ramban was the first to mention this commandment [to conquer and settle in the Land of Israel etc.] as binding for all times. In his notes to Maimonides' *Sefer Hamitzvoth* (Book of the Commandments), in the section on "additional" positive commandments, No. 4, Ramban discusses this opinion at length. Here in his commentary on the Torah, he mentions it briefly, relying presumably on his explanation in the work quoted above.

Land and inherit it, because He has given it to them and they should not reject *the inheritance of the Eternal.*[25] Thus if the thought occurs to them to go and conquer the land of Shinar or the land of Assyria or any other country and to settle therein, they are [thereby] transgressing the commandment of G-d. And that which our Rabbis have emphasized, the significance of the commandment of settling in the Land of Israel, and that it is forbidden to leave it [except for certain specified reasons], and [the fact] that they consider a woman who does not want to emigrate with her husband to live in the Land of Israel as a "rebellious [wife],"[26] and likewise the man[27] — the source of all these statements is here [in this verse] where we have been given this commandment, for this verse constitutes a positive commandment.[28] This commandment He repeats in many places, such as *Go in and possess the Land.*[29] Rashi, however, explained: "*And ye shall drive out the inhabitants of the Land* — [if] you dispossess it of its inhabitants, then *ye will* be able to *dwell therein,* and to remain there, but if not, you will not be able to remain in it." But our interpretation [of the verse] is the principal one.

55. 'L'SIKIM' IN YOUR EYES — " 'like pins' which prick out your eyes. The [Aramaic] Targum [Onkelos] of the Hebrew word *yetheidoth*[30] (pins) is *sikim.* 'V'LITZNINIM.' Translators have interpreted this [word] in the sense of [the phrase] *mesuchath* (*hedged*

(25) I Samuel 26:19. (26) Kethuboth 110b: "If he wants to emigrate [to the Land of Israel] and she refuses, she may be forced to go there, and if she still refuses, she may be divorced without her *kethubah* (marriage contract — see Vol. II, pp. 385-386). (27) "If she wants to emigrate [to the Land of Israel] and he refuses, he may be forced to go there, and if he still refuses, he must divorce her and give her the *kethubah* (*ibid.*). (28) "For all generations, every person being obliged in the performance thereof, even during the exile" (Ramban in his notes to Maimonides' Sefer Hamitzvoth "additional" positive commandments, No. 4). (29) Deuteronomy 1:8. "And when they refused to go up, it is written: *but ye rebelled against the commandment of the Eternal your G-d* (*ibid.,* Verse 26 — Ramban on Sefer Hamitzvoth, *ibid.*). (30) Exodus 27:19.

by) *thorns*[31] encircling you so that they enclose and imprison you and you cannot go out or come in." This is Rashi's language.

Now it is [indeed] clear that *sikim* means "sharp thorns," and is related to [the expression]: *I will take away 'mesukatho' (the hedge thereof)*; [32] *I will 'sach' (hedge up) thy way with thorns;* [33] *Hast Thou not 'sachta' (made a hedge) about him?;* [34] *and put 'sakin' to thy throat*[35] — [all these phrases referring to] something sharp, made from a thorn or from iron. *V'litzninim* is likewise [a term for] a *piercing thorn*[36] related to the expression: *and taketh it even 'mitzinim' out of the thorns*); [37] *'tzinim' (thorns) and snares are in the way of the crooked,*[38] and [the word *tzinim* in these two verses] lacks the double letter ['*nun,*' since the full word is *tzninim,* as in the verse before us]. But the intention of [the expression here] *'l'sikim' in your eyes* is: "to mislead you so that you will not see nor understand," just as in [the expression], *for the bribe 'blindeth' the open-eyed,*[39] and as, *nor put a stumbling-block before 'the blind,'*[40] according to the opinion of our Rabbis. Thus the verse is saying that they [*the inhabitants of the Land*] will "prick out" your eyes by misleading you, because you will not perceive nor understand [the danger], and they will teach you [to do] *all their abominations*[41] and to worship their gods, just as He said, *They shall not dwell in thy Land, lest they make thee sin against Me, for thou wilt serve their gods.*[42] After being *thorns in your eyes* and misleading you to turn away from Me, they will be *pricks in your sides,* causing you suffering and pain, by plundering and despoiling you. And after that *they shall harass you,*[43] meaning that they will fight against you and bring you under siege, and I will then send you into exile, *a whole captivity,*[44] in their place. For *as I thought to do unto*

(31) Proverbs 15:19. (32) Isaiah 5:5. (33) Hosea 2:8. (34) Job 1:10. (35) Proverbs 23:2. (36) Ezekiel 28:24. (37) Job 5:5. (38) Proverbs 22:5. (39) Exodus 23:8. A bribe does not "blind" physically but misleads the recipient to render an unjust decision. (40) Leviticus 19:14. In the opinion of the Rabbis this establishes the prohibition against giving misleading advice to a person who is "blind" (unsuspecting) in a certain matter. See "The Commandments," Vol. II, pp. 277-278. (41) Deuteronomy 20:18. (42) Exodus 23:33. (43) Verse 55 here. (44) Amos 1:6.

them[45] because of you, that is, to send all of them into exile from the Land, so that you should *leave none of them any more there,*[46] but you have not hearkened to My voice, therefore *so will I do unto you*[45] and I will leave not a single one of you in the Land.

In a similar way Joshua said: *And they shall be a snare and a trap unto you, and scourge in your sides, and pricks in your eyes, until ye perish from off this good Land.*[47] Joshua said *a snare and a trap* referring to the errors into which they will lead you, as in [the expression], *for thou wilt serve their gods — for they will be 'a snare' unto thee;*[42] *and a scourge in your sides* which means that they will chastise you with *shotim* (whips)[48] so that they may plunder, despoil and cause you great suffering; *and pricks in your eyes,* this refers to blinding of the perception of the heart, so as to further mislead you after their gods; *until ye perish from off this good Land,* similar to that which it is said, *lest they, seeing with their eyes, and hearing with their ears, and understanding with their heart, return and be healed.*[49]

34 2. 'EL HA'ARETZ KENA'AN' (INTO THE LAND OF CANAAN). "This is like [the expression]: *and the prophecy of Oded the prophet,*[50] [which is to be understood as: *'and the prophecy,* a prophecy *of Oded the prophet'*]. The sense [of the verse thus] is: *'into the land,* the land *of Canaan.'* " This is the language of Rabbi Abraham ibn Ezra, and so also did Rashi write.[51] Scholars have brought a similar example: [*I am*] *'ha'E-il beith eil'*[52] [which they interpreted to mean: "*I am G-d,* who is the G-d *of Beth-el*"]. And I have already explained [there] the secret thereof.

(45) Verse 56. (46) Ezekiel 39:28. (47) Joshua 23:13. (48) The Hebrew word *ul'shoteit* [in Joshua 23:13, which is usually translated: *as a scourge*], is understood here by Ramban as coming from the noun *shot* (a whip). (49) Isaiah 6:10. (50) II Chronicles 15:8. See above in *Seder Beha'alothcha,* Note 284, for the grammatical reason why the verse requires the additional expression "a prophecy" after the initial words *and a prophecy.* Here too, the meaning of the verse is: *into the land,* the land *of Canaan.* (51) This is not found here in our texts of Rashi. However, Ramban may be referring to Rashi on Genesis 31:13, where this interpretation is clearly implied. See Vol. I, p. 382. (52) Genesis 31:13.

The correct interpretation of [the phrase] *el ha'aretz kena'an* appears to me to be that the name of this land is Canaan, like *Mitzraim* (Egypt), and the name of the land is identical with that of the people. Similarly, *the inhabitants of Canaan,*[53] and *O Canaan, the land of the Philistines; I will even destroy thee, that there shall be no inhabitant.*[54] Thus the expression here *el ha'aretz kena'an* is as one says, " 'the' city Jerusalem;" *and 'the' King David;*[55] *and 'the' man Gabriel.*[56]

35 2. AND OPEN LAND — "a space [consisting of] open land outside and around the city, in order to make the city pleasant; and they [the Levites] are not permitted to build any building there or to plant a vineyard, or to sow any crop. 4. A THOUSAND CUBITS ROUND ABOUT. But afterwards [in Verse 5] it says [that it should be] *two thousand cubits!* How can we explain this? He assigned two thousand cubits for them around [the cities], of which the inner [area with a radius of a] thousand [cubits, as mentioned in Verse 4] was to be free [open] space, and the outer [area of a thousand cubits] was to be for fields and vineyards round about." This is Rashi's language taken from the words of our Rabbis.[57]

The correct interpretation according to the plain meaning of Scripture seems to be that Scripture [in Verse 4] is stating that they should assign as open space a *thousand* cubits directly round about the

(53) Exodus 15:15. (54) Zephaniah 2:5. These two verses indicate clearly that Canaan is not only the name of a people, but of the land also. (55) I Kings 1:1. (56) Daniel 9:21. — In other words, *el ha'aretz kena'an* does not mean "into the land [of the people] of Canaan" but "into the land [called] Canaan." There is therefore no problem necessitating the above interpretation of Rashi and Ibn Ezra. See above in *Seder Beha'alothcha,* Note 284. (57) Sotah 27b. Thus, according to Rashi, two thousand cubits were assigned for each of the four sides round about the Levite city. Of these, the *innermost* thousand served as the open space, and the *outermost* was for fields and vineyards. Thus the two verses are harmonized. It will be noted though that Rashi did not assign any dimensions for the city proper. This will be one of the major contentions of Ramban, from which will follow important conclusions (see Note 59).

city, meaning that [the combined open space of *both sides* of the city] should be a thousand cubits long, five hundred on each side, and similarly [the open space of *both sides* together] of the width, should be a thousand cubits, five hundred cubits on each side.[58] After this He stated [in Verse 5] that they should make a square [the dimension of which to be] two thousand cubits by two thousand cubits, and the city should be situated in the center of the square. He thus added to them [the dimensions — in Verse 5] an open space not directly facing the city, equal to the measurement directly in front of the city, so that you find when leaving a thousand cubits as open space round about the city as He assigned at first [in Verse 4], the city, a thousand by a thousand cubits, will be in [the center of] the square.[59] Thus the city given to the Levites was in the form of a square.

Know that the term *pei'ah* [in Verse 5] signifies "a whole side" [i.e., the *whole* length of the distance of any of the four sides of the outer

(58) Thus, where Rashi assigned two thousand cubits for each of the four sides outside the city (as explained in the preceding note), Ramban allocates only five hundred for each side, totalling one thousand on the two opposite sides. (59) Thus, while Rashi did not designate any dimensions for the Levite city proper, Ramban assigned it a thousand by a thousand cubits. [See in Erubin 56b where one of the Amoraim, Abaye, indeed proposes these measurements for the Levite city, and this may well be the source of Ramban's interpretation at which many scholars have wondered.] By placing now this square-shaped city of a thousand by a thousand in the center of the larger outer-square of two thousand by two thousand, some important conclusions follow. Since, as has been clarified before, a *migrash* (open space) of five hundred by a thousand extends in each direction *directly facing* the city, there still remains a space of five hundred by five hundred above and below these *migrashim*, near the corners of the *outer* square. These remaining spaces, Ramban will suggest, were to be designated for fields and vineyards. [In a drawing of Ramban's design of the Levite city, found in my Hebrew commentary, p. 336, there will be noticed a circle encompassing all these four *migrashim* directly facing the city up to the walls of the outer-square. The circle naturally cuts down somewhat on the space allotted for the fields and vineyards. I based this upon the Gemara in Erubin *ibid.*, as interpreted by the commentators, especially the Ritba, in order to bring Ramban's words into consonance with the text there. Ramban's general concept though of the Levite city and its environs as presented here, according to the plain meaning of Scripture, is clear.]

square, and not merely any point along that side].[60] Similarly the expression, a hundred cubits long *'lapei'ah ha'echath'*[61] means "for the whole 'one' side," and so also similar expressions mentioned there [with reference to the dimensions of the Tabernacle]. This is also true of the term *pei'ah* at the end of the Book of Ezekiel[62] [with reference to the dimensions of the city of Jerusalem and the Sanctuary of the future]. Moreover, if the intent of the verse was to have been [as Rashi interpreted] that they were to assign *two* thousand cubits round about the city in each direction, He would have said, "And you shall measure without the city *'l'pe'ath keidmah* ('to' the east side — two thousand cubits) etc.;" but instead He says [in Verse 5] *And you shall measure without the city 'eth' pe'ath keidmah,* which means "the measure of that [whole] side" [i.e., the whole distance along the eastern side of the outer square area, and also on each of the other outer sides, as the verse continues]. Such a four-sided plane figure having all its sides equal [and all its angles, right angles] is indeed a pleasingly suitable appearance for cities to have, not that they should measure two thousand cubits around the city in all directions [as explained by Rashi], thus eliminating the corners. A similar case is the expression, *It shall be eighteen thousand reeds round about,*[63] which means that the city [of Jerusalem] will measure on all of its four sides together eighteen thousand reeds, since he [Ezekiel] assigned there for each of the four sides four thousand and five hundred [reeds]. Now it is correct to say that the thousand cubits which He assigned [in Verse 4] as open space directly round about the city that it is not to be planted, and the thousand cubits He added in the second verse at each of the outer sides [not directly opposite the city] be used for fields and vineyards, as our

(60) Thus, unlike Rashi who explained, for example, *eth 'pe'ath keidmah alpayim ba'amah* (*for the east 'side' two thousand cubits*) as *any point* on that eastern side of the circle, located two thousand cubits away from the city (see Note 57), Ramban applies it to the whole length of that eastern side *alongside the city* [of which a thousand cubits were directly opposite the city, and five hundred were above and below the city, as explained]. (61) Exodus 27:9. See also Verses 11-13 *ibid.* (62) Ezekiel Chapter 48. (63) *Ibid.,* Verse 48.

Rabbis have received by tradition. But the term *migrash* (open space) in Scriptural language applies to both, but in the one case [in the remote corners, not directly opposite the city] it may be cultivated and sown, whereas in the other case [in the *migrash* facing directly the city] it *may neither be plowed nor sown.*[64] That is why Scripture separated them from each other [by giving two commands, in Verse 4 and in Verse 5, and not commanding both of them together].[65]

8. FROM THE MANY YE SHALL TAKE MANY, AND FROM THE FEW YE SHALL TAKE FEW. Here too,[66] in the opinion of our Rabbis [the meaning is that] from *the paternal families* which received a large amount as their inheritance, they should take many [cities], as He mentioned *according to your families,*[67] while each tribe received exactly the same amount of land [and therefore had to provide an equal number of cities for the Levites]. And although you will find in the Book of Joshua that the number of cities which they gave to the Levites was *not* equal,[68] according to the number of tribes, that was because of the [different] value of the particular cities, since some were more important than the others, for the Land was divided according

(64) Deuteronomy 21:4. (65) With this interpretation Ramban solves the apparent contradiction between Verse 4 which speaks of the *migrash* as consisting of a thousand cubits and Verse 5 which assigns it to be two thousand. Ramban's answer is that the term *migrash* applies to both — open space, and land for planting. Thus Verse 4 addresses itself to that *migrash* which was for open space, while Verse 5 speaks of the overall concept of *migrash* which includes both the thousand cubits of open space directly opposite the city, and the five hundred cubits above and below the city for planting, which total altogether two thousand cubits. (66) See 26:54 where Ramban presents a similar explanation about the allocation of the whole Land amongst the twelve tribes; he now applies the same principles to the manner in which the tribes contributed to the number of cities given to the Levites. (67) Above, 33:54. (68) In Joshua Chapter 21, where a list of all these cities is given, it is stated that while most of the tribes each gave four cities to the Levites, the tribe of Judah gave eight, Shimon one, the half tribe of Menasheh in Canaan two, and Naphtali three [thus totalling thirty-eight cities in the land of Canaan and ten on the eastern side of the Jordan]. Ramban's statement that "the number of cities which they gave to the Levites was *not* equal" is thus clear, as is proven in the cases of Judah, Shimon, and Naphtali.

to its value.[69] A proof to this is the fact that from [the tribes of] Judah, Shimon and Benjamin they gave thirteen cities [to the Levites],[70] and from the tribes of Issachar, Asher, Naphtali, and the half-tribe of Menasheh, [also] thirteen [cities were given],[70] and yet these [latter tribes] were larger than the former ones in their population.[71] And from the tribe of Ephraim they gave four cities [to the Levites],[72] and from the tribe of Dan four cities,[73] and yet the children of Dan were double [the population] of the children of Ephraim.[74]

14. YE SHALL GIVE THREE CITIES BEYOND THE JORDAN. "And even though in the land of Canaan there were nine tribes, and here [on the east side of the Jordan] there were only two [and a half], Scripture gave them an equal number of cities of refuge, because in Gilead [on the east side of the Jordan] murderers were numerous, as it is written, *Gilead is a city of wrong-doers; it is covered with footprints of blood.*"[75] This is Rashi's language, based on the words of our Rabbis.[76] Now even though the [cities of] refuge were only for those who killed in error [and these murderers of Gilead killed deliberately], they would kill in treachery and make themselves appear as if they had done it in error, and therefore it was necessary to increase [proportionately] the number of their cities of refuge, in order to be

(69) Baba Bathra 122a. Thus, land nearer to Jerusalem was appraised more valuable than land further away, both because it was nearer to the Sanctuary and also it was further away from the border of the nations (Rashbam, *ibid.*). (70) Thus: Judah gave eight, Shimon one, Benjamin four, totalling thirteen cities. Similarly: Issachar and Asher each gave four, Naphtali three, the half-tribe of Menasheh two, totalling thirteen cities. (71) The figures used here are those of the census, above Chapter 26. Judah (Verse 22 *ibid.*), Shimon (Verse 14), and Benjamin (Verse 41) totalled 144,300. Issachar (Verse 25), Asher (Verse 47), and Naphtali (Verse 50) totalled 163,100. The complete tribe of Menasheh (Verse 34) totalled 52,700. Assuming that the half-tribe of Menasheh mentioned in Joshua was exact half [i.e., 26,350] we have a total for the latter group mentioned of 189,450, which is far more than the 144,300 of the first group. (72) Joshua 21:20-22. (73) *Ibid.*, Verses 23-24. (74) The children of Ephraim totalled 32,500 (above, 26:37), while Dan totalled 64,400 (*ibid.*, Verse 43)! Thus we must say that the cities were not given in proportion to the population of the tribes, but according to the appraised value of the city. (75) Hosea 6:8. (76) Makkoth 10a.

able to take in all of them, since one could not tell who had killed deliberately. If so, [we must say that] the Holy One, blessed be He, commanded this on account of the future [since He knew that murderers in Gilead would be numerous], similar to that which it says [of the future generations], *and this people will rise up, and go astray.*[77] Or perhaps the Rabbis will say that the climate of the land of Gilead was conducive to producing murderers since it became a nation.[78]

But I wonder! For in the opinion of our Rabbis, of blessed memory,[76] the [cities mentioned in the] verse which says, *and beside them* [i.e., apart from the six cities of refuge], *ye shall give* [to the Levites] *forty and two cities,*[79] were all commanded as cities of refuge, and thus there were thirty-six of them in the land of Canaan, and six beyond the Jordan,[80] and they all offered protection, in the opinion of our Rabbis, of blessed memory! Thus the cities of refuge throughout the Land of Israel were [distributed] justly and equally, for each of the [twelve] tribes received four cities of refuge. He also counted the tribe of Menasheh in the land of Canaan,[81] because the majority of it was

(77) Deuteronomy 31:16. (78) Exodus 9:24. (79) Above, Verse 6. (80) Since from the total of *thirty-eight cities* which, as clearly stated in Joshua Chapter 21 (see Note 68), were in the land of Canaan, we must now deduct the three main cities of refuge, leaving us a total of *thirty-five* additional cities of the Levites in the land of Canaan—and consequently a total of *seven* such additional cities for beyond the Jordan to complete the total of forty-two—we must perforce understand Ramban's language in speaking of *thirty-six* cities for the land of Canaan and *six* for beyond the Jordan as based on the theory mentioned above in the text that the factor of appraised value was also taken into consideration, and hence the seven cities on the eastern side of the Jordan were regarded as six, thus leaving a total of thirty-six for the land of Canaan. (81) I.e., in Joshua Chapter 21, Verse 25, the half-tribe of Menasheh in the land of Canaan is mentioned among the other nine tribes as giving cities to the Levites, which served as cities of refuge. This was because, as the text continues, the larger part of the tribe was there; therefore, although their land was smaller, the number of cities they gave to the Levites equalled that of their brethren beyond the Jordan [each giving two cities]. This proves that the determining factor was not because in Gilead murderers were numerous and that therefore the two and a half tribes beyond the Jordan were given a larger proportion of cities of refuge.

there [thus the nine tribes in the land of Canaan together with Menasheh were given thirty-six cities of refuge, i.e., those which constituted the cities of the Levites, plus the original three cities of refuge, making a total of thirty-nine]. Perhaps in [the proportion of] *the* [six] *appointed cities*[82] G-d increased [the number of these cities] beyond the Jordan, in honor of Moses, so that he would set aside half of that number [since he could not enter the land of Canaan], but in their totality [of forty-eight cities] they were all divided up by measure and according to proportion [each tribe receiving four cities].

According to the simple meaning of Scripture, it appears to me that the land on the [east] side of the Jordan was very large, for it contained [the kingdom of] the two great Amorite kings [Sihon and Og], about whose might the verses speak in superlative terms, and [this kingdom became] even greater when Ammon and Moab became a legitimate [conquest for Israel] through them [i.e., through Sihon and Og who captured the lands of Ammon and Moab, and from whom Israel subsequently took them by the right of conquest],[83] whereas the kings of the land of Canaan were merely kings of cities, and every ruler of a city was called a "king," as you see [from the verse]: *the king of Jerusalem, one; the king of Hebron, one,*[84] although between them [these two cities] there is a distance of [only] half a day's walk.[85] Similarly the Sages mention[86] that between Beth-el and Ai is a distance of [only] four miles, and yet each of these cities had its own king.[84] It is possible that it was the custom in those generations to call every ruler

(82) Joshua 20:9. The phrase refers to the six cities that were originally designated specifically as places of refuge. According to the Rabbis, these six cities offered protection whether the murderer knew that they were cities of refuge or not; in the other forty-two cities he was protected only if he knew that they offered protection (Makkoth 10a). (83) Chullin 60b. Israel was not allowed to fight against Ammon and Moab (see Deuteronomy 2:19). But since parts of their lands were captured by Sihon first, this injunction was removed. (84) Joshua 12:10. See also *ibid.,* Verses 9 and 16. (85) This language possibly indicates that Ramban wrote this on the basis of his personal experience, which would indicate that these parts of his commentary were written [or emended] when he was already living in the Land of Israel. See my article on this issue in Hamayon, Tammuz, 5728. (86) Shemoth Rabbah 32:2.

of a city "king," or perhaps [this was only in the Land of Israel] in honor of the Land of Israel, as our Rabbis, of blessed memory, explained.[87] In any case, they were not kings of countries, but only kings of particular cities. And thus it is written, [*And Adoni-bezek said*], *'Threescore and ten kings, having their thumbs and their great toes cut off, gathered food under my table.'*[88] Thus the land on the [east] side of the Jordan was a very large land, and required three cities of refuge just as the whole of the Land of Israel on the [west] side of the Jordan did, and only these six cities offered refuge [to unwitting murderers], and the forty-two cities [set aside] were for the open lands of the Levites and not for refuge.[89]

29. IN ALL YOUR HABITATIONS. "This teaches us that a Sanhedrin[90] may function outside the Land [of Israel] as long as one functions in the Land of Israel itself." This is Rashi's language. This is indeed correct, because after the destruction [of the Temple] the Sanhedrin cannot function in the Land of Israel nor outside it, just as our Rabbis have said in the Chapter *Arba Mithoth Beth Din:*[91] "*And thou shalt come unto the priests the Levites, and unto the judge that shall be in those days*[92] — when there is a priest [performing the Divine Service in the Sanctuary] there is [execution of] judgment; when there is no priest [at the Sanctuary] there is no judgment." And we have been taught in the Mechilta:[93] "Whence do we know that judicial execution can take place only during the existence of the Sanctuary?

(87) Bereshith Rabbah 85:16: "Any king or ruler who had no [seat of] sovereignty in the Land of Israel would consider himself worthless." (88) Judges 1:7. The seventy kings subject to Adoni-bezek were clearly not kings of countries, but of small local areas. (89) Ramban is here explaining the verses "according to their simple meaning," and not according to the opinion of the Rabbis, as mentioned above (at Note 82). See also my Hebrew commentary, p. 338, for further explanation. (90) In our Rashi: "a small Sanhedrin," i.e., a court of twenty-three judges which functioned in every city, and had power over civil and criminal cases. The "great Sanhedrin" consisted of seventy-one judges, and its seat was in a chamber on the Temple Mount, adjoining the Sanctuary Court. (91) Literally: "Four kinds of death-penalty of the court." — The text referred to here is in Sanhedrin 52b. (92) Deuteronomy 17:9. (93) I.e., the Mechilta of Rabbi Shimon ben Yochai (on Exodus 21:14). This

Because it says, *From Mine altar, thou shalt take him, that he may die.*[94] If you have an altar, you may render capital punishment, and if not, you may not do so."

But I have nowhere found in connection with a commandment which is limited to the [duration of the] existence of the Sanctuary that Scripture should say about it, *throughout your generations in all your habitations* [as it does here], because this [expression] indicates [the contrary, namely that it is binding] even during the exile, outside the Land. Thus [it uses this expression] in connection with [the obligation of abstaining from work on the Festival of Shavuoth,[95] and in connection with the prohibition of [eating from] the new crop [before bringing the *omer* on the sixteenth day of Nisan],[96] in order to make [these laws] obligatory even outside the Land [of Israel] and even nowadays [when the Temple is destroyed], so that we should not [think that the prohibition against eating of the new crop is] dependent upon [the actual offering of] the *omer,* and [so that we should not make the commandment to abstain from work on Shavuoth dependent] upon the offering of *the new meal-offering*[97] [on that day]. Likewise [the expression *throughout your generations in all your habitations* is used] in connection with [the prohibition against eating certain] fats[98] so that we should not think that it is dependent upon the offerings.[99] [And so here too the expression *throughout your generations in all your dwellings* would indicate that the execution of judgment including the death-penalty, applies at *all* times, and is *not* dependent upon the existence of the Sanctuary!] Perhaps the Rabbis interpreted the words [in our verse here]: *And these things shall be for a statute of judgment* [as referring not to the criminal cases mentioned in this section, but] to [the general law of] the Sanhedrin mentioned continually in this section, as it is said, [*until he stand*] *before 'the*

work is mentioned by Rambam in his Sefer Hamitzvoth, principle 14, (see "The Commandments," Vol. II, p. 424). (94) Exodus 21:14. (95) Leviticus 23:21: *it is a statute forever in all your habitations throughout your generations.* (96) *Ibid.,* Verse 14. For the explanation of the word *omer,* see Vol. III, p. 368, Note 243. (97) *Ibid.,* Verse 16. (98) *Ibid.,* 3:17. (99) See Ramban's emphasis on this point in Vol. III, pp. 85-88.

congregation' for judgment;[100] *then 'the congregation' shall judge,*[101] and Scripture is thus saying that we should always have, throughout all generations, and even after the destruction [of the Sanctuary], "a congregation that judges" [i.e., a Sanhedrin, or court] in order to adjudicate upon the laws of fines, robberies, personal injury, and all monetary matters, and to deal with the law of forty stripes.[102]

31. AND YE SHALL TAKE NO RANSOM FOR THE LIFE OF A MURDERER etc. The correct interpretation of [the repetition of the phrase *ye shall take no ransom* in Verses 31-32] that at first [i.e., in the verse before us] He warned us against [pardoning] a *deliberate* murderer, [stating]: *And ye shall take no ransom* of monetary payment *for the life of a murderer, who is guilty of death, for he shall* under all circumstances *be put to death,* and shall not be saved from death by any means, neither by exile nor by stripes nor by any other punishment. And afterwards [in Verse 32] He stated, *And ye shall take no ransom* to allow him to flee [from the city of refuge] and return to live in the Land, *until the death of the priest,* and the verse thus refers back to those liable to exile [for unwitting murder] which He had [previously] mentioned, who are the main subject of this section. It is thus as if He would have said: And similarly you shall take no ransom from a murderer [who killed unwittingly] in order that he should flee [from his city of refuge] and return to live in the Land, before the death of the [High] Priest." It was unnecessary to say that we should take no ransom from him [to free him] altogether from fleeing to the city of refuge, because anyone who kills somebody unwittingly is afraid at first that the avenger of blood might kill him in the heat of his anger, or [might kill him] because he suspected him of deliberate murder [and therefore he will always want at first to flee to the city of refuge]. Scripture, therefore, did not have to speak about [not taking] a ransom to free him altogether, but speaks only about [the prohibition against taking] a ransom after he has fled there, to enable

(100) Above, Verse 12. (101) *Ibid.,* Verse 24. (102) Deuteronomy 25:3. All these laws are applied even after the destruction of the Temple.

him to return to his land, and so that he should not have to stay there [in the city of refuge] as long as the [High] Priest is alive. For [it is likely that he may desire to leave it, since] after he has fled [there] and stood [trial] *before the congregation for judgment*[100] and has been acquitted by them [of the charge of deliberate murder], he will no longer be afraid of the avenger of blood, and so he will want to return to his house before the due time [i.e., before the death of the High Priest]. Therefore Scripture warned us against [accepting from him *a ransom* or bribe for] this [purpose]. Or [it may be] that there is a letter *vav* "missing" from the word *lashuv* [in Verse 32 — so that it is as if it said *v'lashuv*] meaning "or to abide."[103] But the first interpretation appears to me to be the correct one.

33. 'V'LO TACHANIPHU' (AND YE SHALL NOT POLLUTE) THE LAND. Because He had said at the beginning: *And these things shall be for a statute of judgment unto you throughout your generations in all your habitations,*[104] meaning that these judgments apply also outside the Land [of Israel], therefore He mentioned additional stringencies applying to the inhabitants of the Land [of Israel], in honor of the Divine Presence which is [especially] present there, and He warned us not to pollute it and not to defile it.[105]

And the meaning of the term *chanuphah* [mentioned here, which literally means: "flattery," or "pollution"] is that which is said with reference to the imprecations: *Thou shalt carry out much into the*

(103) According to this explanation, Verse 32 involves two separate prohibitions: 1) not to take a ransom from an unwitting killer not to go to a city of refuge, and 2) not to take a ransom from him to allow him to return from there before the death of the High Priest (Aboab). Ramban, however, as he states in his concluding words, prefers the first-mentioned interpretation that Verse 32 involves but one prohibition, namely, that we are not to take a ransom from an unwitting murderer after he has fled to the city of refuge to enable him *to return* to his land before the death of the High Priest. This interpretation is to be preferred apparently because it does not necessitate the introduction of a missing letter into the verse, as mentioned in the text. (104) Verse 29. (105) Verse 34.

field, and shalt gather in little; [106] *Thou shalt plant vineyards and dress them, but thou shalt neither drink of the wine;* [107] *Thou shalt have olive-trees throughout all thy borders, but thou shalt not anoint thyself with oil;* [108] *All thy trees and the fruit of thy land shall the locust make bare,* [109] for all expressions of *chanuphah* indicate doing the opposite of that which is seen by or appears to the eyes. This is the punishment [which will come] to the Land because of idolatry, bloodshed, and immorality, just as it is said, *will not the Land 'chanoph techenaph' (become polluted)*?; [110] *the earth also 'chanepha' (is polluted) under the inhabitants thereof;* [111] *'vatachniphi' (and thou hast polluted) the Land with thy harlotries.* [112] And the meaning of the term "defilement" [used in the next verse — *And thou shalt not 'defile' the Land*] is that the Land will become defiled so that the Glory of G-d will not dwell therein if there is innocent blood [shed] in it which has not been atoned for *by the blood of him that shed it.* [113] Thus the Rabbis have said in the Sifre: [114] " *'V'lo tachaniphu' the Land* — this is an admonition against flatterers." For at first [in Verses 31-32] He warned us against taking a bribe from murderers, and then [in Verse 33 here] He warned us against flattering them because of their high position or their power, or the honor of their family, even without taking a bribe, because if we flatter them, we will thereby cause the Land to "betray" its inhabitants [as explained above].

36 7. 'V'LO THISOV NACHALAH' (SO SHALL NO INHERITANCE) OF THE CHILDREN OF ISRAEL MOVE FROM TRIBE TO TRIBE. Scripture was only concerned to improve the situation at that time [i.e., for the daughters of Zelophehad who had raised that problem]. For if there were [then] women in Israel

(106) Deuteronomy 28:38. (107) *Ibid.*, Verse 39. (108) *Ibid.*, Verse 40. (109) *Ibid.*, Verse 42. (110) Jeremiah 3:1. (111) Isaiah 24:5. (112) Jeremiah 3:2. In all these three verses, the earth itself is described as becoming "*chanuphah* (polluted)" because of the sins of its inhabitants, which means, according to Ramban, that it will do the opposite of that which is its nature, for it will be planted and cultivated but not produce fruit. (113) Verse 36 here. (114) Sifre, *Mas'ei* 161.

[already] married to [men of] another tribe, and they [the women] inherited [a portion of the Land] at that time, or would inherit at some future time if their brothers or fathers died without sons, their inheritance would perforce move from one tribe to another [because their husbands, who were of a different tribe, or their sons, would inherit them when *they* died], and *who can straighten out* in time *what they have made crooked!*[115] The Torah, furthermore, did not want to command that the sons or husbands of these women should not inherit them [if they were not of the same tribe], because it did not deem it fit to abrogate [in this case] the [regular] law of inheritance. Similarly Scripture did not concern itself with events which would occur in the future; for even if those daughters who do not possess an inheritance [before they are married] would be permitted to marry [men from] any of the tribes, yet it is possible that at some future time they might inherit some property, if [all] their brothers die in the lifetime of their father, and thus their father's inheritance, or that of their relatives would pass on to them.[116]

But according to the opinion of our Rabbis who interpreted:[117] "This law[118] only applies to that particular generation," it is possible[119]

(115) Ecclesiastes 7:13. (116) In other words, if not for the opinion of the Rabbis on the meaning of Scripture we could say that this prohibition is for all times, applying to such women as the daughters of Zelophehad who stood to be married and who already possessed an inheritance. But women who were already married at that time to men of other tribes and are [like the daughters of Zelophehad] inheriting now [because their fathers who were among those who left Egypt, died without sons], and similarly, women who stand to be married and may yet inherit their fathers if they die without sons — with all these possibilities Scripture was not concerned. Instead, the law for all times was specifically applying to women who stand to be married and have already an inheritance of the tribe, just like the daughters of Zelophehad. All this we might be inclined to say. But according to the opinion of our Rabbis etc. (see text) — (Kur Zahav, quoting Aboab). (117) Baba Bathra 117a. (118) Literally: "this thing," based upon Verse 6 which reads: '*This is the thing*' *which the Eternal hath commanded concerning the daughters of Zelophehad* — that they marry men of their father's tribe. (119) The gist of Ramban's thought is as follows: In the light of the saying of our Rabbis, that this law did not apply for all times [as explained above in Note 116] but only to that particular generation, it is possible then to say that

that [at that time] there were no daughters who inherited a portion amongst all those who were to come into the Land [of Israel] except for the daughters of Zelophehad, and therefore [we do not find that] they [i.e., other women] asked [Moses about it as the daughters of Zelophehad did]. Scripture, then, is commanding that if anyone dies from that day onwards until the Land is divided up amongst their tribes, and his daughter inherits him, she should not marry [anyone] from another tribe, in order that when the Land is divided up, that man should not come to take himself an inheritance amongst another tribe. For the [Torah's] concern about them [i.e., about the separate inheritance of each tribe] was greater at the time of the division of the Land [than afterwards], so that the [different] tribes should not become mixed up with each other when taking their inheritance, whereas afterwards their [separate] inheritance will have already become known, and they would not be so concerned about it. But since the [exact] time of the division [of the Land] was not yet known, He imposed the prohibition on the whole of that generation. And G-d *in Whose hand is the soul of every living thing*[120] did not have to be concerned with future events [which might in certain cases result in the transfer of a particular inheritance from one tribe to another].

This explanation is correct according to the plain meaning of Scripture, for [the phrase in Verse 9] *v'lo thisov nachalah* is not a reason [for prohibiting the marriage of a woman who has already an inheritance, with a man from another tribe] "in order that the

Scripture was also concerned with the above-mentioned possibilities. As for those women who were already married to men of other tribes and are now inheriting, it is possible to say that there was no other case in that generation similar to that of Zelophehad's daughters, the proof being that no other tribe complained. And as for the other possibility, of women who stand to be married and may yet inherit their fathers if they die without sons, we answer, G-d *in Whose hand* etc. (see text) — (Kur Zahav, in the name of Aboab). (120) Job 12:10. Ramban's intent is to state that He *in Whose hand is the soul of every living thing* knew that "until the division of the Land no man would die without leaving a son, so that his daughters would be inheriting him" (Aboab). But such an assurance could naturally not apply if we were to say that the prohibition was for all generations.

inheritance shall not be moved [from tribe to tribe]," but there are two separate commandments [in this section]. He commanded [first, in Verses 6-8] that those women who already possess an inheritance [such as the daughters of Zelophehad, who were not married] should only marry into their father's tribe, and then [in Verse 9] He commanded that [in the case of] those who are already married [to men of other tribes and have no inheritance], or [in the case of all those women] who will come into an inheritance [later on] after they marry a man [of another tribe], *the inheritance shall not move from one tribe to another tribe,* but their brothers or their relatives are to inherit them, and not their sons or their husbands. Thus at first [in Verses 6-7] He commanded [the law] in connection with the daughters of Zelophehad, and afterwards [in Verse 8] concerning *every daughter that possesseth an inheritance;* and then He said in connection with all Israel that *an inheritance shall not move from one tribe to another tribe* [as stated in Verse 9, meaning] that even in the case of women who are [already] married [to men of another tribe], or [unmarried] women who have been commanded [not to marry men of another tribe] and who transgress this commandment, the men of their tribes [i.e., the women's brothers or other relatives] should inherit them, in order that they should be closely attached to the inheritance of their fathers' tribes, and their inheritance should not be severed from them, nor they from the inheritance of their fathers. And all these [restrictions] applied only to the generation which took possession of the Land, at the time that it was divided up. Thus He advised them about unmarried women, concerning whom they had asked, and He also made provision for those that were already married.

Thus is completed the Book of the Censuses[121] [i.e., the Book of Numbers] and the standards of the hosts;

(121) Such is the name given by the Sages to the fourth book of the Torah: "the Fifth of the Censuses" (Sotah 36b).

And to G-d, the G-d of hosts, be praises and thanksgivings, in hundreds, thousands, and myriads.

And as He has done for our ancestors *great and awesome deeds,*[122] may He bring about speedily in our days *the end of the wonders.*[123]

May He build the House and the chambers and *the border before the cells.*[124]

And prepare there *the thrones of the house of David,*[125] and may our eyes behold it!

And may He in His mercies purify us of all [our] hidden [faults] and all errors,[126]

And show us wondrous things from His Torah![127]

Amen. May His Will be so!

Finished and completed.

(122) See Deuteronomy 10:21. (123) Daniel 12:6. A reference to the Messianic era. (124) Ezekiel 40:12. (125) Psalms 122:5. This may also be a reference to the mysteries of the Cabala. See at end of Ramban's Introduction to the Book of Genesis: "And He will show those who are pleasing to Him wonders from His Torah" (Vol. I, p. 16). (126) See *ibid.,* 19:13. (127) See *ibid.,* 119:18.

Index

OF NAMES, PLACES, BOOKS AND SUBJECTS

Index

A

Numbers refer to pages. Names and subjects appearing only in the place of the Biblical test, are not listed.

Abraham ibn Ezra, Onkelos, Rashi and Sifre, because of their constant occurrence, are not listed.

Certain basic terms — such as *konam, ohel,* etc. — because of their familiarity to the student of Jewish law, are also included in this Index.

B

C

D

F

G

H

I

J

K

L

M

N

O

P

R

S